As the Bamboo Shoots

Orange Hat Publishing
www.orangehatpublishing.com - Waukesha, WI

As the Bamboo Shoots

竹

愛　Love

家　Family

和　Harmony

學　Learning

For information, please contact:

Orange Hat Publishing
www.orangehatpublishing.com
info@orangehatpublishing.com

Cover design by Evan Pollock
Editing by Beth Hoffmann and Sandy Sabo

Printed in the United States of America

As the Bamboo Shoots

Adventures of My Life

Celine Tan Robertson

譚渝華

(Tan Yu Hua)

Orange Hat Publishing
www.orangehatpublishing.com - Waukesha, WI

This book, *As the Bamboo Shoots,* is dedicated:

To
My parents, General and Mrs. Nan Kwang Tan,
and my six siblings for nurturing my deep roots.

To
My husband Don, two daughters Joline and Andrea,
sons-in-law, and precious grandchildren for making my life
complete with love and laughter.

To
My students around the world for making my path
joyful, vibrant, and spiritual.

To
All my friends for filling my life with moments of
pleasure and rainbow colors.

As the Bamboo Shoots
Contents

Chapter 1   Love and Laughter

Chapter 2   Roots Run Deep

Chapter 3   Journey to the West

Chapter 4   Transplanting and Transformation

Chapter 5   As the Bamboo Shoots

Chapter 6   Return to My Roots

Chapter 7   The True, the Good, and the Beautiful

Chapter 8   Fruitful Harvest

Chapter 9　Forever

Keelung 基隆

Hsinchu City 新竹市

Taipei 台北

Taichung 台中

Taiping 太平

Taichung City

Hualien County 花蓮縣

Taiwan 臺灣

Taiwan

Tainan City

Kaohsiung 高雄

Kaohsiung City

Taiwan 台灣

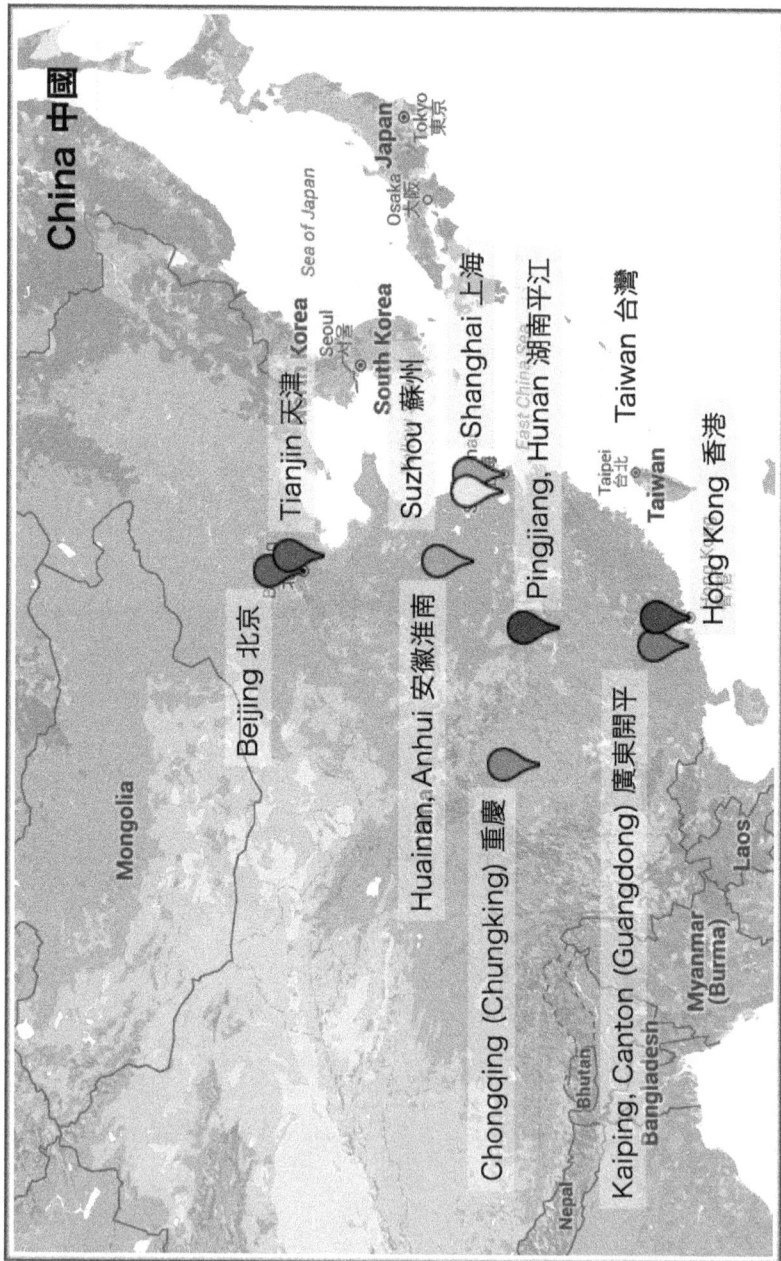

China 中國

Mongolia

Sea of Japan

Japan 日本
Tokyo 東京
Osaka 大阪

Korea 韓國
Seoul 서울
South Korea

Tianjin 天津
Beijing 北京

Suzhou 蘇州

Shanghai 上海

East China Sea

Pingjiang; Hunan 湖南平江

Taiwan 台灣
Taipei 台北
Taiwan

Huainan, Anhui 安徽淮南

Hong Kong 香港

Chongqing (Chungking) 重慶

Kaiping, Canton (Guangdong) 廣東開平

Nepal

Bhutan

Bangladesh

Myanmar (Burma)

Laos

United States of America

Pocatello, Idaho

Lincoln, Nebraska

Milwaukee, Wisconsin

Chicago, Illinois

United States

Edwardsville, Illinois

Wichita, Kansas

Mexico

Gulf of Mexico

Gulf of California

WASHINGTON
Seattle

OREGON

IDAHO

MONTANA

NORTH DAKOTA

SOUTH DAKOTA

WYOMING

NEVADA

UTAH

COLORADO

NEBRASKA

IOWA

MINNES

WISCON

MICHIGAN

San Francisco

CALIFORNIA

Las Vegas

ARIZONA

NEW MEXICO

San Diego

Los Angeles

KANSAS

MISSOURI

ILLINOIS

INDIANA

OHIO

WEST

PENN

KENTUCKY

OKLAHOMA

ARKANSAS

TENNESSEE

NORTH CAROLINA

TEXAS

MISSISSIPPI

ALABAMA

GEORGIA

SOUTH CAROLINA

LOUISIANA

Houston

FLORIDA

Ottawa

Toronto

MAINE

VT

NH

MA

Boston

CT RI

NEW YORK

New York

MD

DE N J

VA

ix

As the Bamboo Shoots

Foreword

If you have a dream, make it come true.
If you have a vision, make it happen.
If you have energy, make it positive.
If you have something extra, share with people.

-Celine Tan Robertson

This is the way I raised my children; this is the way I taught my students; and this is the way I live my life.

I listened to books in the car while driving to and from Arrowhead High School in Hartland, Wisconsin where I established a four-year Chinese language program in 2009—a 40-minute drive each way, every day. In three years, I had listened to many good books.

In the spring of 2012, one of the authors mentioned the growth of bamboo. He said that it takes five years for a timber bamboo to root. When the roots mature, bamboo shoots up to twenty-five feet or higher, non-stop.

Bamboo plays a very important role in traditional Chinese culture. It is even regarded as a model of gentlemanly behavior. As bamboo has some features such as uprightness and tenacity, Chinese people admire bamboo as a symbol of integrity, elegance, and plainness. Ancient Chinese poets wrote countless poems to praise bamboo.

I was amused by a non-Chinese author writing about bamboo. I was even more amazed by bamboo's incredible growth. I know that Chinese people revere bamboo. However, I didn't know much about its growth. It aroused my curiosity, and I started doing research on bamboo, in both Chinese and English.

After the roots are cultivated and secured, the new bamboo shoots spring out of the ground. The shoots may grow more than a foot per day from ground level up to fifty feet in the spring season. They reach their full height in two to three months. They need to be part of a large grove to produce this caliber of growth. Transplanting does not affect the growth of a bamboo.

The beauty of the timber bamboo grove takes your breath away. The bamboo stands fast, tall, and strong with such endurance, air, and energy. The bamboo enjoys the sunshine and absorbs the moisture. With flexibility they sway in the blowing wind, and with endurance they survive the vigorous storms. It is a powerful, gorgeous, and extraordinary plant. It is truly one of most remarkable plants on earth.

I was born in China, lived in Hong Kong for a year, and grew up in Taiwan. I came to the United States for graduate school at a young age.

Did my transplants affect my growth?

Were my roots cultivated and secured solidly?

Is the U.S. like the large grove for a bamboo—the place for me to grow and to transform?

"That's it!" I yelled out loud in excitement. I would name my book, *As the Bamboo Shoots*!

This book is one of my dreams and one of my visions. It is my positive energy, and it is something I would like to share.

This is the way I live my life.

If you have a dream, make it come true.
If you have a vision, make it happen.
If you have energy, make it positive.
If you have something extra, share with people.

Acknowledgments

A bouquet of gratitude goes to each of the many people who have accompanied, guided, and assisted me every step of the way throughout this challenging, amazing journey.

Without them, I couldn't have made one of my dreams come true—to pass the roots to my descendants. Without them, I couldn't make another vision happen—to share my life expeditions.

Sincere thanks to my two wonderful teachers of the Creative Writing for Publication course at Waukesha County Technical College, Gail Grenier Sweet and Kathryn Lytle Rothschadl, for their patience, encouragement, and guidance.

My deepest gratitude goes to all my classmates, the *Borrowed Eyes,* for escorting me throughout the journey.

I thank the *Grammar Guru,* Beth Hoffmann, with earnest gratefulness, for standing by me as a friend and an editor along the way.

My forever appreciation goes to my old friend, Sandy Sabo, for reading my stories on weekends and spending her whole vacation to do the final round of editing for me.

Special thanks go to Chris Roerden, an Agatha Award-winning author, for reading my stories and writing a blurb for my book.

My forever love to my little buddies, my students, Evan Pollock for designing the beautiful book cover and maps and Madelyn Burgdorff for technical assistance.

Many thanks to Xiao Min Sun for helping with the maps and Lillian Wang for scanning all the pictures.

The wonderful articles and pictures in the <u>Lincoln Journal Star</u> in Lincoln, Nebraska, and the <u>Mukwonago Chief</u> and <u>Lake Country</u> in Waukesha County, Wisconsin, highlight many of my stories.

Chapter 1
Love and Laughter

愛

Love and Laughter

Under the blue Wisconsin sky and fluffy clouds, the yellow and orange leaves of the glistening trees were falling. Each leaf was like a flower, swirling and dancing from the tall walnut trees to the ground. Giggling and laughter filled a beautiful backyard. Three happy little kids were swinging high on the swing, sliding down the slide, running, and chasing each other with joyful laughter and smiles. They were precious, they were beautiful, and they were mine.

Holly was going to celebrate her first birthday in a week, and Kiran would be two years old in one month. Casey was a six-year-old first grader. They were our darling grandchildren who made our life complete.

Here I was in the fourth month of my retirement at the home of our older daughter, Joline, and her husband. I was with my three grandchildren, my favorite *toys*, as I called them, playing in the colorful yard on a sunny autumn day in 2012. How much more blessed could a person be?

Holly

Holly was kicking her legs, laughing and excited, and on the swing doing "High Five" with me, a gesture she had just learned. I laughed loud and giggled hard. Who was having more fun, Holly or me?

"Holly, do you know when you laugh, you are as beautiful as a blooming rose?"

She kicked her legs and laughed again.

"*Po Po* [maternal grandmother] is so happy like a little kid and has so much fun playing with you!"

She had her right arm up and wanted to do "High Five" with me again.

Our older daughter, Joline, and her husband, Ken, were engineers. Holly's nanny came at 7:30 in the morning, and I took care of her before her nanny got here. After her nanny came, I taught Casey Chinese and Kung Fu, Chinese martial arts, before taking him to school every morning. What a blessing to have this special bonding opportunity with both of them every day.

Casey practiced his Kung Fu while Holly and I took our walks on the long driveway every morning. Holly was *Ge Ge*'s [big brother] biggest fan.

Holly was so happy looking at the trees, the flowers, and the birds in the sky.

"Do you hear birds singing and saying 'Good morning!' to you?" I asked her.

She looked up to find the birds.

"Do you see the squirrels smiling at you?"

Holly bounced up and down and reached out, trying to catch squirrels from her stroller.

"What are the bunnies doing over there?"

She waved her little fingers at the running bunnies.

"The red flowers are blooming. Aren't they beautiful? But you are more beautiful."

She gently touched the red flowers.

"*Po Po*, watch my new tricks," yelled Casey.

"Wow, *Po Po* can't do that," I yelled back. I was impressed with Casey's creativity with the staff, a martial arts instrument that I made for him with a 5-foot bamboo stick.

"Isn't it fun watching *Ge Ge* practice his Kung Fu?"

Holly waved her little staff *Ge Ge* made for her like she knew how to do it also.

"Do you want to learn Kung Fu too? *Po Po* will teach you when you are bigger."

She bounced up and down again, waving her staff.

"Are you going to be smart, beautiful, pleasant, and happy with a big heart like Mommy when you grow up?"

Holly raised her hand for "High Five" with me again.

"Are you going to be as alert and intelligent as Daddy?"

She had a big smile, with her arms up in the air.

"Do you want to get out?"

She gave me another beautiful smile, a smile like a full bloomed flower. I got her out of the stroller. She put her head against my chest and patted me on my shoulder with one of her little hands.

Kiran

Kiran climbed up the tree house for the slide. As he got to the top, he said, "I made it!" with a million-dollar smile. He headed to the ladder and slid down, again and again.

Our gorgeous second grandson, Kiran, is a gentle, charming, and sweet toddler. He has Mommy's beautiful eyes and Daddy's shiny curly hair. Nobody can resist his delightful smiles.

Whenever he saw me he held up his arms and said, "*Po Po, bao bao* [hold me]."

How could I not hold him, looking at his sparkling eyes and innocent, charming face? No, I was not spoiling him. I just enjoyed him and loved him more in my arms.

"Are you *Po Po*'s *bao bei* [precious treasure]?"

"Yeah," nodding his head.

"Does *Po Po* love Kiran?"

"Yeah," he smiled.

"Does Kiran love *Po Po*?"

"Yeah," he said, leaning his face on my chest and hugging me tight.

In the fall of 2008, Andrea, our younger daughter, gave up a great job at the Capital Group Companies as a compliance specialist in Los Angeles to join our older daughter in Milwaukee, Wisconsin. Joline, our older daughter, has been an engineer at a healthcare company since 2001.

Andrea and her husband, Rylan, had Kiran in November 2010. We bought a house only four blocks from their house because of Kiran.

Don, my husband and Kiran's *Gong Gong* [maternal grandfather], picks him up early from the daycare every day so that we could see more of him. I have been speaking Chinese to him since he was born.

"*Nai, nai* [milk]," Kiran spoke Chinese to his teacher when he started to talk. The teacher would give him milk.

"*Shui, shui* [water]," said Kiran. He would get his water. It was so cute and wonderful that his American teachers learned Chinese from him.

What a blessing that Kiran could play with his cousins, Casey and Holly, at least two times a week. He followed Casey around like he knew what was going on and he did whatever Casey was doing. With his toddler vocabulary, he carried on a continuous conversation with six-year-old cousin, Casey.

"Are you having fun playing with *Ge Ge*, Kiran?"

"Yeah," he said, nodding, giggling, and running after *Ge Ge* again.

He called Holly *Mei Mei* [little sister] whenever he saw Holly. He didn't know what to do when *Mei Mei* was so excited, waving her arms and running toward him. Holly wanted to play with him.

He looked at Holly and started digging into the toy box to get a toy. Holly got more excited and tried to grab the toy Kiran had picked. Well, the fun part started.

"Share! Share!" I told them both.

Holly looked so innocent and stood there watching Kiran cry. You wondered what this nimble little one-year-old was thinking.

"Look, what is this?" I comforted Kiran, wiped his tears, and showed him another toy.

He stopped crying, took the toy, and followed *Ge Ge* around again. Holly was right behind him.

I was always so envious of friends who had cousins to play and grow up with when I was growing up in Taiwan. We didn't even know we had five cousins until 1978 when we finally located our three uncles in China after thirty years of separation by the Taiwan Strait.

It was hilarious to watch a one-year old, a two-year old, and a six-year-old playing together, even though there were tears and fighting at times. They enjoyed one another and had so much fun playing together. What a great delight and fun for me to watch these three cousins playing with one another.

Here came Kiran running to me, holding his arms up in the air and said, "*Po Po, bao bao!*"

How could I not hold him looking at his charming, smiling face?

"Are you *Po Po*'s *bao bei*?" I asked him after I picked him up.

"Yeah," giving me another darling smile.

"Are you having fun with *Ge Ge* and *Mei Mei*?"

"Yeah," nodding his head and leaning his face on my chest and hugging me tight.

I whispered in my heart. *Enjoy and love your cousins. They will be your best friends for life.*

Casey

The International School of Beijing was established by the U. S. Embassy for the children of American diplomats when China was opened to the outside world in 1972. It is a pre-K -12th grade American system school with more than 1,800 students.

The school needed an experienced teacher to lead and coordinate the Chinese Language Department. They first approached me in the fall of 1998. After they had tried to persuade me for three years, I finally decided to go Beijing to teach there. I taught Chinese to international students from fifty-six countries, mostly diplomats and foreign business executives' children during 2001-2009.

I turned in my resignation and announced my second retirement as soon as Andrea, our younger daughter, moved to Milwaukee from Los Angeles to join our older daughter, Joline, in October 2008.

The principal asked me, "Is there anything we can do to keep you?"

"No, I am homesick and I am going home," I answered.

I hung Casey's pictures, big ones, in my office, classroom, and the house when I was in Beijing. How I wished that I could see him, hold him, kiss him, and play with him. I talked to his pictures every day, and I wondered if he could hear me and feel my love.

We came back, not to Lincoln, Nebraska, which had been our

home since 1973, but instead we came to Milwaukee to join our two daughters and their families in June 2009. Joline and Ken's first child and our first grandson Casey was three years old.

I started talking Chinese to Casey after we settled in Milwaukee. He did not understand a word I said although both his parents speak fluent Chinese. I kept talking Chinese to him.

Ten months after I started talking to him in Chinese, he asked me one day, "*Po Po*, would you teach me Chinese?"

I said with great delight, "Of course! I will teach you every morning when you start kindergarten in the fall."

Casey's first formal Chinese lesson began on the day when he started kindergarten as I promised him. I had taught junior high and high school students since I was twenty-one years old. He is the youngest student I have ever worked with.

Casey is a highly motivated and focused student—the best student any teacher could wish for. I was very happy with his amazing progress.

"Aren't you proud that you can read thirty books in less than a year?" I asked him one day in March, with a big smile.

"Yeah, I can count to ten in Spanish too," Casey responded proudly.

He then asked me seriously, "*Po Po*, can your students do what I do?"

"Not all of them. You are one of my best students, and I am so proud of you." I hugged him.

After watching the *Chinese Kaleidoscope*—a 40-minute program, consisted of Dragon Dance, Lion Dance, martial arts, folk dances, and songs at Arrowhead High School, Casey asked me, "*Po Po*, would you teach me the Chinese martial arts, dragon dance, lion dance, Chinese painting and calligraphy, and all the things that you taught your students?"

I responded with enthusiasm, "Sure, you would be a super Kung Fu Kid!"

I started teaching him Kung Fu right away. He loved the Chinese martial arts—Tai Chi, sword, broadsword, staff, and Kung Fu fan. What a joy and privilege to pass on to him the Chinese culture—his heritage.

7

I played some Chinese songs while Casey practiced his Kung Fu after his Chinese language lesson every morning.

"I like this song. What is the name of it, *Po Po?*" asked Casey.

"It is *The Descendants of the Dragon,* one of *Po Po*'s favorite songs," I told him.

"Isn't dragon evil?" he stopped and asked.

"Dragon may be evil to Westerners. To Chinese people, dragon for thousands of years is the symbol of power, wealth, fortune, and emperor. Dragon is China, and Chinese people call themselves, the *Descendants of the Dragon.*" I explained to him.

"Really? So dragon is not evil." He continued with his practice.

I announced my first retirement at my last *Chinese Kaleidoscope* program at Lincoln High School in Lincoln, Nebraska in April 2000. The theme of the program was the Descendants of the Dragon. I bid farewell to my students and 3,600 audience members as a *Descendant of the Dragon.*

"Am I a *Descendant of the Dragon* too?" Casey stopped again and looked at me.

"Yes! You are!" I assured him.

"I know how to say dragon in Chinese. *Long* [dragon]!"

"Great! You have made *Po Po* very happy and proud."

"It is fun learning Chinese and all the Kung Fu."

He smiled and picked up his sword to practice his new tricks again.

Casey asked me one day, "Why did you retire, *Po Po?*"

"*Po Po* did it for you, Kiran, and Holly. I want to spend more time with you."

"I am so glad you are retired. Now you can play with us more." He hugged me.

It has been a great joy working with Casey every morning. He absorbs everything like a sponge. His Chinese characters are beautiful. He started talking to me in Chinese.

"Hey, I can understand what you say in Chinese now!" I said to Casey with excitement.

"I know how to say all the fruits in Chinese too." He looked at me with a big smile on his face.

"I know!"

"I know the twelve animals for the Chinese zodiac also," he added.

He never skips a day practicing his Kung Fu. His body is so flexible, and his forms with different martial arts instruments are very creative and beautiful. He really loves it, and he does it with such a pride—being a Chinese descendant.

"Do you know that you are more artistic and creative than *Po Po* with the Kung Fu forms and movements?"

"Yeah, I can do more tricks, and with both hands too. Look!" Casey, with one sword in one hand and a broadsword in the other, swung around and showed me his new fancy movements.

"Wow! You are truly my super Kung Fu *Kid*," I applauded his creativity.

"I am also a *Descendant of the Dragon*," said Casey without stopping his demonstration.

I agreed totally, "Yes, you definitely are!"

*****

Under the blue Wisconsin sky and the fluffy clouds on a sunny autumn day stood the most blessed *Po Po*, giggling and laughing with three beautiful children in a colorful yard. What a blissful life! This is the life that I have envisioned—a life with love and laughter.

I pondered what stories I should tell my beloved grandchildren—my fabulous *Descendants of the Dragon*. The floating clouds took me back in time to a far-far-away land—a land where I was born, a land where I dreamed, and a land where I was rooted...

Kiran, Casey, and Holly in Minnesota (2012)

Chapter 2
Roots Run Deep

家

Po Po
Ma Ma
Ba Ba
The Tomboy and the Little Lady
Hands and Feet
The Seeds

Po Po

One morning in July 2013, as I was teaching Chinese to our 7-year-old grandson Casey, I was curious. "What do you say about *Po Po* to your friends?"

Casey laughed. "*Po Po* is funny, and *Po Po* is fun."

"You think *Po Po* is funny? Why?"

He laughed. "You are scared of bugs. You are fun too. You know how to do a lot of stuff, like Tai Chi and Kung Fu. You giggle and laugh a lot. It is fun to play with you."

Casey had so much fun scaring me with bugs. He even bought a plastic bug to scare me. He was thrilled as he watched me, screaming and running from the bug.

"What else about *Po Po*?"

"You are a demanding teacher."

"What is a demanding teacher?"

"You make me work hard. I have learned so much from you."

"What will you remember about *Po Po* when you grow up?"

"*Po Po* is fun. *Po Po* teaches me things. *Po Po* loves us."

*****

We sat on the floor. We played with Thomas trains. We raced cars on the wooden floor. We went outside to find bunnies. We picked tomatoes on the deck. We smelled the blooming flowers and we searched for the soaring airplanes in the sky. We counted the steps in Chinese when we went up and down the stairs. It was our special fun time together—Kiran and I played together at least twice a week.

I enjoyed playing with Kiran. "*Hao wan bu hao wan* [Is it fun]?"

"*Hao wan* [It is fun]." He smiled, and nodding his head.

"Is *Po Po hao wan*? [Is *Po Po* fun?]"
He got up and gave me a bear hug. "*Po Po hao wan.*"

*****

"*Po Po! Po Po!*" Two-year-old Holly heard me coming.
"Holly! Holly!" We ran to each other, giggling and laughing.
She hugged my legs, her face leaning on me, to give me love while I kissed her on the head.
She liked to play in my in-law-suite, my special room downstairs. She wanted to go down and play again. "Down. Down."
"Do you want to go downstairs to *Po Po*'s house?"
She smiled, and nodding. "Yeah. *Po Po*'s house."
She snuggled right next to me and watched one of her favorite programs—Curious George. We built tall buildings with Legos. She pulled her little wagon around and around. We ate all the fruit and vegetables from her little basket that I used for teaching. We drew pictures and we colored. We sang Chinese songs and we sang *ABC* and *Twinkle, Twinkle Little Star*.
It was such a joyful blessing to have her and to play with her. "Holly *hao wan* [is fun]."
She stopped everything and climbed up on my lap. She held my face with one hand on either side, and she looked at me, with a smile like a blooming rose. "*Po Po hao wan.*" Then she kissed me.

*****

Our brand new granddaughter, Callie, is so sweet and alert. She loves to smile. I sing Chinese songs to her while rocking her. She is my new *toy*. I love to hold her tight in my arms and talk to her.
"Are you having fun with *Po Po*?"
She smiled, like a beautiful lotus, pure and sweet.
I held her up on my lap, and she bounced up and down.
"You are so strong. Do you want to dance?"
She looked at me, smiled, and bounced more.

"Are you going to be strong like your daddy?"

She smiled, wiggled, and made some noises.

"Are you going to be smart like your mommy?"

I set her on my lap, and she looked at me and gave me another big smile.

"*Ge Ge* loves you. Aren't you lucky to have Kiran as your *Ge Ge*?"

The 2-month-old princess seemed to understand what *Po Po* said. Her beautiful sparkling eyes were smiling; her little mouth was making sounds; and she got all excited and wiggled right and left. My new *toy*, Callie, swayed her little arms and kicked her chubby legs, non-stop.

Po Po

Now I am a blessed *Po Po*, with four darling grandchildren. They have made our lives complete and young—full of joy, love, laughter, and energy.

I have been thinking of my *Po Po* often, ever since I became one. She died when I was eleven. In my memory, my *Po Po* never played with me, and she never smiled. She had little expression on her face. I always wondered why when I was little, and I wondered why when I grew up.

My *Po Po* was born in 1879, during the last dynasty in China, in Hunan Province. The Qing Dynasty was isolated from the rest of the world, and the government was very weak. People suffered tremendously. It was the time of foreign invasion. It was the time Hong Kong was taken by the British. It was a time of change, chaos, and turbulence.

There were also many unreasonable traditions, especially for women. Girls were not allowed to attend school. Women were to be faithful wives and raise children. Marriages were arranged by parents.

My *Po Po* had very small feet. She couldn't walk fast, and she didn't seem very stable while walking.

One day when I was a little girl I asked Mother, "Why does *Po Po* have such small feet?"

"It was a tradition for women. It was considered a symbol of beauty for *Po Po*'s generation."

"How did they do it?"

"They bound each foot tightly with a piece of long cloth every single day. They did this to girls when they were very young so that their feet wouldn't grow any bigger."

I couldn't imagine how little girls tolerated such pain. "Didn't it hurt?"

"Yes. But it was a tradition and the girls had no choice."

"Did they try to bind your feet when you were little?"

"Yes. But my father, an open-minded and liberal man, didn't allow it."

My mother was a tall lady, with big feet. "I am so glad you don't have bound feet."

*****

Through arranged marriage, *Po Po* was married to my *Gong Gong* [maternal grandfather]. My *Gong Gong* was a courageous and knowledgeable man who firmly believed that a new and strong China could end people's suffering. Later he joined Dr. Sun Yat Sen for the revolution to overthrow the corrupted and weak government of the Qing Dynasty.

My *Gong Gong* had three wives. I was curious about his marriage with three wives. I asked my mother, "How could *Po Po* allow *Gong Gong* to have two more wives?

"It was *Po Po*'s idea."

"What? Why?"

"Po Po gave birth to four children, two girls and two boys. I was the third born."

I never heard Mother talking about her older brother and sister, only her three younger brothers. "What happened to your older brother and older sister?"

"They both died of meningitis when I was very little. They died one after the other within twenty-four hours. *Po Po* was heart-broken losing two children in one day. The unbearable grief was so devastating that she didn't want any more children. She told *Gong Gong* to have other wives."

At the time, rich and successful men in China always had more than one wife. The first wife was in charge of the domestic household. Usually there were conflicts and jealousy among wives, especially between the first wife and other wives. My *Po Po*, the first wife, was never jealous. She treated the other two wives as sisters. Each one had a boy. *Po Po* loved them as her own.

Our house, *Yi Yuan* [Garden of Art], was one of the seven most beautiful and well-known garden houses in Suzhou at the time. Suzhou is a city near Shanghai, known for its beautiful garden houses. There were around 20 family members, including some distant relatives, living in the household. There were always nine or ten helpers around the house. *Po Po* kept everything in great order. With fairness, kindness, and genuine, unselfish love she brought harmony to this big family.

I wanted to clarify some facts I never knew before. "So our second uncle and third uncle are your half-brothers?"

"Yes." Mother loved all her younger brothers with all her heart, just as my *Po Po* loved all four children.

Mother was raised by my loving *Po Po,* who embraced everyone around her with a caring heart. Our mother, with a Buddha heart, modeled kindness, empathy, and selfless love. She taught us seven children to always embrace people, especially the less fortunate and disadvantaged people, with compassion and empathy.

*****

The Republic of China was established in 1911 after the Qing Dynasty was overthrown by the revolution led by Dr. Sun Yet Sen, with supporters like my grandfather, who shared the vision: to build China into a strong republic.

The new government tried to build a republic. Because emperors had ruled China for thousands of years, the obstacles and problems were inevitable.

There were warlords. Each of them had his own territory and army. The power struggle among warlords and their fighting against one another and against the new government made China very unstable. People still suffered immensely. In 1927, after many years of fighting and negotiation, Chiang Kai Shek defeated some of the warlords and made agreements with others.

Japan, being a little island country, wanted to expand its territory. The Japanese had been watching China for a long time. The chaos, changes, and unstable state in China provided them the best opportunity to creep into China. It was then the Japanese started to "invade" China.

In 1931, they had total control over the nine provinces in Northeastern China. As they moved to other parts of China, wherever they went, there were massacres. The Nanking Massacre during the war was the most brutal one of all. The Japanese soldiers raped women, young and old. They robbed people, and they occupied land and property. They controlled more and more local governments. This oppression and invasion continued....

The government of the Republic of China didn't have a chance to recover and to unite the country after fighting the warlords. Chinese people couldn't tolerate the ambitious and ruthless Japanese any more. In 1937, the government declared war against Japan.

Japan underestimated China and its people and proclaimed, "We will take China in three months!"

Chinese people, including my *Gong Gong*, my father, and my oldest uncle, fought hard for eight years against the Japanese, from 1937 to 1945.

As my father, an officer, fought in the front lines, my mother and my older brother followed the government and relocated in Chungking, where the temporary capital was during the war. When our oldest uncle graduated from college, he, like countless young Chinese, joined the armed forces to defend the country.

Our family was separated and went in different directions—no one knew how long the separation would be.

Gong Gong and *Po Po* left their garden house in Suzhou for their hometown in Pingjiang, Hunan, for safety—two younger uncles were under ten. They walked hundreds of miles on foot where there was no ride available, and they climbed steep hills and rugged mountains. *Po Po*, with her bound feet and small steps, suffered tremendous physical pain on the journey.

Gong Gong and *Po Po* worried about both their oldest son and my father's safety in the battle fields. They missed my mother and my older brother—their first and only grandchild in Chungking. Although *Po Po* suffered such unthinkable agony, she never stopped, she never slowed down, and she never complained.

When *Gong Gong* was away to rescue some people, she protected her two young boys from the Japanese, often hiding in the mountains for days, without food.

When my second uncle was thirteen, he was captured by the Japanese in the woods and was taken to do hard labor work. He was beaten and mistreated. He managed to escape from the labor camp and returned home.

Po Po held her little boy and gently touched the wounds and scars, as tears rolled down on her face. "My poor baby! What did they do to you?"

Three of them wept together, holding one another.

What an agony and sadness to see your young child was abused by the cold-blooded enemy!

My second uncle suffered physically and emotionally. He lived with poor health the rest of his life due to the abuse at the camp and the hardship during war.

Sixty years later he described *Po Po*'s courage, love, and tenacity to us, with tears in his eyes. "*Ma Ma*'s profound love, courage, and protection sustained us."

In 1943, the Japanese took control of most of Hunan Province. They wanted someone to be the "puppet" governor. *Gong Gong*, a retired army general, was a well-respected and highly influential gentleman in Hunan Province. They picked *Gong Gong* to be their controlled governor.

Gong Gong refused and told them off. "No! I will never do this to my people!"

They let him leave, but they sent a troop of Cavalry and killed my *Gong Gong* on his way home. His body was found in a lake, many days later.

After *Gong Gong* died for his people, poor *Po Po* was alone with two young sons, hiding in the mountains. My second uncle was fourteen, and my third uncle was eleven. *Po Po* lived one day at a time. With courage, endurance, and perseverance, she survived hardship and suffering, pain and grief, and worries and poverty.

Two years later in 1945, the Japanese surrendered. *Po Po* brought her two young sons safely back to their home in Suzhou to reunite with the rest of the family—her oldest son and our family of five. Besides *Gong Gong,* his second wife and second son's birth mother, and some other relatives, also died during the war.

Chinese people's misfortune didn't end after the Japan surrendered. The Communist party was formed in China before the war against Japan. It was led by Mao Ze Dong. During the war against Japan, it got bigger and stronger by the day. The Nationalist Chinese Government didn't even get a chance to breathe and to reorganize the country after the war. The Communists started the civil war—fighting against the Nationalist government and against their own people.

*****

The Communists took over China in 1949. This was the year that families got separated again. It was the time numerous tragedies started—tragedies without an end—for countless Chinese people who escaped the communists and went to Taiwan.

The Taiwan Strait divided the Republic of China and Communist China. It was the *Iron Curtain* separating Chinese people into two different worlds. For numerous families, it was an eternal separation between parents and children, wives and husbands, brothers and sisters, and grandparents and grandchildren…

My father, a Nationalist Army general, followed the government and went to Taiwan in 1949. Father arranged for our mother and us four children, to stay in Hong Kong until an arrangement was made for us in Taiwan. *Po Po* came with us to help us. Our three uncles decided to stay—it was the sons' obligation to guard the properties *Gong Gong* had left in Suzhou. We left on the very last boat for Hong Kong.

That year, Mother was thirty-two years old; our oldest uncle was thirty years old; the second uncle was twenty years old; and the youngest uncle was seventeen years old. *Po Po* was seventy years old.

It was a tragedy of eternal separation for our family. It was the last time *Po Po* saw her three sons, and it was my mother's forever good-bye wave to her three beloved brothers.

There was no correspondence allowed between Taiwan and mainland China. *Po Po* missed her sons and worried about their well-being, day and night. Mother constantly asked friends in Hong Kong to check on her three brothers in Suzhou. But there was no news whatsoever from the other side of the *Iron Curtain*.

Po Po finally stopped asking, "Any news from Suzhou?"

As the years went by, her pupils became duller and her body got weaker. There was no more expression on her face. There was no more sparkle in her eyes. There were no more tears left. Hopelessness, depression, and despair filled her heart.

In my memory, for the seven years when *Po Po* was with us in Hong Kong and Taiwan, *Po Po* never smiled, and she seldom talked. She never played with us.

The unbearable, lingering grief weakened her heart, and the indescribable anguish and hopelessness deteriorated her body. My *Po Po* died broken-hearted, when I was eleven years old.

Po Po, Po Po!

What a courageous and tragic life your generation lived!

What unspeakable pain, grief, suffering, and despair you carried!

What an amazing love, unbelievable endurance, perseverance, and courage you had!

*****

Casey called out to me, "*Po Po, Po Po!* Look what I did. I wrote more than one hundred Chinese characters." Proudly he showed me the beautiful characters he had written.

I patted his head and gave him a big smile and a hug. "Wow! You can write so many words. Show them to Mommy and Daddy."

Kiran ran to me and held one of my fingers with one of his little hands. "*Po Po*, come with me."

We sat down on the floor and raced his favorite cars.

"*Po Po, Po Po*!" Here came Holly running toward me. We hugged and we kissed.

"Down. Down. *Po Po*'s house." She wanted to go downstairs to play in my in-law-suite again.

Our new princess Callie gave me a beautiful smile, like a blooming rose. She kicked her legs non-stop, looking excited as we walked by her.

My precious ones,

May you remember your Po Po—a Po Po who has lived a blissful life, with lots of love, joy, and laughter!

Po Po, Gong Gong, Ma Ma, and three uncles

21

Ma Ma

I finished my sophomore year in college and came home for summer vacation. Since I was away for college, my family didn't want me to worry, so I didn't even know *Ma Ma* [Mother] had been seriously ill for a while. Nothing seemed to help her condition. The whole family was concerned and very worried.

One morning when I went to get groceries at the open market, the merchant of a fruit stand asked me, "Where is your mother? I haven't seen her for a long time."

I wondered how he knew my mother and I were related. "She has been sick."

"What's wrong with her?"

"There is something wrong with her liver."

"I hope she will feel well soon. Your mother is the kindest person I've ever known."

A few days later, the man at the fruit stand appeared at our door, and he brought some herb medicine with him. "This herbal medicine is very effective for liver problems. It cured many people. I got the herbs in the mountain for your mother. Have her try it."

What a caring person this man was! "Thank you so much."

We were deeply touched that a fruit stand merchant in the market cared so much about *Ma Ma*'s wellbeing. We prepared the herb medicine according to his instructions, and *Ma Ma* took it for a week or so. Amazingly, *Ma Ma* got well. Her healing was like a miracle.

We always had one or two helpers doing housework, cooking, and taking care of younger siblings. Every morning *Ma Ma* bought the daily groceries needed at the neighborhood market. I went with her sometimes during winter or summer vacation.

People bargained for everything. Some people were very rude and disrespectful to the merchants. My mother didn't bargain at all.

I was curious. "How come you never bargain?"

Ma Ma, a kind and gentle lady, said to me, "They don't make much, and they need to support their families, too."

The merchants at the market identified *Ma Ma* as the kindest and most gentle lady—the lady who never bargained. They really appreciated her. Although she never bargained, they always gave her fair prices and quality produce.

What she said to me that day has stayed with me forever. Bargaining is still a culture for shopping in China. During the eight years I taught in Beijing, I didn't have the heart to bargain as other people did. My loyal and caring helper, Xiao Mei, was worried about me whenever I went shopping. She thought I was too soft-hearted, and she feared people took advantage of me.

She wanted so much to protect me. "You got taken again! Take me along when you shop next time."

I remembered what my loving mother said to me a long, long time ago. "It's okay. They don't make much, and they need to provide for their families."

Xiao Mei just shook her head.

*****

In *Ma Ma*'s eyes there was no bad person. She never discriminated against anyone. She had a kind heart and a gentle soul; she saw only the goodness of everyone. She always found reasons to forgive people.

When I was in college, I had a friend who was smart and beautiful, but she had trouble getting along with people. I was probably one of a very few people who never had a conflict with her throughout four years of college. She came to our house often, and my family knew her well.

One day I shared with my family an incident related to her at school. "It is so sad to see how much people dislike her. I really feel sorry for her."

Ma Ma remarked with her gentle voice, "Be nice to her. She grew up in an unstable and insecure environment."

"She is truly annoying sometimes." I remarked.

"She needs love and acceptance. If you grew up in her environment, you might be worse and more annoying."

What *Ma Ma* said to me that day has stayed in my heart ever since. Although I didn't approve of this friend's behavior sometimes, I tried not to be judgmental. Instead I tried to feel for her, with empathy and understanding, and I provided her the extra attention and friendship she desperately needed.

I was so thankful that I was born to a stable and loving family.

I understood then why *Ma Ma* was always so peaceful, patient, kind, and understanding. She embraced everyone without any discrimination whatsoever, with empathy and compassion.

With this understanding and realization in my heart, I became more sensitive to people's behaviors and more understanding of their hidden feelings they might not even know themselves. I remember always and constantly practice what *Ma Ma* taught me—to transform the negative to the positive with empathy and compassion.

I was very actively involved at different levels and areas throughout the years, project after project and commitment after commitment, for the community and for my students. I was a recognized and visible figure.

There was jealousy, and there were rumors.

Friends were angry with the people spreading rumors about me. "Aren't you angry at them?"

I laughed at some of the ridiculous rumors. "People who know me will know those rumors are not true."

"You are not going to do anything about it?"

"No."

"Why?"

I was too busy to waste my time and energy on negative people. "When people are jealous of you, they feel inferior and insecure themselves. It's not a good feeling. I feel sorry for them."

When I was stabbed in the back recently by a person who was truly petty and unappreciative, again I let it go.

Friends who witnessed what happened to me were surprised that I didn't let it bother me—as if nothing had happened.

A friend just couldn't understand. "How can you do it? I'd be very angry."

"She grew up in an unhealthy environment, without trust and security, where people stabbed one another in the back for survival. She is still living such a life, in fear and insecurity."

Again I felt extremely blessed and thankful that I grew up in a decent, healthy, trusting, and simple environment—surrounded with lots of love.

Ma Ma's example, guidance, teachings, and wisdom bestowed on us seven children compassionate hearts—empathy and understanding. Her teachings and wisdom have accompanied me and taught me how to transform the negative to the positive throughout the years.

Whenever and wherever I am, I live an uncomplicated and positive life—embracing people with empathy, compassion, and *Ma Ma's* love and guidance.

*****

Ma Ma was born to a wealthy and prestigious family. *Gong Gong,* Min Gang Ling, was a general in the army after the revolution, fighting side by side with Dr. Sun Yet Sen to overthrow the Qing Dynasty. He was an open-minded visionary and a courageous liberal. He didn't like the politics, so he decided to retire early from the army. He gave up his prestigious and well-respected position.

Gong Gong loved land, and he loved Suzhou, a city near Shanghai, known for beautiful garden houses. He worked very hard with his limited funds. He became a very successful developer in Suzhou.

Their house, *Yi Yuan,* was built in the late 1920s. There was a ballroom with a marble floor in the house because *Gong Gong* believed dancing was good exercise for the body and the mind. It also had a tennis court in their yard so that children could play a sport conveniently. There was a big pond with lots of fish, and there were beautiful landscapes with trees and flowers all over the garden. *Gong Gong* truly was ahead of his time with ideas and visions that most people couldn't imagine back in the late 1920s in China.

When *Ma Ma* was around 20, *Gong Gong* decided it was time to choose a husband for his only daughter.

I loved to listen to *Ma Ma*'s stories. *Ma Ma* was a romantic and sentimental person. She always told us stories with her gentle voice. I was very curious. "Were you okay to have *Gong Gong* pick your husband for you?"

She was an obedient daughter. "It was the way at the time."

Gong Gong was a well-respected and honorable man. *Ma Ma* trusted her father totally. *Gong Gong* loved friends, and he had lots of them—different ages and in different fields.

Memories took *Ma Ma* back in time to when she was a young maiden. "When *Gong Gong* decided it was time for me to get married, there were more than one hundred candidates, recommended by his friends."

"Wow! You didn't know any of them?!"

"No. There were lawyers, doctors, engineers, bankers, and scholars, etc., all from prestigious and rich families. Your father was the only soldier, without anything, among them."

"Why did *Gong Gong* pick Father, a poor soldier, for you?"

Father was a brilliant and handsome young man. He had a positive and lively spirit. He was a good-natured and kind man. His parents passed away when he was little. "He was an energetic and genuine person. He had no family. My father didn't want me to marry into a complicated household, a rich family with a lot of conflicts."

"It would be miserable in such a family." I agreed totally.

"Most people would have selected a young man from a rich and prestigious family for their daughter. *Gong Gong* picked a poor soldier, without any family and without money, for me. He didn't want me to suffer and to live in fear with in-laws in a big family."

There were many horror stories about the way daughters-in-law were abused in big and rich families. "What a profound love! *Gong Gong* was truly a wise man. He chose the right man for you."

I wished that I knew *Gong Gong*, but he was murdered by the Japanese before my twin sister and I were born.

Gong Gong's decision—selecting a poor soldier for my mother—

shocked all the people around him.

Ma Ma missed her beloved and admired father. "Yes, your *Gong Gong* was indeed a wise man and a loving father."

After being engaged for two years, *Ma Ma* married my father, a soldier. Father fought hard in the front lines for eight years against the Japanese. He became a general at a very young age right before World War II ended in 1945.

Their first born, my older brother, Karl, is a doctor, and he was a general in the army also.

How unique it was Mother had three generals in her life.

*****

When we were growing up, the first thing *Ma Ma* did every morning was to burn incense and prayed in front of an altar. It was her daily ritual. I was deeply moved by her sincerity and piety. She was praying for us every single day.

I never knew the power of her prayers until later in life.

Ma Ma didn't cook, but every morning she gave each of us vitamins, prepared warm milk, and served breakfast to us, Father and seven children, at different times. Everyone had a full schedule. She made sure each of us had a good breakfast and vitamins before going to work or school.

She never rushed us. "Take time to eat breakfast. Be sure to take your vitamins. Milk will help you grow strong bones and be tall."

When we got home from school, at different times, she asked each of us, "How was school? Are you hungry?" She listened to what we shared with her, attentively and patiently. I've always wondered how *Ma Ma* took care of seven children with such patience.

Ma Ma never pressured us, either to do anything or not to do anything. She took great care of us. She stood by us and supported us as needed, always. She was our forever non-judgmental supporter.

After college, I became a teacher teaching Beginner English to 180 seventh grade boys at Keelung Secondary School. I took the bus and then the train to go to teach. *Ma Ma* served my breakfast and vitamins.

She stayed and chatted with me while I was eating. She opened the door for me when I was leaving. Every morning she stayed by the doorway and waved goodbye to me until I turned the corner at the end of the block.

My classes were all in the morning, and I usually came home for lunch at noon. *Ma Ma* heated up food and stayed with me while I ate lunch. I shared my day of teaching and talked about my students with her.

I was deeply loved and well taken care of by *Ma Ma*'s love and blessings every single day.

Ma Ma had unconditional love, compassion, patience, and wisdom—which all had a lasting impact on us.

She loved to read, and her only pastime was reading. She could sew. She made beautiful dresses, handsome jackets, and the best fitted pants for my twin sister and me. I still have the jean jacket she made for me when I was in high school. She was quite creative with the design, using both sides of the fabric to make it into a jacket with two different colors. Later in life when I learned how to sew, I appreciated even more her creativity with sewing.

Ma Ma never worked outside of the house. She never did anything for herself. She never went out for herself. She was always home. She did whatever we wanted to do, and she went wherever the family wanted to go. She was the only selfless person I have ever known.

I have always wondered:

How could Ma Ma live such a selfless life the way she did?

Ma Ma devoted her whole life totally to Father and us seven children. She was content, and she was peaceful.

We were her life, we were her world, we were her career, and we were her accomplishment.

How blessed we were, being *Ma Ma*'s children!

We are still blessed with our loving, wise, kind, and selfless *Ma Ma*. Her teachings are in our blood. Her compassion is our practice. Her wisdom is our guidance. Her spirit is in our souls. *Ma Ma* accompanies us wherever we are and whatever we do.

Ma Ma lives forever in our hearts. *Ma Ma*'s love is eternal....

General and Mrs. Nan Kwang Tan *(Ba Ba* and *Ma Ma)*

Ba Ba

"*Gong Gong* was fun. He always teased us, and he enjoyed us. He was happy and playful like a kid, not boring at all," Bobby, my twin sister Irene's second son, commented when he was a teenager.

"What do you remember about *Gong Gong?*" I asked our two daughters, Joline and Andrea.

"*Gong Gong* was always in good spirits. He liked to sing. He always had these sparkles in his eyes when he was singing. He loved people. People made him happy." Andrea responded with a smile. She continued. "He was a passionate person, and he enjoyed life. He was alert, positive, and fun. He loved to wear floral Hawaiian shirts."

Joline, our older daughter, smiled and nodded. "I remember his Hawaiian shirts too. When I was little, I thought *Gong Gong* was tough and strict, compared with gentle loving *Po Po*. But as I grew older, I felt different about him. I saw different things about him."

"What different things?" I asked.

"*Gong Gong* was very loving and caring. He was so independent and determined. Nothing could hold him back, and no one could stop him once he decided to do something. He would figure a way to make it happen."

"Yes! That was your *Gong Gong,* my *Ba Ba* [Father]!"

*****

It was Saturday, January 4th, 1975. My husband Don and I were on our way home to Lincoln, Nebraska, after spending the holidays with his folks in Portage, Wisconsin. We decided to spend the night in Iowa City, halfway, since we hadn't left for home until afternoon.

When we exited I-80 to look for a motel, we stopped at one not far from the exit. I saw a billboard, "Free Ride to the Hospital," by the motel. I was curious, and I asked Don, "What's that for? Why free ride to the hospital?"

"There is a very good medical school and hospital nearby. A lot of people come here from different parts of the region for treatment. Some people need rides to the hospital sometimes."

I was impressed with the motel. "What a good service!"

After we checked in and settled in the motel, we went to a nearby restaurant for dinner. Not long after dinner, Don got sick and vomited violently, non-stop. I was worried about his condition, and I panicked. I didn't know what to do!

At that moment, I remembered what my *Ba Ba* always said to me when I panicked about things when I was growing up. "Don't panic! Clear your mind and think. There is always a way to solve the problem."

Yes, I need to clear my head and think!
Don't panic!
I need to get him to the hospital.
I can't drive his stick shift car.
What do I do?
That sign said "Free Ride to the Hospital!"

I called the front desk right away and asked for a ride to the hospital. The manager took us to the emergency room at the hospital. Don had food poisoning. The doctor told us that Don could leave after getting a shot.

We had to get back home the next day since the following day was Monday, a working day for both of us. Don was still pretty sick. There was no way he could drive us home. I had never driven on the highway before, let alone driven a stick shift car.

It was midnight when we got back from the hospital. I was worried; I was quiet; and I needed to prepare for the best as I expected the worst.

How do we get home if Don is too sick to drive tomorrow?
What happens if we get stuck here for more than a couple of days?

My twin sister Irene lived in Iowa City for a few years while her husband was in graduate school at the University of Iowa. Both my younger sister Eileen and my younger brother Ken attended graduate school there also.

I wondered if they still had some friends living in Iowa City. I called Ken and told him what had happened and of course my concerns. "We have a situation here. I can't drive Don's car. We need to go back tomorrow. I am not sure Don will be well enough to drive us home. And I don't know how long we will be here either. If that's the case, we might need some help. Do you still have any friends here who might help us if needed?"

"We have a good friend, Hsiao, still living there. Let me call him to see if he can help you. I will call you back right away."

Ken called back five minutes later. "Hsiao and his wife offered to drive you back if Don doesn't get well tomorrow." He gave me Hsiao's phone number.

I called Hsiao and thanked them for their support and willingness to help.

With this arrangement and assurance, I felt relieved, and I got a few hours of sleep. Don had a good night's sleep after the shot. He was well enough to drive us home the next day as scheduled.

Ba Ba helped me survive this ordeal, even though he was in Taiwan at the time. *Ba Ba*'s words accompany me as I face life's ups and downs throughout the years.

Whenever Joline and Andrea panicked and worried about things when they were growing up, I passed on Ba Ba's guidance to them. "Don't panic! Clear your mind and think. There is always a way to solve the problem."

*****

A Chinese person asks me when we first meet, "Where are you from?"

I answer, "I am from Canton."

I tell them where my ancestors, on my father's side, came from, not

Chungking where I was born. That is the Chinese way.

Canton (Guangdong) Province is on the coast in Southern China. People can go to Hong Kong by train or ferry in less than an hour. Since it is on the coast, Cantonese people had early exposure to the outside world—Southeast Asian countries and Western countries.

In the late 1800s, the Qing Dynasty, isolated from the rest of the world, was very corrupt and weak. People suffered tremendously. A great number of people in Canton and the neighboring province, Fujian, left their hometowns and went to different countries in Southeast Asia and the U.S.A. for a better life.

Ba Ba's ancestors came from Kaiping, Canton. His family, the Tans, was a big clan in Kaiping. It was a well-to-do family. My *Ye Ye* [paternal grandfather] went to Vietnam when things got worse in China, as a lot of Cantonese did during the time of chaos and turbulence.

Ba Ba was born in Vietnam, and he was the youngest of seven children. *Nai Nai* [paternal grandmother] died shortly after *Ba Ba* was born. *Ye Ye* took *Ba Ba* back to his home in Kaiping, Canton.

Ye Ye was a Chinese medicine doctor, and he practiced Taoism diligently. He could tell one's future. When *Ba Ba* was a toddler, *Ye Ye* said to his family one day, "This kid will do well in the future."

Shortly after that, he left to practice Taoism and self-cultivation, and to search for the truth. No one knew where he went, no one knew what he did, and no one knew if he would come back.

Ba Ba was just a toddler, without a mother and without a father, so he became an orphan. He was raised by the clan.

I can't imagine what our childhood would be like without the pampering love from our parents. It gives me heartache just thinking of and visualizing *Ba Ba*'s childhood, without loving care from either of his parents. I've always wondered how *Ba Ba* survived his childhood. How could he be such a positive, good-spirited, compassionate, courageous, and successful person, without any bitterness, complaints, and negativity?

I loved to listen to my parents telling us old stories. One time, *Ba Ba* was telling us some of the things that happened to him when he was a kid. It always made me very sad to know that *Ba Ba* was not always treated fairly while growing up. There was no one there to guide him, love him, or protect him.

I was curious if he joined the army because of that. "*Ba Ba,* why did you become a soldier?"

"Well, after high school, I was working in a theater in Shanghai that was owned by the family."

"Wow! Your family had a theater in Shanghai? You could watch all the movies that you wanted to watch." No wonder *Ba Ba* took us to see movies almost every weekend.

"Yeah, but I was not happy working there. It was not challenging at all, and it was boring. There was no future for me. I knew I needed to do something different, something more stimulating and satisfying."

Ba Ba continued. "When I was at the cross roads, I met a Buddhist monk."

"A real monk? A bald-headed monk?" I interrupted again.

"Yes. What he told me changed my life."

"What did he say to you?"

"After I shared my life and thoughts with him, the monk looked at me and studied me in a profound way for a while. Then he told me something that changed my life."

Ba Ba had a sip of tea and continued. "He told me seriously, 'You should join the army. Our country needs people like you. You will be a general someday. It is your destiny.'"

It sounded amazing. "Really?! He could tell your fortune?"

"I didn't take the general part seriously. But I joined the army and became a soldier. It is truly my destiny."

Ba Ba fought bravely and fearlessly against the Japanese for eight years in the front lines. He became a general at the age of 34, before World War II ended.

"The monk was right. You did become a general."

Ba Ba was very good at languages. He could speak the various dialects spoken in different parts of China. He attended St. John High School in Shanghai, where he learned his Shanghainese and English. When he was a general in the army, there were many American officers in Taiwan. He could communicate effectively with the American officers who worked with him. When he made an official visit to the Pentagon in the U.S., he didn't need an interpreter there, either.

Ba Ba loved learning, and he was a focused and hard-working student. He was one of the top students graduating from the Academy of the Army. Whatever he chose to do, he did well. His determination and will power never let him down. He didn't quit or fail. His mind was working non-stop, always searching for a better way to do things, anything. Working smart and effectively was one of his mottos.

Although *Ba Ba* was very busy as a general in the army, he checked on us seven kids and our studies very closely. In the evening, he patrolled from room to room like a commander checking on his soldiers, to see how we were doing with our studies. The year before I came to the U.S. for graduate school, he provided me opportunities to translate some articles into English so that I could practice my English.

"Learn to use terms in different areas. They will come in handy someday." He gave me articles in different areas, and some of them were related to the armed forces.

I used a dictionary to check on those terms that I had never seen or learned before. I tried my best to translate the articles, and *Ba Ba* always checked them when I finished.

He encouraged me always. "Good job. Keep it up."

Ba Ba was fast with his mind and nimble with his movement. He was intelligent, thorough, and well organized. He was always ready, and he was always ahead of schedule. "Always be well prepared and be ahead of the schedule. This way you have time to react or to amend the plan if anything should go wrong."

One day, my teenage daughter Joline asked me, "Why is it that you are always so well prepared and ahead of the schedule for everything?"

I do feel anxious if I am not well prepared and ahead of the schedule. "Do you think our life would have gone so smoothly if I were not well prepared for everything?"

"No."

I passed on to Joline what *Ba Ba* taught me when I was her age.

*****

Not long before the communists took over China completely in 1949, the Nationalist Chinese Commander in Chief General Fu handed Peking, now Beijing, to the communists without a fight, based on a mutual agreement to preserve the ancient city—not to make Peking a battle field. Several Nationalist Chinese generals were with Commander Fu at the time as he handed Peking to the communist. *Ba Ba* was one of them.

Ba Ba told us what happened when the communists took over Peking. "General Fu defected and joined the Communist Party."

"What? He surrendered just like that? Why?" I asked.

"The communist gave him a great offer. A group of us were with General Fu at the time when he surrendered."

I was concerned. "How did you get away from the communists?"

It took *Ba Ba* back in time. "It was one of the strangest things."

"What did they want? Did they torture you?"

"No."

"Then what happened?"

"One day a communist officer told me that according to their investigation, I was clean, not corrupt. I was given a choice to stay or to leave.'" *Ba Ba* chose to leave. Amazingly, he returned home safely.

"Wow! Just like that?"

"Yeah, I came back safely." He seemed to be in deep thought remembering what happened in Beijing.

It was such a close call, to say the least. *Ba Ba* didn't have any money or property like some other generals. He was a person of integrity, and it saved him from the communists.

There was politics and there was corruption in the army. When *Ba Ba* was in his 40s, he held a position in the Armed Forces in charge of a lot of supplies, biddings for constructions, and budgets for different projects.

One day when I, an eighth grader at the time, came home from school, I saw some fruit and a basket on the ground outside of the front door. I wondered where it came from.

"Take your money and get out of my house right now!" *Ba Ba* said in a very angry tone to a man standing in the living room across from him.

The man picked up the red envelope with lots of money in it from the ground, and he left.

"What happened?" I asked *Ma Ma* timidly since *Ba Ba* didn't look happy.

"That man tried to bribe your father to accept his bidding on a construction project."

Apparently *Ba Ba* threw out the basket full of fruit when he discovered there was money in the basket.

"Oh! No." No wonder *Ba Ba* was so mad. It was such an insult that the man would try to bribe *Ba Ba,* a person of integrity and honor.

Ba Ba's immediate supervisor was a very corrupt and greedy person. *Ba Ba* had known about his corruption for a long time. One day he wanted *Ba Ba* to join him and help him with corruption. *Ba Ba* refused and told him off.

"No! I will not do this to our country! You shouldn't do it either!"

After that day, for ten years, his corrupt supervisor blocked all the opportunities for *Ba Ba*'s promotion.

Although *Ba Ba* was devastated by this unfairness and injustice, he continued to stand by his principles, and he lived his dignified life. *Ba Ba* was truly a person of integrity and honor. It is in our blood to be honorable and honest, always.

When I was the China Link Supervisor at International School of Beijing in China, I was in charge of some purchasing budget. One time after I purchased some costumes for the school, the merchant asked me what amount I wanted written on the receipt.

I was puzzled and wondered why there was such a question. "What do you mean? Didn't we just add up the total cost? Write down the exact amount."

She looked at me in a funny and unbelieving way. "Okay."

I learned later that it was a common practice for corrupt people to have a bigger amount than the actual cost written on the receipts. The difference between the two amounts was their "reward" money. No wonder the merchant looked at me the way she did when I told her to write the exact amount on the receipt.

*****

When we were growing up, we always did something for fun on weekends. *Ba Ba* and *Ma Ma* took us to see either Chinese or Western movies. In the summer, we went to *Bi Tan* [Green Lake] to play in the lake, to row the boat, and to have fun in the water.

Ba Ba was very active and athletic. He was good at whatever sport he tried. He learned how to play tennis when he was 60, and the young people who played with him seldom could beat him. *Ba Ba* had led a badminton team to participate in many Armed Forces tournaments.

Being an energetic and fun person, *Ba Ba* had many interests. He enjoyed Chinese opera and operas from different regions of China. He taught himself how to play the moon guitar, a Chinese stringed instrument. When he was a young man, he competed in track, swimming, and even singing. He enjoyed learning and trying new things.

Ba Ba loved and enjoyed life, and he lived a full and balanced life. He had a pure and happy heart like a kid. He was always ready to help people who needed his help, with compassion and kindness. He was well liked and appreciated by people of all ages.

During the stressful 10 years working under his corrupt supervisor, *Ba Ba* stayed positive. He learned to do Chinese grass writing, a fancy and elegant style of Chinese characters. His grass writing was truly artistic and beautiful. Again he didn't let anyone or anything affect his creativity and passion for life. He stood tall and proud, with a good spirit always!

Ba Ba showed us how to let go of what you can't change and how to let go of the negative. Working hard and playing hard was his way to balance his stressful life. He modeled how to change pace and to regenerate energy while living a busy life. He demonstrated to us how to transform the negative to the positive, with a high spirit that no one can take away.

I practice what I learned from *Ba Ba*: Doing your very best with whatever you do, you won't have any regrets; and making the best out of everything and everyone whenever and wherever, you live a fuller life.

Ba Ba's uprightness, tenacity, wisdom, and insight in life have helped me live a fulfilled and positive life.

*****

Among *Ma Ma* and *Ba Ba*'s generation, love was not expressed verbally. I never heard them saying, "*Wo ai ni* [I love you]" to each other. But the love between them was most profound. Their inseparable bonding—deepest trust and heartfelt sentiment—was reflected in everyday life.

Ba Ba never criticized *Ma Ma*, and he always complimented *Ma Ma* on her selfless love for us. "Your *Ma Ma* is the kindest lady and the most loving mother. We are truly blessed."

Ma Ma supported *Ba Ba* at all times with her loving and understanding heart. She accepted and embraced him—no matter what happened, whatever he decided to do, and however he behaved. She always provided *Ba Ba* subtle and gentle advice whenever needed.

Ma Ma loved *Ba Ba* as a mother loves a child—accepting, embracing, and supporting with love, gentleness, kindness, understanding, and compassion, all her life.

*****

After *Ma Ma*'s passing in 1990, *Ba Ba* lived with Eileen, my younger sister who was single, in Los Angeles. I invited *Ba Ba* to stay with us every summer when I was not teaching. We truly enjoyed his visit. Our house was always full of friends on weekends. He enjoyed all of my friends, young and old, and my friends loved him.

I took *Ba Ba* everywhere I went, and we took walks and chatted every day. One day in the summer of 1995, when we walked and talked after dinner, *Ba Ba* said, "I have been fortunate with a good life, especially having your mother as my wife."

I agreed totally. "Yes, you indeed have lived a good life with lots of blessings, even with all the ups and downs throughout the years."

"You don't know how lucky you kids are for having your *Ma Ma* as your mother. The only thing that I have wished all my life is that I had a mother like your mother." He looked up at the sky in deep thought—great sadness in his eyes.

I understood why *Ba Ba* felt sad. His mother died shortly after he was born, and his father left him with relatives when he was a toddler, so he never had the pampering love from either of his parents while growing up, as we did.

It made me very sad, and my heart was aching inside for *Ba Ba*. I tried to comfort him. "You are blessed with many things in life, *Ma Ma,* for one."

He nodded his head and totally agreed. "Your mother was the kindest lady and the best mother I have ever known."

"She was like a mother taking great care of you and standing by you all her life."

"Yes. She was."

Although *Ba Ba* was 84, he was in great shape—had a clear mind, full energy, and nimble movement. His general pension enabled him to live a very comfortable retired life. "You have a blissful life. You have good health and a good retirement that many people don't have at your age."

"Indeed, I have many blessings." He smiled.

"We kids are very lucky to have a pleasant, easy-going, and open-minded father like you. We may not be the most successful people, but we all are good-natured and kind people like you and *Ma Ma*. We all love you dearly. We all enjoy you."

Ba Ba looked cheerful again. "I am truly lucky to have a great wife and wonderful kids."

I feel genuinely grateful all my life—having *Ba Ba* and *Ma Ma* as my parents.

*****

It was on Sunday, February 18th, 1996, that I received a call from Eileen, my younger sister, in L.A.

She was crying. "*Ba Ba* is gone!"

Ba Ba was in good health and good spirits. I had talked to him on the phone just a week ago. I had invited *Ba Ba* to come to see my biennial production, *Chinese Kaleidoscope,* scheduled in April. He was supposed to spend spring and summer with us in Lincoln, Nebraska.

I was shocked. "What do you mean he is gone? What happened?!"

"We don't know. We are in the hospital." Irene, my twin sister, was there with Eileen.

*****

One day in January, *Ba Ba* said to Eileen, "I am tired. I want to go."

Eileen was sad hearing this, and she tried to distract *Ba Ba* from the idea. She replied jokingly, "I am tired, too. I will go with you."

In the following month *Ba Ba* developed seven sets of pictures that he treasured and sent to each of us seven children. He told Eileen exactly how he wanted everything to be taken care of. He was well prepared and ahead of schedule as always, even for his death.

Eileen didn't want us to feel upset and sad. She kept it to herself and didn't share this with us.

Ba Ba became a vegetarian and practiced Buddhist meditation diligently for self-cultivation after *Ma Ma*'s passing in 1990. He went to a meditation center with Eileen to meditate for three or four hours every Sunday. *Ba Ba*'s spiritual practice brought him peace for six years without *Ma Ma* by his side.

A month after he told Eileen he was ready to go, *Ba Ba* and *Ma Ma* were reunited in heaven, with several hundred people meditating by his side—at the meditation center.

We were devastated and deeply saddened. But we were glad that he didn't suffer with any pain or misery of any kind of illness. He was blessed with safety during the war in the front lines, without injury. He lived a healthy and active life. *Ba Ba* never spent a single day in the hospital throughout his 85 years of life.

We learned only in books that a high monk reaching an extraordinary spiritual level could choose his time to leave the earthly world in

41

meditation. *Ba Ba* had chosen his own time to leave us to join *Ma Ma*, just like a high monk—the hospital couldn't identify the cause of his death.

With flexibility and perseverance like bamboo, *Ba Ba* swayed and stood fast in the blowing wind. With endurance and courage he survived the vigorous storms in life. *Ba Ba* stood tall and lived a remarkable life—a life of love, honor, and pride.

Not a day goes by I don't think of my beloved *Ba Ba* and *Ma Ma*. Not a day goes by I don't thank God for my blessings in life, especially the love from *Ba Ba* and *Ma Ma.Ba Ba,*

Your legacy will live on!
Your courage and your spirit are in our blood.
Your teachings will be passed on to your descendants.
We miss you, Ba Ba, Ma Ma !
We love you, Ba Ba, Ma Ma!
Thank you for being our forever loving parents…

Ba Ba at Pentagon

Ba Ba, Ma Ma, **Karl, Ken, Celine, Irene in Peking (Beijing)**

The Tomboy and the Little Lady

People often looked at Irene and me, dressed alike, when we were little, and they asked, "Are you twins?"

Irene and I answered together. "Yes!"

"Who is older?"

I pointed at Irene. "She is fifteen minutes older."

"*Jie Jie* [older sister] is prettier," people usually commented, insensitively.

*****

Mother always told me whenever I laughed and giggled loudly when I was little, "A girl shouldn't show teeth when laughing." This is how she was brought up to be a lady.

I wondered how to laugh or smile without showing teeth. "How do you laugh with your mouth closed?" My mother truly was a Chinese lady. She really never showed her teeth when she laughed. She covered her mouth with one of her hands when something was really funny.

It was impossible for me. I was a simple, free-spirited happy soul. I laughed at myself being stupid and I laughed at every little funny thing. I couldn't laugh without showing my teeth then, and I can't now.

Mother gave up on me—my being a lady like her. She let me be— to enjoy my happy life my own way.

She smiled and shook her head whenever I was giggling and laughing, non-stop, at funny things. "Silly girl!"

Whenever I told her about things I wanted to do, she never stopped me. Mother, a lady of wisdom, knew too well that this free-spirited little girl had a mind of her own. Nothing and no one could stop her.

But Irene was different. She never laughed the way I did. She was beautiful. She was quiet. She was wise. She was a gentle little lady. She didn't have "crazy" ideas as I did. She never did the "wild" things as I did.

Our father and mother were totally opposite. Father was very fast with thinking, reactions, and actions, and he was always ahead of everyone and everything. Mother never had fast motion or movement. Father was active and alert while Mother was gentle, reserved, and wise. Father was athletic, and Mother never did any sport. Father was decisive, and Mother went along with whatever he decided, with gentle and subtle remarks of wisdom as needed.

Irene was the other half of me, the half I couldn't be. We are night and day different, just like Father and Mother. We were very close. We didn't talk until three years old, but before then, we communicated with each other all the time in our own language.

We loved to listen to Mother talking about us when we were little. Once she said, "Even when you two were babies, you were so different."

"Really? How different?" I asked.

"Irene could play on your oldest uncle's lap for the whole afternoon while he was reading."

I was curious. "What about me? Where was I?"

Mother smiled and continued. "Each one of you had a nanny. You never could sit still at one spot. Your nanny took you to play with all the other helpers around the house. You were playful. You were always so happy and excited, giggling and laughing. You made people so happy."

When we first moved to Taiwan from Hong Kong, Irene and I were five years old. Father was the Deputy Commander of the Port of Kaohsiung in Southern Taiwan. There was no kindergarten then. Our *General* father commanded Irene and me, two untrained *soldiers*, to attend the first grade in a public school, the *battle field*. It was during the second semester.

Irene and I walked quite a distance to school every day, side by side and hand in hand. We didn't know what was going on in the class, since we were younger than other kids and we missed the critical first semester. But we never missed a day of school. Were we learning anything in class? Only Heaven knew!

Mother, with five kids then, tried to adjust to her new life in a much smaller house with only one helper, instead of nine or ten helpers in their garden house in Suzhou. She was overwhelmed, and she had a lot to worry about. She was drained.

Before long, Father got transferred, and we moved to Taipei, the biggest city in Taiwan. We started the second grade. There were 72 students in our class. Irene and I were still totally lost and didn't know what was going on.

Students were always ranked at the end of each year. At the end of our second grade, Irene was ranked 65 and I was 66 out of 72 students. What glorious report cards! But Irene and I didn't really understand what the ranks meant. We, two *special* students, still didn't know what was going on at all.

I bet the teachers I had for first and second grade, whom I have no memory of, would never believe that I made it this far and became a teacher, with a master's degree in Special Education.

Irene and I sometimes talked about our *glorious* past, when we were five and six. I laughed so hard and asked her, with tears in my eyes, "Do you remember how dumb we were? Do you remember the lollipop factory?"

"Of course!" She started to laugh, non-stop.

When we were in first grade in Kaohsiung, every day on our way home we passed a factory where they made lollipops. Very often the two of us stood by the window watching people wrap the lollipops with paper. It was fascinating to watch them make our favorite candy. People must have thought that the twins looked so dumb but cute, and they gave us lollipops whenever we showed up by the window. We were so happy sucking on them while walking the long way home.

We had great fun remembering some of the *smart* things we did together. "They always gave us lollipops. They were very kind people," Irene remarked.

We didn't really know what was going on with our lives until we were in the third grade. We finally caught up and became enlightened, as Chinese people say about the late bloomers.

I became competitive and organized, I moved and learned faster, and I was more alert. I started raising the bar for myself. I was more observant and curious about what was happening around me. I was elected president of my class, and I was ranked number 1 student when I was in ninth grade.

Irene was different. She was still the beautiful little lady, without fast motion. She was easy going, not competitive at all. She was quiet and could stay at one spot daydreaming for a long time. I always wondered what it would be like to be her.

I usually did my homework right after I got home from school. As soon as I finished, I went outside to play.

A girl next door liked to play with me. "Would you ride bike with me?"

"Sure!"

One time I was steering and she was pedaling, on the same bike. Suddenly a duck appeared from nowhere, right in front of us. I had no time to steer away. I panicked and yelled, "Duck! Slow down!" Too late! We ran over the tip of the duck's tail. Luckily we didn't fall, and the duck survived. We laughed so hard afterward.

Where was Irene? She was probably at home sitting somewhere quietly daydreaming.

My brother Ken is two years younger than we are. He was the president of his class, a selected model student of his class every year, the captain of the baseball team, and the leader of our neighborhood. Almost everyone followed him around, including me, but not Irene.

We played soccer in the street. We played marbles on the ground. We flew the kites we made ourselves from bamboo and newspaper. We did high jump holding the rope made of rubber bands. I was quite flexible. I could run fast, jump high, and jump far. It was great fun. I was always the only girl playing all these activities with the boys.

With the swords we made for ourselves, we did sword fighting against one another.

"Fight me!" It was more fun to fight people who were better than I.

Fighting them helped me improve my skills. I always wanted to fight against my younger brother Ken and my older brother Karl, the best ones of all.

I wanted to be a knight and to fight like a Round Table Knight of King Arthur. I admired their loyalty, courage, and code of honor, and their fighting for justice. I wanted to be knighted at our round table as *the Knight of Magnificent Eagle*, a name I picked for myself.

Where was Irene? This little lady stayed at home.

When we were in junior high, I loved to run. I competed in dash and relay races on field day. I was on the school softball team. Irene almost failed the physical education class that year.

My older brother, Karl, was really skillful at making things, especially bows and arrows. I helped him to sand the arrows to make them round and smooth. He showed us how to use a bow and arrow for target shooting.

"Let me try it again!" I loved aiming at the target with the fancy arrows Karl made for us. I tried it again and again until I was very good at it. What a heroic feeling, with the bow and arrow in my hands, to be like Robin Hood, another legendary hero I admired.

I wondered why Irene was not interested in such fun sport.

When we were little, we loved to hike at Neihu, one of my favorite places for outings near Taipei. With my brothers, not Irene, I climbed rocks, jumped off boulders, and ran on pebbles to cross the little stream. What an adventure!

Giggling and laughing happily, I yelled to my siblings, "Look at me!" It was great fun swinging on the rope that we brought to climb the trees and the steep hill, like adventurers in the movies.

Ba Ba noticed I could run fast and jump high, with good flexibility. He taught me how to play badminton. For at least five years before I went away to college, my father and I played against my two brothers, Karl and Ken, on weekends. Again, Irene, the quiet little lady, never played with us.

We had military training in high school. We learned to use rifles. I thought it was fun, and I was one of the top shooters. I represented our homeroom for competition.

I asked Irene, "How did you do with the rifle?"

"It was so loud. And it really hurt," she responded.

Irene and I attended the same school all the way through junior high. We were always together. We had to take an entrance exam to get into any junior high, high school, and college. After junior high, we were separated. We went to different high schools and different colleges.

It was quite an adjustment not to have Irene with me in school. She'd always been by my side, except for the wild things I did with our brothers and the other boys.

Irene was a great story teller, like our mother. I loved her detailed stories. I enjoyed listening to her telling me slowly in detail what happened in her school with her friends, when we were home together at night.

I loved singing and Irene loved dancing. She danced beautifully.

I wanted to dance as well as she did. "Would you teach me how to dance?"

"Sure! It is easy." She taught me how to rock and roll and how to dance other dances. She was a good teacher.

I loved the rhythm and the music. After I learned how to dance when we were in high school, dancing became one of my favorite activities. I love dancing. I love the floating motion of slow dances, and I enjoy the energy that goes with fast dances. I could really dance all night, even with cramps in my legs.

Irene is brave in her own ways, and I am a "chicken" in other ways. We know each other well. We enjoy being together.

*****

People ask Irene and me all the time, "Are you really twins?"

"Yes, we are."

"You are so different." We agreed.

Irene was a pretty little girl then, and she is a beautiful lady now—a kind, loving, gentle, and patient lady. She still enjoys dancing, and she still loves to tell stories. A couple of years ago she wrote a book, a collection of her beautiful spiritual stories, in Chinese.

I was a tomboy then, and I am still one now, full of action. I love to play, to learn, to do new things, and to challenge myself. I love to have fun as always, with people I enjoy whenever and wherever. I am in the process of recollecting and writing my "wild" stories in English.

Yes, Irene and I are so different. But we really are twins. We truly love each other and really appreciate each other, even with all our differences.

We, a tomboy and a lady, are forever best friends....

Tomboy Celine in action in Taiwan (1984)

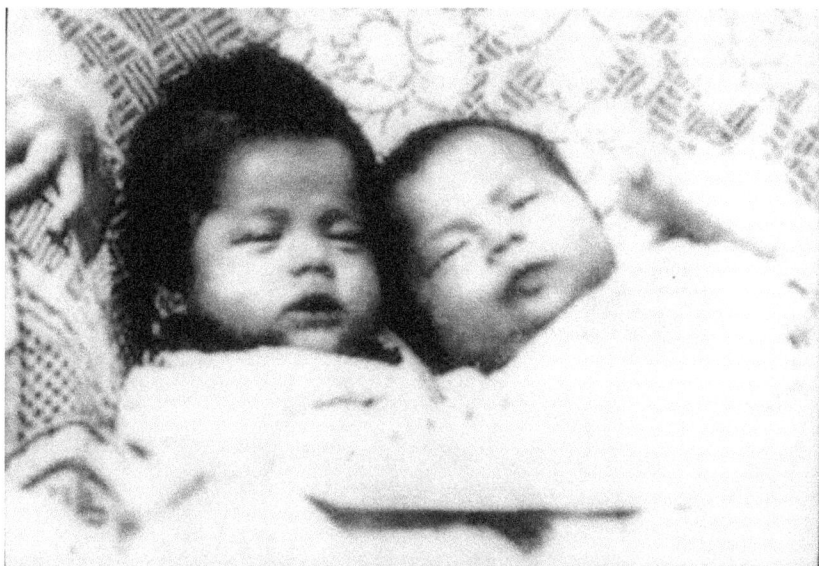

Irene & Celine

Karl, Ken, Irene, & Celine

Lady Irene & Tomboy Celine

Irene, Ma Ma, & Celine

Hands and Feet

Brothers and sisters are born your lifetime friends, and friends are brothers and sisters you choose for yourself.

Chinese people call siblings, *shou zu* [hands and feet], part of you, inseparable.

*****

In high school we lived under the constant and tremendous pressure of taking the college entrance examination. Lunch time was the break that we all looked forward to every day. It was a time to be with friends. We, four friends and I, always had lunch together.

"What's wrong with you? You look so tense today." I was concerned when a close friend, Chen, looked so unhappy.

"I got in trouble with my oldest sister last night."

"What happened?" I was curious.

"She always orders us around. She told me to do something while I was in the middle of something else. I didn't do it right away, and she got so mad at me."

"What did she do?" Lin asked.

"She told our parents when they came home that I didn't obey her."

"My oldest brother does that to us also. We are all so scared of him. He sometimes hits us if we don't follow his orders." Lee shared a similar experience with her oldest brother also.

With respect, we call older brothers *Ge Ge* [older brother] and older sisters *Jie Jie* [older sister], instead of by their names. In Chinese families *lao da* [the first born] is like a parent, in charge of the younger ones, especially when parents are absent. The *lao da*, either the oldest brother or the oldest sister, is the figure of authority to the younger siblings. Some of them can be bossy, strict, and demanding, even more so than the parents sometimes.

Karl

Our oldest brother, Karl, is six years older than my twin sister Irene and me. He is the *lao da* of us seven. He is not like some friends' oldest brothers or sisters. He was protective of us when we were young, and he still is today.

In my memory, Karl was never a kid. He seldom played with friends on the block like my younger brother Ken and I always did. He usually stayed at home, either studying or doing things inside the house.

Karl taught us how to make kites with newspaper and bamboo. "You need to have long enough tails to balance the kite."

He showed us the techniques to fly the kites high in the sky. He spun the string on spinning wheels he made for us so that we could have better control with the string. After watching the movie, Robin Hood, we talked about how heroic Robin Hood was and how fun it would be to shoot arrows. Karl made the most beautiful bow and arrows for us. He showed us how to aim at the targets.

He made swords with wood and showed us how to fight like the Round-Table Knights, with an emphasis on their code of honor.

"You have to have an honorable character with outstanding sword-fighting skills to be knighted."

I was knighted by King Karl, as the *Knight of Magnificent Eagle* at our Round-Table, after learning how to fight with a sword.

He kept an eye on us at all times, and he knew what was going on with each of us.

Karl never was harsh to us. Instead, he was like a pampering parent. He enjoyed watching us play and have fun, even though he didn't always play with us.

He is the most humble and modest person I have ever known. "I will not tell you what to do or not to do since I am not perfect myself."

He never bossed us around or criticized us. He instilled the most important values and principles in us while spoiling us and playing with us.

To us, he is truly perfect—a perfect son, a perfect older brother, and a perfect person. He has the biggest heart. He is never demanding or critical. He is one of the most caring, kind, genuine, humble, and loyal people I have ever known. He has lived an honorable life with dignity, pride, uprightness, compassion, and integrity.

We know of all his friends' strengths, not weaknesses, for Karl sees only the best in everyone and truly appreciates the talents and positive character of each of his friends. We learned from him to appreciate our friends' strengths, enjoy their gifts, and embrace their weaknesses. Our loving and peaceful older brother never has conflicts with anyone. He always puts other people before himself, especially his family and siblings.

Being a high school student, Karl knew so many things and stories. He could identify and draw different airplanes and ships of the U.S. Armed Forces. He knew what was going on around the world. He even knew about the lives of Walt Disney and many other great people around the world. I never knew and still don't know how he could be so knowledgeable back then at a young age, without the Internet.

He helped me with geometry when I was a ninth grader. With clear concepts learned from him, I always got the top scores in math. He showed Irene and me how to use colors with art projects. He was artistic; he was eloquent; he truly knew how to teach when he was just a high school student.

We adored our perfect, amazing older brother. He not only was our idol, but also our first mentor.

We loved to listen to his stories. He told us about lives of great people, both Chinese and Westerners, whom he admired. I can still remember most of the stories he told us.

After telling us the Chinese story of *Three Kingdoms*, a popular historic story, he said to us, "Patriotism and loyalty are noble characters."

He continued, "Once a promise is made, you are committed to whatever you have promised. Being on time shows your respect to other people, and it is also a sign of being trustworthy."

I have followed his teachings all my life, in this respect.

He also taught us about character and honor. "Never do anything that is against your principles to damage your character. Without any wrong doing, you can stand tall and be an honorable person, always."

Through different stories, he taught us different virtues. Karl helped shape and mold our characters through a wide range of fascinating and interesting stories, along with his modeling and teachings. What we learned from him when we were little had a powerful lasting impact on us.

The eight virtues for Chinese people are:

忠 Loyalty; patriotism
孝 Piety to parents
仁 Kindness
愛 Love
信 Trustworthiness
義 Righteousness; loyalty to friends
和 Harmony
平 Peace

When I was in junior high, Karl was a high school student. One day he shared something sincerely with us as we were talking about the future. "You can all study abroad when you grow up. I will stay behind to take care of Father and Mother."

He already had such a strong sense of responsibility of being the *lao da*, the first born, to take care of our parents—the virtue of piety to parents.

After high school, he attended National Defense Medical School, the military medical school, to be a physician. After he finished medical school, he pursued and received his master's degree in Public Health. Being an outstanding student, with noble character and great potential, he was chosen by the school and the government to study Hospital Administration in the U. S. The expertise was desperately needed in Taiwan.

In 1972, he was accepted by Columbia University for his advanced studies. In 1974, when he received his master's degree in Hospital Administration, he became the first and only physician with formal hospital administration training in Taiwan.

The U. S. Navy was very impressed with him and offered him a great job.

I told my siblings, "I know he will not accept the offer."

To him, accepting the offer, he would betray his country since the government sponsored him for his training and studies in the U.S. To him, accepting the offer, he couldn't stay in Taiwan for his piety to our parents—to take care of them as the first born, especially since four of us siblings were already living in the U. S. then.

He declined the offer and went back to Taiwan in the summer of 1974.

With his training, knowledge, and experiences, he became a most respected professor at the National Defense Medical School where he was the deputy director.

Later, he was promoted to general—one of the few in the medical division of the Armed Forces. He became the third general in our family, after our maternal grandfather and father.

After he retired from the army, Karl was appointed as the Director of the Bureau of Health Promotion and Health Protection. Later he became the Director of the Bureau of Medical Affairs, in charge of the affairs of hospitals, pharmacies and medical professionals. He has been an active contributor in the field of medicine in Taiwan since 1974.

All these years, Karl has been living on the other side of the Pacific Ocean. Distance and time didn't keep Karl and us six siblings in the U. S. apart. Whenever we go back to Taiwan, Karl always makes sure we are well taken care of—housing, transportation, and even pocket money—just like when we were growing up.

With both of our parents in heaven, Karl is our beloved "parent" on earth. He was our pillar then, and he still is now. Taiwan is still our home because Karl is there. How blessed we are, having Karl guide us and love us throughout our lives.

Karl is our forever idol and our lifetime mentor.

Irene

People ask me when I tell them I am a twin, "Are you identical twins?"

"No. We are very different, like night and day."

"Really?!"

"Can you imagine two of me?" I always laugh as I say this, for I can't even imagine that myself.

Irene, my twin sister, is 15 minutes older than I. She is my older sister and I am her younger sister. She is like our mother, patient and gentle, without any fast movement. I am fast and active like my father.

Having Irene by my side always while growing up, I became very spoiled and dependent—having someone with me whatever I did and wherever I went. She looks gentle, but she is pretty brave in her own way. I look so brave, but I am such a chicken with many things. Even now, I don't like to do some things alone.

Xiao Mei, the helper I had in Beijing, said to me, "Your twin sister is so genuine, loving, and kind. She is such a great person. I wish I had an older sister like that."

I totally agreed. "Yes. She is a very kind lady. She is a better person than I."

"What do you mean?"

"She is more patient with people."

Irene has a very good business mind. She knows how to manage money, and she had a few successful businesses. I am a people person. I worked with students all my life. Irene is a total lady, always beautifully dressed. I sometimes don't even see myself in the mirror in the morning, even standing right in front of it. She changes jewelry to match her outfits every day, and I have had the same gold necklace around my neck for years. I was a wild tomboy, still one now, and she has always been a gentle and pretty lady.

Irene and I are blessed with genuine, appreciative, and embracing hearts. We are never jealous of each other, siblings or others. We have different personalities, but we share the same values and principles in life.

Irene, my older sister, is a loving and caring lady. I respect her; I love my twin sister; and I appreciate Irene, even though she is so different from me.

Irene and I are forever best friends.

Ken

It was the during the winter vacation of 1963. My younger brother, Ken, was a sophomore in high school and I was a freshman in college.

I loved to sing, and Ken loved to play guitar. He taught himself how to play. I couldn't read music, but I enjoy singing. I learned songs by listening. We loved learning new songs, both Chinese and English songs.

One afternoon, Ken heard me singing and he got out his guitar. "I will play while you sing." He started playing the song that I was singing.

I just watched him play the whole song. When he finished the song, he looked puzzled. "Why didn't you sing?"

"I didn't know when to start."

He played the song again to show me the note where I should start singing. I missed it again. "Sorry!"

"It's okay. Try it again." I felt so stupid, but he was very patient with me.

We tried it a few more times. I just could not identify the note to start singing. He finally said to me. "Why don't you sing first, and I will play after you start."

It worked, and it was great fun.

Ken was very mature and smart. He was active and handy. He was the president of the class; he was the captain of the baseball team; he received the Model Student Award many times. He was such a great leader and organizer at a very young age. People followed him around. Although I am his older sister, I followed Ken like a younger sister following an older brother when we were kids.

He was in the marching band, playing drums. He played guitar well, and he even performed on TV with some of his friends. He seemed to be a very balanced student, with good grades and fun hobbies at the same time, while under the constant pressure of the college entrance examination.

Both Ken and his wife, Yolande, have bachelor's degrees in Architecture. Ken has a master's degree in Structural Engineering, and Yolande has a master's degree in Landscaping. Yolande is an intelligent and thoughtful lady. She is most thorough and capable. Together they make perfect life companions, for better or for worse. They also were the best business partners for their successful consulting company in Houston.

When I helped design a curriculum for an internet Chinese language program, Ken and Yolande were my most valuable and reliable resource and support.

How fortunate can a person be, having a brother like Ken whom you can lean on all your life!

Eileen

It was the unforgettable fall of 1987. One day, Karl called us from Taiwan. "*Ma Ma* has brain cancer."

It shattered our blessed lives. "Oh! No! How serious is it?" I started to cry, non-stop.

Karl sighed and said, "It is one of the most vicious kinds. It needs surgery right away."

Our hearts sank.

Karl was the only one with our parents in Taiwan while six of us were in the U.S. He had been taking care of our parents all along. We didn't think it was fair for Karl to take care of our parents alone at a time of crisis. Eric, my second younger brother, flew back to Taiwan the next day for a month to help take care of Mother. Irene, Ken, and I took turns going back to help take care of Mother afterward.

Eileen was five years younger than Irene and I. We called her *Xiao*

Mei [the youngest sister]. She knew that Karl was busy being the deputy director of the hospital where Mother had her surgery and care. She understood that none of us five could be away for a long period of time, since Irene, Ken, and I had jobs and small children, and the two younger brothers, Eric and Ray, had just started with new jobs.

Eileen was single, with a variety of work experiences. She told us, "Mother needs long term care. It is too much for Karl. I will go back."

She quit her job as a manager at the gas company in Boston and went back to take care of Mother. That was Eileen—selfless, loving, and decisive.

After one year, Mother got better. Our parents agreed to come to Boston to live with Eileen and two younger brothers, Eric and Ray. They were all single and lived together. Three of them took great care of Mother and Father before the recurrence of the cancer that took our mother. I was deeply touched by their piety and devoted loving care for our parents.

After Mother's passing in 1990, Eileen moved to Los Angeles. She asked Father to live with her. She tried to make him feel at home. She bought a house in Monterey Park, where people were mostly from Taiwan. It was in a convenient location. Father could be independent and get around by himself while she worked during the day. With Irene and Ray in Los Angeles also, Father was well taken care of.

We invited Father to stay with us for a few months every year. Ken and Yolande invited him to spend time with them in Houston periodically. Sometimes Father visited Eric in Boston. He was happy to spend time with each of us regularly.

Eileen was very sharp, smart, and alert. Nothing was difficult for her. She could pick up anything and absorb so thoroughly and so quickly, you would think that the subject was her background. She had a MBA degree, but she was a manager in the field of computers. Later in life, she became a realtor and was one of the top agents at her company.

Whatever she decided to do, she did an outstanding job. She worked hard and worked smart. She also was playful and fun.

Eileen was always ready to help people who were in need. She took great care of two younger brothers, Eric and Ray, like a mother, before they got married. She remained single. She stood by us to support and to provide assistance, always.

She loved all her nephews and nieces dearly. Casey, my grandson, was her joy to talk about, especially during her last days on earth.

"She was so happy whenever she talked about your Casey," a friend in Beijing told me.

She went to Beijing to search for different treatment after having chemo treatments in Los Angeles. We lost our *Xiao Mei*, Eileen, in June 2010, after she battled colon cancer bravely for two years. In a Beijing hospital, Karl and I were holding our beloved *Xiao Mei*'s hands as she joined our parents in heaven. At her final moment on earth, she was surrounded by all the friends who provided loving care to her during the last three months of her life, in Beijing. She was deeply loved.

Eileen had devoted her life to our family—her genuine and profound love. The forever void can't ever be filled, and the ache in our hearts will never stop.

Xiao Mei,
We miss you tremendously.
Thank you for your love.
We are blessed having you in our lives.
You will live in our hearts always.
You are forever our beloved sister…

Eric & Ray

When I went away for college, Eric was ten and Ray was seven. Five years later I left home to pursue my advanced studies in the U.S. I didn't have the chance to get to know my two youngest brothers when they were growing up.

Ray, the youngest came to Lincoln, Nebraska for school where we lived in 1980. I was supposed to know this handsome and charming 6'1" tall young man since he is my brother, but I didn't really know him.

Ray has a gentle soul and a kind heart. He was fun and interesting. His life style was quite different from ours. It took some time to figure him out—one surprise after another.

Our younger daughter Andrea loved her fun uncle. Whenever she got up in the morning, this eighteen-month old niece wanted to see her Uncle Ray who lived downstairs.

"Down, down!" she said, and sliding down the stairs on her little butt by herself to Ray's room. She climbed up on the bed and sat on her Uncle Ray, like riding a horse. "Up! Up! High! High!"

She wanted him to swing her up and down again.

He got up and played with her. "Okay. Up and down, up and down!"

"More! More!" She giggled and demanded for more.

Poor Ray; he had just gone to bed a couple of hours earlier.

Ray has a brilliant mind. When he worked at a computer company after he got his master's degree in Computer Science, he solved a long existing problem for the company in no time. His work was displayed at the company for a long time afterward.

One day in the summer of 1998, Karl called from Taiwan and alerted us with something shocking. "Lao Liang refuses to eat."

Lao Liang was our loyal helper for more than forty years. He took care of Ray and Eric since they were babies. He was family. He didn't want to join his own daughter in China after locating her after forty years of separation. We were his family, and he wanted to stay with us forever.

Lao Liang was a very smart man. During the time of chaos, turbulence, and changes in China, he never got the chance for an education. He joined the army. He followed the government and settled in Taiwan. He learned to read throughout the years with our help and newspapers. He could fix anything, especially umbrellas. He could make scales to weigh things accurately. He was always busy fixing or making things for us. I had always wondered what he could have done if he had a formal education.

Whenever I took my two little daughters back to Taiwan to visit, they loved Lao Liang, whom they called *Liang Gong Gong* [Grandpa Liang], and the little turtles that he bought for them. He loved and spoiled our children.

We didn't tell him about our parents' passing, Mother in 1990 and Father in 1996, so that he wouldn't be sad. Somehow he knew, and he missed them and all of us. He decided it was time to join them.

Lao Liang lived in the house where we grew up. Karl checked on him regularly since none of us lived there any longer.

Karl told us, "Lao Liang told me what to do with everything after he is gone. He handed me all his IDs and documents. He refuses to eat. He is going to starve himself to death."

Ray couldn't let it happen. "I will go back right away." He went back to Taiwan the next day.

Lao Liang was so happy to see Ray. Ray said to him, "I am hungry, and I don't know how to cook. Would you fix something for me to eat?" Lao Liang happily cooked something for him, and he started eating again, with Ray.

Lao Liang loved to play Chinese chess. Ray had played chess with him every day before he left to study in the U. S. Here Ray was playing chess with Lao Liang again. One day, he asked Lao Liang, "Would you like to go to the U.S. with me?"

Sparkles appeared in his eyes again. Without hesitation Lao Liang answered, "Yes!"

Ray brought Lao Liang back with him to his home in Boston. He and his wife Julie took great care of Lao Liang, like a son taking care of a father, for eight years before he died at the age of 93.

Eric was the last one who came to the U.S. to study. He came in 1982 and stayed with Irene in Los Angeles while studying computer programming. Irene and Eric finally got to know each other after 14 years of separation.

When Eric and Ray were little, Ray didn't like eating meat and Eric never ate vegetables. Ray was always funny while Eric was very serious. They were very different, but they were very close, like twins.

In 1988, Eric and Ray pursued and started to practice Buddhist meditation for self-cultivation at the same time. They have been promoting a healthy and merciful vegetarian diet ever since.

Eric worked as a field service engineer for a company in Boston until he retired in 2013. Although these two younger brothers have been apart in distance—one on the West Coast and one on the East Coast—they remain attached as always.

*****

No matter what happens in our lives and wherever we may be, we are never alone. Each of us has six siblings—*shou zu*, allies, and best friends for life. We are indeed intertwined and woven together—truly part of one another, forever inseparable.

**The last whole family picture in Taiwan (1967)
Back row: Karl, Eric, Ray, Eileen, Ken
Front row: Celine, Ma Ma, Ba Ba, Irene**

**Karl, Eileen, Eric, Irene, Ray, Celine, Ken
at Eric's wedding in Boston (1990)**

The Seeds

Seeds planted in the soil, either intentionally or by accident, will grow with sunshine and water. There are countless seeds planted in the heart at different stages of life and from different sources. Some were planted purposefully, and some were planted randomly or accidentally. Nurtured with loving care and guided with wisdom, the seeds in the heart will take root in the soul…

Yi Yuan

I am not sure how far back a person can remember. When we left China, I was a toddler. I didn't remember much of anything that happened in China or in Hong Kong where we lived for one year before settling in Taiwan.

Ma Ma and *Ba Ba* were good story tellers. We loved to listen to their stories—the true stories of our roots. I always tried to picture them in my little head while listening when I was a little girl.

One day, we siblings gathered around *Ma Ma* as she told us stories about her three brothers again—we didn't know what happened to them in mainland China for many years. Not until I grew up did I realize that *Ma Ma* told us stories about her childhood whenever she missed her family, which was very often.

There were a couple of images that had popped out once in a while since I was very little. One day I asked *Ma Ma*, "I remember that I was a baby lying on my tummy on a cool floor in a huge room. Did I really do that?"

"Yes. You loved to lie on the marble floor during the hot summer." *Ma Ma* smiled, and I saw a twinkle in her tender and loving eyes.

I knew we lived in Suzhou when I was a baby. "So it was true I did that as a baby. What room was it? Why a marble floor?" I got more excited and curious.

Ma Ma smiled again, with love in her voice. "That was the ballroom for dancing. Your *Gong Gong* loved dancing."

Ma Ma continued, with that sparkle in her eyes, "My father believed dancing was good exercise for the body and the mind."

I was very surprised that *Gong Gong* had a dancing ballroom back in the 1930s in his house. "Gong *Gong* must have had a very modern mind."

As she remembering her honorable father, *Ma Ma* beamed like a deeply loved young maiden—a blooming rose. *Ma Ma* nodded her head and smiled again. With admiration and pride, she commented, "Yeah, he was a very open-minded and liberal man. He was smart and well educated, with visions and principles. He even built a tennis court for us children."

"Wow! A tennis court too? That would be great fun!" I couldn't believe it.

"Your oldest uncle is two years younger than I. He loved to play tennis. *Gong Gong* thought it was a good sport and exercise, so he built the court for us."

Her gentle and loving dream-like gaze took her back in time when she was a happy young girl. I could tell that *Ma Ma* missed her father and brothers profoundly again.

"Did you play tennis?" I was wondering if *Ma Ma* played the sport since they had a court.

Ma Ma shook her head. "No."

"Why not?" My twin sister Irene asked.

"Back then girls didn't play such sport."

"What a shame! I would play tennis every single day!" I yelled.

Ma Ma smiled, and my siblings laughed.

For the longest time, I had another image—a young man holding a long bamboo pole, with two young boys next to him. One was very skinny and tall and the other one was short. They tried to reach for some oranges in a pool.

I asked *Ma Ma*, "Was there a swimming pool also? I remember a pool. A young man and two young boys were by a pool in a big garden. Who were they? Where were they?"

Ma Ma was surprised and smiled. "It was a pond, not a swimming pool. We had some orange trees by the pond."

Ma Ma continued, "The three people you saw were your three uncles. The oldest one is the brother who is two years younger than me. The other two are my half-brothers. The skinny, tall one is my second brother, and the short one is the youngest brother. They are much younger than we two. How did you remember all these?"

"I don't know. These images pop up sometimes. I've always wondered if they were my imagination."

I felt happy that I had not imagined things in my little head. They were true memories of my past at *Yi Yuan*, our home in Suzhou—my only memories of my roots in China.

I had more questions. "Why didn't they come with us to Taiwan?"

"They are boys, and they felt it was their obligation to guard the home and all the property our father left to us."

The decision they made changed their fate—a life that descended from heaven to hell…

Hong Kong

We lived in Hong Kong for a year before joining *Ba Ba* in Taiwan. Eileen, our younger sister, was born there. I don't remember much. I only remembered a couple of things vividly, but I wasn't sure if they really happened or was just my imagination.

There was a huge fire. People were crying, screaming, and running. My twin sister and I were standing and watching the non-stop fire, with our helper Lao Zhang, on the top of a hill not too far from where the fire burned.

I asked *Ma Ma*, "I remember a big fire in Hong Kong. Was there really a big fire? What happened?"

"It was the refugee camp. Many people escaped the communists and went to Hong Kong like us. Most of them lost almost everything, and they were very poor. They lived in temporary housing. They were poorly built with boards and aluminum. It caught on fire somehow and the whole place burnt down just like that."

"What did those people do then? Where did they live after the fire?" I was concerned.

"I don't know what happened to them. It was so sad. It was a time of endless suffering and countless tragedies for Chinese people." With compassion in her eyes and sadness in her voice, *Ma Ma* sighed deeply.

"I also remember my right hand was hurt." I recalled an image that my right hand was in a bandage.

There was pain in *Ma Ma*'s eyes. "We lived in an apartment of a gated compound. One afternoon you and Irene were playing by the gate."

"What happened?" I couldn't wait to find out.

"You had your little hand between the hinges of the metal gate. A boy closed the gate and you screamed. You lost all five fingernails on the right hand."

It sounded extremely painful. "I lost all my fingernails?!"

It still hurt *Ma Ma* as she talked about it. "It took a long time for your little hand to heal. We had to feed you since you are right-handed. Thank God, your fingernails grew back."

My only memories about Hong Kong were not so pleasant ones.

Miracles

My parents, like many Chinese people of their generation, were born in the era of chaos and turbulence. They lived through war after war in China. With perseverance they survived the losses and tragedies. With courage, love, and faith in humanity they lived through painful sufferings and unspeakable hardship, without bitterness or complaints.

I often wonder if I could ever live their lives and survive what they had been through.

I asked *Ba Ba*, "How did you survive all those years during the war in the front line fighting the Japanese? How could you handle all the horrible things that happened to you?"

70

With spark of life and gratitude in his eyes, *Ba Ba* looked at us. "You just do what you need to do and make the best out of every day, everywhere, and everything. I was so blessed to come back alive, without a scratch, after all those years fighting the Japanese." I still couldn't imagine how he did it.

"Yeah. We are truly blessed." With gratitude, we all agreed totally.

I was always worried about everything when I was growing up. I asked *Ma Ma*, "How did you live through all the unknown, uncertainty, and constant worry, especially when *Ba Ba* was fighting the Japanese in the front line?"

Ma Ma sighed deeply. "It was very hard. Many soldiers didn't make it back to the compound the government provided us during the war. You heard new widows crying every single day. It was horrible to see them grieve and their children suffer."

She continued, "Nobody knew who would be the next widow. I just prayed and lived one day at a time, numbly."

Ma Ma looked at us, and saying, "During war, anything can happen. You never knew what would happen the next day. We almost lost your older brother Karl during the war."

"What do you mean? Was he sick? What happened?" Again Irene and I were so concerned and I couldn't wait to find out what had happened.

Something terrible happened beyond our imagination.

Ma Ma looked calm remembering the horrifying incident. "One day during the war before you and Irene were born when Karl was four, *Po Po*, Karl, and I were traveling to somewhere by train."

"What happened? Did the Japanese bomb and hit the train?" I asked anxiously.

"No. I told Karl to stay on the platform to wait for me as I helped *Po Po* to get on the train." *Po Po* had small bound feet.

Ma Ma continued, "As I was getting *Po Po* situated on the train, the air raid alarm sounded off."

"Japanese were coming?"

"Yes. Japanese airplanes were approaching."

"Did they bomb the place?"

"Not at that time, but the train started moving—very fast, and Karl was still on the platform."

I could picture how horrified my mother was and how terrified four-year-old Karl must have been—left behind and alone on the platform, with Japanese airplanes in the sky. "What? My God! What did you do?"

"The train was moving so fast, and *Po Po* was on the train. I couldn't leave her and jump off the train." I saw an agonizing expression on *Ma Ma*'s face. Poor *Ma Ma*!

How could anyone survive such torture? "What happened then?"

"The train went back after the raid was over. Each minute felt like a day. Karl was nowhere to be found at the train station. It was the most horrifying moment in my life." We could hear the anguish in her voice and feel the unbearable ache in her heart.

"What did you do?" I couldn't wait to know what had happened to Karl.

"*Po Po* and I searched every corner and all the restaurants in the area."

"How did you find Karl?" I couldn't wait any longer.

"We searched and searched, hopelessly. When we almost gave up hope, we saw Karl sitting with a man and eating noodles in the restaurant." There was relief on her face.

Thank God! Someone was watching over our family. I yelled, "It was a miracle!"

With deep thought in her eyes, *Ma Ma* echoed. "It was truly a miracle. We are so blessed."

Ma Ma continued, "This man saw Karl standing on the platform alone. He took care of him during the raid and waited for us to come back in a restaurant. We owe our lives to this kind man."

I can't imagine—we would have had to live our lives without our beloved older brother Karl if *Po Po* and *Ma Ma* didn't find him. What an unbearable and scary thought!

It still gives me chills and petrifying fright whenever I think of this incident that happened long ago and the *what ifs*.

*****

"Did anything happen to us when Irene and I were little?" I wanted to know more about our past.

"You are especially blessed also." *Ma Ma* looked at me lovingly.

I was surprised and wondered what had happened. "What do you mean? What happened to me?"

Ma Ma said to me gently, "You were almost taken by people a couple of times."

"What?! Who took me?" I was shocked.

"We were in Chungking. Not long after you and Irene were born, a couple who couldn't have children came to visit. When they saw I had twin girls, they asked me to give one of you to them. They liked you and wanted to take you with them. I told them no."

Ma Ma continued, "There was another couple who didn't have any children. They wanted me to give one of you twins to them. I told them no, but they took you and ran. I ran after them, hill after hill, and I finally got you back."

Ma Ma was brought up a graceful lady—without fast movement, and she had never run before. *Ma Ma*'s love enabled her to run like a marathon runner, for the first time in her life, to rescue me. *Ma Ma* was glad that she got me back.

"Neither of these two couples escaped when the communists took over China."

What a petrifying thought—what if I had been taken by them?

When we were growing up, we liked listening to our parents telling us the stories of our past. They were real yet somehow remote to us. We shared their worries and felt their anxiety and pain only when we were listening to their stories. But our parents, grandparents, and uncles lived through every second of it.

We could never completely feel the regrets, tragedies, sufferings, grief, and sometimes hopelessness behind each of their stories. We merely grasped the stories with our innocence and imagination at the moment, long, long ago. Not until we grew up did we truly understand their sentiments, profound love, gratitude, and deep commitment to all the people they loved.

The Seeds

As we seven siblings were growing up, there were many seeds embedded in our hearts. *Ma Ma*'s unconditional love, selflessness, and kindness nourished and flourished the seed of compassion. The perseverance was manifested and cultivated securely by *Ba Ba*'s courage, determination, wisdom, and fearless and unbeatable spirit. *Ma Ma* and *Ba Ba*'s gratitude and blessings, faith—in God and in humanity—not only were instilled in us but also were cherished with much thankfulness. Integrity, decency, honor, and pride flow in our blood. Witnessing *Ma Ma*'s profound love for her three brothers made love among us siblings genuine and forever.

These seeds in our hearts, nurtured with lots of love and guided with blessings and wisdom, have taken roots—deep roots in our souls…

Chapter 3
Journey to the West

學

Row, Row, Row Your Boat
Flying Tiger

Row, Row, Row Your Boat

Life may be full of dreams—small dreams, big dreams, achievable ones, and impossible ones. Some people dream their lives away. Some people fill their lives with colorful dreams that come true. Life can vanish like a dream without any trace. Life can be a legacy leaving visible marks.

> *Row, row, row your boat*
> *Gently down the stream,*
> *Merrily, merrily, merrily, merrily,*
> *Life is but a dream.*

When I rowed the boat singing this song with my precious two-year-old granddaughter Holly, on the floor, she giggled and laughed. "More! More!"

"Ok. More! More!" I responded happily.

Facing her pretty smiling face and holding her little hands, gently and merrily I rocked her back and forth and rowed the boat down the stream.

Her sweet angel voice was singing, "Row, row, row your boat…"

*****

When I was little, I didn't know anything about dreams. I knew only there were things I really wanted to do and to learn. It made me happy and satisfied once I did something or learned something.

When I was about seven or eight years old, I saw people ride bikes in the street. How carefree they looked! I wanted to have the carefree feeling on the bike too. I shared this with my twin sister Irene. "Wouldn't it be fun to ride a bike?"

One day, I told my older brother Karl, who is six years older than

76

Irene and I, how much I wanted to learn to ride the bike. "Would you teach me how to ride the bike?"

"It is pretty dangerous. You will fall and get hurt."

I wanted to learn so badly that I was ready to face the falls. "It's okay! I am not afraid."

Back then the only little bikes for kids were for rent from the bike shop. Karl rented a little bike and took me to the track field at our school. I was on the bike, feeling so grown up, excited, and ready for this big dream of mine—to ride a bike.

I learned how to ride the little bike in a short time. I wanted to ride the big bike. I asked Karl, "May I ride your big bike?"

"It is too big for you. You can't reach the ground."

"May I try it, please?"

Karl was a loving older brother then, and he still is now. "Okay. But be careful!"

I tried to ride the big bike. But I couldn't get on the bike and get it going by myself. Karl helped me get on the bike and pushed me to start my ride. I couldn't get off the bike by myself either. I rode around and around the block. When I was ready to quit, I yelled out loud as I approached our house. "Come and stop my bike!" Poor Karl and younger brother Ken ran out of the house to stop my bike and get me off the bike.

One time I didn't know what happened, but the front wheel of the bike got stuck in one of the neighbors' broken bamboo fence. I could not get off the bike. I yelled out loud, "Come to get me down!" Again they came to my rescue. My dear brothers never complained about this troublesome sister of theirs.

Of course, I fell many times and left many scars on my knees and legs. But I didn't care and I kept at it. Before long I could ride the bike like others, including getting on and off the bike by myself. I had a big carefree and proud grin on my face whenever I rode the bike.

I followed my feelings, and I followed my heart. I learned and did all kinds of things that seemed exciting, challenging, necessary, or fun to me. It made me very happy.

In junior high and high school we had to wear uniforms. There also was a very strict rule—short and straight hair, no longer than the bottom of the earlobes, for girls. Although we knew that schools wanted us to concentrate on our studies, not to waste time on our hair, we thought it was pretty ugly, and nobody liked this rule. Regular checking on the length of our hair at school was the most annoying thing throughout secondary schools.

We, Irene and I, were dreaming together when we were seventh graders. "I wonder how we will look with long and curly hair. Won't it be beautiful?"

"Yeah! It will be great to fix our hair however we want, instead of the straight, short hair like ours." She tried to picture how we would look with long hair.

When we graduated from high school, we and many of our friends yelled happily, "Hurray! No more uniform! No more hair checking!"

We let our hair grow long, and sometimes we added curls. I felt like a young lady, not a kid anymore! I had long straight hair to my waist for many years.

*****

English has always been a required subject for junior high and high school students in Taiwan. Mother taught us the first lessons in our English book the summer before we started junior high. The first English sentence I learned, from my mother, was "This is a book."

She taught us how to write the 26 letters of the English alphabet. "This is how to write a, b, c…" Mother had beautiful penmanship. It was fun learning to read and write a different language, and I loved it.

Father took us to see movies almost every weekend. "What movie would you like to see?"

"Snow White! Snow White!" Irene and I jumped up and down.

Our family enjoyed watching movies, both Chinese and foreign movies, especially the American movies with subtitles, such as the Disney cartoon classics, mysteries, romance, and westerns. Their lives and values were so different from ours. It was fascinating. How I wished I could understand the language they spoke in the movies.

Back then, each year only the top 30% of the 100,000 students from all over Taiwan who took the college entrance examination, could get into any of the colleges. It was so competitive, and it was out of anyone's control. Thus, people who wished to go to college lived under the constant pressure day after day and year after year throughout grades 1-12 until they entered college.

In high school, we had to decide which field to pursue in the future: science, engineering, medicine, liberal arts, business, etc.

I knew what I wanted to study in college. I told my family and friends, "I want to major in Western Languages—English."

Western Languages—English, the international language, was my first choice for college. I got into a Roman Catholic college, Providence College (Providence University now), majoring in Western Languages—English.

I was seventeen—a freshman in college and a girl with many dreams.

After I finished my first semester I told my parents and family, "I want to see the world. I want to go to the U.S. for graduate school after college."

There were other classmates who shared the same dream, to pursue advanced studies in the U.S. We discussed the possibilities sometimes.

"You need a full scholarship from a college in the U.S. to obtain a passport," Alice, one of my close friends, commented.

Another friend Dorothy added, "Or you can take the Overseas Examination."

"For us liberal arts students, it is not likely to get any scholarship, let alone a full scholarship," I pointed out.

"The test is very hard. Each year only 1,500 people pass the test, out of tens of thousands of people who take it," Josephine emphasized, and she was concerned.

I was determined. "I know. I will take the Overseas Examination."

The Overseas Examination test included English, Chinese, Government, Chinese history and geography, and one's major in college. Since I was majoring in English, English literature was required.

My journey to the West began…

I heard the English literature test was extremely difficult. So I started studying English literature on my own. I always loved Chinese poetry for the hidden meanings and profound emotions. I truly enjoyed American literature and English literature also. I felt and shared the insightful feelings—romance, melancholy, joy, and sorrow—of the poets. I loved Shakespeare, and I understood and felt the struggles of: *To be or not to be?*

Books became my constant companions. English literature was my Utopia. It enriched my life—a life of different dreams. The enrichment helped and reinforced my search for the true, the good, and the beautiful in life.

I started collecting my feelings and thoughts in English on a small notepad I carried day and night. I started my creative writing and translation to practice my English.

With great pleasure and enjoyment, I spent countless hours in the library throughout my four years of college to study, to learn, to absorb, to imagine, to dream, and to prepare for a destiny where my heart was leading me—my journey to the West.

Gently and merrily I rowed, rowed, and rowed the boat down the stream of the life I chose for myself when I was 17…

Flying Tiger

My eyes welled with tears, showing the deep sadness in my heart whenever I thought of Joline, our older daughter, leaving home for college someday soon. It was 1993, and she was a junior in high school.

She was accepted by seven good universities and had been offered scholarships by five schools.

I wanted the best for her. "Pick a school you really like. Don't pick the school just because there's a scholarship."

I didn't want her to pick a school because of the scholarship, as I did when I came to the U.S. for graduate school. There were other schools that I would have preferred to attend, but no scholarship. The exchange rate between the U.S. dollar (USD) and Taiwan currency was US$1=NT$40 back then. My parents provided for and supported us seven kids all the way through college. The scholarship really helped.

I emphasized it again. "Your job is to pick the best school for yourself. Tuition is not your problem."

We visited every school that had accepted her. Her favorite schools were the University of Illinois and the University of Texas-A & M, two of the top schools for Electrical Engineering. We compared the two schools, with pros and cons. She decided to attend the University of Illinois in Champagne.

I was curious. "Why do you select this school?"

"The students looked bright, and everyone was studying. The campus was full of good energy," she responded.

It was interesting. "Yeah, I noticed that, too. Good observation and good choice!"

The time had come. It was so heartbreaking to let go of my baby.

It was August 1994. We loaded her stuff in the van and drove her to the University of Illinois. It was an eight-hour drive from Lincoln, Nebraska. My heart was bleeding.

We got her settled in her dorm, and we met her roommate. We toured all over campus so that we were familiar with the environment where she would spend the next four critical and important years of her life. Her orientation program started, and we had to leave her and go home.

I will never forget the heart-breaking good-bye moment. Both Joline and I cried hard, holding each other. She cried all the way back to her dorm, and I cried all the way to Nebraska.

Not until then had I truly realized how cruel I was to say good-bye to my parents when I left home for graduate school in the U.S., a land far, far away from home, on September 15th, 1967.

*****

It was the spring of 1966. Before long, I would be graduating from college. And before long, I needed to take the Overseas Examination that I had prepared for since I was a freshman.

Some classmates were looking for jobs, and some of us wanted to study abroad for an advanced degree.

One day, some of us were chatting about the future. "Only three people in our class will pass the Overseas Examination," one friend commented.

"Yeah, only three," others agreed and echoed.

It was interesting, and I was curious. "Really? Which three?"

"You, Lisa, and Juliet," one responded.

"Really?" I wondered how they figured that.

The Overseas Examination was a two-day test. I was very nervous and anxious those two days. It was the first step toward my dream, to attend graduate school in the U.S.

Will all the hard work pay off?

Have I prepared myself enough to pass the test?

Guess what? My friends were right. We were the only three who passed the test, out of fifteen or more people from our class who took the test.

*****

After passing the test, I planned to work for a year. I had been away from home for four years of college. I wanted to spend a year with my family before going abroad for my advanced studies.

In college, I was very fortunate to have two great teachers who left a profound impact on my life.

Mr. Thomas Ganchow, a young American teacher from Minnesota, was such a passionate instructor. He taught us with his heart. I could feel his energy and excitement being a teacher, and it touched me deeply. He was well-respected and liked by students. He was the one who took time to check my creative writing, with feedback, encouragement, and praise.

One time, I expressed my sincere gratitude for his help and encouragement. "Thank you for taking the time to help me. I really appreciate it."

He responded, "You know what? '*Thank you*' are words often used, but it is from the bottom of my heart. Students like you make me want to be a teacher. Thank you!"

I shared his passion and dedication when I became a teacher.

Professor Pang-Yuan Chi taught us American literature. She was the one who showed me how to appreciate literature in a profound and insightful way. She was the one who showed me how to look for and to enjoy the treasures hidden in literature.

Her knowledge and keen insights really enlightened me—a romantic girl with many dreams. She had reinforced my search for the true, the good, and the beautiful in life. Studying English literature for the Overseas Examination was not a burden to me, but a pleasure and a source of enjoyment.

Once when I shared with her how devastated I was with one relationship, she shared with me her own experience and insight. "Sometimes we feel devastated and sad, not necessarily because of the person or the relationship, but because a dream for perfection has shattered." How true it was!

In 2009, Professor Chi, at the age of 85, published her memoir *Ju Liu He* [Ju Liu River]. Ju Liu River, Liao River now, is one of the seven rivers in China. It is in Northeastern China where Professor Chi was born and raised. People there called it *Mother River*. The book revealed her roots, life stories, and over a century of Chinese history. It has been not only one of the bestsellers in Taiwan, China, and Hong Kong but also a most popular book for the Chinese people around the world.

These two teachers inspired and touched me immensely. If great teachers could have such an impact on me, I wanted to be a teacher—an influential teacher who touches lives.

I became an English teacher at Keelung Secondary School, grades 7-12. I taught Beginner English to four seventh-grade classes, 180 boys. I was 21, and my students were 13 or 14. I loved teaching. I enjoyed and loved my students. I tried to fill—with some happy colors—the first chapter of their experience learning English. Many of them still have close contact with me even after so many years.

I talked about my students a lot at home. One time I said, "Some of the students really have a hard time learning the language."

"Anyone can teach smart kids, but it takes a genuine master teacher to teach the special and disadvantaged students," my mother, a lady of wisdom, pointed out to me.

How true it is! Helen Keller's teacher, Miss Sullivan, was such a magical teacher. Mother's insight helped me choose my major for graduate school—Special Education.

Time flew, and that year of working so I could be at home passed quickly.

In June 1967, I was accepted by more than five schools in the U.S., and I also received scholarships from two schools. I decided to go to Southern Illinois University in Edwardsville, Illinois, with a scholarship.

I was glad things went smoothly as planned and scheduled. But there was such sadness deep in my heart. When the time got closer for me to leave my beloved family and home, I often hid in my room and wept. I already missed my family.

My family was sad that I was leaving for a far, far away country very soon. No one knew when I would be back. It was not likely they could visit me very soon, either. They were also worried about how I would survive by myself in a foreign land. They knew all too well that I was active and determined, but I was such a timid girl in many ways—being scared of living alone, darkness, animals, and many other things.

My youngest brother Ray was 12, and he would be going to junior high in the fall. I taught him the two books of Beginner English for seventh grade so that he had a good start with the new language. Eric was 15, a ninth grader. I helped him with English as much as I could throughout the year. Eileen was a junior in high school, and Ken was a sophomore in college.

Karl, my older brother and a doctor doing an internship in a hospital, gave me his favorite English-Chinese dictionary. It accompanied me throughout the years. I still use it and feel his love. Irene, my twin sister, and I talked and talked. Together we sobbed and wept.

Ba Ba purchased a one-way ticket for a chartered flight to Seattle on September 15th, 1967.

I was leaving the following week. I didn't want to say good-bye to my family. With deep sorrow, Mother said to me, "No one wants you to leave. You don't have to go."

"I have prepared for it for a long time. If I don't go, I will regret it. I'd better go." I tried hard to fight back my rolling tears.

It was September 15th, 1967. It came too soon.

I started sobbing non-stop as I woke up from a restless night. I didn't even know how I got to the airport. My vision was blurry from tears in my eyes. I didn't know who all gave me the beautiful leis around my neck. The intercom announced my name many times. Friends who came from far and near tried to locate me at the airport. There were more than sixty people at the airport to see me off.

A student wrote and told me that my students looked at the sky whenever there was an airplane soaring in the air on that day.

I boarded the Flying Tiger chartered airplane, with lots of love, blessings, and unspeakable sadness, to the destiny I chose for myself when I was 17—the journey to the West....

Chapter 4
Transplanting and Transformtion

學

Sweat, Blood, and Tears
The American G.I.
A Giant Step
Double Happiness
The Helping Hand
The Chicken of the Sea
A Bridge

Sweat, Blood, and Tears

"Where am I?" I asked myself every morning. It took me a few minutes to get oriented emotionally and physically before getting out of bed to face my new life, alone in a strange land. A scholarship for graduate school had brought me to the U.S. from Taiwan.

There was no dorm on campus. I rented a room from an American family. I shared a room with Mary, a freshman majoring in music. Carol and Barb, two other freshmen, shared another room. They had classes during the day, and my graduate courses in education were offered in the evening.

Our landlord, Mr. Bob McIntyre, was a high school science teacher before. His teacher's pay couldn't provide for his family of six. He became a truck driver, and he was away from home most of the time. They rented out two rooms to college girls. There were ten people in a four bedroom house, their four children of ages 2-19, plus us four college girls.

Mrs. McIntyre, a gentle and caring landlady, managed a harmonious and pleasant household. She was always positive, helpful, and hard-working. I never heard her complain about anything. From her I witnessed how strong and independent American women were. She was truly an inspiring role model to me—a girl grown up in a sheltered home like a flower grown in a greenhouse.

I cried when I received letters from home. Tears smeared my writing when I wrote letters back home. I fought back my rolling tears when I saw people with their families. I could not bear to look at the full moon on the Chinese Moon Festival, a holiday similar to American Thanksgiving. I closed the curtain and wept. People were very friendly, but they were not friends. They all looked the same. No family, no friends, and no food.

Tears were my only companion. I cried every day for three months.

A few months before my journey to the west, my father had said to me, "You might want to learn how to cook now that you are going to the U.S."

I looked at him and puzzled.

What does cooking have to do with me? Isn't food always on the table?

Lao Liang, our helper, always prepared the food. Mom always got milk and vitamins for us at breakfast and prepared snacks for us at night while we studied. Food was always on the table. My mother never cooked, for we had always had one or two helpers.

*****

Here I was in the shared kitchen in the house where I lived with an American family.

I looked at the kitchen and I looked at the dining table. Not until then had I understood what my father was trying to tell me before.

There is no food on the table. What do I eat? What do I do?

Father knows the best. I should have listened. Too late!

Since I did not know how to cook rice, I thought it might be easier to cook noodles. I was wrong. They were either overcooked or still raw. They never tasted the same. I finally asked my landlady, Mrs. McIntyre, to show me how to cook noodles.

She smiled and told me, "Boil the water first. When the water is boiling, put in the noodles."

"How can you tell the water is boiling?"

"When you see bubbles."

"What bubbles, small ones or big ones?"

"Big bubbles." She laughed.

"No wonder my noodles tasted funny. I have been putting noodles in the cold water to cook them." She and I laughed hard together.

I felt so dumb. But I was glad I had finally learned how to cook noodles, my first cooking lesson. I had never eaten so many noodles and so much bread before. I was so hungry for rice. Back home people used a rice cooker to cook rice. I had never cooked rice, not even with a rice cooker. I asked Mrs. McIntyre to show me how to cook rice in a regular pan, the American way.

She handed me a measuring cup and told me, "Put one cup of rice in the pan, and add two cups of water."

I measured the rice and water carefully with the measuring cup. "Okay, one cup of rice and two cups of water. What to do next?"

"Boil them on high heat."

"Okay." I turned on the stove and watched the rice closely.

"Water is all gone! What happened? What do I do?" I panicked and called out to Mrs. McIntyre.

She laughed and came to me right away. "It is okay. Turn the heat to low and cover it. Let it simmer for ten minutes or so. It should be ready."

I stood by the stove waiting and checking my rice the whole time. I did not want to burn it, and I couldn't wait to try the first rice that I had cooked.

Wow! That first bowl of rice looked beautiful, smelled so good, and tasted great. I was so happy I could finally have rice as I always did back home from then on.

Wasn't it ironic that an American lady taught a Chinese girl how to cook rice?!

Before learning to make rice and noodles, I had been eating bread with cold cuts, just to survive. In Taiwan I had bread only when we went on outings, not very often.

There was no supermarket in Taiwan then. Every morning people went to the open markets to buy fresh vegetables, meat, and food needed for the day. I had not seen or eaten canned food before. I bought a whole bunch of canned food at the supermarket. I hoped the cans would make my life easier. But the food didn't look as good as the pictures on the cans. It didn't taste good either. I gave all the cans to my American roommates.

I had taught for one year in Taiwan. My students learned that I couldn't cook, so they sent me a Chinese cookbook. I didn't even know what some ingredients were in the recipes, and I didn't understand some of the cooking terms either.

I started my journey of learning to survive everyday life while pursuing my advanced studies in the new world. I closely watched people, both Chinese and American, as they cooked, and I asked a lot of stupid questions. Whenever I learned a new recipe, I would make the dish right away while the memory was still fresh. The first American food I learned how to make—from my landlady—was fried chicken. It turned out pretty good. I was very proud of myself.

I also learned the hard way that you cut the slippery peppers from the inside so that you don't cut yourself adding the unnecessary flavors—blood and tears—to your food. Little by little, cooking became easier for me. I was learning new things in the new world all the time…

My landlord and his family had great fun telling their friends about all the silly things I had done with cooking. I laughed with them, too.

They were also amazed by what I wanted to learn and what I had learned in such a short time. They always told people, "This little Chinese girl learns so fast!"

There was so much to learn, and I wanted to learn.

I have been saying this to myself and people around me ever since—"Learning to do things is to bring convenience to yourself."

In 1985 with ease and pleasure, I single-handedly prepared a ten-course feast for seventy-five people to celebrate the first Christmas at our brand new house. It was the biggest dinner party I ever gave at our home in Lincoln, Nebraska.

Indeed, my learning how to cook has brought fun and convenience to me and enjoyment to others.

My first year in the United States was the toughest year of my life. I survived. Since then, I realized and truly believed that challenges are opportunities to discover one's hidden talents and potential. With this belief in my heart, I faced the challenges in the years that followed, without fear.

The American G. I.

Here I was in the U.S. My limited survival skills made adapting to my new life very tough; slowly I acquired new skills to enhance the life I had chosen for myself.

There was no regret, although I cried a lot and had many struggles. There was no turning back.

I told myself every day,

I will make the best out of everything and every day.

I will learn, I will grow, I will survive, and I will get my master's degree as scheduled.

One day in late October, a man called. He spoke Chinese to me.

"Who is this? Are you Chinese?" I asked.

"No, I am American." He laughed.

I was curious. "How come you can speak Chinese?"

"I was in the service, stationed in Taiwan, for two years."

"Did you learn the language in Taiwan?"

"No, I learned it at the Army Language School in Monterey, California."

"Your Chinese is pretty good. How did you find me?"

"I got your name from the International Students Services when I went to check to see if there were any students from Taiwan."

"Oh. What do you do?" I asked.

He told me in Chinese, "I work at the university." We talked for a few minutes in both Chinese and English.

"May I come to see you after work tomorrow?"

"Okay." I told him where I lived.

Since he used the Chinese term *zuo gong,* which means laboring as a blue-collar worker, I was expecting a husky middle-aged man, maybe with a big beard.

*****

Ding dong!

It was misting, it was gloomy, and it was Halloween. There stood a refined-looking young man in a suit, with a gentle and friendly smile, holding an umbrella.

"I am Don," he introduced himself politely.

"I am Celine, nice meeting you. Please come in."

We spoke to each other in mostly Chinese, which made me feel closer to home.

"What do you do at the university?" I wondered if the other blue-collar workers in the U.S. wore suits also.

"I am working in the library. I am a librarian." So he was not a blue-collar worker. No wonder he wore a suit. He had used the wrong Chinese term. He was a white-collar librarian.

"Oh." I didn't correct him, but I asked, "Are you from here?"

"No. I am from Wisconsin."

"When did you come here?"

"After I received my master's degree in Library Science at the University of Wisconsin- Madison this past summer, I got my first job at the university. I came on October 1st. How about you?"

"Really?! I came here on September 15th." I was so excited that both of us were newcomers at the university.

I grew up in an army family. Both my grandfather and father were generals in the Nationalist Chinese Army. Young men were drafted in Taiwan after college, and they had to serve in the armed forces for two or three years. People who did not attend college would get drafted at the age of 18 or after high school.

I was very curious about the American armed forces, especially because there were so many American soldiers in Taiwan.

"Were you drafted?" I asked.

"No, I enlisted."

"Why did you enlist?" I was surprised.

"When you are drafted, you have no choice but go anywhere they send you. If you enlist, you have choices and you can choose what to

93

learn and where to serve. So I enlisted after college."

"Oh. Where were you stationed in Taiwan?" I asked.

"I was stationed at the Air Force Base in Lin Kou."

"Really?! I grew up in Taipei!" I exclaimed.

"Yeah?! I went there very often. I really liked it there." He looked excited too.

Lin Kou was very close to Taipei, where I grew up. We talked about different places in Taipei and the good Chinese food we both liked and missed. It made me so hungry and so homesick.

"How long were you in service?"

"I was supposed to be in for two years. But I liked Taiwan and the people there so much that I extended my service for another year. I served three years." *It was unusual.*

I wondered why he had chosen to learn Chinese and to serve in Taiwan, so I asked, "Why did you want to go to Taiwan?"

"Well, in college I had some Chinese friends from Taiwan. I got interested in Chinese history and language. When I enlisted, I decided to learn Chinese and go to Taiwan."

"Did you know any Chinese people there?"

"Yes, the family of one of my Chinese friends in college."

"I bet they took very good care of you." It is the Chinese custom to offer hospitality.

"Yes. They were very nice to me."

"How long did you study Chinese?"

"I was in the intensive Chinese language program at the Army Language School for eleven months before I was sent to Taiwan," he replied in Chinese.

"Only eleven months? You speak very well." I was impressed.

"Not too good," Don said humbly.

The many American G. I.s in Taiwan in the 1960s had quite a reputation overseas with girls, especially with the bar girls. Decent girls wouldn't want to associate with them. Here in front of me was a G. I. whom I wouldn't have felt very comfortable with if I were in Taiwan.

After our meeting, Don checked on me regularly to see if I needed anything or any help. He got some chopsticks for me when he noticed I didn't have any. I mentioned that American bowls were too heavy to hold up to eat rice, the proper Chinese table etiquette. He found some Chinese rice bowls for me in St. Louis, an hour away.

One day, I invited him to try the food I made. I fixed three dishes and a soup for my first guest. The soup was hot and the bowl was full. It took me a few minutes transporting the soup, with a hunched back and baby steps, from the kitchen to the table. The food was a bit too salty.

He knew I never cooked before. "It tastes pretty good." He said, encouragingly.

After dinner, I put all the dirty pans, dishes, knife, and glasses in the soapy water to wash them.

"Don't put the knife in the soapy water, you could cut yourself," he told me right away. He added, "Do the glasses first, then utensils and plates. Do the pots and pans last because they are greasy."

He helped me get everything out of the sink and said, "It's all right. You've never done it before."

I bet he was shocked watching how I did dishes. It was an American G. I. who showed me how to do dishes, the safer way.

What a pampered and sheltered life I had lived in Taiwan! I didn't even know how to do dishes.

I also never knew washing dishes would take such know-how. No wonder there is a Chinese saying, *"It is hard to learn how to do anything. Once you have learned how to do it, the task won't be hard at all."*

One day I was at his place. He asked, "Would you like to stay for dinner?"

I was hungry. "What do you have?"

"TV dinner."

I asked, "What is TV dinner?"

He showed me the box. The picture looked good. I wondered if it would taste better than the canned food I bought.

I asked, "How do you fix it?"

"It is easy. Just put in the oven and bake it."

It sounded pretty easy, although I had never used an oven before. "Really? That's it?"

He went to the living room for something, and I was trying to be helpful. As I was putting the TV dinners in the oven, he walked in and asked me in a panicky tone, "What are you doing?"

I stopped and wondered what was wrong, "Cook the TV dinners."

He said, "You have to get them out of the boxes before baking them."

I never even thought of that. "Oh, yeah?!"

Chinese people didn't use the oven for cooking, and there was no oven in any household. That was the first time I tried to use an oven. Again, I had no concept that the box might burn in the oven.

*****

Babu and Florence were Don's friends. They had a one-month-old baby boy. One Saturday Babu needed to teach Florence how to drive. They asked me to babysit.

We always had a helper taking care of my younger brothers and sister. I had never babysat before. I was worried. I told Don I didn't know how to take care of a baby, so he went with me.

The baby was crying, and I went to check on him. He was on his tummy on his parents' big bed. I needed to turn him over. He was crying hard, and it made me very nervous.

God, how can I turn him over? What do I do?

I held one of his arms with one hand and held one of his legs with the other hand. I still didn't know how to turn him over, even holding his arm and leg. I was just standing there and pondering. *How do I "flip" the baby over?* Don walked in to check on us because the baby was still crying.

He almost died when he saw me holding the baby's one arm and one leg. "It is not a flour sack!" I let go of the baby. He turned the baby over, and he changed the diaper.

Wow, what an experience!

This 27 year-old American G. I. just wanted to have a conversation partner to practice his Chinese. Here he was! He not only wiped my tears when I was homesick or discouraged, but he also taught me how to wash dishes and how to use the oven. Now he was showing me how to *flip* the baby and change a diaper. Poor Soldier Boy!

He was a kind and true gentleman. He respected and understood my culture and my background. He never took advantage of me, and he remained as a true gentleman. I felt safe being with him. He appreciated so much how Chinese people helped him to enjoy life in Taiwan. He tried his best to help me, a girl from Taiwan, adjust to a new life in the new country. He was the only American young man I dared to go out with. This G. I. became my very first friend in the U.S.

He was looking for a better apartment to rent. One of my landlady's friends had an apartment across the street available. Not long after we met, Don moved into a better apartment right across street from where I lived. He had a brand new green Volkswagen. We named it *Qing Long* [The Green Dragon]. There was no public transportation available for me to take to school. He gave me rides to and from school every day.

People saw us together every day. Sometimes they would ask me, "How is your boyfriend?"

I would smile and say, "He is not my boyfriend. We are just good friends."

At that time it was unthinkable and unacceptable for a Chinese girl to marry an American. Besides, there were a few Chinese young men in St. Louis trying very hard to get close to me. In my heart, Don was just a sincere and caring good friend.

The friendship between this American G.I. and the little Chinese girl was solid as a rock.

A Giant Step

All the beautiful multi-colored leaves vanished from the trees. Autumn ended, and then came winter.

In Taiwan, where I grew up, trees stay green all year long. In the U.S., it was exciting to see such distinctive changes from one season to another.

I had been dreaming of a white Christmas ever since I learned to sing *White Christmas* in college. But my first Christmas in the U.S. was not white. The weather was cold, but the ground was not white.

Birds started singing, trees were full of tender leaves, and flowers were budding one by one. The pasture was fresh and green, beautifully dotted with different colored flowers. Spring of 1968 had arrived.

My studies went well. By the end of the spring quarter I would be half-way finished with the required courses for my master's degree in Special Education. I felt more settled, emotionally and physically. Although I smiled more and cried less, I still worried about everything.

One day in late spring I felt anxious again. Don, the American G.I., noticed. He asked me, "What's the matter?"

"I am thinking about what I am going to do this summer."

He asked me, "What are you going to do?"

"I don't know. Some Chinese friends told me that Chicago is a good place for summer work." I was concerned. "How far is Chicago from here? How do I get there?"

"You can take a bus or find a ride. It takes about four or five hours by car."

It sounded scary. I tried to blink my tears away.

"What can I do in Chicago? How will I get a job? I am scared."

He comforted me, "Don't worry. It will be all right."

I was not just apprehensive; I was petrified about going to Chicago.

Although I grew up in Taipei, a big city, going to a big city alone in a foreign land would be a totally different story.

Don found a ride to Chicago for me. I started my journey for another challenge—to find a summer job in Chicago.

I stayed with my college classmate, Corina Liu, for a couple of days. She and her husband took me to a housing complex for Chinese students, owned and managed by a Chinese Catholic priest.

I was excited to see so many students from Taiwan. I ran into a childhood neighbor, Yun, and another college schoolmate, Jackie, at the housing complex.

Since they got there one month earlier than I, they had gotten jobs already. I was anxiously asking them a lot of questions about the public transportation, how to get a job, and life in Chicago, among other things.

"Where do I go to find a job? Is it hard?"

Yun opened a newspaper and showed me the want-ads section, "You can look at want-ads in the newspaper."

"How did you guys find the jobs?" I asked.

"I got my job through an employment agency," Jackie said.

"How did you find the agency?"

"Somebody told me about it. I can give you the contact information, and you can give it a try," she suggested.

I still had many questions. "Great! Where is this agency?"

"It is downtown."

Nervously I asked, "Where is downtown? How do I get there?"

"You have to take a bus first, then a subway, depending where you are." She opened a map and showed me where downtown was on the map.

Jackie handed me a subway map and a downtown map. "You will need these."

It sounded so complicated. I had never used a map before. We always had a driver back home. I didn't even know where I was.

I was totally lost, even with maps in my hand.

Luckily I met a nice young man at the housing complex. He was a graduate student from Kansas. He had a day off, and he spent the day showing me how to get tokens and how to take the bus and the subway. He taught me how to make the transfer from bus to subway and how to use the maps.

He explained to me, "Remember, Michigan Avenue goes north and south, and it is on the east side. Then you can figure out where you are on the map."

He also reminded me, pointing out one section on the map, "Never go to any place in this area. It is not safe there."

The next day I took my first step—a giant step to a new adventure. I was petrified and nervous, holding two maps in my hand.

I had never had so many rejections in my life, day after day for many days. Most companies didn't need short-term summer employees. I felt so discouraged, so frustrated, and so alone. I was so homesick. Many times I put my sun glasses on and hid my face and sobbed at the corners of big buildings.

It took eleven days before I finally found a job as a typist in an insurance company. I didn't eat lunch during those eleven days because I had never eaten alone in a restaurant.

I was not a great typist. My supervisor, Mrs. Theo McDonough, was an intelligent and caring middle-aged lady. She hired me for my high score on the aptitude test, not for my typing skills. I really appreciated the opportunity she gave me. It ended my misery. After that summer I kept in touch with her for a long, long time.

After I had settled, my brother-in-law asked two of his best friends in Chicago to look after me. Both of them were good friends and both of them were engineers. I called them both *Ge Ge* [Big Brother] respectfully, the Chinese way.

They took me to beautiful and fun places all over Chicago. We went to many different restaurants. Chicago was beautiful at night looking down from the Sears Tower. The Lake Michigan boat ride was too rough for me, but I loved the bright stars in the clear sky. I enjoyed the ride on Lakeshore Drive looking at the water and singing songs. I was so happy and fortunate to have two *Ge Ge* I could lean on and trust.

The adventure in Chicago started out with quite a challenge. With a job, a good house in a nice neighborhood, new and old friends, and two thoughtful *Ge Ge* by my side, life in Chicago turned out to be fun, exciting, and colorful.

The summer ended, and I said good-bye to Chicago. It was truly a blissful summer that I have always treasured and will remember forever. Since then, Chicago has always held a special place in my heart, with memories of all kinds.

One day at a time, one challenge at a time, and one step at a time, I had survived my first year—four distinctive seasons in the new country—the toughest year of my life.

It was a giant step to be transplanted in a new land with different roots. It was a giant step for a flower grown in the greenhouse to survive in the wild. It was a giant step to follow the heart and chase the rainbow for a dream.

Double Happiness

I started my second year of graduate school in the fall of 1968—studying in the morning and working in the afternoon. Special Education was my major. I attended classes in the evening, since that was when graduate classes for teachers were offered.

A year ago I had left my home in Taiwan to attend graduate school in the United States. My family missed me. They wanted to know what was going on with my life on the other side of the Pacific.

Back in the 1960s, international calls were very expensive. The procedure was complicated and the connection was bad. I wrote one letter home every week. I numbered each one at the corner of the envelope.

I told them everything—studies and people around me—in detail, except my tears and struggles. They knew about all the "boys" around me, including Don, the American G. I. I met on Halloween the previous year.

One day in the fall, out of the blue, Don asked me, "What do you think about marriage?"

"How do I know? I have never been married before." I truly did not know and I really hadn't thought much about it.

When my Chinese friends asked me if I would consider marrying an American, I said, "No way! I am not that brave!"

I didn't give too much thought to it at this point since I was not ready for anything beyond friendship with any of the boys around me. No commitment!

My response was just like any conversation. Don was a very conservative and reserved person. He was not an expressive person. He realized that this little girl truly didn't know what he was trying to say.

It took a lot of courage, and finally he asked me, "Would you marry me?"

Wow, what is this?

"What happens if there is a war between the U.S. and China?" I asked. How romantic!

"It is not going to happen," he responded.

"I would be sent to an internment camp as the Japanese were during the war."

He must have wondered what this little girl was thinking. "It was wrong. The government will not do it again."

I was curious about the interracial marriage. "What language will the kids speak?"

"Both." He was sure of that. He had all the answers.

I expressed one of my impressions of Americans. "American people divorce too easily." There were very few divorces in Taiwan back then.

"I don't believe in divorce." He looked anxious.

Don was a gentle, kind, decent, and genuine soul. I trusted him. I felt safe with him. We had been such good friends. I said to Don, "I will check with my parents. I will consider it if my parents approve it."

I wrote a letter home to ask for approval. Don also wrote a letter to my parents to ask for my hand in marriage.

When Don was in college, he'd had a Chinese girlfriend from Hong Kong. Her father made her promise at his death bed that she wouldn't marry the American boy.

I could tell that Don was very concerned and apprehensive that his "love history" would repeat.

It took seven days for letters to reach Taiwan back then. It was a torturing wait for Don.

"My parents will not approve it."

"We can elope," he suggested.

"Are you kidding?! It will bring great shame and disgrace to the family."

The wedding ceremony for Chinese people is for a couple not only to be legally married but also to be witnessed by heaven and earth and recognized and accepted by both family clans and their friends. Elopement may be romantic to Americans, but it was a great dishonor to a Chinese family. In some cases, the family would put an official notice in the newspaper to disown their child, especially a girl, for eloping.

What a difference between two cultures.

In China during the olden days, the ceremony would take place in the groom's home. Relatives and friends were invited to witness, recognize, and accept the couple while they paid respect to parents, to heaven and earth, and to each other. The fancy characters of 囍*Xi* [Double Happiness] in red or gold would be all over the courtyard, on the doors and windows of the house and the new couple's room. Red is the color for weddings and all other happy events.

Nowadays, no matter where the wedding takes place, in a church, in a restaurant, or in the big ballroom of a hotel, the tradition stays the same. The character of 囍*Xi*, the decoration for wedding ceremony, has always been valued and kept throughout the years. The囍*Xi* is the symbolic blessing not only to the couple but also to the two families.

My parents knew that there were a couple of Chinese young men who were very serious about me. One in particular, whom I'd met in Chicago the previous summer, was a decent, genuine young man. Chinese courting between a girl and a boy was very different from American way. I was more cautious with the Chinese boys. The aggressive and serious approach of some of the boys had made me very uncomfortable sometimes. I discouraged them right away to avoid hurting them, because most of the Chinese boys, especially in the U.S. back then, were very serious about courting.

I have always cherished people who are natural, gentle, kind, genuine, and decent, with a beautiful heart. These were my standards then and these are my standards now.

In one of the letters my father wrote, "If both the American and Chinese boys score the same according to your standards, pick the Chinese."

Is now the time for me to "pick" as my father advised?

Both of them were decent and highly educated young men. One was an engineer and one was a librarian. They both spoiled me and treated me with respect. They would do anything for me. With the same heritage I had more in common with the Chinese boy, and he was artistic, sensitive, and sentimental. He was very thoughtful and spoiled me more. The American boy had a brilliant mind and a simple big heart that was so pure. We had a deeper friendship and a solid foundation.

I truly didn't have the heart to break either one's heart.

Which heart am I going to break, the Chinese heart or the American heart?

Before I quit my summer job in Chicago at the end of summer, the Chinese boy gave me a small framed portrait of me—drawn from his memory. He named it, at the bottom of the picture, *The Image in the Heart*. The portrait has remained, but unfortunately his heart was broken.

Our family, my parents and siblings, had a family meeting to discuss this serious matter. They discussed and voted. My father was out-voted by 7 to 1. He was the only one against it.

My mother, a lady of wisdom, said to him, "She wouldn't have asked for our permission if she herself did not want to marry this boy."

In my father's letter, he gave us approval under one condition. Don's parents had to ask for the marriage. My parents wanted the assurance that Don's parents accepted their beloved daughter and the marriage was legal. The marriage needed to be recognized, accepted and respected by the family. What a profound love from my parents!

Don asked me if I got the letter. I said, "Yes."

"What did they say?"

"They said 'no'."

"Why?" He looked so sad.

"Americans divorce too easily."

He was frustrated and depressed. "Not every American divorces!"

I didn't have the heart to tease him anymore. I laughed and told him what my parents' condition was.

What a relief for him! He said excitedly, "I will call my parents right away!"

I had met his parents and one of his younger sisters before. He called his parents, but he didn't know how to ask them. After several minutes, marriage was still not brought up. Mother knows best! His mother finally asked him, "Are you getting married?"

His parents were very happy for him, and his mother wrote a letter to my parents to ask for marriage for their son.

Blessed by God, our wedding was witnessed by heaven and earth and recognized and accepted by our families and friends. It took place in Edwardsville, Illinois on December 15th, 1968. My twin sister Irene came to the U.S. in October after marrying her husband Lawrence. She was my Maid of Honor. My family had a banquet to celebrate the special day with family and friends in Taiwan. A big golden character of 囍 *Xi* [double happiness] on the wall, a traditional Chinese wedding decoration, bestowed on us *Double Happiness* ever after!

**Wedding in Edwardsville,
Illinois**

**Don, Celine, Irene (Maid of Honor),
and Lawrence Leang (Brother-in-law)
Celine in traditional Chinese gown for wedding reception**

The Helping Hand

Life is full of surprises and mysteries. Do you believe in miracles? Do you believe that everything happens for a reason?

It was the summer of 1983. We lived in Lincoln, Nebraska. Joline was seven and Andrea was four. I was a special education teacher, and Don, worked at ISCO as an electronic technician. He was also in the Army Reserve. He had to report for duty one weekend each month.

No school for me in the summer—a special time with my two daughters. In the morning, Joline read, wrote, and practiced violin while Andrea read her little books. In the afternoon we met with some friends and their children at the Able Hall swimming pool of the University of Nebraska. The pool was always filled with our splashing and laughter.

We hadn't taken any trips since Joline was two months old. We decided it was a good time for a two-week family vacation.

We planned and scheduled an adventure to the East Coast in August—between Don's monthly duty weekends and before my school started.

Everyone was excited, especially the girls.

"I want to see the Statue of Liberty in New York and Lincoln Memorial in D.C.," Joline yelled out with excitement.

"Me too! Me too! I want to see Niagara Falls!" Andrea joined in and clapped her hands.

One week before our trip, Don came home with a cast on his left hand after his weekend Army Reserve duty. I was stunned. "Oh, no! What happened?"

He responded, "Well, I missed a step going upstairs and fell. I cracked my left hand on the step."

Joline and Andrea came running to check the cast. "Does it hurt,

108

Daddy?" They touched his cast gently.

"Not too bad. Daddy will be okay." He patted their heads.

We had to cancel the trip since it would be difficult for him to drive long distance with a cast on one hand, and I could not handle highway driving. We just had to enjoy the rest of the summer in Lincoln.

I comforted the girls. "We will go next summer when Daddy's hand gets better, okay?"

"Okay." Although disappointment was written all over their little faces, they didn't fuss.

Don was in good health, and I was anemic. The doctor wanted me to check my blood periodically. I decided to make an appointment to have my blood checked now that the trip was cancelled.

Don's mother died of colon cancer a year before. His father had died of a heart attack six months before Joline was born. An article "Colon Cancer Screening Saves Life" in a medical magazine caught my eye while I was waiting in the doctor's office. I had never heard of it or known anything about it before. I was curious.

The article was my first reading and understanding on any kind of cancer even though my mother-in-law died of cancer. She was in Wisconsin, and we were in Nebraska at the time. Her illness and death were somewhat of a mystery to me. Don didn't talk about it much at all. The only thing I knew was that she complained about abdominal pain when she visited us in the spring of 1982. She was admitted to hospital shortly after she returned to Wisconsin. She passed away a month later.

As our family doctor, Dr. Schwenke, was checking on me, I said to him casually, "Don wouldn't come in for a physical exam. His father died of heart attack and his mother died of colon cancer. May I have the slides for colon cancer screening for Don?"

"Sure!" He gave me an envelope, a kit for colon cancer screening.

I took it back to the doctor after Don had collected his samples. It showed blood in the stool. Dr. Schwenke immediately referred him to Dr. Moore, a colon specialist, for further diagnosis. Don went to see Dr. Moore right away. They did a biopsy. It seemed serious and I was very worried. "When will you find out the result?" I asked Don.

He responded, "On Friday."

The new school year was going to start in a week. My best colleague friends, Nancy, Lois, Joan, Mary Lu, and I had lunch together on Friday. I didn't mention anything about Don's biopsy. I felt very uncomfortable the whole time. I was extremely uneasy and didn't have any appetite.

When I got home, I called Don right away. "Did you find out the result from Dr. Moore?"

"There was a tumor, and it was malignant." This was Don, few words without reaction and expression.

"What?! How serious is it?"

"They don't know yet."

It was like a death sentence, and our happy world had shattered. I started to cry. I didn't know what to expect and I didn't know what to do. "What's wrong, Mommy?" Joline was concerned.

I wiped my tears. "Daddy is sick and he needs to go to the hospital."

"Will doctor help him?" Andrea asked.

"Yes." I hugged them and kissed them on the head. I needed to be strong for them.

Don was diagnosed on Friday. He was admitted to the hospital on the following Tuesday. The surgery was scheduled for three days later.

I was so frightened, so worried, and so devastated. I couldn't sleep, and I couldn't eat. I lost a pound a day. When we, a few friends and I, checked Don in the hospital, I was a basket case. Don looked healthy and normal, with a smile on his face. I looked so bad that the nurse thought I was the patient.

"How serious it is?" I asked Dr. Schwenke when he came to check on Don.

"We can't tell until we see it inside." No comfort or encouragement from him.

Pam, a close friend, had moved in with me, for she knew that I was scared. Eddie, a brotherly friend, took me to and from school after I got a ticket for driving the wrong way on a one-way street before Don's surgery.

Early Friday morning, as the nurse pushed Don on the rolling bed to the operation room, I asked him, "Are you scared?"

He responded loudly, "I ain't going yet!" I was glad that he was brave and positive.

I could hardly breathe normally while sitting in the waiting area, even with Reverend Jerry Lundby, our minister and a fatherly friend, and five close friends right next to me.

I prayed and I prayed.

After three or four long hours, Dr. Schwenke came out of the door, finally. I ran to him. "How is Don? How did it go?"

He said, "The tumor was removed. It was at the earliest stage, and it hadn't gone through the wall of the colon. Don is considered cured."

I grabbed his arm tightly, and I almost fainted with the good news. "Thank you! Thank you!"

Don was in the hospital for 17 days. Nai Yu Chen, a dear friend, stayed with Don in the hospital after the surgery during the day while I was teaching. Yi Long, Randy, Man, Eddie, Nai and many other friends were by my side to take care of the girls and to do whatever was needed in the house, especially when I visited Don in the evening.

How blessed and grateful we were—having so much love and support during this tormented time.

*****

Many years later I was chatting about the past with Bea, Don's youngest sister, when she visited us. "Because of Mother's colon cancer, the article on colon cancer screening caught my eye and saved Don's life."

Bea looked puzzled. "What do you mean? Mother didn't die of colon cancer. It was the recurrence of her breast cancer, and it had spread."

"What? Really? All these years I thought she died of colon cancer." Since my mother-in-law complained so much about her abdominal pain before she was admitted in the hospital, I thought and assumed she had died of colon cancer. How ignorant I was.

Don has been cancer free for more than 30 years now. We are

forever in debt to Dr. Schwenke for his prompt action and Dr. Moore for his skillful surgery. We are grateful for the support and love we received during the ordeal.

If he didn't break his hand, we would have gone on the trip to the East Coast. I wouldn't have gone to check my blood, and I wouldn't have read the article on colon cancer screening. It stills gives me chills whenever I think of all the "what ifs".

Don's broken hand turned out to be a life-saving blessing. My ignorance on cancer had saved Don's life. What a mysterious way being blessed.

Yes, indeed life is full of surprises and mysteries! Yes, I believe in miracles! Yes, I believe everything happens for a reason.

Life is truly beautiful with love and faith!

The Chicken of the Sea

One hot day in July 2013, I took my seven-year-old grandson Casey to the YMCA. We were in the current pool, and the waterslide next to it was open also. I thought Casey might like to do the waterslide.

"It looks fun. Do you want to go down the slide?" I asked Casey.

He replied, "Only if you go with me."

"Oh, no, not me!"

*****

Although I grew up on Taiwan, an island, I never learned how to swim. I played in the water very often. The pool was always crowded, and there were no swimming lessons.

My father often took us to Bi Tan [Green Lake] in the summer. I had great fun playing with my siblings on the beach. I learned to row a boat, and I challenged myself to row the boat across the lake alone.

I could only float and kick, with my face down in the water. But it was not swimming, it was only playing. Although I love the water, I am still scared of deep water where my feet don't touch the bottom.

In the summer of 1970, we lived in Pocatello, Idaho. I decided it was time for me to overcome this obstacle—being scared of deep water. Since I had the summer off, being a teacher, I signed up for a beginner swimming class.

Our instructor was a very solemn-looking lady, and the teaching assistant never smiled either. There were around twenty students in the class. The instructor was teaching us on the side of the pool.

I was apprehensive about the class already. I became even more worried, having two serious-looking instructors.

The teacher provided the guidelines and expectations to the class.

"By the end of the semester, you need to know how to swim four different styles, to tread water, and to swim five to ten minutes without stopping."

"The first stroke you are going to learn is the backstroke," she added.

This must be a magic class to achieve all that in eight weeks!

Everyone in class learned the backstroke within a week, except for a young man from India, and, of course, me. We still stayed in the shallow end, trying hard to float on our backs. It was so scary to let go of myself and trust the water. It didn't happen to either of us.

"Do you think you can do it?" I asked him.

He frowned. "I'm not so sure."

I tried to encourage him and myself at the same time. "We just have to keep trying until we can do it."

After two weeks, we still couldn't float on our backs. The Indian student disappeared from class one day. I, the lone *special* swimmer, still tried very hard to float on my back. Other people were swimming like sharks by then. Three weeks had passed. I was still in the shallow end, by myself, trying to float on my back.

I bet the teacher had never had such a *unique* student in her teaching career. She finally got in the water and tried to work with me. It was the first time she needed to get in the water.

As she held me under my arms, I twisted, giggled, and fought. I grabbed her and messed up her hair.

She let go of me and asked me, "What is wrong?"

"You tickled me," I replied.

My solemn teacher laughed for the first time.

It took me four weeks just to lie down and float on my back. Would you believe that the backstroke has been my favorite stroke ever since?

Although I finally learned the backstroke, I was still a shaky swimmer. The teacher assigned the teaching assistant to hold a 10-foot rescue pole over me wherever I swam. That was her sole job for the class was to follow the *best* swimmer closely with the pole over me throughout the class every single day.

One day, we were supposed to swim different styles for five minutes, non-stop. Of course my *security* pole was over me the whole time. I felt so proud that I could swim finally, although with the pole over me.

I've finally overcome the obstacle I had with deep water.

I was on my back doing the backstroke, and the pole was over my head. Suddenly I felt very tired. I panicked. I grabbed the pole and stood up. The water was only to my chest. The TA burst out laughing. I was so embarrassed, and I laughed, too.

She asked, "You are in shallow water. Why did you grab the pole?"

I felt so stupid. "I didn't know where I was. I thought I was in the deep water."

Well, at least both instructors had a good laugh because of me. I bet that they would never forget the *outstanding* student they had in the summer of 1970.

*****

I didn't want my daughters to fear water. Joline, my older daughter, started water-baby class when she was nine months old. Andrea started going to the swimming pool when she was three months old.

In 1983, when Joline was seven years old and Andrea was four years old, they could dive and swim with ease and pleasure. We went swimming almost every afternoon in the summer.

They dove and they swam in different styles. When they went to the diving board or deep water and left me behind in the shallow end, they always kept their eyes on Mommy.

They would call out to me, "Mommy, be careful!"

*****

In 1990, I decided to "polish" my swimming skills. I signed up for a beginner class in the evening, sponsored by the Red Cross. The instructors just so happened to be the parents of Becky Martin, one of my colleagues and a Physical Education teacher.

I did all right this time with all different styles, but deep water still scared me. I could not dive from the diving board. To me it was like

115

committing suicide. The instructors didn't push me.

In the very last class everyone, except for me, of course, had great fun diving over and over again. Mrs. Martin said, "You don't have to dive from the diving board. You can jump from the side of the pool if you want to."

I didn't want to let her down. "Okay. I will jump from the side."

I took several deep breaths. Both instructors were by my side waiting for this "big event".

I screamed so loud that everyone could hear me. The divers stopped diving. It startled my instructors! Poor instructors! Well, I was still on the edge of the pool. They said together, "You don't have to do it! You don't have to do it!"

*****

Casey asked me, "*Po Po*, why won't you go to the waterslide with me?"

"I can't go to the slide with you because *Po Po* is the *Chicken of the Sea*!"

I told him my funny swimming stories.

He laughed so hard. "Ha! Ha! *Po Po* is *the Chicken of the Sea*!"

A Bridge

On a Sunday morning in the spring of 2013, I switched the channels to see if anything worth watching was on TV. Sidney Poitier, the legendary actor and one of my favorite stars, was on the screen. It was the Master Class, one of Oprah's OWN productions. I was curious about what he had to share.

I knew nothing about his personal life. I was surprised to learn that Sidney Poitier grew up on a small Bahamian island with no electricity. He was born early and unexpectedly when his parents were in Florida for some business. So he was born a citizen of the United States, but he did not grow up in the U. S. When he was eighteen, he decided to come to the U. S. to explore opportunities for his future.

He was working at an establishment in the U.S. When people wanted to talk him, they would call out to him, "Hey, Nigger!"

He answered innocently, "My name is Sidney Poitier."

People kept calling him, "Nigger."

He would tell them each time, "My name is Sidney Poitier."

He didn't understand why they didn't call him by his name or even care to know his name. Instead, they always called him, "Nigger!"

I laughed, but not because it was funny. I laughed because I could really relate to what had happened to him.

*****

I was accepted by five universities for graduate school in the U. S. in the spring of 1967. I had decided to attend Georgia State University in Atlanta in the fall. The school had arranged a host family for me. I had started correspondence right then with Susan Swint, the daughter of my host family.

One day I went to a dentist to have my teeth checked. The dentist had studied in the U. S. When he knew that I was going to Atlanta to study, he said to me, "Be aware of the racial discrimination in the U.S., especially in the South."

I wanted to know more. "What do you mean?"

He said, "For example, when people take the bus, white people board the bus from the front door and black people board the bus from the back door."

I was curious. "What about Chinese people?"

"Some people think you are white and some people think you are 'colored.' It will make you feel very awkward."

I couldn't imagine how it could be. Chinese people have the same color of skin, the same color of eyes, and the same color of hair. Even with 56 different ethnic groups, we are without distinguished differences in appearance. I didn't know how I would feel and react if this would really happen to me.

"Wow! What should a Chinese person do?"

"That's why you need to be aware and be prepared."

This was my first orientation to American culture and society.

In June 1967, I received scholarships from both Southern Illinois University-Edwardsville and the University of New York in Syracuse. Instead of going to Atlanta in the South, I decided to attend Southern Illinois University. A couple of family friends lived in St. Louis, an hour away.

In the U.S., I learned that discrimination was not completely determined by geography.

Even though I had decided not to attend Georgia State, I kept in touch with my host family in Atlanta. Susan Swint and I remained good friends until her fatal car accident a few years ago.

In Taiwan, I had taken twenty-nine credits for most semesters throughout my four years of college. A full-time American graduate student needed to take only twelve credits, three courses, each quarter. My major was Special Education. All graduate courses were offered in the evening. After adjusting to my life and studies for a month or so, I felt more comfortable with everything. I decided to find a part-time job on campus.

My job was to check in new periodicals in the periodical department of the library. Mrs. Mosley was the supervisor. She looked old and unhappy.

When I first reported to her, she said to me out of the blue, "Why do you foreigners work in the U. S.?"

What is this? I was caught off guard and didn't know how to respond. I just smiled and said nothing. I sensed the unfriendliness.

Later I found out that she had lost her husband not too long ago. She looked weary, unhappy, unfriendly, old, and miserable. I felt sorry for her.

Not long after that, she was saying something about "laundry" to me. I was really confused.

Why does laundry have anything to do with me?

I had just learned how to do laundry by myself, since my laundry was done mostly by the helper when I was back home. I was puzzled. Again, I just smiled and said nothing.

She always was nice to the other student workers, who were white. But she always said something either negative or unpleasant to me. Whenever the work hours needed to be cut in the department, I was the only one whose hours got cut. Incidents like these went on throughout the year.

I finally asked myself, *"Is this 'prejudice' and 'discrimination' that my dentist had warned me about?"*

It was hurtful and painful to feel discriminated against. I had kept all these insults to myself. When I was 100% sure that Mrs. Mosley was not treating me fairly, I quit my job. Again, I did not say anything.

After my encounter with Mrs. Mosley, I appreciated even more the kind people who had helped me adapt to my new life. Since then, I have always believed and shared with people, "People who are kind to you when you don't have anything to offer are truly kind people."

Not until a few years later, when I had learned something about the history of Chinese immigrants, did I understand why Mrs. Mosley was talking about laundry to me. Many of the immigrants from China, without language and skills, had opened laundry businesses to survive their hardship as immigrants in the early 1900s.

I was like Sidney Poitier, with limited understanding of the American culture, and I had no idea why people acted the way they did and said the things they said. When people called him "Nigger," innocently he responded, "My name is Sidney Poitier." When Mrs. Mosley was mean and unfair to me, I didn't know how to defend myself. Instead I just smiled and said nothing, feeling deeply hurt inside.

Remembering my own experience with discrimination, now I laughed about what had happened to Sidney Poitier and me. Both Sidney Poitier and I were simply too innocent to understand then what was happening.

*****

The moment I landed in Seattle on September 15th, 1967, I had a new very strong sense and awareness: in this new country I was no longer just Celine Yu Hua Tan any more, I represented not only my family but also all Chinese people, the *Descendants of the Dragon.*

With this strong and honorable sense of representation, my perception has widened, my heart has enlarged, and my vision has expanded throughout the years.

A seed had been planted in my heart, and a mission had taken root in my soul.

Since then, sharing my heritage with people has become my obligation. Sowing seeds—the seed of exposure to Chinese culture, the seed of understanding, the seed of appreciation, the seed of friendship, and the seed of celebration—has had been my obligation.

With the seed in my heart and the mission in my soul, I became a bridge, a bridge to connect two groups of wonderful people and a bridge to link two beautiful cultures.

I shared my heritage in a number of ways, as a speaker, a teacher, a friend, a colleague, and a resource person at numerous organizations and schools. I also carried out the mission to educate the Chinese students who came to study at the University of Nebraska, beginning in 1973. I wanted to prepare and help them face their new life in the

U. S. with a positive and healthy attitude. It was important for them to know and understand that it was their duty to share their heritage, and it was also their job to learn about the American culture.

I could not emphasize enough to the Chinese students that American people are the most loving, caring, and giving people. I always reminded them, "Don't accuse people of being prejudiced unless you are sure of it. Some people are ignorant and say or do things due to their limited exposure and experiences, not necessarily prejudice."

I always defend American students and people whenever I hear negative comments on them. I feel obligated to correct misconceptions of American people whenever necessary. This was true especially during the eight years I was teaching in Beijing, China, from 2001 to 2009.

In order to provide my American students with in-depth experiences, I took my Chinese language students to travel in China. I instilled in, and demanded and expected from, my students a sense of honor and pride as they represented their families, schools, and the United States while they traveled in China.

"Don't be the ugly American! Be the beautiful one! You are representing not only yourself but also your family, our school, and the U. S. Take pride!"

Chinese people were impressed with my students' Chinese language skills and great behavior wherever we went.

"Your students are great, courteous, and delightful."

I always replied proudly. "Yes, I love them."

They truly were my wonderful American ambassadors.

*****

In the summer of 1991, my father was visiting us in Lincoln, Nebraska. Someone had damaged my Honda Accord, and with my father and two daughters I went to the Honda body shop for an estimate. A man told us to wait in the waiting area while he was helping someone else. We waited for a long while. Another customer came in. When the man was done with the previous customer, he went to the person who came in after us instead of to us. The customer was a white man.

This is not right.

I was no longer the little girl who would take this with a smile as I did in 1967.

My father, a retired Nationalist Chinese Army general, had never experienced such discrimination. My two daughters needed to know when and how to stand up for themselves when such incidents occurred. I couldn't let this man disrespect my honorable father and pollute the innocence of my two daughters.

I reminded him, "We were here first. We have been waiting here for a long time."

He said, "It will be a few more minutes."

I said, "You are not being fair. Is this some kind of discrimination? Where is your manager?"

"I am the manager," he replied.

I protested, "You are not being fair! We were here first! We have been waiting for a long time."

"I am not prejudiced. My uncle adopted Korean kids."

I firmly repeated myself. "We were here first! You are not being fair!"

This big man was surprised that a little Asian lady would challenge him. He might have thought that I could not even speak English, let alone challenge him. The other customer looked ashamed, hanging his head way down.

I pointed it out to this manager. "How can you behave like this? You are working for Honda!"

He apologized. "I am sorry. It was not called for. I will give you 20% off if you want to do it here."

I didn't report him to Honda. I had given him a chance to grow and to change. Both my father and I hoped he had learned his lesson.

*****

Yes, representation of the Asian community was urgently needed. I accepted the Mayor's appointment as a Human Rights Commissioner of Lincoln, Nebraska, and I served for three years.

I firmly believe that exposure to a culture different from yours will stimulate interest; interest brings understanding; understanding leads to appreciation; appreciation brings connection; and connection brings friendship and harmony among people.

It is my vision and it is my mission.

It is my duty.

It is my honorable obligation to be a bridge.

I brought people of different heritages and professions together to serve on the board of Nebraska Asian Community Center that I co-founded. Working side by side, we provided opportunities and a platform for the community to learn, to educate, to communicate, to share, and to celebrate together.

I established a sister-city relationship for Lincoln with Taiping City in Taiwan. Friendship between the delegates of the two cities really touched many hearts during the process, which included exchange programs on both sides.

Tom was a banker, and he was a kind and sensitive man. We were in the Leadership Lincoln XI class, a non-profit organization to connect community leaders. I believed that I was the first Chinese person he had known. I invited him to be a member of the sister-city delegation. He wholeheartedly supported the mission, absorbed the experiences, and enjoyed the hospitality and friendship we received in Taiping City.

His eyes were filled with tears when he bid good-bye to his friends in Taiping City in Taiwan.

"Thank you, Celine, for providing me the opportunity to be a delegate. It was once-in-a-lifetime experience that I will always remember and treasure." Since then, he has served on the board of the Nebraska Asian Community Center for many years, helping with my *bridge* mission when I was the president of the center.

*****

To broaden students' horizons and perspectives I helped connect four public schools with schools in Taiwan for many exchange programs. I also planned, designed, and set up a three-week summer program at the University of Nebraska for Chu Lin Middle School and Chu Lin High School students to learn English and to experience American culture. The programs continued for many years.

When students of Chu Lin Sister School visited Park Middle School in Lincoln, they brought popular Chinese games as gifts. They taught the American students how to do the activities. What a delight, to watch American and Chinese children playing together.

Becky Martin, a physical education teacher, was thrilled with the challenge and fun of the Chinese pull bells and shuttle cocks. "They are great physical activities. Students loved them." Since then, she has included these two popular Chinese activities as a part of her curriculum.

*****

For many years, I arranged for the Taiwan Youth Chinese Opera Troupe and the Mei Chiang Chinese Folk Dance Troupe to make annual 21-day tours in the U. S. Their outstanding performances received warm welcome and great appreciation in many states, countless schools, and communities throughout the U.S., from Alaska to Washington D.C. and from Minneapolis to New Orleans.

Margaret Wang, a Chinese teacher in Minneapolis, told me, "The whole school loved it. The impact on my students of direct contact with the performing artists was incredible and inevitable. Some of my students want to go to Taiwan to attend the Chinese opera camp in the summer. We would love to have them again for our school."

For many summers Kathy Li, one of my student teachers in Nebraska, took her students from New Orleans to attend the Chinese Opera workshop in Taiwan.

*****

People often asked me, "What holidays do you celebrate?"

"Both. We celebrate the American holidays with Chinese friends, and we celebrate Chinese holidays with American friends. Double celebrations, double fun!"

Since I always had to work on the Chinese New Year's Day, I decided to celebrate this most important holiday with my colleagues. For many years when I taught at Park Middle School, I made one hundred *chun juan* [spring rolls/egg rolls], a food for Chinese New Year. I celebrated the Chinese holiday with all of my American colleagues and friends at school.

I was either the first Chinese colleague or the first Chinese friend of most of my colleagues. Many of them had told me, "You are the one who started me and my family eating Chinese food. We love it."

*****

On the Easter gathering in 1982, when I saw more than forty Chinese children run at Holmes Lake Park to hunt eggs, I said to myself, "It is a Chinese school right there."

With overwhelming support from the Chinese community, I founded Lincoln Chinese School for Chinese children to learn language and Chinese culture at our church, American Lutheran Church, two months later. After thirty-some years, the school is still going strong.

I established a four-year Chinese program for the Lincoln Public Schools in 1988 and at Arrowhead High School in 2009. With language and experiences with Chinese culture, my students broadened their horizons and perspectives and expanded their vision. They are well prepared to be global citizens.

*****

Chinese Kaleidoscope was a program that I directed and produced every other year. It showcased the integrated cultural activities that my students learned in class. Students in Nebraska shared with 3,600 peers, staff, parents, and community members of Lincoln High School. Later, students in Wisconsin shared with 800 people at Arrowhead

125

High School. It was a 40-minute program including Lion Dance, Dragon Dance, martial arts demonstrations, folk dances, songs, and a fashion show of ancient clothing. The very first one was presented at Lincoln High School in 1992, and the very last one was presented at Arrowhead High School in 2012.

My students enjoyed learning and took pride in sharing the Chinese cultural activities that they had learned in class. They couldn't wait to share again. They would ask me before the program was even over, "What will we do next time?"

Lion Dance and Dragon Dance are colorful traditional Chinese cultural activities for celebrations and parades. I organized and led the very first Lion Dance Troupe to represent the Asian community at the annual Nebraska Star City Parade. It was a 100-people Chinese Lion Dance Troupe consisting of people of all colors and all ages. Our unique Lion Dance and colorful troupe won the Specialty Award for both years we participated in 1993 and 1996.

Park Middle School, where I taught, has a diverse student body. I initiated, planned, designed, and coordinated the Park P.O.W.E.R. (Positive Opportunity for Wisdom, Excellence, and Respect) Conference to promote multicultural education. It was a multicultural conference with 29 workshops for 800 students and staff. I involved not only all the staff, from the custodians to the principal, but also community leaders and ethnic group leaders. The mayor and many community leaders joined us for the fun and learning experiences at the conference—the very first one of its kind in the Lincoln Public Schools, which included 48 schools.

My principal, Mr. Tim Carroll, being a minority himself, could see the noticeable and positive impact the conference had on the staff and students. Whenever he saw me in the hallways, he would say, "You are wonderful!"

*****

I have given numerous speeches at different occasions and organizations. One year I was one of the speakers for the Nebraska

126

Martin Luther King celebration in front of an audience of 800 government officials, business executives, and community leaders. There were people in tears while I was delivering my message, and afterward a few people even asked me for a copy of my speech.

These are the remarks I delivered to honor Dr. Martin Luther King at the Freedom Breakfast on January 16th, 1998:

> When you find that a person who came 15 minutes later than you is being served while you are told to wait in an isolated room for 30 minutes, you know that prejudice is there. When you pay for your groceries, the food stamps key is automatically rung; you know the ignorance is there. When you pay by Visa and only your ID is requested, you know that discrimination is there. When the store manager instructs employees to call 911 for shoplifting when people of a certain ethnicity come in the store after certain hour of the day, you know that hate is there. When young children ask why they are being followed in the stores, you know that their innocence is polluted. When people give you the finger while you are driving on "O" Street, you wonder if their parents are their models. When you come back in 45 minutes as told and find out that you must wait longer because your name has been moved from the top of the list to the bottom, you know that you will never go back even if you are starving to death. When young people yell "Japanese" at you on Vine Street, you know that education is needed. And when your children come home crying because of unfair treatment, you know you must teach them in a positive way to be stronger and tougher in facing the cruel realities of life that lies ahead of them without losing faith in humanity.
>
> Diversity is not just numbers on paper. Multicultural living is to enrich your life with your own heritage and with other cultures. Multicultural living is to celebrate your heritage and others' heritage as well. Multicultural living is people living together and caring for one another. Multicultural living is people to live side by side in harmony.
>
> To achieve the harmony of a multicultural life, education is the key. And the most effective way of

learning is through personal experiences and friendship. Friendship is the basis of understanding and appreciation, and understanding and appreciation are the foundation of respect and caring. Please open you mind, open your heart, and provide opportunities to share your heritage with people and learn from them as well. It is everyone's job to share and to educate one another.

Yes. Dr. King had a dream! Yes, he had a vision! It is our duty to honor his vision, and it is our obligation to carry out his mission. With shared vision and mission, we can make a difference.

America is a wonderful country, Lincoln is our home, and the world is ours. With us side by side we can make anything happen. We can make America a more beautiful country; we can make Lincoln a more wonderful home; and we can make our world a more peaceful place for everyone. Thank you!

As the keynote speaker for the National Honor Society Induction Ceremony at Southeast High School in Lincoln, Nebraska, I shared some of my insights and experiences with 1,500 students, parents, and staff.

I shared with them my firm belief in the way I consider my challenges.

Challenges are opportunities to find your hidden talents and potential.

I shared with them the way I have been living my life.

If you have a dream, make it come true.

If you have a vision, make it happen.

If you have energy, make it positive.

If you have something extra, share with people.

Being an educator since I was 21, I truly believe education is the seed; society is the ground; and experience is the water. We need to plant good seeds, to provide healthy soil, and to nurture the seeds with good water.

I have been a seed sower to spread the seeds, and I have been a bridge to bond two groups of wonderful people and to link two beautiful cultures.

My students who have graduated from Arrowhead High School, Hartland, Wisconsin, have close contact with me. Whenever they come home from college, we have a reunion to catch up and to have fun together.

During their winter break they would go with me to celebrate the Chinese New Year with more than 100 little kids at Bright Days, my granddaughter's daycare, and at Big Bend Elementary School, where my grandson Casey attends school. To celebrate July 4th, they led a Lion Dance parade with me for 70 kindergarteners at a summer school.

They help me sow the seeds and they pass on what they learned with pleasure and pride. They share my vision and honor my mission.

I plant the seeds with my heart. I carry out my missions with my soul. Providing good water to nurture the seed is my duty.

I am a seed sower, and I am a bridge. It is my job, a passionate duty of an educator and an honorable obligation of a *Descendant of the Dragon* that I have served with great pleasure, honor, and pride since 1967.

Lincoln
Nebraska
U. S. A.

Taiping
Taiwan
R. O. C.

**Top: The mayors of Lincoln, Nebraska and Taiping City, Taiwan
at the ceremony of establishing the sister city relationship in Lincoln
Bottom: The delegation of Lincoln in Taiping City in Taiwan**

LINCOLN
Journal Star

LINCOLN, NEB.   THURSDAY   APRIL 30, 1998

Celebrating Asian culture

ROBERT BECKER/Lincoln Journal Star

A member of the Taiwan Youth Fu Hsing Chinese Opera Mission performs Wednesday at Lincoln High School. The group is touring the United States, doing shows in eight cities in four states over 24 days. The group is scheduled to perform Saturday at 7 p.m. at Kimball Recital Hall. The performance is sponsored by the Asian Community and Cultural Center to celebrate Asian Heritage Month, which is during May. Tickets are available at the door.

Staff photo by Carol Spaeth-Bauer

Dancing in the halls

Big Bend Elementary Principal Shawn Waller leads the dragon dance for the grand parade through the halls during the Chinese New Year celebration on Jan. 8. For more photos see our online photo gallery at LakeCountryNow.com.

Chinese New Year Celebration at Big Bend Elementary School

Big Bend Elementary student Jackson Miller tries kicking a shuttlecock during a Chinese New Year celebration.

Big Bend Elementary second-grader Casey Hsieh waits in costume to lead the grand parade. The celebration was lead by his grandmother, retired Arrowhead High School teacher Celine Robertson.

Chapter 5
As the Bamboo Shoots

竹

The Wild, Wild West
Touchdown
The Lost Immigrant
Beyond Imagination
P.O.W.E.R
Windows on China
Orient Express
Friends without Borders
Friends from Afar

The Wild, Wild West

As I arrived at Franklin Junior High on the first day of school, students gathered at the entrance. The door was closed. There was a man standing inside the door. I tried to open the door to enter the building.

"You have to wait for the bell," the man at the door said.

"I am a new teacher."

"Sorry! I thought you were a student," he said and let me in.

It was August 1969. I was the new special education teacher at Franklin Junior High in Pocatello, Idaho—my first school in the U.S.

*****

Don was born and raised in Wisconsin. He attended college in Logan, Utah, for four years. He was a passionate hunter and fisherman. He loved the mountains and rivers in Utah. He talked about his life in Utah a lot, especially about the beautiful scenery.

Here we were in southern Illinois, nothing but flat lands. I could tell that he missed the beautiful mountains and rivers in the West.

"You will love it. It is so beautiful there. The mountains and rivers are nearby and great hunting and fishing!" He described the beauty with such delight.

"Do you wish to go back to the West?" I asked.

"Yes!"

He applied for jobs in the western states—Utah, Idaho, Wyoming, Montana, and Colorado, as I was finishing my thesis for my master's degree in Special Education.

Don attended Utah State University for his bachelor's degree. He obtained a master's degree in Library Science at the University of

Wisconsin-Madison after serving three years in the army. He was a librarian.

One day in the spring, Don was so happy and excited. "I got a job offer from Idaho State University in Pocatello, Idaho."

"Where is Idaho? How do you pronounce the name of city? What is it like there?" I had never heard of this state, let alone the city of Pocatello.

"It is right above Utah. There are mountains and rivers. Yellowstone Park is not very far from there. You will love it."

Yellowstone Park was one of the places I always wanted to visit. "It must be very beautiful there."

My mother instilled in us girls that the husband is the head of the household and the center of our lives. "Support whatever your husband wishes to do, always."

"Okay. We will go!" I supported Don's excitement.

People often asked me, "How did you end up in Idaho?"

This is what I told them. "Well. There is a Chinese saying: *If you are married to a rooster, you follow the rooster; and if you are married to a dog, you follow the dog.*" Rooster and dog are two animals of the twelve animal symbols for the Chinese Zodiac.

I got a teaching job offer shortly afterward, as a special education teacher at a junior high. After I obtained my diploma in June 1969, we said good-bye to our first home and all our friends in Edwardsville, Illinois, to start a new chapter of our lives in Pocatello, Idaho.

*****

Idaho is indeed a beautiful state and a great place to live— surrounded by high mountains and clean rivers. With its high altitude, summer is not too hot, and winter is not too bad either.

My colleague, Mrs. Leona Thurman, the other special education teacher, was my mother's age. She was a veteran teacher and an energetic caring lady. She took me under her wing and became my mentor. She had a successful and loving husband and three daughters who were about my age. She was generous and kind. Mrs. Thurman was a cheerful, caring friend.

Mrs. Thurman and I learned oil painting together. Mr. Koval, the art teacher, helped us. We had fun teaching and learning to paint together. She later became quite a Chinese painting artist.

One time when I took one of my oil paintings, my third painting—a scenery painting with trees, rocks, and a river—for a frame, a customer at the shop kept looking at my painting. "Would you sell the painting to me? I really like it."

"Thank you. I like it, too. I want to keep it for myself," I laughed and responded.

Wow! Someone wanted to buy my painting.

But my painting was not for sale, it was *priceless*!

Mrs. Thurman was like a mother to me. I respected her as a mentor and loved her as a motherly friend. She told many people, "I would have adopted Celine if she were not my colleague." I was very touched when people told me that.

When I had my first student teacher, a 6'4" football player, I shared with him my experiences. He had to look down while I looked up as we talked. It was very tiring since we talked about serious things every day. I decided that it was easier for both of us to sit down to talk.

Mrs. Thurman was so amused looking at us, a 5'1" little girl having a "giant" as a student teacher. She told other colleagues, with such delight, "Little Celine got this giant under her thumb!"

She knew how much I missed my family. She told me more than once, sincerely, "When your parents come to visit you, I would like to take them to our cabin in Yellowstone Park."

I was grateful, and I treasured her genuine caring love. "Thank you. I will definitely bring them to visit you."

Many years later, my parents came to visit us for the first time when we lived in Nebraska. I took my parents to meet Mrs. Thurman, my dear motherly friend in Idaho. We stayed in their cabin in Yellowstone Park, which her family had for many generations. My parents and I spent a joyful week together in the amazing and beautiful park, accompanied by the very best tour guide.

When I visited her again in 2000, she was in her 80s. She was almost totally blind due to diabetes. She was still so cheerful and laughed a lot—the hearty laugh that I remembered. What a lady!

We enjoyed our time together remembering the good old days. We even visited some of our old colleagues, including Mr. Koval, our oil painting teacher.

Mrs. Thurman, my dear motherly friend and mentor, passed away shortly after my visit. I was so glad that I went back to see her for the last time. I will always remember her cheerful laughs and her motherly love.

*****

Mrs. Webber, the mother of our neighbor Judy, was a friendly lady. She knitted a lot of beautiful things for her granddaughter. It amazed me how she could make such beautiful things with two needles and yarn.

I was fascinated by her work. "Would you teach me how to knit, Mrs. Webber?"

"Sure!" She was so delighted that I wanted to learn.

I bought some yarn for my first knitting project, a scarf for Don. Mrs. Webber showed me how to knit it. I finished it in a few days, and I wanted to make something else. I asked her, "Now what do I do?"

She showed me a beautiful knitted pillow. "You are so fast. Try to make this round multicolored pillow."

"It is beautiful. I want to make a few." I got the yarn right away and started my second project. In no time, I made four for us and a couple for my twin sister.

Mrs. Webber was so surprised by my speed and impressed with my work. I wanted to make something more challenging, like a sweater with fancy designs.

"Would you teach me to knit sweaters with fancy designs and stitches?"

"It is not easy. But I think you can do it."

She showed me some books, and I picked a pattern for my first sweater. She told me what kind of yarn and how much to get for a sweater.

I always felt that watching TV in the evening was wasting life. So I knitted as I watched TV. I could knit one sweater in five evenings. In a year, I knitted 30 some sweaters of fancy designs. Everyone in my family got one or two sweaters. I learned how to crochet at the same time also, and I made quite a few pieces of different things, just for fun.

What would be fun to learn next?

Sewing looked challenging and fun to me. I told Don one day, "I would like to learn how to sew."

"There are classes you can take if you want to learn."

Don looked up the information on classes for me. He bought me a Singer sewing machine. Like I've always said to myself and others, "Learning to do things is to bring convenience to yourself." I was ready to learn how to sew—a challenging and useful skill.

I challenged myself after learning the basics. I made lingerie and swimming suits for myself, and I made a sports coat, swimming trunks, and some slacks for Don. For many years, I made all my clothes that I wore to work.

It was fun learning new things and new skills. It was always such a joyful satisfaction once I learned what I wanted to learn.

*****

"I can't swim. Are there classes I can take at the college?" I asked Don one day.

"Yes. You can take Beginner Swimming in the summer."

I took my first swimming class in the summer of 1970, and I learned how to swim—in shallow water only.

I took a woodworking class with my students. I made a few bookcases. My grandchildren love the cute little wooden stool with a heart on either side that I made more than 40 years ago. The two wooden ottomans with padded cushions that I use every day are still in good shape after so many years.

While I was learning new things in Idaho, Don enjoyed his hunting and fishing. Don was so happy that he could go fishing in the clear water rivers and reservoirs in the nearby beautiful mountains. There were so many big trout. One summer we caught eighty of them, big ones. We had to rent a locker to freeze them.

Don, a serious fisherman, showed me how to fish. I am scared of worms, and he had to put them on the hook for me. I screamed with excitement whenever I got a fish. "A big one! Help!"

Don had to get the fish off the hook and put another worm on the hook for me. Sometimes the fish fought so hard that it frightened me, and he had to help me reel in the fish. My skillful fishing was: to throw the bait in water, to wait for the bite, and to scream for help whenever I caught a fish. Poor Don!

Don, a cautious and good hunter, often hunted deer and antelope with friends. He brought back seven ducks, the limit, each time he went hunting for ducks. I had to learn how to cook them.

I wanted to see what hunting was like. Don took me dove hunting once. When I saw doves flying not far from us, I got so excited. "Over there!" I tried to help, but I scared the birds away. Don didn't know what to do with me. He just shook his head. That was the only time I went hunting.

The three years we lived in Pocatello, Idaho—1969-1972—I became an American teacher; I was a cooperating teacher helping student teachers; I knitted sweaters, I crocheted baby blankets, and I sewed all kinds of clothes; I fished with some help and some screams; I scared the birds away while hunting; I learned how to swim in shallow water; I painted oil paintings; and I made cute little things with wood.

I lived a busy and productive life, just like a pioneer, in the Wild, Wild West.

Touchdown

In November 1996, after a lengthy final panel interview, I—one of the five finalists—was selected by the Nebraska State Department of Education to be the 1997 Nebraska Teacher of the Year.

Throughout the year of 1997, I, with great honor, participated in various national programs, representing Nebraska teachers.

*****

I, in a swimming suit and a jumbo life jacket, climbed up a three or four-story high tower beside a lake. When I finally reached the top, the lady fastened something on me and told me, "Sit!"

I looked behind me, and I didn't see any chair. "Sit? Where?"

She commanded, with no patience or expression. "Sit!"

I sat, and "Zip!" I was "flying" down backward into the lake. Everyone at the lake could hear my horrified scream.

Well, I had just done one of the things that an astronaut has to do—the zip line.

After I zipped into the water, I was supposed to undo the life jacket and swim to the bank. But the life jacket was too puffy and too big, and my short arm could not reach over to the other side of the life jacket to unbuckle myself. I couldn't even turn over after trying several times.

Here I was on my back like an overturned turtle in the lake. "Help! I can't turn over."

Then came the lifeguard to rescue the helpless "turtle"—the only one out of the 75 participants that needed help to get out of the lake.

It was July 1997. I was at the NASA International Space Camp in Huntsville, Alabama.

Cornhusker

The summer of 1997 was a busy summer. I was the president of Chinese Language Association for Secondary-Elementary Schools (CLASS). It is an international association for teachers of the Chinese language. In June, I coordinated a two-week summer workshop for more than 30 Chinese language teachers from different countries, at a culture and language college in Beijing.

I rushed back from China to report to NASA in Huntsville, Alabama, for the International Space Camp.

The International Space Camp was designed especially for us 75 teachers—50 State Teachers of the Year from the U.S. and the Teachers of the Year from 25 other countries. Each of us received a scholarship for this International Space Camp, and each of us represented either a U.S. state or a country.

"Go, Big Red!" I cheered loudly when I, a Cornhusker in the red jersey and helmet, was introduced as the Nebraska Teacher of the Year in the parade.

When I found out that each of us was to wear something to identify the state in the U. S. or the country we represented, I decided to be a Cornhusker to represent Nebraska. I went to the office at the Nebraska Cornhusker Football Stadium to see if they could help me.

"I am a teacher at Lincoln High School, and I am the Nebraska Teacher of the Year. I am going to represent Nebraska in a parade at the International Space Camp at NASA. Is it possible that I wear a Cornhusker jersey for the parade?"

They were delighted and congratulated me. "Sure! Let's see what we can do."

They enthusiastically provided me the whole outfit, including a helmet and a pair of cleats. "Let us know what else we can do to help you."

I tried them on at home. My number was 97. Gosh! How can anyone function wearing all this gear, let alone run, tackle, and fall? The helmet was heavy and tight, and it pinched my head. I needed to hold my head really straight to have good balance. The pants made me two sizes smaller—that was a plus. Well, here I was, a Cornhusker, ready for the grand parade at NASA.

The parade was colorful and fun. Just imagine the costumes and the energy that 75 Teachers of the Year brought to any place, especially to an exciting place like NASA. It was electrifying, and it was wonderful.

Astronaut

After the parade, we started to learn and to try whatever an astronaut has to do, in the water and in the air. The journey to space began!

The Moon Walk was easy and fun. We felt no weight. The spinning machine was a challenge. It spun so fast in different directions that many people got sick. Some people didn't even try it. I wanted to try everything. I get dizzy very easily, even on a Merry-Go-Round.

"Would you stop the machine as soon as I yell 'stop'?" I asked the attendant who was in charge of the machine.

He laughed. "Sure!"

Terrified, I lay on the circular machine and took a few deep breaths. It started! My body was going all directions. What a horrible feeling! After I was spun around for about forty-five seconds, or maybe less, I screamed, "Stop!" I didn't get sick, but I would never do it again.

Later we were divided into different teams for simulation missions in space, as astronauts do. Each group was assigned a mission. Each person was assigned a job. My job was to watch and to ensure the safety of the astronauts who were doing jobs outside of the space shuttle. I needed to bring them back as soon as I knew there was any possible danger for them. I had to stay alert with any situation that might endanger my people.

We were in our space suits and ready to go on our mission. Everyone was very serious, excited, and intense, and some were more so than others. We couldn't fail the mission.

The captain of our team was totally uptight about the mission. When I received a notice that my people were about to encounter danger out there, I alerted my people outside of the space shuttle right away through the communication system.

"Danger! There is a situation out there. Come back in now!"

The captain tried to have the communication system to himself for the whole mission, and he cut me off. I reminded him of my duty. "I received a danger notice. My people are in danger, and I need to bring them back in!" I brought them back safely.

Wow! Talk about being competitive, and talk about tension! Can you imagine being on a mission in space with 75 Teachers of the Year, from the U.S. and around the world?

Well, our mission was successful. It was quite an experience indeed.

I couldn't swim if my feet couldn't touch the bottom. I didn't know how to dive, and I couldn't tread water. I believed that I, *the chicken of the sea,* was the only one who was so glad and relieved that the diving into deep water activity was cancelled due to some kind of maintenance problem.

There was another activity in the water. We needed to escape from an airplane in the ocean as an astronaut must do.

The water was up to my neck in the airplane. I was petrified, and I asked one of the teammates before the activity. "Would you help me out of the airplane in the water if I have trouble getting out?"

He said, "Sure!"

With his assurance, I swam under water and got out of the airplane safely all by myself. It was sensational!

In the Sky

The director of our program was pleased. "Congratulations to all of you. You have passed all the activities in the water."

He continued. "The astronauts have to know how to fly an airplane also. That is what you are going to do next—fly an airplane."

"What?" "Really?" "Wow!" "When?" He received our different responses.

Some people clapped their hands and cheered. Enthusiasm and excitement filled the room. We couldn't wait for the once-in-a-lifetime experience—flying an airplane. I was scared of heights, but I was excited too.

It was a beautiful day, a blue sky with a few white clouds. I was standing on the runway of a small airport.

A handsome young man approached and asked me, with a friendly smile, "Are you ready to fly?"

"Yeah!"

We got into a two-seat small airplane, no bigger than a truck. I sat in the pilot seat. My instructor sat in the passenger seat. I fastened my seatbelt and waited for instructions. I was really frightened and didn't know what to expect.

The instructor sensed my fear. "It's easy. Just relax and follow the directions. Okay?"

"Okay." I did whatever he told me to do, without really knowing what was going on.

The airplane started moving forward slowly on the runway. I followed more instructions. Our airplane moved faster and faster! The noise was getting louder and louder! My anxiety level got higher and higher, as the airplane started "floating" in the air.

I grabbed the instructor's thumb as the airplane ascended. As we got higher and higher in the blue sky, I grabbed his left arm, instead of his thumb, tighter and tighter, with silly and fear-filled giggles.

When I looked at the beautiful sky, it was unbelievably extraordinary! When I looked down from the plane, my feet and legs felt a continuous tingling. It was a petrifying but brilliant sensation.

He laughed so hard at me, and I giggled, non-stop, my right arm holding his left arm tight against me. I bet he felt the pain on his arm and sensed my fear. "Are you scared?"

I was still giggling and holding his arm tightly. "Yes!"

We flew around and around in the gorgeous blue sky above Huntsville, arm in arm. He kept laughing, and I kept giggling. I didn't let go of his arm.

"Do you want to go down?"

"Yes!" I made the landing safely, and I was thrilled and proud.

Finally I let go of his sore arm. He told others, "I never laughed so hard in my life!" This handsome young instructor of mine was still laughing.

I laughed with him. "Sorry that I almost tore your arm off in the sky!"

Down in the water, and up in the sky, this Cornhusker Teacher of the Year advanced through all kinds of challenges and made a *Touchdown* at NASA in Huntsville, Alabama, in July 1997, with thrill, enjoyment, and great honor.

Go, Big Red!

Go, Cornhusker Teacher of the Year!

Celine at the International Space Camp

International Space Camp Parade

The Lost Immigrant

On Friday, April 18th, 1997, I was at the Northwest Visitors Gate of the White House. As I was waiting to go through the security check and looking at the blue sky and floating clouds, I went back in time to when I first visited Washington, D.C.—a long, long time ago…

Lost

In the summer of 1975, our parents came from Taiwan to attend the wedding of my younger brother Ken and Yolande in Boston. Ken and Yolande took off for their honeymoon after the wedding.

We three girls, my twin sister Irene, our younger sister Eileen, and I, decided to take our parents to visit New York and Washington, D.C.

Here we were, three sisters, and each one assumed the other two knew what to do and how to get to New York and D.C.

Eileen held a map in her hand and suggested we take a look at a map the night before the trip. "We need to take a look at the map."

I was surprised we needed a map to go to New York. "What? Don't you know how to get to New York? Isn't Boston very close to New York?"

"I never drove there by myself. Ken always did the driving. We need to look at the map."

I responded, "I don't know how to use the map."

Eileen was shocked. "You have traveled so much, and you don't know how to use maps!"

"No. Whenever we traveled, Don always drove his stick shift car. He knew how to get to places with maps."

Whenever we traveled, I was never involved with planning the routes, looking at the maps, or driving. I just sang, ate, drank, and

147

slept. Traveling was effortless for me. I had never driven on the highway. Don didn't come with me to the wedding, and Irene's husband couldn't come to the wedding either. Here we were, three inexperienced drivers, looking at the map for the trip.

"What about you, Irene?"

"I don't know how to get there," she responded—simple as that.

Eileen was the only one who might get us there. Not until then did I realize it took some planning and a map to travel by car. I had been so spoiled and had taken everything for granted.

We made it to New York without any trouble. We watched *Mary Poppins* at Radio City Music Hall, visited the Statue of Liberty, and enjoyed authentic Chinese food in Chinatown. We had a great time, and of course we got lost a few times driving in this big city.

It was time to move to our second destination—Washington, D.C. I drove on the highway for the first time. I screamed with fear when I saw so many cars on both sides while driving in the middle lane. "There are too many cars on both sides of me! It's scary! What do I do?" I bet I scared my parents. They didn't say a word while I was driving.

Eileen and Irene kept saying, "You are doing fine. Don't look at those cars."

What a frightening experience!

Mark Luong, a very good friend who lived in the D.C. area, invited us to stay with him. We found his house without any trouble.

He had been hit by a car, one of his legs was badly hurt, and he was on crutches. He apologized to us, "I am sorry I can't drive you around."

We assured him, "Don't worry about it. We will be okay."

Mark showed us on the map how to go to the White House, the Lincoln Memorial, and other places.

We took our parents to visit all the places as planned. We looked at the White House from outside, and we joined the crowd and visited the Lincoln Memorial and other places. Father, a General, had come on an official trip to the Pentagon before. It was the first time for the rest of us visiting D.C. It was great fun being together again—with my parents and two sisters—after so many years.

It was late, it was dark, and everyone was tired. We decided to go back. It was supposed to be a 40-minute drive back. After two hours, we still saw the Lincoln Memorial, from different directions. We stopped to ask a policeman for directions, and we ended up at an airport. The policeman didn't know his way around either. Other people pointed different ways, and we got to Baltimore and some other places. We just couldn't find our way back.

We three took turns driving, and we took turns getting lost. We were hungry, we were tired, we were frustrated, and we had no more energy or patience.

"Look at the map again!" Eileen demanded.

"I don't know where we are. Where do I look on the map?" I was useless sitting in the front seat with a map.

"Can you find it, Irene?" Eileen asked Irene impatiently.

"I will get sick if I read a map in the car." Irene was no help either.

"We will find it. Don't worry!" Father tried to calm us.

When we finally got back, it was midnight. Mark had been standing by the window, on his crutches, for three hours, waiting for us. There were no cell phones then, and we couldn't contact him for directions.

He was so worried. "I was going to call the police if you didn't get back in a half hour."

"We just couldn't leave the Lincoln Memorial. We really don't know how we got back, either." We tried to tell him our stressful and horrible experiences getting lost, even with a policeman's directions.

He kept apologizing. "I wish I could drive you and show you around. This wouldn't have happened."

To this day I still don't know how we made it back to his house.

It was quite an adventure for all of us, especially for my parents traveling with us—three "brave" drivers.

When Ken came back from their honeymoon and found out what we did, he scolded us seriously, "It was so dangerous. Don't you ever do this again, especially with *Ba Ba* and *Ma Ma*!"

We were too naïve to know how dangerous it could have been. How we wished he had been with us on the trip. "No way! I will never do it again," I assured him.

Both Irene and Eileen, after living in Los Angeles for many years, became great and brave drivers. I never forgot the experiences of getting lost in D.C. I still don't drive to any place by myself if I don't know the way. What a chicken!

We three felt so dumb and laughed so hard whenever we talked about our first trip to New York and D.C., with our parents in 1975.

The White House

Here I was in D.C. again—standing in front of the White House on a pleasant sunny day in the spring of 1997.

President Clinton was hosting the recognition ceremony to honor us, the 50 State Teachers of the Year. It was the big day we had been looking forward to—meeting President Clinton at the White House.

Each of us could invite one guest. My husband Don was my guest. Everyone was excited and thrilled. We went through the security check at the Northwest Visitors Gate to enter the White House.

Every one of us was going to have one-on-one time with President Clinton. We were so overjoyed, waiting eagerly outside of the room.

"Celine Robertson, Nebraska Teacher of the Year," someone called my name.

There stood President Clinton—with his left hand holding onto a crutch due to a knee surgery, Vice President Gore, and Secretary of Education Riley in the middle of the room, waiting for me. Can you imagine it?!

With a happy smile I walked into the room toward them, feeling like *Miss Nebraska*.

Each of us spent a few minutes meeting and talking with President Clinton individually. I didn't know what other people talked about. Everyone seemed cheerful and excited while talking to the President.

I decided to say something meaningful that would make a point. "I am an immigrant from Taiwan. I appreciate all the opportunities I have had in the United States."

President Clinton looked surprised to learn I was an immigrant from Taiwan. "Really?! Congratulations! Thank you for your contribution to the United States."

The White House photographer took my official photos, with President Clinton, Vice President Gore, and Secretary Riley.

After the President met and had pictures taken with all 50 State Teachers of the Year, the ceremony started. President Clinton gave a warm speech to welcome us. He shared many of his experiences with his teachers while growing up—with appreciation to his teachers, humor, and tears in his eyes, mentioning one special teacher in his life, his second and third grade teacher. He also commented on many issues in different areas, especially on education.

He remarked, *"... Among the Teachers of the Year here today, we have an immigrant from Taiwan making a great contribution to the United States..."*

It was a great honor to be the first teacher he recognized at the ceremony. President Clinton's good memory, sincerity, and of course his eloquence were most impressive. Vice President Gore also gave a wonderful eloquent speech afterward. Both of them were warm, sincere, handsome, and charming.

It was such a great fun and unique event meeting and talking with President Clinton. I will always remember and treasure this once-in-a-lifetime, extraordinary, unforgettable, and honorable experience at the White House.

*****

A month later, in May, my students asked me to join them to do some high jump activity. I had great fun doing it with them. I forgot I was not 18 anymore, and I forgot I was no longer 99 pounds. I kept jumping higher and higher, over the elastic rope. I fell. I broke my little toe on my left foot, and I was on crutches for six weeks.

When people saw me on crutches, they asked me, "What happened to you?"

I laughed and answered, "Don't you know '*being on crutches*' is contagious? I shook President Clinton's hand last month, and he was on a crutch."

Beyond Imagination

When we seven siblings were growing up in Taiwan, we never missed any Disney movies, especially the classic animated ones. My twin sister Irene and I often talked about all the pretty girls in different movies—Cinderella, Snow White, Sleeping Beauty, and of course hair styles, dresses, and handsome princes. I loved carefree Peter Pan and the adventure at sea on a pirate ship. Together we dreamed that we would be at Disneyland someday to see all the characters that were in the movies.

Life is full of dreams, surprises, and adventures. Some dreams come true in the most wondrous and surprising ways—beyond anyone's imagination...

Surprise

On June 3rd, 1998, during my sixth period Chinese class, Dr. Wortman, the principal of Lincoln High School, asked me to send all of my students to the multi-purpose room down the hall to help him with something.

A few minutes later, he came back. "Would you come to help me?"

"Sure!" I went with him to check things out.

When I walked in, the room was full of people—my students and colleagues, all wearing Mickey Mouse hats and yelling, "Surprise!"

Wow! I was truly surprised! The big multi-purpose room was beautifully and festively decorated with balloons, Mickey Mouse posters, and flowers.

A lady representative from the Walt Disney Company had come from Chicago to our school, to cheer me on for my final competition for the American Teacher Award on June 10th, 1998.

"We wish you the best of luck for the American Teacher Award," she said as she put on my head a cute Mickey Mouse hat, with my name, Celine, on it.

She also presented me an award made of glass with Mickey Mouse on it, and a beautiful Mickey Mouse watch. "Congratulations! Good luck with your final competition at Disneyland."

She then handed me a Mickey Mouse carry-on suitcase for my trip to Los Angeles, where the American Teacher Awards activities and competition would be held. "This is for your special trip to Disneyland."

What a pleasant surprise! I was honored. Four days later, on June 7, I wore the Mickey Mouse watch, carried my Mickey Mouse luggage, along with the heartwarming support, and boarded the airplane for Los Angeles.

Honorees

The Walt Disney Company presents the American Teacher Awards every year. Thirty-six teachers—honorees—from across the country are selected from a pool of tens of thousands by the Educational Advisory Committee, comprised of members from different American educational councils and associations.

Three honorees are selected for each of the twelve areas of instruction, ranging from social studies to physical education, from foreign language to performing arts. One of the three honorees of each category is chosen to receive the American Teacher Award—the highest honor for American teachers.

Fifty judges select the winner for each of the twelve categories. A teaching video of each honoree, filmed by the Disney production crew, is the first part of the two-part competition. The second part is a three-minute speech that each honoree presents during the pre-ceremony activities in front of 50 judges, 36 honorees, and their guests. There is no restricted topic for the speech. Honorees share whatever they wish to share. Whoever has the highest combined scores of the two parts is the award winner for his or her category.

The American Teacher Awards ceremony has the same format as the Oscar Academy Awards ceremony. A celebrity introduces the three honorees, with profiles for each one shown on the big screen, and then he/she opens an envelope to announce the award winner.

I was honored to be selected as one of the 36 honorees for the 8th Annual American Teacher Awards in 1998—competing in the category of Foreign Language/ESL (English as a Second Language).

My personal photographer and producer from the Walt Disney Company came to film me on April 3rd, 1998. The producer followed me throughout the school day and filmed my teaching and all the activities in my classrooms. He also interviewed my students and colleagues to collect additional information to make a profile of me.

The profile was reviewed by the 50 judges of the selection committee. A short clip was also made for the 8th Annual American Teacher Awards ceremony on June 10, 1998, and for the premier broadcast around the world on the Disney Channel ten days later.

Each of us also received the profiles of all of the 36 honorees before meeting one another in Los Angeles. What an impressive group of teachers!

When we met, we exchanged comments on one another's remarkable profiles. We humbly expressed sincere admiration to one another.

Could you imagine if a student has these teachers for all their subjects?

Speech

The critical and nerve-wracking second part of the competition—the three-minute speech—was scheduled after breakfast on June 8, the first day of the pre-ceremony activities at the luxurious Ritz Carlton Hotel in Pasadena, California, where we stayed.

How could anyone eat under such pressure and anxiety?! What a waste of the abundant breakfast!

This was the three-minute speech I presented to the honorees, guests, and 50 judges:

To teach is to touch a life forever is on a magnet from Lecia. She knows my philosophy and my passion for teaching. Eric writes, "When you walk in her class, you walk in her life," in the school paper to salute me as Nebraska Teacher of the Year. He feels my love. "My teacher, my friend!" is on a wooden bell from Ashley. She trusts me with all her heart. Dawn says, "I always do my very best," because I once told her, "Never settle for a B if you can get an A."

A perfect letter from Eric, a special needs student, shows he remembers the grammar and spelling I taught him 20 years ago. Yvonne donated money to honor me, because I never gave up on her son. Robert's grandma told me that my impact on him will be forever. Students follow me for four or five years, they grow up with me.

They asked me to play a high jump game with them, and I broke my foot. They don't see my wrinkles and weight; they see my forever young heart. They all performed like super stars with pride and excellence in the *Chinese Kaleidoscope,* a biennial Chinese cultural program, presented to 3,600 people to honor me.

Amy is in Nanjing, Ling is in Beijing. Howie was in Taiwan for two years as a missionary. Becky and Bart studied Chinese in Taiwan; Josh got a degree in Chinese; Jason works in Shanghai; and Justin majors in Asian Studies. Laura is going to Taiwan. Katie and Jeremy are going to Beijing. Jenny is going to be a teacher of Chinese. Many others have done exchange programs and traveled in Asia.

A call across the Pacific, five students that I taught for one year when I was 21 in Taiwan, donated $20,000 within a week. This partial but crucial funding made it possible for me to bring the Taiwan Youth Chinese Opera Troupe to tour the U.S. for 24 days again this year. Even in another land, they share my vision and honor my mission. Now, after so many years, they are still in my life and I am still in their hearts.

Yes, to teach is to touch a life forever. My relationship with my students goes beyond classrooms, time, and distance. Teaching is my life, and it is forever for me.

I wrote my speech, and I practiced in front of a mirror numerous times, with a timer. When I delivered my speech at the podium, I didn't mess up. It went perfectly—two minutes and forty-five seconds—as I planned and practiced. What a relief.

Later in the day when we were at Disneyland, a couple of judges specially approached me to tell me they really enjoyed and appreciated my speech. It was a much appreciated affirmation.

Disneyland

Competing with the nation's top teachers was an extraordinary once-in-a-lifetime challenge. It was truly a humbling experience.

After the nerve-wracking speech presentation, the fun started. Each of us, our families, and special guests received a green VIP bracelet. We were to spend the rest of the day at Disneyland. We could cut in line with our VIP bracelets—another incredible and fantastic privilege!

My two daughters yelled, "Hurray! We don't need to stand in line for any rides."

Mickey Mouse, Donald Duck, Minnie Mouse, Pluto, and Goofy were there to welcome us. What an unbelievable reception. We had so many pictures taken with each of them individually.

A childhood dream had come true not only for me, but also for my two daughters, Joline and Andrea—a day at Disneyland with Mickey, Donald, Minnie, and many more.

When we went back to the hotel after a long thrilling day, there was a beautifully wrapped gift on the bed. It was a collectable "Donald Duck," carrying books on his back.

It was indeed a memorable day for all of us!

Mulan

The Walt Disney Company provided our formal attire for the American Teacher Awards ceremony. Designers and their assistants helped us, honorees and our guests, select, fit, and alter our gowns or tuxes for the award ceremony. Ladies had more than 100 gowns to choose from, and they also provided jewelry to match our gowns.

Everyone was treated as a super star for the awards ceremony.

June 9th was another extremely brilliant day. The Walt Disney Company conducted a premier showing of *Mulan* for us, all our families and special guests, in the theater of the Walt Disney Company. Each of us was sitting in a huge, comfortable seat to enjoy the amazing animated movie. Another once-in-a-lifetime privilege!

Each of us received a sketch of a character in the movie drawn by the artists who created *Mulan*. Mine was a portrait of *Mulan*.

Before the showing at the reception, there were Lion Dance, Chinese food, music, and performances. There was also a fortune teller. Everything seemed to be arranged especially just for me this day. It was most entertaining and gratifying to enjoy the unique event, with my family and my twin sister Irene by my side.

Irene saw the fortune teller. "Let's ask the fortune teller if you are going to get the award." My two daughters, Joline and Andrea, seconded the idea and grabbed my hands. "Yeah, let's go and ask her."

Even though we enjoyed every moment during these couple of days, everyone was extremely apprehensive about what would happen at the award ceremony the next day.

The honorees kept the fortune teller busy.

When we returned to our room after another incredible day, there was another beautifully wrapped gift on the bed. It was a handcrafted leather photo album with my name on it—to collect and to treasure the memories of the three dream-like days.

Honor

June 10th, 1998, was the big day for all of us—a day I will always remember and cherish.

We all were formally dressed like super stars for the Oscar Academy Awards, anxiously and tensely waiting for the start of a most critical and sensational event in our lives.

The awards ceremony was held at the historic Dorothy Chandler Pavilion, where the Oscar Academy Awards ceremony was held numerous times.

Jeff Goldblum was the host of the ceremony. He was more handsome in person than in the movies. The celebrity presenters for the American Teachers Awards were: Hector Elizondo, Tia and Tamara Mowry, Tahj Mowry, Matthew Broderick, Dennis Franz, Scott Hamilton, Candice Bergen, Rob Estes, James Cromwell, Ryan MacKnight, Jenna Elfman, Kathy Kinney, Dave Koz, Kim Delaney, and Shelly Long.

Finally it was time for the Foreign Language Award. Dennis Franz came to the podium. He introduced each of us three honorees. After our profiles were shown on the big screen, he opened the envelope and announced the winner, "The Outstanding Foreign Language Teacher of the Year—Celine Robertson."

It was like being in a dream. It didn't seem real at all. I didn't scream for excitement. I was calm—numb. I just smiled and walked slowly (so I wouldn't trip on my gown) to the stage to receive my award and gave my acceptance speech:

> I would like to dedicate this great honor to my parents, General and Mrs. Nan Kwang Tan. I would like to thank my husband, two daughters, and all my siblings for their forever love and support.
>
> I also would like to thank Lincoln Public Schools for the opportunities. I'd like to express my sincere appreciation to Lincoln High School and Park Middle School staff

and students, especially to all my students for making my teaching and life exciting and fun.

Being a world language teacher, I would like to encourage everyone to learn a second language. Second language will bring you adventure and excitement, and it will bring you friendship and appreciation.

I would like to salute all teachers. Please take great pride being teachers. We, the teacher, make all professions possible. Thank you!

My presenter, Dennis Franz, was very sincere and friendly, and we chatted all the way to a room to have pictures taken together.

As my two daughters were growing up, I didn't allow them to watch TV after 7:00 PM during the week. In order to be a good model for them, I didn't watch TV either. I really didn't know who Dennis Franz was.

I asked my family, "Who is Dennis Franz? What is he famous for?"

Don watched quite a bit of TV. He told me, "He is the big star in the TV show, NYPD Blue. He is very famous."

After I found out who Dennis Franz was, I started watching NYPD Blue. I really enjoyed the show and became a big fan of his.

Beyond Imagination

A high school buddy, Mei Xin Lee, called me from Taiwan and told me excitedly, "We saw you on TV getting the Walt Disney American Teacher Award."

I knew the program was broadcast around the world on the Disney Channel. I never expected any of my friends in Taiwan would see it. "Did you really see me on TV?"

"Yes. I got so excited and I called some of the classmates right away."

Uncle Barry, an American fatherly friend living in Indiana, knew I was in the competition. He called me after the premier broadcast of the award program, "I watched the program with our family and many neighbors. We were so happy for you. I am so proud of you."

One day when I was shopping in the grocery store, a little girl came to me and said, "I know you. You are the Walt Disney Teacher of the Year."

I was curious. "Yeah? How do you know?"

"I saw you on the Disney Channel. The whole city of Lincoln got free Disney Channel that day because of you."

I was surprised to learn that. "Wow! That was nice. I didn't know that. Did you enjoy the program?"

"Yes. I loved it. Great teachers!"

That is the Walt Disney Company—thorough, considerate, thoughtful, creative, and influential. Disney again provided spectacular world-class presentations and heartwarming experiences to honor teachers and to share, to reach, and to touch people around the world, as always.

My American Teacher Award is displayed in our living room on top of a cabinet that I designed and had custom made in China. The award itself is a piece of art—with a child sitting on a book and holding the world that he is curious about. It is a bronze sculpture designed and made by an artist in Italy especially for the American Teacher Awards. It is truly a very unique piece of art.

My life has been blessed with dreams, honors, surprises, and adventures. An impossible dream, a highest honor for an American teacher, had come true in the most wondrous, astonishing, and blissful way—beyond anyone's imagination...

The fortune teller was right, she said I would win.

Joline, Celine, Ken (son-in-law), Andrea, & Don

Fun with Disney characters

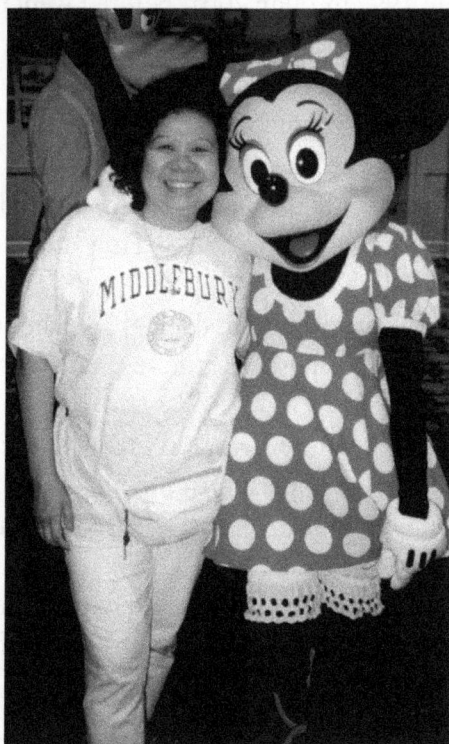

P. O. W. E. R.

A Dream

On January 16th, 1998, I stood at the podium in a big hall in front of several hundred government officials, business executives, and community leaders of the State of Nebraska. It was the Dr. Martin Luther King Freedom Breakfast—an annual celebration of Dr. King's birthday.

In 1992, I was one of the co-founders of the Nebraska Asian Community and Cultural Center. I was the president of the center in 1997 and 1998. I was actively involved as an executive board member for the Center from 1992 through 2001, before I went to China to teach.

A few months earlier, a committee member for the Dr. Martin Luther King Freedom Breakfast asked me, "Would you be one of the speakers for Dr. King's birthday celebration?"

"Sure! What would you like me to speak about?"

"Would you make the final remarks for the special event?"

I was curious. "Who will be there? How many people are you expecting?"

"There will be several hundred people. The Governor, other government officials, business executives, and community leaders will be there."

I gave much thought before I worked on my speech for this special event. What a wonderful opportunity for me, an Asian, to share my vision and mission with the Governor, other government officials, and community leaders in Nebraska.

Some people were in tears when I delivered my final remarks. Afterward some people approached me and asked for copies of my speech.

It was a great honor to be part of the 1998 Dr. King's Freedom

Breakfast—sharing his vision and honoring his mission. With the voice from my heart I delivered my speech. With my faith in people, I shared my experiences. With my hope for the world, I invited everyone to be by my side to make the world a more wonderful place for all.

The World

Being a teacher all my adult life, I truly believe that to achieve the harmony of a multicultural life, education is the key. The most effective way of learning is through personal experiences and friendship. Friendship is the basis of understanding and appreciation, and understanding and appreciation are the foundation of respect and caring.

With this belief in my heart and with vision and mission in my soul, I involved many non-Asian community leaders as active board members of the Nebraska Asian Community and Cultural Center. Together we provided the platform for numerous intercultural programs and learning opportunities for the community.

The sister city relationship between the City of Lincoln and the City of Taiping, Taiwan, was formally established in the City of Taiping in 1997. The Lincoln Sister City Delegation visited Taiping periodically, and the Taiping delegation came to visit Lincoln a couple of times. The friendship touched many hearts.

In order to help students recognize that the world is bigger than what they can see with their eyes, and to open their young hearts to friends afar, during 1995-1999 I initiated and established sister school relationships for four Lincoln public schools and schools in Taiwan. The positive impact on both American and Chinese students, from direct contacts and lasting friendship through the exchange programs, was evident over many years.

P. O. W. E. R.

I taught at Park Middle School, which has a diverse student body—Vietnamese, African American, and Hispanic, as well as white students. There were racial conflicts among them. I always felt a multicultural education was desperately needed to promote respect and harmony among students.

In August 1994, Tim Carroll, an intelligent and gifted young African American, became our new principal. He arranged individual interviews to meet each of the faculty before school started.

I was impressed with his creative way to start his new position at a new school. After my introduction I commented to Mr. Carroll, "What a smart way to get to know your staff!"

"Thank you. I would like to get to know each of you before school starts."

He continued, "I see you have been involved with various things at different levels. What would you like to see happen at Park?"

"I am glad you asked. I have had this vision for a few years now."

"What is it that you would like to see happen at Park?"

"Our school has a diverse student body. Students need to learn to respect the differences and get along with one another."

"Do you see there is a problem here?"

"Yes. We really need to have a multicultural conference for the whole school, students and staff, to promote respect and understanding toward cultures that are different from their own."

I could see he was excited about this. "It sounds like a great idea. Would you do it?"

Without any hesitation, I responded, "Sure!"

Immediately I started working on all the details for the first multicultural conference. I was excited to make one of my visions happen and to carry out one of my missions at Park Middle School, where I had been teaching since 1974 for twenty years.

With Tim's total support of the program, I shared the ownership of the conference with all my colleagues. They supported the project positively and were involved actively in the preparation process. It was smooth, pleasant, and fun—working together side by side to provide positive learning for our students. What a wonderful staff!

At the opening program of the conference, all staff, from principal to custodians, wore clothes from different cultures and countries. I borrowed the clothes from friends and community people. Staff walked into the auditorium to the stage in pairs, and one teacher held a globe. Together we presented the globe—the world and the multicultural conference—to our students.

Students were so excited to see their teachers in ethnic garb on stage. They clapped and cheered for their teachers as the staff walked in. After presenting the world to the students, there was a short program of performances. Following the opening program, each student attended three workshops they chose from a total of thirty workshops on different multicultural topics and interests.

Our first conference in the spring of 1995 was a great success— well received by all the students and staff. They had fun learning in 30 different areas from community experts. Mayor Johanns was invited to participate in the first-of-its-kind conference in the Lincoln Public Schools.

A positive and pleasant atmosphere filled the whole school. Everyone wore a big smile throughout the day. It was truly a happy and productive event. More than 800 students and staff participated in what became a yearly event for several years. Presenters from the community volunteered their time, energy, and expertise for the multicultural experiences and education at Park Middle School.

I named the Park Middle School multicultural conference Park P. O. W. E. R. for Park Positive Opportunity for Wisdom, Excellence, and Respect.

The assistant principal, Don Woodburn, said to me, "You made such a big project so easy and fun!"

The positive impact on students and staff was obvious. For a long time, whenever Tim Carroll saw me in the hallways, with both thumbs up he would say, "You are wonderful!"

Tim was a fun person with sense of humor. With giggles I always responded jokingly, "I know!"

Whenever I needed some funding or approval for special projects or initiating new ideas, I would tease him, "It's a great investment." He always laughed and agreed.

He told other people, "Celine comes to me for many things, but never for herself, always for her students and our school."

Mission

With Tim's full support, we established a very close sister school relationship with Chu Lin Middle School in Taiwan in 1995. Every year, we had homestay for 30 or more Chinese students and various exchange programs to promote understanding and friendship for students and staff.

In the summer of 1999, I took a delegation from the two schools where I taught, to visit Chu Lin Secondary School where high school and junior high are on the same campus. Principals Mike Wortman of Lincoln High School and Tim Carroll of Park Middle School were in the delegation. I was very happy a few of my forever supportive colleagues and great friends—Nancy Larsen, Lois Alward, Diane Reinsch, and Susan Hertzler were among the delegates.

The welcome reception for us was grand and impressive. The delegation was overwhelmed by the hospitality, warmth, and friendship of our Chinese hosts. It was not only an eye-opening, exciting event but also an educational and memorable experience for the delegation.

I share Dr. King's vision and honor his mission. I do my part and I do my best to make the world a more wonderful place for people around me. I have been blessed with full support from Tim Carroll and many others throughout the years.

It is my obligation to share my heritage; it is my duty to educate my students and friends; and it is my mission to provide people the P. O. W. E. R.—Positive Opportunity for Wisdom, Excellence, and Respect, whenever and wherever.

A Principal Friend

P. O. W. E. R. is dedicated to Mr. Tim Carroll—one of the best principals I had ever had, and a good friend. Tim Carroll died in a car accident on November 21, 2010. Tim was a true and caring educator. He always wanted the best for the students and for the school. Tim shared my visions and honored my missions. I greatly appreciated his total trust and support for the various programs and projects I initiated or was involved with throughout my six years under his leadership before I took early retirement from Lincoln Public Schools in 2000.

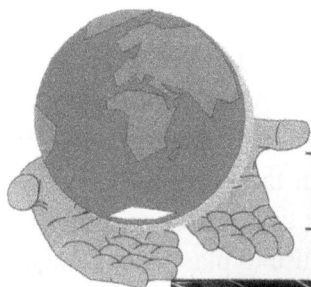

Park
POWER

Windows on China

Norman worked with me closely for many years. He and I were two of the co-founders of Nebraska Asian Community Center. The executive board members continuously planned and provided opportunities and platforms throughout the years for the community to learn, to communicate, to share, and to celebrate together.

During one board meeting at our house to plan for the Asian Night, a cultural program for the community, I had some ideas that would add some color and more excitement and meaning to the program.

He asked me, "Would you take care of it?"

"Sure!" I responded without hesitation.

Later he said to my two daughters—a big smile on his face, "When your mother finishes her sentence, the job is considered done."

My two daughters laughed and agreed, "Yeah! We know!"

Detour

In 1984, I was a special education teacher at Everett Junior High in Lincoln, Nebraska. David Van Horn, our principal, approached me one day. "We need a different social studies class. Would you be interested in teaching a class on China?"

"It sounds fun! Sure!" I responded with excitement.

I designed this one semester social studies class, Discovering China, for the following school year.

I introduced language, history, culture, traditions, and arts and crafts. The class was well received by the students, the administrators, and the school district. We were in the newspaper for this one-of-a-kind class in the state, and maybe in the country at that time. I was excited and happy to share my heritage with motivated students.

One day in the spring of 1985, Sue Smith, the foreign language consultant of the school district, came to see me. "I heard great things about your Discovering China class."

"It is fun teaching the class. I have great students."

"Are you interested in starting a Chinese language program for Lincoln Public Schools?"

"I have never taught Chinese language before. But it sounds fun. Okay!" I responded, again without hesitation.

"We can write the proposal together to apply to the Geraldine Dodge Foundation for a three-year grant for the program."

"Sure!"

I knew nothing about writing such a proposal. I learned a lot throughout the process working with Sue.

In the spring of 1986, the Geraldine Dodge Foundation selected and provided funds for ten more school districts in the U.S. to start Chinese language programs. Our school district, Lincoln Public Schools, was one of them.

I became a pioneer in the field of Chinese language teaching in secondary schools. With very limited resources and no suitable materials for secondary school students, I had to create materials and handwrite every character and every worksheet I needed to teach my students.

In 1987, I formally joined the other pioneers in the field of teaching the Chinese language to secondary school students in the U.S. During the year of planning, I visited schools in Minnesota, and I attended a workshop in Hawaii sponsored by the Geraldine Dodge Foundation. I met and made connections with other Chinese language teachers. We, the thirty-five Dodge Foundation teachers, established four-year Chinese language programs in secondary schools in different states.

What a vision the Geraldine Dodge Foundation had!

Lincoln Public Schools is truly a great school district, one with a vision. The proposal to start a Chinese language program was approved, encouraged, and greatly supported.

In the fall of 1988, after one year of planning, I established my first four-year Chinese language program at Everett Junior High and Irving

Junior High in Lincoln, Nebraska.

A new chapter of my life began, and a sensational journey was underway.

Network

The Geraldine Dodge Foundation provided opportunities for us teachers to learn, to share, to support, and to connect among ourselves. The Chinese Language Association for Secondary Schools (CLASS)—was formed and formally established in the summer of 1989 at Middlebury College while we were participating in another workshop.

After that, Chinese language programs grew like bamboo shoots. More schools in the U.S. and many other countries adopted Chinese as part of the world languages programs in both secondary and elementary schools. In 1994, CLASS became the Chinese Language Association of Secondary-Elementary Schools, and it expanded to be an international association for Chinese language teachers in many countries.

Being an executive board member for ten years—two terms as treasurer, president-elect, president, and Midwest coordinator, I was actively involved with the association.

We established a close network among the Chinese language teachers to share and to support one another. We set up many workshops throughout the years to provide teachers opportunities to learn and to share in the U.S., Taiwan, and China.

It was an honor to be part of it from the very beginning of the association for the development of the Chinese language programs for secondary and elementary schools in the U.S.

A Vision

Here we were backstage in the auditorium at Lincoln High School in the spring of 1994. We were presenting the second *Chinese Kaleidoscope* program, a 40-minute Chinese cultural program, to

3,600 students, staff, parents, and guests from the community.

"*Lao Shi* [Teacher], what are we going to do next time?" Students were excited and proud, and they wanted to do it again.

I was deeply touched by their enthusiasm. "Let's talk about it when this is over. Okay?"

"We are going to do it again, right?" They so enjoyed doing the program.

I assured them, "Sure! We will do it again."

Chinese Kaleidoscope was a program that I directed and produced every other year. It showcased the integrated cultural activities that my students learned in class. It included Lion Dance, Dragon Dance, martial arts demonstrations, folk dances, songs, and a fashion show of ancient clothes and so on. The very first one was presented at Lincoln High School in 1992, and the very last one was presented at Arrowhead High School, Hartland, Wisconsin, in 2012.

People asked me, "How could you get your students to do what they did on stage, especially those big boys?"

"They love it. They want to do it again." My students shared my passion and enthusiasm, and they shared what they learned in class with pride and pleasure.

People were impressed with the programs. "Wow! How did you ever get the idea to do such a program?"

"Well, I had a vision and some guts!" I said with a laugh.

In the fall of 1991, my first group of Chinese language students was in the fourth year of studying Chinese, and they were going to graduate in the following June. I wanted to provide them some unique experiences that no one had done with them before and no one would do with them in the future.

Learning the culture is a big part of learning a foreign language. I integrated Chinese cultural activities regularly to provide my students with hands-on experiences and in-depth understanding of the Chinese culture, which was so different from their own.

I wanted to prepare them to be global citizens. With language and experiences with Chinese culture, my students broadened their horizons and perspectives and expanded their vision.

Wouldn't it be a unique and awesome experience if my American students demonstrate Chinese cultural activities on stage, to share with other people?

I don't even read music, let alone have any training for performing. The only thing I knew was that it would be an experience for my students that they would always remember and treasure.

With this vivid vision in my heart, I singlehandedly choreographed, directed, and produced my first 40-minute *Chinese Kaleidoscope* program in the spring of 1992.

There was no funding. There were no costumes and no equipment. There was no audition. There was no assistant or assistance. There was no training or practice after school. I integrated all the learning and practice in class.

Every single person in the Chinese language program went on stage and performed to share Chinese culture, including myself. I performed the Tai Chi Sword. I was very anxious and nervous about the whole thing—the presentation and, of course, my own performance.

My students sensed my concern, and they encouraged me. "*Lao Shi*, don't worry about it. It will go well. You will do fine. If you make a mistake, no one will know. Just keep going."

I was deeply touched and I didn't feel alone any more—having my wonderful students by my side.

How I loved my students!

Wow! It went well, including my Tai Chi Sword, and it was well received by all our spectators, in three performances.

The costumes I made looked very good on my students. The two dragons my students made for the Dragon Dance worked. The presentation of Ancient Fashion that I borrowed from the Taipei Economic and Cultural Office in Kansas City, Missouri were very colorful and beautiful. It provided a brief introduction to Chinese history through ancient fashion. The props students made for the background looked professionally done. I didn't faint on stage performing the Tai Chi Sword. I didn't mess up either.

Students received compliments from their peers and teachers after the program and throughout the year. We were in the newspaper and on TV news. My students were so proud and encouraged. It was the first time for most of the students, as it was for me, to perform on stage in front of so many people. The impact on the students was immense and long-lasting.

I was so proud of my students, and I jumped up and down with them. "We did it! You are my Super Stars!"

My students, after so many years, still remember the program as their favorite experience of high school. They are proud that they had shared what they had learned in class with so many people. After that, the *Chinese Kaleidoscope* program became a tradition for Lincoln High School. In the following years, many schools called and wanted to reserve seats, a year in advance, for their schools.

Well, we had made another one of my visions soar!

Gratitude

I went to Taiwan many summers to learn martial arts, folk dances, arts and crafts to better prepare myself for my students, since I was their only learning channel, *the Window on China*, for Chinese language and culture.

My award money from different awards was spent on costumes and equipment we needed for the program. The $5,000 grant I received from the Nebraska Arts Council enabled me to provide opportunities for my students to learn folk dances, Chinese opera, and martial arts from experts from Taiwan.

I announced my early retirement from Lincoln Public Schools at my last *Chinese Kaleidoscope* in the spring of 2000, twelve years after I established the language program.

I didn't tell my students that I was going to retire in June until the day before the program. They were so sad. The next two days they did their very best on stage to honor me, with such pride and sincerity. They received a standing ovation for each of the three performances, from 3,600 people.

There was a budget cut in the school district. There was no fund for buses, and there were no field trips in the year 2000. But the school district provided me 10 buses, free of charge, to bring students from all over Lincoln to come to see my last *Chinese Kaleidoscope* at Lincoln High School.

I felt honored, and I was grateful that I taught at a school district where my effort was appreciated and my vision and mission were shared for 26 years.

Extended Experiences

"*Lao Shi*, I can understand what people are saying." Jason Christie told me with great excitement.

"Me too! People are so friendly," Jason's twin sister, Jennifer, echoed.

Josh Campbell joined in. "*Lao Shi*, it is so interesting and different here. They understand my Chinese. I am so glad that I came."

"Great! Talk to people whenever you can. You'd be surprised how much you can speak and how much you can understand," I responded with great delight.

We were in Beijing. We were on the Great Wall, and we were surrounded by Chinese people.

In order to provide Chinese experience in depth for my students, I took nine students to China in the summer of 1992. Students received some scholarships from a foundation in the school district. We sold pizzas, and we sold fortune cookies. We raised $2,000. I gave each of the nine students $200 for their trip.

It was my first trip back to China since I left the country when I was a toddler. I was curious and excited, as were my students.

My students were wonderful. They absorbed and enjoyed everything with respect, excitement, and appreciation. Not many American people were traveling in China at that time. Chinese people wanted to have pictures taken with them. My beautiful students became movie stars wherever we went. They were patient, friendly, and courteous. They represented Americans well. I was very proud of my fabulous ambassadors.

The trip had quite an influence on my students. Two years later, Jennifer and Jason—the twins—went back to Beijing for a one-semester exchange program in college. Josh is now an executive in an American company in Shanghai, with a bachelor's degree in Chinese language from the University of Chicago. Jason, an engineer with a MBA degree, has his own company, and he is also the managing director in charge of the factory in China for a company in Lincoln, Nebraska.

Enlarged World

I tried my best to provide experiences and opportunities for my students to expand their horizons, vision, and perspectives. I wanted them to know the world is bigger than what they could see. I prepared them to be global citizens with understanding and respect for other cultures.

With all these in my heart I established a four-year Chinese Language Program for Arrowhead High School in Hartland, Wisconsin, in 2009. We did two *Chinese Kaleidoscope* programs during the three years I taught there, to audiences of 800-1,200 people each time.

I coordinated and led a two-week China Experience Trip for 22 students and staff in the summer of 2011. Students talked about the trip throughout the year. Many of my students continue with Chinese in college.

It had quite an impact on the teachers also. Kathy Nelson, an English teacher and a good friend, went on the trip with us. She called me one day. "Celine, guess what class I am taking?"

"What class?" I wondered.

"I am taking Asian Literature. It's so interesting. I am reading a lot of great books. I love the class." She took such an interest in China and its culture after the trip. She started drinking tea every day. We exchanged different views on some of the books she was reading throughout the semester.

A dedicated teacher is constantly learning to develop new skills, to expand horizons, and to broaden knowledge in order to enrich students' learning and experience. Kathy Nelson is such teacher.

Windows on China

My students, after graduating from Arrowhead High School, still share my vision and honor my mission. They keep in close contact with me and help me to celebrate the Chinese New Year in different schools during their winter and summer breaks from college.

On January 10th, 2014 during their winter break from college, nine students came and helped celebrate the Chinese New Year of the Horse at Big Bend Elementary School where my grandson was a second grader. They performed the Dragon Dance. At the workshop they taught 60 second graders how to dance the Dragon Dance, to play the pull bells, and to kick shuttle cocks. After the workshop, they helped lead a 120-people parade.

The Kelly brothers were among the nine students. David had so much fun teaching pull bells while his brother Steve laughed and kicked the shuttle cocks with the second graders. David said, "It's really fun." Steve smiled and echoed, "I enjoy teaching the little kids."

Some of the parents and I have become good friends. Austin Kissinger brought his mother Nancy to help with the music and Ryan Anderson's mom Terry filmed for us.

Both Mrs. Nancy Kissinger and Mrs. Terry Anderson were most supportive during the three years when I taught their sons. They continued to be supportive of what I do. They had fun helping with the celebration. Terry said, "Just let me know whenever you need help." And Nancy echoed. "It is fun!"

The dragon is almost 50 feet long, and its head is pretty heavy. Evan helped second graders with the dragon head while Maddie showed them what to do with the dragon tail. She laughed the whole time while helping them. "They are so cute!"

Evan said, "The little kids really enjoyed learning the Dragon Dance. It took two of them to hold the dragon head."

Austin and Evan treasured the experience and posted all the pictures provided by the reporter of the Mukwonago Chief on Facebook.

Kyle played the Gu Zen, a 21-string instrument. He said to me after the program, "Let me know whenever you need me to perform Gu Zen."

"Thank you. You did a beautiful job. They had never seen Gu Zen before." I was so proud of him.

I has told Kyle be sure to learn a Chinese instrument while studying in China. He spent a year in China, and he learned to play my favorite Chinese instrument, Gu Zen.

This 21-string instrument plays beautiful and amazing music. You can hear the sound of running water if the song is about the river. If the music is about a battle, you feel all the energy and the urgency on a battlefield. It is truly an incredible, unique instrument.

Emily was leaving for an exchange program in Spain the following week. She took time and came to help. Emily said to me, "I want to see you before I go to Spain." She was giggling with the kids while teaching the pull bells the whole time.

Some of them also celebrated July 4th with 70 kindergarteners at a summer school, with Lion Dance and a parade in 2013. We also celebrated the Chinese New Year with more than one hundred little kids at the Bright Days Daycare every year since 2010.

Sophie Peterson taught her friends in college Lion Dance, and they performed for the 2014 Chinese New Year celebration program at her school in Chicago.

With great joy and pleasure I was the learning channel—the *Window on China*—for my Chinese language students for 23 years.

My students around the world have also become *Windows on China*—sharing what they had learned in class with families, friends, and community whenever they have the opportunity.

Orient Express

On June 14th, 1999, after a one-day orientation in San Francisco, I boarded the airplane for another adventure—to spend three weeks in Japan as a member of the 1999 Delegation of U.S. Educators. It was the beginning of my 1999 adventurous expedition in the Orient.

A panel of educators selected 200 American teachers from a national pool of more than 2,700 applicants to participate in the Fulbright Memorial Fund Teacher Program to promote greater intercultural understanding between the U.S. and Japan. The program was fully funded by the Government of Japan.

We began our adventure in Tokyo. After we received a practical orientation on Japanese life and culture we met with Japanese government officials and educators. We then traveled in groups of 20 to prefectures outside of Tokyo to have direct contact with Japanese teachers and students. We also had a homestay scheduled to spend a day and a night with a Japanese family besides visiting cultural sites and local industries.

Another privileged, extraordinary, and adventurous experience unfolded…

Japanese

Lincoln Public Schools in Lincoln, Nebraska, is truly an outstanding school district. It not only provides great programs for special needs students but also provides challenging programs for gifted students as well. A highly gifted student could choose a subject area to be taught by a one-on-one mentor at school or take a college class at the University of Nebraska.

Andrea had creative writing with a mentor from fourth grade

through sixth grade. When she started junior high school, she had a broader choice.

When it was time to plan and to select her junior high courses, I asked her, "What would you like to learn with a mentor?"

She responded, "I want to learn something that is not offered at school."

The world is so inter-connected, politically and financially, that foreign languages have become an essential and critical tool. I suggested, "You are very good with Chinese. Would you like to learn another language?"

"Yes. Joline told me the Spanish class at school was too slow and boring for her."

"What about a language that is not offered at school?"

"What about Japanese? I know Chinese, and I really like it. Are they alike? Daddy speaks Japanese."

"They are quite different. Japan is a very different country, with its own characteristics. Japan invaded China, and the Japanese murdered your great-grandfather. It might be a good choice to learn Japanese and to learn more about Japan—to know China's old enemy."

After talking to Don, Andrea decided to take one-on-one Japanese lessons from a mentor in junior high. "Japanese sounds interesting. I'd like to learn that with a mentor."

Japan

Japan and China have had ongoing ties, wars, and complicated relationships throughout history. My maternal grandfather, Min Gang Ling, a well-respected patriot, was murdered by the Japanese when he refused to be their puppet governor for the Province of Hunan during World War II.

Japan invaded China and caused much chaos, uncountable tragedies, and incalculable bloodshed across China for many years. The Japanese killed my grandfather before I was born. Knowing my mother's deep love for her father, I couldn't even imagine how she and her family suffered the unbearable pain, misery, and grief that the

Japanese caused my family and the Chinese people.

For as long as I could remember, I had no desire to do anything with Japan or even to visit there. I had complicated feelings toward that country.

What kind of country is that? I decided to see this country myself.

In November 1998, I told my family, "I decided to apply for the Fulbright Memorial Fund Teacher Program." On December 1st, 1998, I submitted my 10-page application with recommendations.

Since Andrea was learning Japanese and was thinking of participating in the study abroad program in Japan during her junior year in 1999, she was excited. "I hope you will get it."

"Me too. It is very competitive. If I am selected, I will spend three weeks in Japan this summer."

In order to better learn the language and understand the Japanese culture during her junior year in college, Andrea decided to attend Sophia University—a study abroad program in Japan. She also worked as an intern at the Standard & Poor's office in Tokyo, from June 1999 through July 2000.

On April 23rd, 1999, I received a letter from the Institute of International Education. I was selected as a member of the 1999 Delegation of U.S. Educators to Japan—an honored guest of the Government of Japan.

I was excited to be selected. "I got it! Andrea, I will meet you in Tokyo." Andrea and I jumped up and down together. She left for Japan two weeks before I did.

Andrea called and asked, "Do you have any free days?"

"Yes, I am free on the first weekend in Tokyo."

"Wonderful! Do you want to visit Kyoto and Nara, beautiful cities not far from Tokyo?"

"Sure! How do we get there?"

"We can take the bullet train. It is very fast."

"Great! Would you make the arrangements for our trip?"

"Sure! I will get everything ready. I can't wait to see you, Mom."

On June 18th, Andrea met me at the Hotel New Otani Tokyo—one of the most luxurious hotels in Tokyo, where we stayed. The next morning, I followed my personal guide, Andrea, to the train station to start our two-day adventure in Kyoto and Nara.

In Kyoto we visited the Imperial Palace, where the emperors lived before the Meiji Restoration in 1867, and the Nijo-jo where Tokugawa Shoguns lived in Kyoto. The floor is known as a "nightingale" floor—it squeaks and chirps like nightingales whenever anyone steps on it, so no assassin could sneak into the place.

Andrea commented, "What a smart alarm system!"

The Golden Pavilion, with its reflection in the pond and the beautiful landscaping around it, was most elegant and gorgeous. It was peaceful and serene.

"It's beautiful, just like the postcards," I remarked.

Andrea appreciated its beauty also. "Yes. It's gorgeous. I am glad we came."

There are so many temples, just like in China. There are 1,001 statues of the Goddess Kannon (Kwan Yin) in the Sanjusangen-do Temple. Kwan Yin is the Goddess of Mercy for Buddhism.

"Why are these Kwan Yin different from the ones in China?" Andrea wondered.

I shared my understanding. "I guess that every country has its own version that looks familiar to their people so that they can relate to the Goddess."

"It makes sense."

"I have seen the statues of Kwan Yin for Indian people. They look different as well. Even Buddha looks different in different countries."

There were Geishas walking around at the Gion District. I was excited and surprised to see real Geishas. "They look just like in the movies."

"Yeah. They have the same make-up, same hair-do, and same traditional clothes."

We went in the shop nearby and bought a gorgeous kimono for Andrea—a green and red one with beautiful designs that a bride wears for her wedding ceremony.

Nara was an ancient capital of Japan. In Nara, there is a park called the Nara-koen where there are more than 1,000 deer running around.

We had never seen so many deer before. They were gentle, beautiful, and friendly—not scared of people at all.

Andrea got excited. "Look there! The babies!"

I was thrilled to see all the deer. What an amazing scene. We were so happy, like two little kids running toward the fawns.

Andrea exclaimed, "What a unique experience being among so many deer!"

A long time ago, on a flight I was sitting next to a Japanese man. He was reading a book in Japanese, with a lot of Chinese characters in it. We got to talk some. I was curious, "When do you use Chinese characters?"

He told me something interesting. "The higher education a person has, the more Chinese characters are used."

I looked at his book, and half of the page was in Chinese characters.

With Andrea's Japanese, we had no trouble traveling around. Although I can't speak or understand Japanese, I could read the language—since Chinese characters are part of Japanese written language. It was quite interesting.

At one of the temples, people could ask for their fortunes. Their fortune notes were written totally in Chinese characters, just like the ones you get in a Chinese temple in Taiwan or China. Since I could read Chinese and speak English, many Westerners asked me, "What does mine say?"

One American girl got a bad one for her love affair. She started crying, "What do I do?"

I comforted her and told her, "Tie the bad one on the tree. It will be blown away. You can try to get another one. Be sure to pray first." The young girl was smiling again afterward.

I often asked Andrea to say them in Japanese whenever I saw any street signs or store signs that looked interesting to compare them with Chinese. I was learning about this country every chance I got.

Andrea was my dictionary. "How do you say that in Japanese? Do they mean the same in Chinese?"

I constantly compared the two countries, China and Japan—languages, cultures, and people. Although they are different in many ways, Japan didn't seem a totally strange place to me after all.

During the two-day adventure in Kyoto and Nara, our lives were enriched—filled with pleasure, excitement, new knowledge, and colorful memories.

Imari, Saga, Japan

On June 21st, our 10-day expedition in Imari, Saga, Japan, started. Our group of 20 flew to Imari—a city in Southwest Japan. It is a city known for its fine porcelain. It was especially interesting to me, since both China and Japan produce fine china.

We visited a porcelain factory, and I learned how to paint flowers on my little dish before firing it. I had never done anything like this before. I couldn't wait to do one.

After I stenciled my design on my dish, I asked the artist, "Could you show me how to paint my dish?"

He pointed at the ink and gave me a small brush. "Paint with the ink and the brush. You need to go over the design many times to make the color darker."

The paint looked black. "Will the design be in black color?"

The artist smiled and shook his head. "No. It looks black now, but it will turn blue after firing. It is a very pretty blue."

Everyone concentrated and worked hard on the designs on their dishes. Our dishes were delivered to us at our hotel after they were fired. My little dish turned out very nicely—beautiful flowers in different shades of blue.

We visited different schools in different parts of the city. In the morning, we saw students learning the primary colors in an art class and doing the calligraphy writing of Chinese characters in a language class at one school.

Since I knew how to do the calligraphy, I joined the students and wrote a few characters with the calligraphy brush. The students were surprised and impressed with my fancy character, especially the character of *long* 龍 [dragon].

In the afternoon at a different school in another part of the city, students were doing exactly the same thing in the art class and writing the same calligraphy characters. I didn't think this would ever happen in American schools.

I asked some of the teachers in our group, "Do you think this will ever happen in the U.S.?"

They all shook their heads, "No way!"

Schools were well equipped. Classes were big, with thirty or forty students. We visited music classes and physical education classes. English was a required subject for junior high and high school students—as it is in most Asian countries.

The host teacher who was showing us around told us, "Girls also learn how to serve tea the traditional way for the tea ceremony."

We were curious. "Are we going to see that?"

She answered with great pride and a smile on her face, "Yes, you are invited to one later."

The girls served the tea gracefully. The tea cup was small, and the tea was quite strong, stronger than what I was used to. The tradition of the preparation and serving of the tea was very elegant and formal. It takes training and practice to know how to serve the tea properly. Chinese people brew the tea and serve tea differently. The Chinese enjoy the fragrance and taste of the tea and the company while drinking tea, but the Chinese are not as formal as the Japanese.

People without Borders

Homestay was another highlight of the program. I spent a day and a night at the home of a high school English teacher, Akira.

I visited Akira's school. Since I loved Chinese martial arts, I asked him, "Do you have a martial arts club or class in your school?"

"Yeah. We have a sword fighting group for students to learn after school."

"May I try it to see if it is the same as Chinese sword fighting?"

"Sure. I can arrange it."

I bet he was surprised that I wanted to try sword fighting. "I love Chinese martial arts, and I teach my students martial arts sometimes,"

I explained.

I joined him and two of his friends to learn Japanese sword fighting. As he provided me the uniform and a sword made of bamboo, he said to me, "We will show you the basic techniques of sword fighting."

I had fun learning and fighting with my bamboo sword. It was quite different from Chinese sword fighting.

At Akira's home, there were three generations living in the same household—Akira, his wife, and their three children, and Akira's parents, just like some families in China.

Tsuya, Akira's mother, was 71 years old. She was a very nice and gentle lady. Apparently she was in charge of the domestic household. She didn't speak English, and Akira translated for us.

"What would you like to have for dinner?" she asked me, with her daughter-in-law Tomoko by her side.

"I am a vegetarian. Would you teach me how to make vegetarian Sushi?"

They were very happy that I liked Sushi, and they smiled and nodded their heads.

I offered, "If you have extra rice and some vegetables, I will show you how to fix fried rice."

Tomoko, Akira's wife, and Tsuya nodded their heads again, and they wanted to learn how to make fried rice.

They went to their vegetable garden right away to pick vegetables I could use for my fried rice. Three of us ladies in the kitchen, with hand gestures, head-nodding, and guesses, made a delicious meal together—Japanese Sushi, Chinese fried rice, and a few other tasty dishes.

With Akira's translation, Chinese characters, and both of their children's phrases in English, Akira's family and I enjoyed a delightful dinner together.

Their house was a traditional Japanese house with a big yard, no beds. Everyone slept on the floor. My room was the room where the family shrine was, a special room for guests. My sweet hostess, Tomoko, made the bed on the floor for me right before bedtime. She put the bedding away as soon as I got up in the morning.

The one-day homestay experience with this lovely Japanese family was one of my most remarkable and enjoyable days in Japan.

How precious, harmonious, and pleasant to be people without borders!

Complicated Feelings

A few days later, we had another unique cultural experience—staying in one of the most luxurious traditional Japanese hotels. Four people shared a room without beds. One of the roommates opened the curtain for the sliding door and yelled, "Look! How gorgeous it is outside!"

The garden was lovely, with Japanese landscaping. There was a little running stream, a few feet wide, just outside of the sliding door of the room. Sunlight shone on the clear water and sparkling water flowed over the beautiful pebbles in the stream. The sound of the running water was soothing and tranquil, like a stream in the high mountains.

We all adored the beauty and the serenity, and we truly cherished the unique experience. I loved it. "What a peaceful and beautiful place to spend the day!"

When we turned around, we found tea on the table. At bed time, the attendants took the table away and made four beds for us. In the morning, beds disappeared without any commotion, and our shoes were ready for us when we were ready to leave. All of the attendants wore kimonos. The service was unbelievably efficient and amazingly quiet. In the evening we had a traditional Japanese feast—sitting on the floor and eating authentic Japanese seafood and many other dishes at a low table in a big room.

It was truly a privilege being an honored guest of the Government of Japan. During the three weeks in Japan, we not only enjoyed world-class luxury but also had the most unique and unforgettable experience that we will always treasure.

The 1999 Fulbright Memorial Fund Teacher Program provided us opportunities to better understand Japan and its people. The mission of the Government of Japan—to promote intercultural understanding—was well accomplished. Since then, I have been able to compare the U.S., China, and Japan more accurately. I have shared my delightful adventures and fond memories with many people.

Like my forgiving mother, I never hated Japan. Like my kind parents, I didn't really hold what Japan had done to China and the Chinese people against the Japanese people I met throughout the years. I even had a couple of Japanese friends. People such as my friends and my host family in Japan were not responsible for what had happened in the past.

I could really share and appreciate deeply our parents' compassion and forgiving nature that enabled them to bring only peace and love to our lives, never hatred.

With different complicated feelings, I left Japan—the first expedition of my 1999 adventures in the Orient…

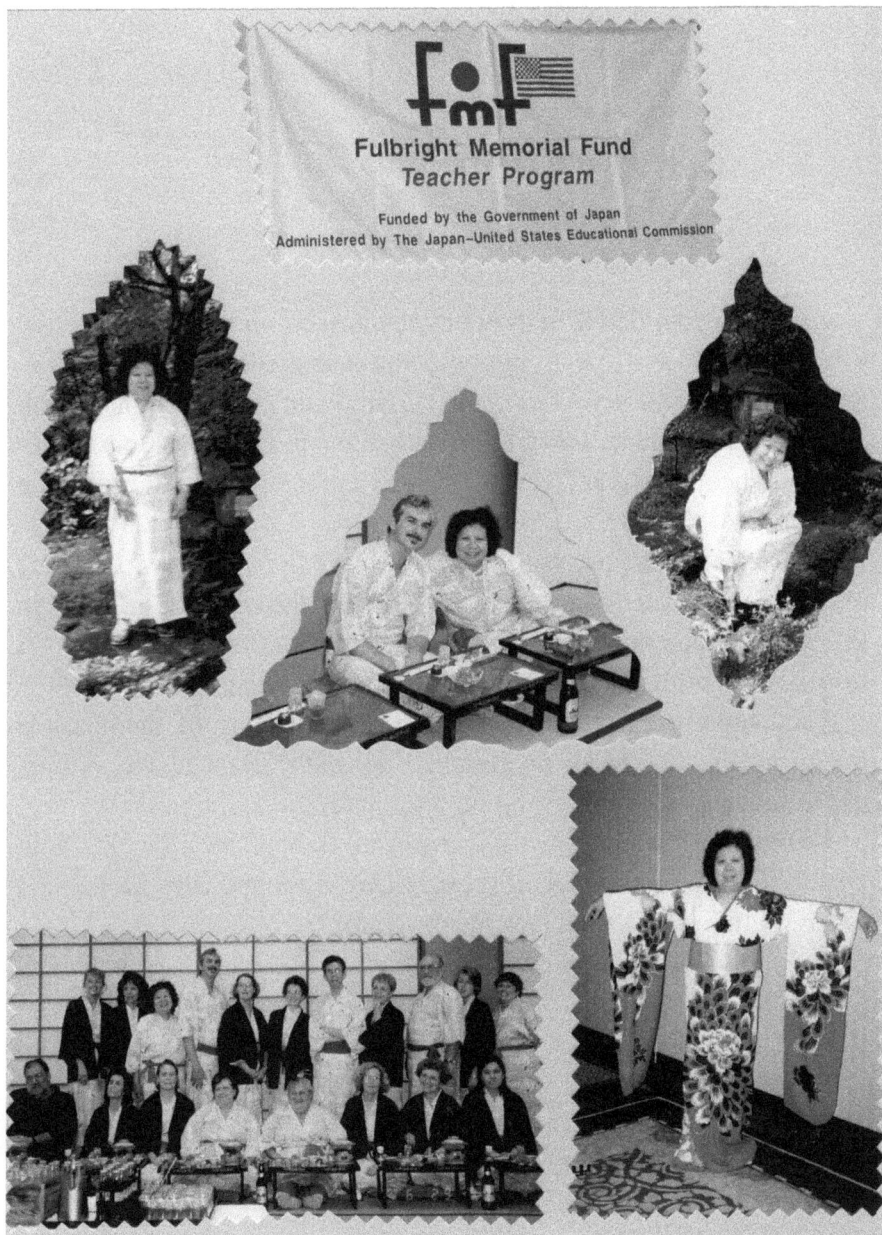

Friends without Borders

Wall of Honor

On April 3rd, 1998, a production crew from the Walt Disney Company followed me throughout the school day and filmed my teaching and all the activities in my classroom at Lincoln High School.

While the producer was filming to make a profile of me, a reporter of the Lincoln Journal Star was there taking my pictures for the newspaper.

At the same time, two representatives from the selection committee of the Scottish Rite Award—the most distinguished award in Lincoln Public Schools, a district of 48 schools—came to Lincoln High School to notify the principal and the recipient of the award.

They noticed the reporter's car was there. One of them asked the principal, Dr. Mike Wortman, "We haven't made the official announcement yet. Why is the reporter here?"

Mike smiled and said, "The reporter is here because the Walt Disney Company production crew is here filming Celine Robertson for the American Teacher Awards program."

They laughed and one of them said, "She is the one we came here to see."

I got a note from Mike, "Please come to my office after your class and filming are done."

After school, when Disney's filming and the reporter's interview were completed, I went to see Mike. Two strangers were sitting in his office. They smiled at me as I walked in.

After introductions, one of them said to me, "It looks like we have picked the right person. You have been selected as the 1998 Scottish Rite Distinguished Educator of the Year."

"Wow! Really?!" I was overwhelmed.

"Yes. Congratulations!"

"Thank you!"

"We will select a day to present the award to you."

I appreciated their coming to school to tell me the good news.

I couldn't believe I won this great award. Whenever I went to the administration building, I admired the wall in the main lobby full of pictures of the distinguished educators.

I was the 34th recipient of this prestigious award. On November 16th, 1998, I hung my picture on the Wall of Honor in the lobby— Lincoln Public Schools Hall of Fame.

Exchange Programs

Chu Lin Secondary School in Taipei, Taiwan has a junior high school and a high school on the same campus. I helped establish the sister school relationship between Chu Lin and Park Middle School and Lincoln High School in 1995.

Each year during spring break in early April, 60 to 70 students from Chu Lin came to visit Park Middle School and Lincoln High School. Students stayed with host students, and staff stayed with host teachers.

In 1998, the Chu Lin delegation was to arrive in the evening on Sunday, April 5th. Host students and families were excited about their 5-day visit. Students asked, "When do we meet at the airport?"

"Get there half an hour before they arrive. We will go over the schedules for the next five days once more with all the host families."

Jeremy Jewel's family always hosted four students each year. He was extremely excited. "I will take the welcome banner."

Since we received guests from the sister city and sister schools often, we had a welcome banner—in both Chinese and English, made to welcome our guests at the airport. "Great! You will be in charge of the banner."

At the airport, many families were waiting excitedly for their guests. Some of them had flowers, and some of them held balloons. It always touched my heart when I saw the excitement on their faces, welcoming friends from afar. The impact of this experience has a lasting effect on the families.

Lincoln High School principal, Mike, decided it would be great to have the Scottish Rite Award presented to me while the sister school delegation was visiting our school on Tuesday. "How about having a whole school assembly in the gym to welcome Chu Lin students and staff and to present the award to you?"

"Great idea! Our students and staff will meet the guests, and Chinese guests can see what an assembly in an American school is like also."

On Tuesday, there were 2,500 Lincoln High School students and staff at the assembly. A lion dance, performed by my students, started the program to welcome our guests from Taiwan.

At the assembly, I received the Scottish Rite Distinguished Educator of the Year Award officially in front of the whole student body, colleagues, and our friends from Taiwan at Lincoln High School.

Park Middle School and Lincoln High School provided great experiences and activities for Chu Lin students during their annual visit. Both Chinese and American students enjoyed the exchange programs.

Right after seeing the Chinese students off at the airport each year, my students often asked me, "Will they come back again next year?" They missed their friends already.

"Sure!" I smiled.

"Great! We want to host them again next year!"

I wanted my students to develop a global vision. Not everyone can visit other countries. I shortened the distance and made it possible for students and staff to embrace friendship through school exchange programs. Some of my students and staff maintained long lasting friendships with the Chinese friends they hosted.

At the Pyrtle Elementary School welcome assembly for their guests, Chinese students learned how to dance the polka, and kids at Pyrtle learned how to do the fan dance. Students from both countries giggled, sang, and danced together.

May Morley Elementary School students and staff also had delightful experiences with their visitors from their sister school in Taiwan.

The delegation from May Morley also brought back unforgettable memories visiting their sister school and Chinese friends in Taiwan.

This was what I had envisioned when I initiated and helped these four schools establish sister school relationships with schools in Taiwan. The new bonds between children will continue to reach across the globe.

It is indeed a small world after all.

**Welcome friends from Chu Lin Sister School
at the Lincoln Airport**

Sister School Delegation

The summer of 1999 was a busy summer. On July 3rd, 1999, I bid farewell to friends who traveled and learned together during the three weeks in Japan—the Fulbright Memorial Fund Teacher Program. Andrea, our younger daughter, who worked as an intern at the Standard and Poor's office in Tokyo, met with me for our next expedition in the Orient.

A delegation of 16 administrators and teachers from Park Middle School and Lincoln High School, including principals from both schools, met me in Taipei, Taiwan, on July 4th for an adventure they would never forget. For a week we were to be the honored guests of our sister school Chu Lin Secondary School in Taipei.

With my connections in Hong Kong, some of them took advantage of the trip and went to Hong Kong before we met, and some of them went to Hong Kong and China afterward.

Mike, his wife, and Pam Carmichael, the assistant principal of Lincoln High School, went to Hong Kong first and had a grand time there. "Thank you for all the arrangements. Everything went as smoothly as you planned. It was so colorful and fun there."

I was happy everything went well for them. "I am glad you had fun there. Now you can compare Hong Kong with Taiwan after next week."

My best teacher friends at Park, Nancy Larsen, Lois Award, and Diane Reinsch were so excited to hear about their adventure in Hong Kong. They and Tim were to go there after their visit in Taiwan. "What was most fun there?"

Mike told them, "Everything. It is so different, and there is so much to see."

I was so excited the delegation—my friends and colleagues—were going to see Taiwan, where I grew up. "Wait until our program starts here in Taipei."

Eye-Opening

The next seven days in Taiwan were especially memorable—a once-in-a-lifetime remarkable experience for all my American colleagues and friends.

On July 5th, our adventure began. More than 2,000 students in uniforms lined up on both sides of the walkway—from the main gate, up the hill to campus, and all the way to the auditorium, approximately 800 feet, where the welcome ceremony would take place.

The mayor of Chong He, with Chu Lin administrators, welcomed us at the bottom of the hill. There were bouquets of flowers for each of us. Everyone was clapping as we entered the school gate, and the applause continued as we walked all the way to the auditorium.

The delegation was overwhelmed with the warm welcome from the sister school.

Everyone was impressed and moved by such a grand reception—they had never experienced such an enthusiastic welcome in their lives. Everyone smiled and waved to the students on both sides of the path.

Tim Carroll, the principal of Park Middle School, said to me, "Wow! I knew it would be big, but I never expected it to be this grand. It is amazing!"

I knew what it would be like, but it was an eye-opening experience for my American friends. "It is the Chinese hospitality for their special guests. You can't imagine unless you experience it."

"Now we understand what you were trying to prepare us for before the trip," Nancy commented.

"Yeah. I am so glad I came with you," Lois added.

My colleagues absorbed the new and exciting experiences Chu Lin provided for us.

At the ceremony, we received not only heartwarming welcomes, but also many great gifts. There was a reception with tea and lots of good food afterward. We watched a video presentation introducing the history and structure of Chu Lin. We visited classes, and we met with teachers and students. We saw the students' art work and different projects displayed around the school. We toured the campus, which is very different from our schools in America—with many buildings, a big outdoor stadium, and a huge closed campus with security guards at the main gate.

Mike was impressed. "The school is so well planned and organized. Students are courteous and well behaved."

Tim said, "Uniforms are a good idea."

I laughed. "It's really not a bad idea for students. But I hated it when I was a student."

In the afternoon, we visited the Palace Museum, where the ancient Chinese treasures are stored and displayed, and the Chiang Kai-shek Memorial. We watched a special performance of Chinese opera when we visited the National Fu Hsing Dramatic Arts School, where I learned Chinese opera and martial arts during many summers. I had arranged for the Fu Hsing Youth Chinese Opera Troupe for a three-week tour in the U.S. many times. They had performed at Lincoln High School and Park Middle School.

The next four days, Chu Lin arranged a tour across Taiwan for us. Our sister school paid for our 7-day visit in Taiwan. What a treat!

We enjoyed the great company of the Chu Lin staff who accompanied us on the trip; we traveled from north to south on the island; we ate all kinds of delicious authentic Chinese food; we visited many popular points of interest across Taiwan; we were in high mountains; we looked at the beautiful ocean from the Su Hua Highway on the east coast; and we picked colorful smooth pebbles on the beach of Qi Xing Lake.

Nobody wanted the trip to end. Lois said, "It's so beautiful and fun. I don't want to leave."

"Yeah. I want to stay longer too," Nancy agreed.

"It is amazing! What a vacation!" said another dear friend Diane Reinch.

Nancy was a devoted special education teacher, a close friend. We had so much fun together. I called her "Crazy Lady," and she called me "the Craziest." Lois was an outstanding special education teacher. The three of us worked closely together for many years when I was a special education teacher. We became very good friends—with a long and lasting friendship.

Diane worked with students at risk. She was a great friend and a forever supporter of my activities or projects.

What a joy to watch my friends enjoy a different culture and experience Taiwan—the place where I was raised!

I smiled. "Now you know where I grew up."

Nancy teased me again, "No wonder you are so crazy!"

"You are the craziest!" We all laughed together.

With deep appreciation, my colleagues took the friendship, hospitality, and beautiful experience home with them. They will always remember and treasure the opportunity, hospitality, experiences, and fun they had with their Chu Lin friends in Taiwan. They talked about the trip for a long time, and they shared their experiences with many people. They couldn't wait to see their Chinese friends visit our schools again.

Every one of the delegation told other colleagues they should go with me on my next trip.

My colleagues thanked me numerous times. Tim said, "Thank you for the memorable experience. You picked a great sister school for us."

Mike commented, "You've really shortened the distance between the two schools. Thank you!"

I smiled. "It's my pleasure! I am so glad that you went. You guys were great!"

How beautiful it is to be friends without borders!

Taiwan was the second destination of my 1999 adventures in the Orient...

Chu Lin Sister School
Taipei, Taiwan

200

Friends from Afar

Life is indeed full of dreams, surprises, opportunities, and sometimes unexpected journeys.

The year 1999 was a year of adventures. It was a year in the sky—flying over the Pacific, soaring over the Atlantic, and traveling across the Land of Liberty.

Honor

In the fall of 1998, I received a letter from the American Councils for International Education to invite me to apply for the 1999 United States-Newly Independent States (former Soviet Union) Excellence in Teaching Award. Apparently they invited only the American teachers who had received high honors to apply for this international award.

This program was funded by the United States Information Agency. It was designed to foster contacts between teachers and schools in the United States and the five NIS (Newly Independent States of the former Soviet Union) countries—Kazakhstan, Kyrgyzstan, Russia, Ukraine, and Uzbekistan.

I chose Kazakhstan as my first choice. Kazakhstan is located northwest of Xinjiang Province in China. Xinjiang was a place I had always wanted to visit ever since I was a little girl in Taiwan where I learned to sing the romantic love songs that originated there.

In April 1999, I received a letter from the Office of Faculty Exchange of the American Councils for International Education. I was one of 28 American teachers selected to receive the 1999 US-NIS Excellence in Teaching Award.

I was excited and yelled, "I am going to Kazakhstan!"

My husband Don asked, "Great! Isn't Kazakhstan your first choice?"

"Yes!" I couldn't believe that I was really going there.

At the same time, the selection committees in these five countries were selecting the winners from their respective countries. In June, 70 teachers from NIS would arrive in Washington, D.C., for a six-week professional development program.

As a participant in this award program, I would represent American teachers and visit Kazakhstan in October. I was to visit the capital, Almaty, for a couple of days, and then I would spend ten days in the school and community of a winning teacher of the Excellence in Teaching Award in Kazakhstan.

Connections

The summer of 1999 was indeed a fully-booked summer. In June, I spent three weeks in Japan as a member of the American Teachers Delegation. Following that, I met and led the Sister School Delegation to the Chu Lin Secondary School in Taipei and to tour Taiwan for a week. I had to rush back to report at the University of Delaware in Newark on July 16th for the international conference: Celebrating Teaching Excellence Across Cultures.

The award winning teachers, 28 American teachers and 70 NIS teachers, met at the conference for four days. Each of us American teachers prepared a poster session and a presentation to help our guest teachers learn about the U.S., our states, American schools, and different education programs.

Here I was at my poster station with pictures, posters, and information on the State of Nebraska. I was surrounded by the teachers from Kazakhstan.

One teacher pointed to a picture of Lincoln High School and asked, "Is this your school? It is so big. How many students are there in your school?"

"Yes, it is Lincoln High School. There are around 2,400 students at our school."

"What is your state?" another person asked.

"Nebraska."

They had never heard of the state, just as I had not when I first came to the U.S. in 1967. "Where is Nebraska? Close to here?"

It was a question often asked by foreigners. This is how I always showed them. I smiled and folded a U.S. map. "No. It is located in the middle of the U.S. If you fold the U.S. map in half, Nebraska is in the middle of it."

They all laughed and looked at the map as I pointed to the State of Nebraska on the map. Nobody will forget where Nebraska is after that!

An NIS teacher pointed at another picture—American students in Chinese costumes. "What are they doing here?"

"Oh. My students were performing at the *Chinese Kaleidoscope* program to share with 3,600 people the Chinese cultural activities they have learned in class."

"Really? They know how to dance Chinese dances? Did you teach them?"

I nodded my head. "Yeah, I integrate different cultural activities, like games, songs, dances, and martial arts, into the Chinese language program."

Another teacher commented, "They looked beautiful in Chinese costumes."

"They are my beautiful students!" I said proudly.

One of the teachers saw the picture of me at the White House standing next to President Clinton, Vice President Gore, and Secretary Riley. She got excited. "Look! President Clinton!"

Other teachers gathered around her and looked at the picture. One of them asked, "Where was this taken?"

"It was taken at the White House," I told them.

"You were at the White House?"

"Yes!"

Another teacher asked, "Why were you there? You met the president?"

I chuckled. "I was the 1997 Nebraska Teacher of the Year. I was honored by President Clinton at the White House."

They were so impressed. We started to chat about their schools and their country.

"Would you come to visit my city and school?" Many of the teachers invited me.

I giggled. "It will be great to see you again, especially in your country."

They were all English teachers. They could communicate pretty well in English. We had fun learning about one another and our countries throughout the poster session. At my other presentation session, I presented my *Chinese Kaleidoscope* program to the whole group. I met all the teachers from Kazakhstan throughout the three-day conference. It was quite a helpful, exciting, and pleasant conference. I knew that wherever I would be assigned to visit in October, I would have a friend there.

When the NIS teachers returned to their countries in mid-August after six weeks of professional development in the U.S., they would apply to host a U.S. teacher. The visit of the American teacher ambassadors to their cities and schools was part of the NIS teachers' "prize" for winning the Excellence in Teaching Award.

Since more Kazakhstan teachers requested me to visit their cities and schools, I was to visit two places in southern Kazakhstan in October-November 1999. One of the places, Georgievka, was a rural community not far from Almaty, and the other one, Taraz, was a city in southern Kazakhstan.

In the fall, when I was notified that I had more requests from the teachers and I was going to visit two places, I called the two host teachers to see if they needed anything from the U.S.

I called Danibala in Georgievka, whom I would visit on my first stop. I asked her, "What would you like for me to bring?"

Danibala said, "Jeans for me and my husband, wireless phone, and materials…" It was a long list.

I was surprised that she wanted all those personal things for herself and her family. But I said, "Okay."

I called my second host teacher, Galina, in Taraz, a good-sized city.

I asked her, "Do you need me to bring anything for you?"

She answered courteously and thoughtfully, "If it is possible for you to bring some materials we can use to teach English, it would be wonderful."

I said, "I'd be happy to bring some materials for you."

So I got busy shopping for the things my host teachers in Kazakhstan needed.

Another remarkable expedition of my 1999 adventures in the Orient unfolded ...

First Reception

I was excited for the adventures, and at the same time I was apprehensive traveling to a communist country that I was not familiar with at all.

We, the 28 American Teacher Ambassadors, met in Washington, D.C., for an orientation before our departure to our assigned destinations in the NIS. Nobody knew what kind of experiences each of us would bring back after two weeks.

Three of us were going to Kazakhstan. It was a long flight over the Atlantic and Europe. The airport at Almaty was very dark and backward. The atmosphere was tense and unfriendly, nobody smiled. A representative picked us up and took us to a small hotel, smaller than any motel in the U.S.

We used the next day for an orientation and a short tour in Almaty. Our host teachers were to pick us up at the hotel in the afternoon. The other two teachers left with their host teachers. My first host teacher, Danibala, didn't show as scheduled. I waited and I waited. I was so tired and thirsty, and I couldn't communicate with the lady at the reception desk in the lobby—the only hotel personnel there, and she couldn't speak English.

I remembered Danibala from the conference. She was a native of Kazak, and she was very aggressive at the conference. I noticed how other teachers reacted to her—avoiding her. I didn't expect her to be irresponsible and unreliable—treating a friend from afar this way.

I didn't feel safe being by myself in this dark and deserted-looking hotel—without any local money or anyone I could talk to. I was worried and wondered if she would show up.

I prepared for the worst...

Almost two hours past the scheduled time, Danibala and her husband finally arrived to pick me up. Her husband had been to a horse race. They didn't even apologize!

The next five days with them will be interesting and challenging!

When we got to their house, it was dark. They took me to one room and told me, "You can sleep in our room." There was only one bedroom.

"Where will you sleep?" I asked.

"We will sleep in the living room."

"No, I can't take your room. I will sleep in the living room."

The living room was like a walkway, very small, with a couch facing the front door. Their kitchen was in the courtyard outside. They didn't stay with me after dinner. They went out. They didn't even ask me if I needed anything. They left for their own business and didn't come back until very late. The commotion woke me up as they entered the house. *What a considerate host!*

The next day I went to visit her school. I had prepared a few lessons on American holidays and traditions to teach students. Before I came, on the phone I had told Danibala, "Invite other classes to join your class for the lessons on American culture." Before I visited her school, I told her again to share this opportunity with other teachers.

She didn't share or involve other colleagues or other students. At the welcome assembly, she used the platform to show off and brag about herself instead of letting me talk to the students and staff. Even though I didn't understand Russian, I knew exactly what she was doing.

A Neighbor

There was a young American man working as a Peace Corps volunteer in this rural community. His parents had contacted me from Minnesota before I left the U.S. "Our son John is a Peace Corps volunteer where you are going to visit. Is it possible for you to take something to him for us?"

"Sure! I'd be happy to take whatever you want to send to him."

I met this young man John, and I gave him the package from his family and some of my favorite peanut M & M I took along for snacking. The rural community outside of Almaty is very backward. John lived a very poor and deprived life. He showed me around, but there was not much to see. He bought some kind of flat bread at a small store, which had very few items. The owner handed the bread to him, without a wrapper or box. He just held the bread in his hand on a windy day, with dust blowing all over the bread.

"How long have you been here?" I was concerned about his wellbeing.

"About a year."

I wondered, "How did you adjust to such a different life here?"

"It's very tough with our limited allowance and supplies. But I've survived."

"I admire you guys with such will and strength, working in a backward country like this. You looked happy teaching the students." I admired his spirit and passion.

"The best part is working with the kids. I am the assistant to the English teachers here. I get a chance to practice my Russian."

A Unique Community

Denibala told me we would go to a school in a *Dongang* community. I didn't know the significance of such community, since I didn't understand Russian. She didn't provide me any information or any reason we would visit this particular school. John went with us.

I was surprised as I walked into the school. It was a Chinese community. They spoke Mandarin, with a regional accent. Students wore Chinese costumes, and they performed Chinese dances, like the ones in Xinjiang Province, to welcome us. Families had kept the Chinese traditions, and they taught their children Chinese, just as I had—to preserve the Chinese traditions and language as the *Descendants of the Dragon* wherever we are. I was deeply touched.

I was curious and I asked the principal, "How did you end up here?"

"Our ancestors came to Russia in the late 1700s from Shangdong Province in China when things were getting very difficult in China"

There were a great number of Korean people in Kazakhstan also. They too came to Russia in late 1700s. Very interesting!

The principal invited us for dinner at his house. In rural Kazakhstan, to honor their honorable guests, they kill a lamb to prepare the meal. The head of the lamb is set right next to the honored guest. Here we were in the dining room in a big house, with farmland around it. There was the head of the lamb right next to me—for me to eat. I am a vegetarian, and I felt so bad for this poor lamb killed because of me.

I offered to John, who sat right next to me, "John, you can have the head of the lamb."

"Great! Thank you." John enjoyed the big feast our host had prepared for us, especially the lamb's head.

When I needed to go to the restroom after dinner, it was outside—thirty feet from the house, in the middle of an open field. It was dark, and there was no light. Under the moon, five people went outside with me to show me the restroom—the outhouse in the field, without door, without light, and without paper. I was worried the whole time that I would miss my footing and fall in the dark field or into the toilet! What an experience!

Friendship in Taraz

It was time for me to visit my next teacher, in Taraz—my second destination. I said good-bye to John and gave him some money. "Take good care of yourself and stay healthy." I worried about him.

Again, Denibala and her husband took their time to take me back to Almaty to meet my second host teacher, Galina, from Taraz.

We traveled in a car across a long stretch of dusty dry country. The edge of the endless brown land touched the skyline. We were the only travelers on the road. Then I saw camels, quite a few of them.

"Look! Camels!" I pointed and yelled.

I was excited to see camels on the road instead of cars. "Can we stop? I want to take pictures."

We stopped. I took a few pictures with camels in the background.

Galina from Taraz was there when we finally arrived in Almaty. Galina and I were so thrilled to meet again. Galina was a beautiful, gentle, and smart Russian lady. We had to take an overnight train ride to get to her city. Since the country was newly independent, it had limited resources. It was not too stable, and there were a lot of problems across the country. The government was ruled by Kazak natives, and the non-Kazak natives felt their lives were degraded with the new government.

On the train, people tried to take our assigned seats, but Galina got the seats back. We shared a cabin with two rough-looking people who stared at us the whole time. I could sense the instability and danger on the train. Galina, my guardian angel, was so protective of me, and I felt safe. I was so grateful that she was with me. It gave me chills to imagine what could have happened if I had to travel by myself.

Galina told me a lot of things that were going on in their new country. "Life hasn't gotten any better, but worse. There are a lot of problems and more poor people. It is not always safe."

"Does it affect you and your family?" I was curious.

"Yes, it has really affected my parents' life. They can't do what they could do before. You have more opportunities if you are Kazak natives."

"How about teachers? Is your job secure?"

"I am okay since I am an English teacher." English was the most in-demand language there.

"Will I meet your family?"

She got excited and smiled. "Yes, you will meet my family. You will stay with Natalya, another English teacher. You will like her and her family. They are wonderful people."

She continued, "All the English teachers in our city will meet you for a welcome dinner at Zina's home when we arrive. Zina is our department chair. They are all excited to meet you and to learn from you."

"Great! It sounds fun." I laughed.

"You will have a conference with students of second grade and older. They are so thrilled that they can ask you questions in English."

It sounded like a remarkable event. "Awesome! Will I get the chance to teach a few classes also? I'd love to teach American culture and traditions to your students."

"Yes, we will combine English classes so that they all can learn from you." Everything seemed to be well planned.

What a true professional Galina was to share her honor and opportunities!

My mission, being an American Teacher Ambassador and traveling this far, was to learn, to share, to interact, and to connect the U.S. with students, colleagues, and community in this far- away country!

My host family, Natalya and Andrey, took great care of me while I stayed with them. Whenever I turned around, there would be hot tea and a snack for me. Natalya was such a thoughtful hostess, and she was by my side all the time. I enjoyed their two happy children, a boy and a girl. Andrey had his own business. He didn't speak much English. His gentle smiles made me feel welcome even though we couldn't communicate without translation from Natalya. They made me feel at home. What a pleasant and lovely family! I was so touched by their hospitality and friendship.

One evening, I met Galina's sweet family—her husband, her daughter, and her parents. Again how precious it is to be friends without borders—communicating with translation and the most beautiful universal language—smiles!

I spent the next few days working with teachers in Taraz and students at Galina's school.

The hallways in the school were so dark that I could hardly see. I asked Galina, "Why is it that lights are not turned on? Are there lights in the hallways?"

"The school has a limited budget, and we need to save energy."

What we take for granted in the U.S. was a luxury in this country. The chalkboards were in bad condition, and the teachers used rags to clean them. I was glad I had brought a lot of teaching materials for

Galina and her school.

Students were well behaved and motivated, especially to learn English. They had an Olympia English contest every year. Students competed with high motivation and tremendous effort. Even with limited resources and a deprived environment, they learned English so well. As a world language teacher, I was impressed and amazed by what the teachers had done with their English program.

I decided to do something to encourage this group of motivated students.

At the conference with 300 students, I was so awestruck by their English skills. They asked excellent questions in good English. Their teachers had prepared them well.

At the end of the conference, I smiled and complimented all of the students, "Your English is very good. You are wonderful! I am so impressed with every one of you." I continued, "I know you have the Olympia English contest each year. I would like to sponsor the contest and provide prizes for you."

The students were so happy, and their excitement filled the auditorium for a few minutes. I was so touched and happy that I could encourage these motivated students in a far-away land.

I took home with me the friendship and great memories my colleagues had given me during the five days I was in Taraz—precious experiences and friends I will always treasure.

I left some money with the school to purchase prizes for the Olympia English contest for the year. I continued my sponsorship for several years until I lost my channel for sending money, a missionary organization in Indiana.

With great appreciation, admiration, and respect for my colleagues in Taraz, Kazakhstan, I invited Natalya, Galina, and their husbands to spend two weeks in the U.S. the following summer. I sent the traveling fund for their trip through the same organization in Indiana to bring my friends from Taraz to the U.S. in the summer of 2000.

With fond memories and new friendship, I left Taraz in Kazakhstan, the last stop of my 1999 adventures in the Orient…

Friends from Afar

My friends from Kazakhstan and I screamed with excitement and happiness when we saw one another at the airport in Lincoln, Nebraska.

I showed them the beautiful State Capitol and took them to meet the Governor. I introduced my friends to Governor Johanns, "These are my friends from Kazakhstan. I am showing off our state."

Governor Johanns welcomed my friends warmly, "Welcome to Nebraska. You have the best host in the state. Have a great time here!"

The Governor presented special certificates to them. They could not believe they met the Governor in person. Meeting government officials was not possible in their country. Galina commented, "I can't believe it. We met your Governor just like that. He was so friendly."

"The Governor's son was my student, and I serve on the Governor's advisory board on quality education." I told her, "He has been very supportive of all the projects I have done for the schools and the community ever since he was the mayor of the City of Lincoln."

We visited the schools where I taught and we visited the Mayor of Lincoln.

During their two weeks of visiting, I tried to provide them different experiences to enrich their knowledge so that they could take home what they learned in the U.S. to share with their colleagues and students.

After spending a few days in Lincoln, I took them to Disneyland and Universal Studios in Los Angeles and also Las Vegas.

They were so happy. "Thank you, Celine, for the once-in-a-lifetime treat and the fun," Natalya said to me every day.

Before they came, I collected four suitcases full of teaching materials and gifts for their schools and friends. Galina and Natasha greatly appreciated the materials, the pictures taken during their visit, and the gifts. Galina said, "I will share all these with all the friends you met when you were there."

We enjoyed every moment we were together, for we didn't know when we would meet again. With lots of tears and many hugs, I said good-bye to my friends from afar…

*****

Sixteen years later in 2015, Natalya, Galina and I are still connected. Natalya has moved to Russia where she teaches English. Galina is still living and teaching English in Taraz, Kazakhstan.

The Lincoln High School Newsletter   January 2000

LINKSLetter

Lincoln High School • 2229 J Street • Lincoln, Nebraska 68510 • (402) 436-1301 • (Fax) 436-1540

NEWS RELEASE:

AREA TEACHER VISITED KAZAKHSTAN AS PART OF TEACHER EXCHANGE PROGRAM

Area teacher, Celine Robertson, from Lincoln High School in Lincoln, NE, visited Kazakhstan from October 18 to November 1, 1999 as part of the 1999 United States-Newly Independent States Awards for Excellence in Teaching program. The program is administered by the American Councils for International Education: ACTR/ACCELS and funded by the Bureau of Educational and Cultural Affairs of the United States Department of State under the authority of Fulbright-Hays Act of 1961, as amended.

After meeting with government and educational officials in Almaty, the capital of Kazakhstan, Mrs. Robertson traveled to Zhambyl to meet with award-winning teachers and visit their schools and communities.

Celine Robertson visits Kazakhstan.

HIGHLIGHTS OF THE TRIP INCLUDE:

- US-NIS (newly independent states of former Soviet Union) Awards for Excellence in Teaching
- Celine spent two weeks in Kazakhstan as a winner of the US-NIS Award for Excellence in Teaching. See news release. Celine is going to invite four friends from Kazakhstan to visit the U.S. in the summer of 2000.
- 300 student press conference in English
- presentation on Nebraska, American football, American holidays and traditions

- workshop sharing with 50 English teachers across the city
- meeting government officials
- Independent Day celebration
- The passion for teaching and faith in children and education are well shared among teachers around the world.

For further information about the Awards for Excellence in Teaching Program, contact Karen Hollis Program Officer, American Councils for International Education at (202) 833-7522.

213

Chapter 6
Return to My Roots

家

A Gift
Cold as Ice
A Dream and A Promise
Hooked
Little Monkeys
A Big Small World

A Gift

There were noodles on the dining table. I asked Ma Ma, "Whose birthday is it today?"

"Today is your youngest uncle's birthday," *Ma Ma* responded, with such a deep sorrow in her eyes.

"How old is he now?"

"He is twenty years old today." It was December 20th, 1953.

Noodles—a symbol of longevity—are always served to celebrate birthdays for Chinese people. It's tradition not to break the noodles, the longevity, when you prepare them.

When the communists took over China in 1949, my father—a Nationalist Chinese Army general, followed Chiang Kai-shek and went to Taiwan. He arranged for us, *Ma Ma, Po Po* and us four children, to stay in Hong Kong until he had everything ready for us in Taiwan.

At their parting, with tears and unspeakable sadness, *Ma Ma* waved her final good-bye to her beloved three younger brothers who decided to stay and guard the property their father had left to them. *Po Po* bid her eternal farewell to her three sons. We boarded the ship and left for Hong Kong. At this heart-breaking moment, *Ma Ma* was 32 years old and her youngest brother was 16 years old. My twin sister and I were just toddlers.

There was no correspondence allowed between Taiwan and mainland China—especially since Father was a general and our older brother Karl was a doctor in the army, and later became a general.

We, the Nationalist Chinese in Taiwan, referred China as *Tie Mu* [the Iron Curtain]. China was closed, isolated, and blocked from the rest of the world, especially from people like us in Taiwan. We didn't know what had happened to our uncles—alive or dead, behind the *Tie Mu* separated by the Taiwan Strait. We celebrated our three uncles' birthdays every year.

Day after day, month after month, and year after year, thirty years had passed. *Ma Ma* never stopped missing and loving her brothers. We, seven children, shared her unspoken deep-rooted pain and grief and felt her invisible tears of sorrow. *Ma Ma*'s love for her brothers profoundly moved our hearts and touched our souls. We had an unspoken wish deep in our hearts and we prayed for a miracle—to find *Ma Ma*'s brothers for her someday...

Despair

In 1969, Nixon abandoned the long-time World War II ally—Republic of China in Taiwan led by Chiang Kai-Shek, and established a diplomatic relationship with Communist China, led by Mao Ze Dong. In 1972, China pulled the *Iron Curtain* and opened up to the rest of the world after 23 years of isolation.

In the fall of 1972, our older brother Karl, a doctor in the Army, was selected by the government of the Republic of China in Taiwan to study Hospital Administration at Columbia University. He received his master' degree in the spring of 1974. In July, on his way home to Taiwan, he came to visit us in Lincoln, Nebraska.

It was a precious and treasured week for both of us. We hadn't really talked, heart-to-heart, since I left home for my advanced studies in the U.S in 1967. We had a lot of catching up to do. During his seven-day visit, we talked and we talked, non-stop.

We had shared the same vision and mission in our hearts for a long time—to find our uncles for *Ma Ma*. Karl said to me, "China is open now and has a diplomatic relationship with the U.S. I wonder if we can try to locate our uncles from the U.S."

"I have been thinking about the same thing also. Let's write a letter and send it to our old address in Suzhou to see if they are still living there."

"Yeah. Let's write a simple letter so they won't get in trouble having a connection with anyone outside of China."

People were closely watched in China. There was no private telephone, and the mail was always censored. "You are right. You never know how the communists will take this letter coming from the U.S. We'd better be careful."

We decided to take our first step in searching for our long-lost uncles. To avoid any possible complication, it was safer for all of us—our family in Taiwan and our uncles in China—to have my husband Don, an American, write this letter.

I asked Don, "May we use your name to write this letter to our uncles?"

Don was well informed, and he knew our background and how the communists were in China. He agreed without hesitation, "Good idea! Go ahead."

We drafted a simple letter. In the letter, Don, as a friend, merely described how our family was doing and where everyone was residing. We sent the letter to *Yi Yuan*, our home in Suzhou where *Ma Ma* and her three brothers were born and raised. We used our address in Lincoln as the return address.

We decided not to tell our parents of this letter. We prayed and we waited.

It was like a rock sunk in deep sea—no news.

Our hearts sank, with great despair.

Slightest Hope

I was a special education teacher, having worked with special needs students at Everett Junior High School in Lincoln, Nebraska since 1974. Rex Scott, a colleague, taught social studies. His classroom was very close to mine. Sometimes we chatted in the hallways between classes.

Being a social studies teacher, he watched the changes of the world closely. One day in early spring of 1978, he said to me, "Hey, do you know Nebraska is sending a delegation to visit China."

"Really?" I was amazed that Nebraska was making a connection with China.

"Yeah!"

I was very curious. "When are they going and who all is going?"

"Very soon. Government officials and community leaders. My mother is a member of the delegation. They will visit Beijing." He was excited about his mother's trip, representing Nebraska to visit the newly opened China.

China was a mysterious and dangerous place to me under the communists, even though I was born there. I didn't know if I would ever go back. With complicated feelings—profound distrust and fear of Communist China, I said, "Really? That's great. I hope someday I will go back to China. I still have three uncles there. I don't even know if they are alive or not."

Although I was born in China, we had left China when I was a toddler. I hardly had any memory of our uncles, let alone China. I only knew that the communists did a lot of horrible and brutal things to people like us who had strong ties with the Nationalist Chinese Government.

Over the weekend, I got this notion that maybe it was worth trying.

On the following Monday, I talked to Rex. "We haven't had any contact with our three uncles since 1949. Would you check with your mother to see if she would deliver a letter to the Red Cross in Beijing to locate my uncles?" I assumed that there was a Red Cross in Beijing.

Rex thought it was a good idea. "Sure! I bet she'd be happy to do that. I will check with her tonight."

I appreciated the slightest hope to find our uncles in China. "Thank you! Thank you!"

Rex came to my classroom early the next morning. He was excited and told me, "My mother said that she would be happy to deliver the letter for you."

I was so grateful for this opportunity and Mrs. Scott's willingness to help. "Thank you! Thank you! I will get the letter ready before she leaves."

I didn't know what to expect, but I was going to give it a try again— to locate *Ma Ma*'s three brothers.

Special Delivery

In the late spring of 1978, when Mrs. Scott came back from her trip to China, she told me what she had seen and learned there. She made a special request to the Chinese government to visit the Red Cross in Beijing and to deliver the letter for me in person. "I delivered your letter myself. I was the first foreigner that the Red Cross received in 30 years."

With earnest gratitude I thanked her again and again for taking the trouble to help my family. "Thank you so much for delivering the letter for me. This is our only and last hope to locate our uncles."

"It was my pleasure. I hope you will get some responses."

"I do too!"

I tried to be positive and hopeful.

I wished and I prayed.

I hoped since it was an official visit, maybe there was a better chance they would take some kind of action on the request to locate my three uncles.

Anguish

I checked the mail anxiously every day. A few months had passed and still I didn't receive anything from China. I was so devastated. I shared my despair with my siblings in the U.S. "Well, it looks like our effort is in vain again."

My twin sister Irene in Los Angeles said, "With our family background, I wonder if they are still alive."

Ken, my younger brother in Houston, commented, "Being the landlords and with our family background, they are classified as *Five Black Groups*. I can't imagine what they would have been through if they are alive."

Landlords and people with any tie with Nationalist Chinese in the family were categorized under the *Five Black Groups*—the enemies of the people—and had received brutal treatment, exile, or execution in China since 1949. Our grandfather owned a lot of property in

Suzhou, and both he and my father were Nationalist Chinese generals. We were very worried about our three uncles.

Our younger sister Eileen said, "Don't give up hope yet! Give it more time."

I waited and I waited. I was not hopeful any more. Finally I let it go and tried not to think about it or even talk about it.

No hope! No miracle!

My heart ached for *Ma Ma*..

A Best Gift

Two more months had passed. On day in late August, I received a letter from the American Red Cross. I wondered if it was for some kind of donation.

I opened the letter and I was so stunned that I almost fainted!

It was an official document written in Chinese.

It said,

> 'We located your family member, Ling Ze Ji. His address is as follows…'

Uncle Ji was Mother's youngest brother. "They found him! Uncle Ji is alive!" Even though I was alone, I jumped up and down and screamed with disbelief.

Suddenly I realized something.

How come only one name?

Where are Uncle Lin and Uncle Pei?

Are they still alive?

Don was at work, and Joline was only two. I needed to share this with someone right then. I called Irene in Los Angeles. "I got a letter from the Red Cross. They found Uncle Ji. He is alive and he lives in Shanghai!"

Irene cried, tears of joy, and she was worried about the same things. "Only one? Where are Uncle Lin and Uncle Pei?"

"I don't know. I will write to him right away to find out what happened to them."

Later I called my younger brother Ken in Houston and younger sister Eileen in Boston to share the news. They too were worried about the same thing.

I wrote a letter and mailed it to Uncle Ji in Shanghai. It took at least a week or longer for any letter to get to or from China.

I shared the progress with the search for our uncles with my three siblings in the U. S. during the whole process. We decided not to tell our parents about the news just yet, not before we found out what had happened to the other two uncles.

Again, it was such torture—waiting restlessly, like sitting on a seat full with needles.

The unknown and frightening apprehension drove me crazy. Poor Don! I asked him countless times every day, "Do you think they are still alive?"

He was very calm and patient with me. "Just wait and see!"

In late September, after almost a month, I finally got a long letter from Uncle Ji in Shanghai.

I jumped up and down holding the letter. "They are alive! They are all alive!"

It was a miracle! Thank God! All three of them were alive!

Mother's oldest brother, Uncle Lin, and his family lived in Huai Nan, Anhui Province, and her second brother, Uncle Pei, was a science teacher at Nan Kai High School in Tianjin, not far from Beijing. The youngest brother, Uncle Ji, was a second mate of a domestic coastline ship.

I was expecting my second daughter, Andrea, the following February. Our parents were scheduled to come to the U.S. in October to visit us four siblings and to help us with our new baby. We decided to surprise them with the great news when they arrived in a couple of weeks.

As soon as they arrived at Irene's home in Los Angeles, we told them the great news. Mother was so shocked that she couldn't talk for a while. With tears of joy in her eyes, Mother murmured, "Thank God they are alive. My prayers were heard."

When they arrived at our home in Lincoln, Nebraska, I presented *Ma Ma* with all the letters from the three uncles. She touched the letters gently and held them close to her heart. She then opened each letter carefully. After reading the letters, she was speechless for a long time—tears she had held back and hidden for the past 30 years rolled down on her cheeks, non-stop...

It was truly the best gift I could ever give to my dearest *Ma Ma*.

Cold as Ice

In 1998, Theresa Chao, a good friend of mine, went to live in Beijing when her husband Roger was offered a great opportunity there. Just as I was wondering how they were doing in China, I received a call from her.

"Hey! I was just thinking of you. How is Beijing? Do you like it there?" I was delighted to hear from her, and I was curious about how they adjusted to such a different life in Beijing.

"We are doing fine. It is very different here. But China is changing, very fast." She filled me in.

"Are you working? What have you been doing there?"

"I am teaching math at the International School of Beijing. That's why I am calling you." She was a certified math teacher in Connecticut.

"Oh. Why?" I wondered.

She asked me, "Would you be interested in teaching here in Beijing? Our school…"

"Teaching in Beijing? No way! I don't like Beijing at all!" I blurted out before she could finish her sentence.

"Listen! The International School of Beijing is an American-system school for children of diplomats and foreign business executives around the world. It is like the Taipei American School in Taipei. The students are very good and the school is well equipped."

The Taipei American School is a very good international school. It has a very long history, and I had known about this school since I was a child.

She continued, "We need a person to lead the Chinese department, and the school asked me to recommend someone. You are my first choice."

223

"Thank you. But I really don't want to go to Beijing."

Theresa couldn't understand why I turned her down instantly. Well, it was because of some experiences I had in Beijing in 1997—I seldom talked about it and yet I never forget.

As the president-elect and the president of—Chinese Language Association for Secondary-Elementary Schools (CLASS), I had many responsibilities. One of them was to coordinate, organize, and provide learning opportunities that were desperately needed for our members—the pioneers in Chinese language teaching to secondary school students in the U.S. and other countries.

Two summer workshops were held at the Mandarin Center of the National Taiwan Normal University in Taipei. The staff and the instructors were professional, caring, and personable. Director Teh Ming Yeh of the Mandarin Center made the workshops pleasant, comfortable, and productive.

The Chinese Opera Workshops for both students and teachers were held at the Fu Hsing Performing Arts Academy in Taipei. Again, it was a great experience for the attendees. When a student got sick, the activity director, Mr. Tien Yu, took the student to the hospital immediately for medical care. The school even paid for the medical expenses.

Theresa was a CLASS member. She was actively involved with the Chinese program at the heritage school for Chinese children in Stamford, Connecticut. She participated in two of the workshops that I coordinated and organized. We had a lot in common—both born in China and grew up in Taipei; we came to the U.S. for advanced studies; and we were actively involved in the local Chinese community and heritage schools. With some shared visions and missions, we hit it off instantly and became good friends.

After three workshops in Taiwan, I decided to arrange a workshop in Beijing to provide different learning experiences to broaden resources for CLASS members. The workshop was to take place at a Beijing language and culture college in July 1997.

The director of the Chinese language department and I worked closely the previous year through phone calls and documents by fax.

I went to Beijing a few days earlier, hoping to get things in order before members arrived. It was our first workshop in China—an unfamiliar place to most of us.

The director was supposed to pick me up at the airport. I didn't see any sign with my name on it when I arrived. I wanted to call him, but I couldn't find a phone. I waited and waited—worried and scared in this unfamiliar communist country, all alone. The driver finally came—holding a sign with my name on it, and found me. The director didn't come. The unfriendly driver dropped me off at a very old hotel. Without any instruction or word, the driver left. I didn't expect such "courtesy" and "hospitality" that was so different from the Chinese way I was used to.

I hadn't eaten any lunch. "Are there any restaurants nearby?" I asked a man at the hotel.

"No." He was pretty stingy with words, and he ignored me afterward.

It was very hot, dry, and uncomfortable. I was tired, hungry, thirsty, and worried—alone without anything to drink or to eat. I went out and looked around. I didn't see any restaurants—only some food stands in the street by the hotel. I bought a couple of plain Chinese buns and a bottle of water at the closest food stand.

Later I felt the chills and I had a fever. My friends and members would not be here until two days later.

I went through a lot of trouble finding a phone and made a call to the director, the only person I knew in Beijing. A woman answered the phone, in a rough tone and manner, "Who is this?"

I said to her, "May I speak to the director? I am the person from the U.S. in charge of the workshop at his school."

She answered abruptly, "He is not home."

"Would you have him call me at the hotel? I am sick and I need help." I left a message, the phone number, and my room number at the hotel.

I waited for two days for him to contact me, but he never called. I couldn't understand how he treated me—a guest from afar and a person working closely with him for the past year. It was totally not the Chinese way.

I wondered and I pondered:

What had happened to the Chinese people here?

What had happened to the Chinese courtesy, hospitality, and caring good nature?

What would happen if there would be a life and death emergency for any of my members?

Should I have this workshop in Taiwan instead?

Is this a mistake?

Although I was born in China and I speak the language, this China was such a foreign country to me—so different from my up-bringing and what I was used to. I was in such "culture shock" and I didn't want to go out by myself anymore. I just stayed in my room waiting patiently for my friends and members, Nancy Liu and Catherine Wu, to arrive from Taiwan to rescue me.

"Thank God! You are finally here." I hugged Nancy and Catherine tightly when they arrived and found me at the hotel.

Nancy noticed my fever. "What happened to you? You are so hot!"

"I have been sick!" I told them what had happened fighting back the tears.

"The director never called or came to see you?" Nancy was so angry.

"Go! Let's find a clinic for you." Catherine grabbed my hand.

They found out there was a clinic not too far from the hotel. As we walked into the clinic, a woman was giving a shot to a woman patient in the open on her butt with a big needle, not a disposable kind.

She lifted her head and asked us, "What do you need?"

"She is sick, with a fever," Nancy said to her, pointing at me.

"Okay. She needs I.V.," she said it without even checking on me.

I screamed, in fear, "No I.V.! No shots!"

Nancy and Catherine agreed with me. It wasn't safe. "Do you have any medicine for fever instead?" Nancy asked her.

We paid the woman and got some pills for my fever.

"You haven't been eating. Let's find a place to eat." What a blessing to have wonderful friends to take care of me!

We asked around and we searched. We walked a long distance, and we finally found a little eating place—a few dirty tables under some kind of temporary roof. The service was so bad. The food was served like a Frisbee—it was thrown at us. We looked at one another and smiled, and we ate our food very fast and left.

We tried to take a taxi back to the hotel since I was too weak to walk. It was so hot. There were three kinds—a little yellow van for transporting goods, a taxi without air conditioning, and one with air conditioning. We decided to take the most expensive taxi, with air conditioning, but the driver refused to turn it on even though we paid for it.

After spending seven days in Beijing to ensure the workshop was in order, I rushed back to the U.S. I was to represent the State of Nebraska in the International Space Camp in Huntsville, Alabama. The space camp was designed especially for the fifty American State Teachers of the Year and twenty-five Teachers of the Year around the world.

It was an unbelievable and unforgettable week in Beijing! I turned down the invitation to meet and to have dinner with the president of the school. I didn't respond enthusiastically to the director when he approached me to discuss a possible workshop in the future.

The scorching sun and the dry wind in Beijing turned my hair into hay, but the rough unprofessional and uncaring treatment had turned my warm heart cold as ice.

Do I want to teach in Beijing?

No way!

A Dream and a Promise

Although China was open to the rest of the world in 1972, people were watched closely and the mail was censored. Father had retired from the army, but our oldest brother Karl was an active army officer in Taiwan. After we located our three uncles in 1978, Mother corresponded with her three brothers only when she was in the U.S. or through us when she was in Taiwan.

In March 1979, our parents were with us to help with our new baby daughter, Andrea. Mother received a letter from Uncle Pei in Tianjin. She quietly read the letter as tears rolled down her cheeks.

I wondered what happened. "What's the matter, *Ma Ma*? Is Uncle Pei okay?"

Ma Ma nodded and handed the letter to me. In the letter, Uncle Pei described their "abundant" Chinese New Year Eve feast:

> '…With ration allowance we were fortunate to have a chicken and some extra ounces of oil for the Chinese New Year Eve dinner this year. It was the best New Year feast we have had for a long, long time. We were so happy to have this abundant feast to celebrate the Chinese New Year…'

I was in tears and speechless like Mother.

"What's wrong?" Father was concerned watching us two crying.

I handed him the letter. Father looked sad, and he sighed deeply. He comforted us. "Things might get better. At least they had a chicken to celebrate the New Year this year."

To celebrate the Chinese New Year, we always had ten or more courses—a feast for the New Year Eve dinner, the highlight of the 15-day Chinese New Year celebration. It is the most important holiday to Chinese people, like Thanksgiving to Americans. I have kept the tradition with my family for more than four decades in the U.S.

Uncle Pei was very tall, 6 feet and 4 inches, and skinny. He suffered greatly during World War II. When he was about thirteen, the Japanese captured him and brutally abused him at a hard labor camp. It permanently damaged his growth and health and caused a lot of health problems for him later in life.

Mother was in tears again. "I have always worried about his health. He now has only one-fourth of his stomach after the surgery."

She continued, "He was buried for many days under a collapsed building after the Tang Shan Earthquake." *Ma Ma* wiped more tears from her face.

Since 1949, Uncle Pei and his family had also gone through a lot and suffered tremendously due to our family background. During the Cultural Revolution they were banished to be peasants and couldn't raise their only son. A farmer raised our cousin for ten years.

Both Uncle Pei and his wife were science teachers at Nan Kai Secondary School in Tianjin until they retired. They were poor and lived a very simple life.

Banished

Uncle Lin was two years younger than Mother. He was a Chemical Engineer. When he graduated from college, he joined the army to fight the Japanese during World War II. Since he had good English skills, he was an interpreter.

His past—being a rich landlord and a Nationalist Chinese general's son, serving in the Nationalist Chinese Army during World War II, and having a Nationalist Chinese general brother-in-law in Taiwan—had caused him tremendous injustice, unbearable humiliation, endless physical abuse, and unspeakable anguish, day after day and year after year.

He was banished to work at a paper mill in Huainan, Anhui Province—a remote and backward place. He had lived through hell and suffered the most out of our three uncles under the communist regime. His loving wife had shared much of his physical abuse to protect him by shielding him from brutal beating and humiliation in front of a crowd, very often. Since then she had suffered severe chronic pain in her legs. Their three children couldn't get quality educations while growing up in Anhui.

I always remember *Ma Ma*'s comment about our aunt. "I am so glad that your oldest uncle has a great wife. She sacrificed a great deal and suffered so much for him."

Chinese people, especially our parents' generation, seldom say, "I love you" to their loved ones. The deepest love and most profound commitment were in actions of everyday life, for better or for worse, reflected especially during difficult and challenging times.

Uncle Lin's decision to stay in China with his two younger brothers in 1949, changed his fate from a prestigious life of the young master of *Yi Yuan* to a life in hell for the next forty some years...

Mother was consumed with sorrow and worry before her brothers were found, and now she was so devastated and miserable knowing what each one of them had been through. "Why is it they had to suffer so much?" she seemed to ask God, often.

Feeling her pain, we couldn't and didn't know how to comfort her. "China is changing. Their life is getting better. We will do whatever we can to help them."

Branded

Under the communist regime, the *Five Black Groups*—landlords, rich farmers, rebels, the capitalists, and of course the Nationalists— were the enemies of the people. Our family was in three categories out of five.

Our youngest uncle, Uncle Ji, graduated from college with a major in Marine Transportation and Operation. With this label—*Five Black Groups*—on his head, he received unjust treatment and limited opportunities. Even though he was one of the most experienced, educated, and qualified sailors on the coastline ship, for a very long time he was not promoted, as he should have been, beyond the position of a second mate on the ship.

Mother always tried to look at the good in people and see the best of everything. With a deep sigh she said, "At least he was allowed to attend college. He got married and settled in Shanghai, not far from home."

"Could he go back to our home in Suzhou?" I wondered.

"Our house was taken by the government a long time ago." *Ma Ma* wiped her wet eyes again.

A Patriotic Hero

China's policy on overseas connections, people like us, changed constantly and tremendously during the 1980s. The government of Suzhou not only issued an official document to clear my grandfather's name from the *Five Black Groups* to a patriotic World War II hero against Japan, but also compensated Mother and our three uncles for their house *Yi Yuan* that was taken away a long time ago. A historical museum displays a picture of Grandfather and Dr. Sun Yet Sen that was taken after overthrowing the Qing Dynasty.

With the compensation money, Uncle Lin bought a house in Suzhou where he planned to return when he retired. He also bought one for Mother there. Uncle Pei purchased a house in Tianjin where they lived for the rest of their lives.

Uncle Ji bought a house in Shanghai. Since our grandfather's name was cleared and with overseas connections, Uncle Ji finally got the long overdue promotion and became the captain of the coastline ship where he had worked as the second mate for many years.

Mother really wanted to help her brothers to live a better life. She sent money to them frequently. All three uncles' lives improved a great deal. "I am so glad my youngest brother finally became a captain of a ship. All of them now have settled in their own houses."

"What are you going to do with the house they bought for you in Suzhou?" I asked.

"Your oldest uncle has three children, and they need more help. I will give it to him." It was a good idea.

"What happened to *Yi Yuan*?" I was curious.

"Who knows? It is not ours any more. I really miss it. Hope I can see it again someday." *Ma Ma*'s gaze took her to a far, far away land…

Crushed Dream

We had close correspondence with our three uncles after we located them in 1978. China was very backward then. Common people didn't have telephones. Letters were the only way to communicate with them.

Mother couldn't go to China because Karl was an active army officer in Taiwan. It was impossible for our uncles to go overseas. We continuously tried to figure a way for *Ma Ma* to meet her brothers. Maybe they could meet in Hong Kong if our uncles were allowed to go to Hong Kong.

In the fall of 1987, nine years after locating our three uncles in China, Mother was diagnosed with a vicious brain tumor. We all were saddened by her illness.

I shared my worry with my six siblings after Mother's surgery. "We have to get *Ma Ma* to see her brothers soon."

Eileen, our younger sister in Boston, quit her manager job and went back to take care of Mother. A year later we decided it was best to move our parents to Boston to live with Eileen and two younger brothers since it was too much and unfair for Karl to take care of our parents alone in Taiwan, especially since Mother was not well.

"Now what to do? There is no way *Ma Ma* can travel to China or Hong Kong." We siblings continued our conversation on how to get Mother to reunite with her brothers.

"I will check to see if it is possible for our uncles to come to the U.S. to visit Mother." Eileen suggested.

Eileen found out that with a medical document on Mother's health condition, our three uncles could get passports to come to the U.S. to see Mother. Everyone was so excited that finally there was a solution. We then made arrangements for their visit.

On August 4th, 1990, while our three uncles were anxiously and hopefully waiting for their passports, Mother left us and went to heaven—six weeks after her surgery from the recurrence of the brain tumor.

It was so close, and yet too late…

We and our three uncles were devastated and tragically saddened. Uncle Pei took it especially hard, and with his poor health he fainted many times after receiving the news.

Ma Ma's life-time dream—to reunite with her three brothers, was crushed completely.

Mother's farewell wave to her brothers on the deck of the ship, heading for Hong Kong, 41 years ago in 1949, had been her eternal good-bye to her beloved brothers. It was the beginning of a life-time tragedy for Mother and her brothers…

What a forever heart-aching regret and unbearable tragedy for us all!

Going Home

In order to provide an in-depth experience for my first group of Chinese language students before they graduated from high school, I decided to take them to experience China and to use the language. Our trip was set for June 1992.

I was looking forward to this trip, especially because we were to spend two days in Suzhou—where Mother was born and raised. I wanted to see my three uncles, who I hardly remembered, and all the cousins I never met. I sent them the itinerary.

I told my students excitedly, "On the trip we will visit many places, and you are going to meet all my uncles and maybe a couple of my cousins."

"Really?" Jason was thrilled. "Where are they?"

"The one in Tianjin will meet us in Beijing. The other two will meet us in Shanghai." My students knew my family background, and they were especially happy to have the chance to meet my family in China.

"I will also take you on rickshaws to see our house in Suzhou." I told them about our home, *Yi Yuan*.

There was a hidden promise in my heart—to see my three uncles and *Yi Yuan* in Suzhou for *Ma Ma*.

Messenger of Love

In Beijing, the first stop on our China trip, from Mother's description throughout the years, I recognized my very tall and skinny Uncle Pei instantly, even from a far distance. There was no gap of time or distance whatsoever, even though we had been separated since I was a toddler. He spent a day with my students and me. We shared stories; we asked questions; and we provided answers.

I delivered Mother's deepest love to him. "We grew up listening to stories about you three uncles. We celebrated your birthday every year. *Ma Ma* prayed for you all her life."

"It was a life-time dream to be connected with our long lost older sister." He wiped his tears from his cheeks. "We received your first letter in 1974, but we dared not respond because we were watched closely. We were so happy to have received news of your family."

"Mother missed you and loved you so much all her life." I, too, tried to fight back my tears.

"How I wish we could see her again, even just for five minutes." There was unspeakable pain and sorrow in his voice. His eyes welled with tears again.

Forever Shattered

"Would you take us to this address? We will need five rickshaws." Surrounded by my eager students, I handed the address of *Yi Yuan* to one of the rickshaw drivers along the street by the hotel.

My students waited eagerly to go on this excursion with me on rickshaws—to find *Yi Yuan*, my home, in Suzhou. They seemed to genuinely care and share my personal mission.

The driver took a look at the address and said, "I know this address, but the house is no longer there."

"What? What do you mean? What happened to it?" I knew it was taken by the government, but I didn't know it disappeared totally from the earth.

I was devastated, and my heart ached intensely.

"The house is gone. Many factories were built there by the government a long time ago." He looked regretful, for me.

Tears rolled down my face, non-stop.

My memories of our home, *Yi Yuan* [Garden of Art] in Suzhou, and a dream and a promise—going home for *Ma Ma*—were forever shattered...

My students looked stunned, and they tried to comfort my dismayed heart for many days afterward.

Reunion

Uncle Lin and his younger daughter came all the way from Anhui to meet me in Shanghai—the last stop of our trip. Uncle Ji lived in Shanghai. They came together to meet me at the hotel.

"Uncle Lin, you look just like Mother!" I yelled out as I opened the door for them. His lips were quivering. My beautiful cousin Xia tried to comfort him. Uncle Ji wiped his eyes also.

Uncle Ji came alone. I asked him, "Where are aunt and cousin Bei?"

"Bei has college entrance examination soon, and she needs to study. Aunt needs to stay with her."

"Last time I saw you, you were just this tall." Uncle Lin laughed, his hand in the air by his thigh and tears in his eyes.

Uncle Ji commented. "You twins were so different. Irene was a total girl, and you were such a little tomboy." We laughed together—tears rolling down at the same time.

"How is she doing?" he asked.

"She is still a lady, and I am still a tomboy." We laughed again.

I wanted them to feel Mother's love. I told my uncles, "Mother told us stories about you three all the time. Not a day went by that she didn't miss and love you."

Both uncles sobbed.

I wanted to know about our home, *Yi Yuan*. "What happened to our house in Suzhou? I tried to see the house, and they told me it was not there anymore."

Uncle Lin sighed deeply. He looked so painful, regretful, and helpless. "It was taken away by the government long time ago, along with all our property. We lost everything our father left to us."

Uncle Ji seemed so devastated and heart-broken. "*Yi Yuan* was torn down to build several factories many years ago. We couldn't even guard our home."

The choice they made to stay behind to guard the home and the property their father left to them in 1949 indeed changed their fate—a life descending from heaven to hell, from wealth to poverty.

We laughed and cried, and we talked and talked—to fill in the blanks of the preceding 43 years...

Hooked

Since I turned down the opportunity to teach in Beijing in 1998, Theresa Chao took the position herself as the coordinator of the Chinese Language Department in the fall of the next year. She reorganized the Chinese language department and led a department of twenty-some teachers.

My persistent friend Theresa never gave up on me. She called me again. "China is really changing, for the better. There is a new airport, and things are in better order now."

"There is new airport now?" I still remembered the dirty, shabby old airport.

"Yes!" She continued, "I go to a Chinese medicine doctor every week to have adjustments done. I have massages done at home every week. You can get a helper to do house work. Car with a driver for hire is around $50 for a day. There is so much to see and do in China— things that you can't do or have in the U.S. You can travel in China and to the neighboring countries very easily."

"I don't know. Besides, I am not old enough to retire from here yet." I turned her down again, without much thought.

In June 2000, I decided to take an early retirement after teaching for 26 years in Lincoln Public Schools.

In September, Theresa called again. "Now you are retired, would you consider teaching here at the International School of Beijing next fall?"

"I would like to take a year off." I really needed a break to do whatever and to go wherever just to have fun—without using much of my brain.

She then suggested, "Now you are free! Why don't you come to take a look at the school?"

After retirement, I visited one place each month to see friends or family, and I had just returned from a two-week trip to visit friends in Seattle and Vancouver. It was late September.

"It's so far. I haven't recovered from my last trip yet."

She persisted. "Well, you can come to visit in November. You and Don can stay with us."

"I will think about it." I didn't really want to go.

Jason Christie, one outstanding student of mine, had been working in Shanghai since he graduated from college a few years earlier. He kept in very close contact with me. He called me one day. "*Lao Shi*, you are retired now, come to visit me in Shanghai."

"It's so far!" I responded.

He said, "You don't have to worry about anything, just come."

Don had never been to Beijing or Shanghai. "We can go in November. You have a month to recover from your last trip."

Well, what could I say?

I surrendered. "Okay. We will go to Beijing and Shanghai in November."

Hooked

On November 5th, 2000 we arrived at the new Beijing airport. Our flight was delayed, and we couldn't find our luggage. It took forever to fill out the form for the missing luggage. It was one o'clock in the morning when we, the last two people, finally walked out of the airport. Theresa and her husband Roger waited patiently outside for us.

Without our luggage I had nothing to change into for the night or to wear the next day. I was not sure when our luggage would arrive. The next day was Saturday. Theresa invited a few Chinese language teachers for dinner. She borrowed some clothes from one of the teachers, Tuanmu, for me to wear for the next two days in case my luggage didn't arrive.

Theresa took me shopping for some underwear. We looked and we searched at one of the open markets where Theresa went sometimes.

But we couldn't find any stand to buy such things.

It was not funny at all, but there was nothing we could do but laugh!

What kind of place is Beijing?

When my luggage finally arrived the next day, I was so happy to wear my own clothes. As we planned our itinerary for our seven-day stay in the evening, Theresa said, "I will take you to visit the school tomorrow. I have arranged for you to meet our director, Dr. Paul Dulac, in the afternoon."

"Okay." I didn't think too much about the whole thing.

The next day Theresa gave me some background of the International School of Beijing (ISB) community on the way to school. "We have very good students here. Parents are highly educated, and they are very involved and supportive." She continued, "We are well equipped, and teachers have all the supplies they need for their classes."

As we toured the campus, I was surprised. "This campus is pretty beat up compared to schools in the U.S."

"It's getting too old and too small. We are building a new school near the airport. Wait until you see the new campus!" Theresa showed her pride teaching at this school.

"A new school?"

"Yes. It's in the final stage now. There are more and more students wanting to get into our school every year. We need a bigger school. We are very selective of our students." There were high standards for admitting any students at ISB.

I saw smiles on students' faces around the campus. "Students look happy and content here."

Theresa took me to meet Dr. Dulac after visiting some classes and touring the school. I didn't bring a resume. I brought a book—*My Mentor Celine Robertson* written by a fifth grader Philip Yao—to share with him. Philip is the son of an old friend. I helped him with English when he first came to the U.S. from Taiwan. He wrote this book as a class project on a person who had great impact on him. He did a great job with the book—with a lot of information on me and many pictures.

After I talked with Dr. Dulac for a couple of minutes, he said to me,

"We don't have any opening at this time, but I will not let you go. I want to hook you now." We both laughed.

Theresa was surprised to receive the call from him before she even got back to her office. Diane Wong, the secretary for the Human Resource director, was stunned that I was offered a teaching job instantly.

Coming to Beijing to teach at ISB hadn't really been on my mind at all. I had been resisting the idea of teaching far away from family in this backward and rough communist country. I was even reluctant to make this trip to visit the school.

"When do I need to get back to you?" I was astonished by his offer and my unexpected response.

"Please do consider it and get back to us as soon as possible. We really would love to have you here at ISB. We will fax you the contract when you get back to the States."

Not until I saw students in classes, did I realize how much I missed working with the students and the action of teaching. "Okay, I will think about it and get back to you."

Am I really hooked?

After a week in Beijing, we went to visit Jason Christie in Shanghai. He looked happy, content, and confident. Jason spoke fluent Chinese. He not only made all the arrangements for us but also paid for everything during our visit, the Chinese hospitality.

New Adventure

I wasn't sure if I would like it in Beijing, and I didn't want Don to quit his job to go with me in case I didn't like it there. We decided I would go by myself first. If I liked it there, Don could join me later.

Don encouraged me to take the job. "Don't worry about me. I will be okay. It's a good opportunity for you."

My two daughters assured me, "We will be fine. We will check on Dad and each other." Joline was an electrical engineer at Chrysler in Rockford, Illinois and Andrea was a senior at Middlebury College in Vermont. Four of us would be at four different places.

I accepted the position and became the first Chinese language teacher hired from overseas at ISB.

Life indeed is full of surprises. If it is your destiny, you can't escape it no matter how hard you try to talk yourself out of it or to avoid it. Things sometimes just happen—beyond your understanding and your imagination.

In the fall of 2001, there were many changes with our lives. Joline started her new job as an engineer at a healthcare company in Milwaukee. Andrea started her first job after college to be a TAP (The Associate Progam) at an investment company in Los Angeles. I returned to the classroom—my passion and my joy—at the International School of Beijing in Beijing, China.

Another new chapter of my life and adventures unfolded…

Little Monkeys

I believe foundation building is the most critical process for learning anything. It has a lasting impact on students' learning, which greatly affects their interest and motivation later.

When I first went to teach at ISB, I was assigned to teach three high school classes and two middle school classes of 7th and 8th graders. I noticed the middle school students didn't have a solid foundation for the language. They had trouble writing basic sentences in Chinese.

I made a request to Theresa. "I would really like to teach sixth graders to build a solid foundation for them, if it is possible."

Theresa was a passionate teacher herself. She understood. "Sure! It will be excellent. I will see what I can do for next school year."

The following school year I switched to teach two classes of sixth graders. It was always a big transition and a big challenge for this age group—both mentally and emotionally—moving from elementary school to middle school. They have to adjust—from staying in one classroom to traveling to seven different classrooms and from one homeroom teacher to many teachers. A lot of teachers don't enjoy middle school students, but I think they are fun and exciting to work with. They are genuine and honest, and they let you know how they feel most of the time. It is a perfect time to guide them, train them, and mold them.

My sixth graders looked excited and restless. They seemed curious but scared. They appeared to be fun and innocent. They were hyper-undisciplined, like little monkeys—sparkles in their eyes showing curiosity and a desire to learn.

On the first day, I taught them the daily Chinese ritual—bowing to the teacher to show respect and appreciation before and after class, as I did when I grew up in Taiwan. I gave them clear guidelines and expectations for the class.

I started the first few lessons slowly and closely monitored each one's progress and learning. Being very consistent with rules and expectations with them, I did not let them get confused. With my background in special education I knew each student's strength, weakness, and learning style in a very short time. Constant encouragement and different approaches to reach individual students—differentiation in action—was the way I worked with my little monkeys.

One day, Seth, a bright American boy, didn't leave after class was dismissed. Instead, he approached my desk and bowed to me.

I stopped what I was doing. "What's up, Seth? May I help you?"

He had a big smile, from ear to ear. "*Lao Shi*, I just want you to know that I have learned more from you in a month than I did five years combined in elementary school."

"You are such a winner. You are doing a wonderful job." It was great to have this affirmation.

I saw sparkles in Seth's eyes—pleased and gratified. "*Xie xie ni* [Thank you], *Lao Shi*, for being my teacher."

"*Xie xie ni*! It's my pleasure to have you in my class, Seth. Keep up the good work!"

He bowed to me again before leaving. What a delightful and appreciative student.

The following fall, not long after school started, I was walking down the hallway after class. Connor, another American student about my height, caught up with me. He had his left arm around my shoulders walking with me side by side. "*Lao Shi*, you should be the Teacher of the Year again."

I laughed. "Thank you. Why?"

"I used to hate Chinese. Now Chinese is my favorite subject."

"Wonderful! You are doing a good job." I was happy that he enjoyed learning Chinese.

"I love it because you make our learning fun. You make it so easy and interesting for us to learn. I have learned a lot." A big smile filled his face.

"*Xie xie ni*. You have made my day!" My heart was warmed by his change.

One day I ran into Mr. Callahan, a middle school Physical Education teacher. He said, "Hey, you should be proud of yourself."

"Oh? Why?"

"I took some boys to a game over the weekend. Two of them were your students. They both said that you are their favorite teacher. Chinese is their favorite class."

"How sweet! Thank you for telling me." It was great to know they enjoy learning Chinese.

These were my sixth graders—my lovable little monkeys. They wanted to learn. They didn't mind how demanding I was. They worked hard and they were proud seeing their own progress. They appreciated teachers who helped them learn—getting rid of their frustration, gaining confidence, and seeing their own accomplishments.

The feeling of achievement, success, and self-assurance gained throughout the foundation building process will make anyone soar without fear, for a very long distance…

Sweet Little Monkeys

It was after lunch, ten minutes or so before class. One by one, students entered the classroom and took a white board and an eraser from the corner of the room. They then sat in their assigned seats. Every student started practicing the vocabulary projected on the screen, quietly.

This amazing sight appeared before me when I returned to my classroom after lunch, every day.

One day Theresa and I had lunch in the office next door. I asked her after lunch, "Want to see something incredible?"

She smiled and stood up. "Sure!"

"Come with me!" I took her to the doorway of my classroom to peek at what was happening—ten minutes before class.

She couldn't believe her eyes. She walked in the room and applauded the students. "Wow! You are such motivated learners!"

"Aren't they wonderful? I'm so proud of them."

All my sixth graders in Chinese II looked so happy and satisfied, but they didn't stop writing the characters.

"It's truly incredible!" Theresa couldn't believe what she witnessed.

"Nobody will believe they are the wildest little monkeys I have ever had."

This group, 19 of them, came to my class in the fall of 2006. They were a happy and active group. They were hyper and connected—bunches of good friends in the same class starting middle school together. It was a group of extremely "wild" little monkeys. They were restless and talkative. These "wild" monkeys were busy doing all the wrong things in class. It was indeed a challenging group.

I used different behavior modifications to reinforce their good behaviors, and I worked closely with both students and parents on unacceptable behaviors. It didn't take long for them to realize I was a demanding but caring teacher; I was strict but fair; I wanted them to learn; and I helped them to learn. They soon appreciated the fun of learning the language and the progress they made in class.

By the end of the first quarter they were so surprised and couldn't believe how much they had learned and could do. They could write 14-character complex sentences correctly and independently. At the end of the first semester they proudly showed off their 150-character essays to their parents and peers.

My little monkeys had great fun learning the language from different hands-on projects and different activities throughout the year.

For the Shopping Unit, everyone brought money and shopping list. We walked to the nearby open market where no merchant spoke English. They not only had to speak Chinese but also bargained for whatever they wanted to buy. They were so proud of themselves getting what they needed with a good price.

Opening restaurants in the classroom was the final project for the Food Unit. They prepared the decorations for their restaurants; they made their menus in Chinese; they prepared or bought the food based on their menus; and they made ordering tickets and receipts.

They were waiters and waitresses taking orders in Chinese on Restaurant Day. All the customers were Chinese—friends, teachers, or staff from different departments. I gave the customers fake Chinese money to use at the restaurants. They were to communicate with my students in Chinese. The customers voted for the best decorated restaurant and the best waiter or waitress. All restaurants also competed for "The Best Restaurant"—making the most profit. It was a fun project that went smoothly and successfully. Everyone—my little monkeys and all the customers—had a grand time. Students asked me afterward, "Can we do this again?"

For the Home and Family Unit, we went to visit one of the twenty-two mansions—a $3.4 million mansion—right next to our school. This four-story house had an elevator. Each student was to be a realtor to gather information at the mansion. They were to prepare an oral presentation for a promotional advertisement and a written one for the want-ad, including the price, names of different rooms, descriptions and special features of the house, etc.

I asked my little monkeys sometimes, "What do we do in this class?"

"Work hard and play hard!" they all yelled in unison.

Indeed, we worked hard and we played hard. I integrated many cultural activities in class as part of language learning. I taught them how to do Lion Dance and Dragon Dance in addition to many other Chinese activities and games. They became the most lively, active, and popular Lion Dance and Dragon Dance Troupe at ISB and in the community.

We were invited to perform at school and outside of school for special celebrations such as the Moon Festival and Chinese New Year. None of my little monkeys was late or missed the performances. They performed with all their hearts, like pros. Watching them share everything I taught them brought tears to my eyes, every time.

I truly enjoyed and loved my little monkeys. "Do you know I love you guys?"

All of them nodded their heads. They yelled loudly, "We love you more!"

Ben, a handsome American boy, was born in Beijing. He could speak Chinese fluently, but he couldn't read and write as well. He made tremendous progress in reading and writing, and he became a motivated and confident learner. Many days he didn't leave class until he sang to me the key phrase of one of the most popular Chinese love songs—pointing at me with his index finger just like the singer on TV, *"Wo ai ni, Wo ai ni, jiu xiang lao shu ai da mi..."* [I love you, I love you, like the mice love rice...]

What a charming and heartwarming gesture!

Valtter and Idalina were cute and playful twins—their father was from Finland and their mother was from Brazil. Ben was their buddy. They did juggling and a lot of other things together. They were always willing to perform juggling and other performances in addition to the Lion Dance and Dragon Dance, whenever and wherever I needed them for the special occasions I organized for the school and the community. They were my little shining stars.

This group of wild little monkeys—became my most motivated, hard-working, and fun sixth graders. What a joy to watch them grow!

Good time soars like flying arrows. It was time for them to move on to seventh grade.

Ben, Valtter, Idalina, Lana, Isabella, and all the other kids begged me almost every day in May, *"Lao Shi*, please teach us again next year. Please!"

"All of you are being promoted, but *Lao Shi* got retained—sixth grade again next year." They didn't know I already missed them.

The following year, whenever they went by my classroom, they yelled at the doorway, *"Wo ai ni!* [I love you.] *Wo men xiang ni!* [We miss you!]" Sometimes I found notes from them on my desk saying, *"Wo ai ni!"* signed by several students. One day when I came back from lunch, I saw *"Mrs. Robertson Rocks!"* on the board. How sweet!

Lana and Isabella often came by to hug me. "We miss you so much."

"I miss you guys too."

Theresa and the Chinese Language Department organized a surprise farewell party for my retirement from ISB on my birthday, April 10th, 2009. I was deeply touched and truly surprised with the creative and heartwarming program they planned for me. Surprisingly appearing in front of me were all my wild monkeys I missed so much, including

Asia who had moved away and came back from Hong Kong just for the occasion. They performed the Dragon Dance for more than one hundred guests—all my friends at ISB and Chinese friends in Beijing. I couldn't hold back my tears any longer—tears of heartfelt joy and sweet sorrow.

How I loved my little monkeys! My sweet little monkeys will be in my heart, always…

A Big Small World

United Nations

When I first went to Beijing to teach at the International School of Beijing (ISB) in the fall of 2001, I really didn't know what to expect from my time in Beijing. It was quite an adjustment for me, teaching at an international school and living in China—where I had been born and yet a foreign country to me.

I taught three high school classes and two middle school classes—seventh and eighth graders. ISB's students were from all over the world. I had a student from Iceland. The Australia ambassador's daughter was in my class. Many students were from countries I had never heard of, and they had to show me on the map where their countries were.

Most of the ISB faculty was from five English speaking countries—the U.S., Canada, the United Kingdom, New Zealand, and Australia. The majority of the Chinese language teachers came from China. The staff was from all over the world—different races and nationalities. ISB was indeed a very interesting and different community—like a little United Nations. I lived in a gated villa compound of western style apartments and townhouses, the Capital Paradise, near school. Most of the residents were expatriates from different countries.

I also needed to adjust my listening skills to different English accents in order to understand not only my students but also some of the staff. This made my teaching even more challenging and interesting.

It took me a long while to understand a teacher who had a very strong accent from an island in southern Australia. When he first talked to me, I didn't even realize that he was talking to me, since I couldn't understand him at all. I didn't respond. He must have thought that I ignored him. His son was in my high school class. I could understand his Chinese clearly, but I couldn't understand his English sometimes. It was so funny that I had to remind him sometimes when I had trouble understanding him, "Please speak Chinese." The whole class laughed whenever I did that.

Since Don didn't go with me, adjusting my life—living alone for the first time in my life—was quite an adventure. With an open heart, I accepted the surprises and with an open mind I welcomed new experiences. Theresa and new friends helped me feel at home slowly but surely. I learned to enjoy my life in Beijing—a city where I had endured horrible experiences not too long before.

Teaching at ISB was a totally different experience. I adjusted my teaching at ISB very quickly, and I enjoyed my students. One day during the third week of school, Theresa smiled as she walked toward me. "Guess what?"

"What?" I didn't know what she was up to.

"A parent just told me that the school should give you a lifetime contract." She laughed.

"Oh, yeah?" I laughed and wondered what had happened.

"Her daughter is in your high school class. She loves you! She said you are the best teacher she has ever had."

"Really?!" I was glad that my adjustment to a new life in China didn't affect my teaching.

ISB is also an International Baccalaureate (IB) school—students can either take six IB classes to get the IB diploma or take four classes for the certificate. It is like the AP program in the U.S., but it is more complex. It is a very intensive two-year program—compact and with college-level classes. Students who pass the IB tests with a score of six or seven can obtain credits in most of the colleges around the world. The passing score is four and the full score is seven.

In the following fall, I started teaching an IB Mandarin Ab Initio class, a beginner Chinese class for non-Chinese speaking students. I developed and integrated seventeen units for three semesters in order to prepare my students well for the required IB tests in three components: oral communication, comprehension, and writing. During the fourth semester I needed, not only to review all materials, but also to administer the oral test, and prepare my students for the other two tests. It was extremely stimulating and challenging for both students and teachers.

Each year, at the orientation for both IB students and their parents, I introduced the program, guidelines, and expectations.

"The passing grade is four. The highest score is seven. My goal for my students is six or seven."

I continued, "If your child follows me closely, I guarantee that he/she will be able to write a five-hundred-character essay and give a five-minute speech without looking at his/her writing, at the end of the third semester."

My students worked very hard, and the test results were very strong, above world average, for the seven years I taught IB classes. My last group's average—before my retirement from ISB—was 6.85 out of 7.

My students attended different colleges in different parts of the world. Katie went to Columbia University in the U.S, and she did well with the placement tests. When she came back to visit, she told me, "I was placed in the third level Chinese class. I could do it without any trouble."

I was very proud of this bright and motivated student. "You are such a winner!"

Katie went back to China after college, and she is currently working in Beijing.

Robin attended the University of California in Davis. He wrote me an email. "*Lao Shi*, I want to thank you. I was placed in the fifth level Chinese class. My teachers and classmates were so impressed with my Chinese."

Gregg Smith, the ISB elementary school principal, came to see me one day. "I thought you might want to know Justine's Chinese teacher moved her to the highest level Chinese class after one week. She is the only non-Asian student in the class."

His daughter, Justine, was a smart and diligent student—one of my top students. She went back to Australia for college. "Impressive! She is such a winner! Tell her I am so proud of her."

In the spring of 2006 after the IB tests, Mr. Magnusson came to see me. He was the father of my Icelandic student, Bjarni. I was happy to see him. "Congratulations! Your son did a great job."

He laughed. "It was amazing! I came to thank you. When you told us at the orientation last year that my son would be able to write a 500-character essay and give a five-minute speech by the end of third semester, I didn't believe you. But he really did it. Thank you so much. He gained so much confidence being in your class."

"He is a bright kid. He can do whatever he wants to do, with true effort. I really pushed them hard. Guess what?"

"What?"

"Your son came to thank me also." I smiled.

"He did?" He seemed surprised.

"Yeah!" I told him what happened.

Earlier in the spring, Bjarni came to me. "*Lao Shi*, thank you very much. You not only taught me the language but also showed me how to put forth effort in whatever I do. I learned to work hard with all my subjects."

He continued, "I have learned so much from you. You have changed my attitude. Thank you, *Lao Shi*."

"Thank you. You did it yourself." I saw the changes in him also. I was pleased to know that he applied and expanded what he learned in my class—always set high expectations and strive for excellence—to his life. What a smart young man.

He was excited as he told me his future plan with the language. "I decided to stay in Beijing to spend a year to study at the University of Beijing before going home for college."

"Great! It will really reinforce what you have learned." It was a wise move.

"Thank you again for everything you have done for me." He bowed to me and left.

The following year Bjarni came to visit me many times while studying at the University of Beijing. He conversed with me in Chinese, fluently. He looked happy and confident. I still remember the grin on his face—from ear to ear.

Adhira, an outstanding student from India, found me on Facebook not long ago. She told me, "I think of you often. I am getting my PhD degree in Chinese at the University of Chicago."

I wrote back, "I am so proud of you!"

Sensational

The international school students at ISB don't usually stay in any city or country very long. They attend different international schools in different parts of the world—wherever their parents get transferred—which happens very often. Most of them speak more than two languages—English, their native tongues, and whatever languages they can learn. Some of them don't have a home base in their own countries. They live and travel around the world. They are indeed global citizens. With their exposure, connections, and experiences, they will continue to be global—whatever they do and wherever they are in the future. I don't doubt some of them will make leaders somewhere in the world someday.

Most of the international school teachers move from one international school to another. Many of them stay in one part of the world for a few years and then move to another part of the world to teach for a few years. What a way to see the world and to be global and well connected. On Facebook, we keep in close contact with friends—the ISB Alum. Suzanna, a friend currently teaching in Japan after leaving ISB, received birthday greetings on Facebook from friends in twenty-four countries. When I was in China, people asked me often, "Where do you like it better, the U.S. or China?"

"I like both. When I am in China, I enjoyed what the U.S. doesn't have. When I am in the U.S, I enjoy what China doesn't have."

We spent summer and winter breaks in the U.S. I enjoyed the space, the fresh air, clean water, the blue sky, and all kinds of salad. Driving was one thing I missed in China.

In China, I had a helper doing the housework. I dared not drive in China. We hired a car with a driver on weekends to enjoy Beijing. Masseuses came to the house to give me massages regularly. I had my body adjusted weekly at a Chinese medicine clinic by an excellent and caring Chinese medicine doctor, Dr. Yan. Acupuncture treatment helped my seasonal allergies and other problems without my taking any medication. We enjoyed cuisines not only from different parts of China but also from around the world. I had my hair done weekly at the salon—I seldom did in the U.S.

I started to enjoy Beijing as I adjusted my life gradually. Don took an early retirement and joined me two years later. His fluent Chinese and a map enabled him to explore Beijing independently, every day. Having a helper to take care of housework, he lived a totally free, luxurious, and pampered retired life during his six years in Beijing.

We wanted to see more of China. After my first not-so-good trip with a couple of friends, I decided to plan my own trips. I organized my trips to places I wanted to see, and many friends joined us. Whenever we had a week-long break—two to three times a year—we traveled around China and neighboring countries.

Our traveling pals—Liming Wong, Betty and Tien Shaw, Sabrina Yeung, Cindy Campbell, Barbara Hurwick, Shirley and Stanley Lam, Susanne Voigt, Wendy Chou, Francoise Nedellec, Mary Ann Drakulovic, and many more—became our friends throughout the years.

We laughed so hard when guys went on one side of road and girls went on the other side of the road in Tibet to take care of nature calls—there were no rest stops. At the Yue Ya Shan in Gebi Desert on the Silk Road, I screamed the whole time on the camel ride on the edge of the mountain. I was the only one having a person holding the rein and leading my camel while the rest of them looked like locals on the camels. They laughed at me whenever I screamed at scary spots. We saw the changes in the three gorges of Yang Tze River—many villages under water and different water lines. The Yellow River was even more muddy and rapid than I imagined.

Climbing up more than one thousand steps in the huge cave in Guiyang was quite a challenge. The hot spring felt great after walking down the endless narrow steps of steep Lu Shan [Mt. Lu]. We shopped for porcelain in Jingdezen where china was most famous, and we bought the best silk and gorgeous embroidery in Suzhou. Huang

Shan [Mt. Huang] looked just like the paintings many Chinese artists painted. We sweated and laughed in the rainforest in Yunnan. More than fifty people joined us to go to see the spectacular ice sculptures in Haerbin—the China winter land. We enjoyed the gorgeous beach on Hainan Island—the farthest south of China.

In Vietnam, we tried very hard to guess what the tour guide with his broken English tried to tell us about his country and our daily itinerary. We enjoyed tranquility at the temples in Burma. People in Thailand were friendly and peaceful. The trip to Egypt to see the Pyramids was like being in a dream—unreal and different.

It was great fun spreading our footprints side by side with our traveling pals in China and other countries. They filled our lives with moments of pleasure and unforgettable and joyful memories.

Sometimes before one trip was over, some of them couldn't wait for our next trip. "Celine, where are we going next time?"

"Where do you want to go?" I laughed and asked for ideas and suggestions. I was flexible since there were so many places we could go and see.

I worked with the most reliable and trustworthy travel agents, Zhen Yan and Wendy Pan, for all our trips. One day Zhen Yan suggested, "So many people travel with you each time. You could have a free trip if you add your expenses on the other travelers."

"Don't do that. I will pay my expenses like others. Just lower everyone's cost." I enjoyed the trips and my traveling pals. I organized the trips to have fun with them, not to have free trips. I paid for all my trips in full.

Our traveling buddies made our trips and lives more colorful and memorable in China. Although most of them left Beijing after Don and I left, we still have close contact with one another. We hope to travel somewhere in the world together again someday.

Life was very interesting and exciting in China, and we truly enjoyed our lives there. When I decided to retire from ISB to join our two daughters in the U.S., Don was sad. "Economy is not good. Why do you want to go back?"

"What does it have to do with me? I am not looking for a job."

I knew he enjoyed Beijing so much—using his Chinese, searching through ancient Chinese coins for his collection, enjoying great food and beer, and living a spoiled life—of course he didn't want to come back to the U.S.

Casey, our first grandchild, was turning three. Nothing can top being together with family—especially playing with Casey. We came back, not to Lincoln, Nebraska—our home since 1973—but to join our two daughters to start our new life in Milwaukee, Wisconsin in June 2009.

Teaching at ISB—a mini United Nations; witnessing China's rapid and amazing development to get ready for the Olympics of 2008; and living a pampered and exciting life in Beijing—a fast growing international city; my life was enriched tremendously and my perspectives expanded a great deal in those eight years.

I truly feel blessed to have had the opportunity to teach at ISB and live in Beijing for such a long time. My great appreciation and thanks to Theresa for her trust in me and her persistence—not giving up on me for three years.

Life is truly beautiful and exciting when you accept opportunities with an open mind and a welcoming heart. Teaching students and having friends from all over the world, including great friends from China, indeed enhanced my life. All the new experiences enabled me to discover the world with a bigger heart. It helped me understand China and its people better. I felt and related to my heritage more profoundly when I returned to the land where I was born.

My world became bigger and yet smaller at the same time—a sensational big small world!

Celine, Don, & Chelsea on a camel ride in Gebi (Gobi) Desert

Celine and traveling pals in Yunnan

Chapter 7
The True, the Good, and the Beautiful

和

A Big Sister
A Beautiful Couple
Motherly Lady
A Dear Uncle
Noble Love
Life Savers
Blessed
Spiritual Journey
Enriched
Dairyland
Borrowed Eyes
Dreams
The True, the Good, and the Beautiful

A Big Sister

To a flower grown in the greenhouse, a summer shower may feel like a storm. To a 17-year-old girl grown up in a sheltered home, going away from home for college was like an exile to Siberia.

I waved a teary good-bye to my family and started the journey to my independence at Providence College in Taichung—five hours from Taipei by train.

Through one of my older brother Karl's buddies in medical school, I met Alison Mok in college. Alison was a sophomore and two years my senior. She laughed a lot, and she looked mature, confident, and intelligent.

Alison is a person of integrity—genuine and straight forward. She might sound sharp to people who are out of line at times, but she has a tender caring heart. A Chinese description about such a person—*The mouth is sharp as a knife, the heart is soft as dou fu* [tofu]—describes her perfectly.

Alison was my first trusted friend in college. Little did we know then we would be forever connected.

Whenever I was homesick, Alison comforted me and made me smile again. Whenever I needed advice, I went to her. When I was sick, she was the one who took me to see the doctor or nurse. When I screamed while getting a shot, she held my hand, scolding me and laughing at me. She was the one I leaned on throughout my freshman year and many, many years after.

Alison came to the U.S. for graduate school a year before I did. After she obtained her master's degree in counseling, she became an outstanding counselor in public schools.

When I first arrived in the U.S, she was in Kalamazoo, Michigan—her second year of graduate school. I was in Edwardsville, Illinois.

The first thing she told me, "Don't hold hands with any female friends as we did back home. It is not acceptable here." She gave me tips for studying and surviving in the U.S. Alison sent me a package containing things I needed to start my new life here. She was more than a friend. She was a caring sister.

Alison and I lived in different states throughout the years. We seldom saw each other. But we always kept in close contact.

In 1983, my husband Don had colon cancer. I was devastated emotionally and physically throughout the ordeal. Even though Don was considered cured after his surgery, I lived in the shadow of despair—frightened and worried—for a long time afterward. Although I was surrounded by people, no one knew my untold feelings, not even Don.

One day Alison called me. After talking with me for a few minutes, she sensed something was wrong with me. "Celine, you sound sad and depressed. You need to get out of it before it gets worse. Exercise will help you." I couldn't hold back my tears any more. We talked for more than an hour.

I followed her advice and joined a gym. Alison gave me a one year subscription to the magazine *Guideposts*. Realization of my emotional condition, exercise, and *Guideposts'* uplifting stories helped me get out of the depression that I hadn't recognized or acknowledged.

When I was honored as the 1997 Nebraska Teacher of the Year, Alison came from Schenectady, New York, to Lincoln, Nebraska, to attend the award ceremony.

I was to be honored by President Clinton at the White House in April 1997. At the same time, our younger daughter Andrea was invited by Middlebury College in Vermont to attend a special program designed for potential students. I didn't know what to do. I told Alison about the situation.

Alison said to me, "Don't worry about it. Have Andrea come to our place. We will take care of her." They made all the detailed arrangements for her. After so many years, Alison still was the person I leaned on.

With Alison and Walter as Andrea's acting parents at Middlebury

College, I had nothing to worry about. Don and I enjoyed the State Teachers of the Year program in D.C. I had a life-time memorable moment, meeting and talking with President Clinton at the White House.

When Alison retired as a high school counselor in 2003, I invited her and her husband to visit me in Beijing. They stayed with me. Don was still in Nebraska. One morning I had a dizzy spell that lasted a long time. They urged me to see a doctor. I didn't want to go.

Alison insisted, "You'd better find out what the problem is."

"I don't even know where and how to find a doctor." I had seen only a Chinese medicine doctor in Beijing.

"Xie He Hospital is the oldest hospital in Beijing. It should be all right. Let's go!"

When we got there, we were shocked. There was such a stressful and frightening scene in the lobby—a crowd of several hundred people waiting in different lines. We didn't even know where to start, what to do, and how to find a doctor. I would have turned back if Alison and Walter hadn't been with me.

We finally found out—after half an hour circling around in the lobby—there was a VIP department located on the second floor where you paid twenty times more than common people to register. There was no line.

The doctor was very thorough and wonderful. But the facility and the system in the hospital were so different that it made me very uncomfortable.

It turned out my blood pressure was high. When I had a scan done on my brain in the U.S. the following summer, it showed I had a mild stroke. Two of my brothers had bad strokes a few years later. It still gives me chills whenever I think what if Alison and Walter weren't with me when I had the dizzy spell. Alison came to my rescue again.

Alison is an energetic, conscientious person of strong principles and high standards. She is witty with a great sense of humor. We are very much alike in many ways—having high self-expectations, a sense of responsibility, and a passion for our professions.

She was a dedicated and caring school counselor for many years.

I urged her, "You are still very young and you have so much to offer. Why don't you join me and be a counselor here at the International School of Beijing (ISB)? Wouldn't it be a beautiful blessing if we could be together again?"

She listened and pondered for a while. "I will think about it."

The following school year, out of thirty-six candidates, Alison was chosen to be one of our middle school counselors. Students loved her, parents trusted her, and the staff respected her.

When Alison's buddies and roommates in college—Mimi, Lena, and Rosary, visited her in 2005, Alison invited me to join them for the reunion.

There was so much to catch up on, since I had not seen them since college. We laughed and screamed remembering our college lives together. Alison asked her friends, "Do you still remember how Celine was when she was a freshman?"

Mimi chuckled. "How could we forget?!" They all burst into laughter.

I was puzzled. "Why? What?"

Mimi continued, "Whenever we saw you approach our place, we told Alison, 'Crying Baby is coming'."

I couldn't believe I earned such a nickname. "What?! Did you really? " I laughed so hard with them.

Alison knows me the best. She exclaimed, "Celine has changed the most throughout the years."

I agreed. "No one believes I was such a wimpy crybaby when I was young." It was such an amusement recalling with old friends how dependent I was when I was in college.

Alison has been a true friend ever since we met when I was seventeen. She feels my pain whenever I struggle; she shares my joy without the slightest jealousy; and she stands by me no matter what, whenever, and wherever. She is not only a treasured friend but also a beloved sister.

It was truly a great blessing to be with Alison again—teaching at the same school and living in the same compound for two years in Beijing—after more than four decades of separation.

What a heavenly gift to have Alison—a God-sent big sister and a forever best friend—in my life!

Alison & Celine celebrate Chinese New Year at ISB

A Beautiful Couple

I often said to friends, "The genuine kind people are the people who care for you and help you even though you have nothing to offer in return." They are the people who warm your heart, give you hope, and make your world more beautiful.

I was apprehensive the day before I left for Chicago to look for a summer job—my first summer in the U.S. I worried about the giant step I was to take—alone in a big city looking for a job. Mrs. Bao Hua Luan called, "Be sure to come to dinner tonight. Our tradition is to have *jiao zi* [dumplings] whenever a family member leaves home." She is a northerner from Shanxi province in China.

Tears rolled down on my cheek. They treated me as a family member. "Thank you. I will be there." After one year, the toughest year of my life, in the U. S., I was still homesick, feeling all alone and scared.

Mrs. Luan, six years my senior, was a traditional Chinese lady. She married Dr. David Luan, an economics professor, in December of 1967 in Taiwan. I met them shortly after she arrived in Edwardsville, Illinois—where Dr. Luan taught and I attended school. We became very close friends. She invited me often to share the warmth of their home.

Although I went back to see them only once since we moved away in 1969 after obtaining my master's degree, I've never forgotten how their caring friendship helped me survive the most challenging year of my life.

I think of them often and phone them regularly to check on them. I called them recently. Mrs. Luan answered the phone. "This is Celine. How are you doing? How is Dr. Luan?" Her husband is seventeen years her senior.

Mrs. Luan laughed. "Hi! How are you? Dr. Luan is 93 this year. He is doing great!"

"How wonderful! How are the kids and grandchildren?" They raised two outstanding children, a boy and a girl. Both of them are physicians. Their spouses are also doctors. Each couple has two children.

"Fine, fine! We had a family reunion on a cruise not long ago to celebrate Dr. Luan's birthday." She sounded happy and proud telling me how everyone in the family was doing.

We talked for a long time, laughing and remembering our time together decades ago in Edwardsville, Illinois. Mrs. Luan giggled and said, "I am not like you. I don't have a career."

She dedicated her life to her family. It has touched me deeply witnessing the happy and harmonious life she and Dr. Luan have had together.

"Your career is a great one. Look how happy and healthy Dr. Luan is. You have two wonderful children. Your love and dedication to your family is the greatest achievement anyone could have," I complimented her with true respect and admiration.

Before saying good-bye I told her, "Thank you and Dr. Luan again for sharing the love and warmth of your home with me when I needed it the most. I will never forget your kindness and friendship."

"You are welcome. We had so much fun with you. I tell people about you often."

Dr. and Mrs. David Luan made my tough life easier; they reinforced my faith in people; and they made the world more wonderful for me.

Motherly Lady

When I first came to the U.S., I rented a room sharing with a roommate from an American family. One morning my landlady, Mrs. Claudia McIntyre, said to me as I walked to the kitchen, "I heated your milk for you. It's on the stove."

"Thank you. My mother always prepared hot milk for us back in Taiwan."

Mrs. McIntyre knew I was homesick again. "A couple of friends and I are going to the woods to pick mushrooms in a little bit. Do you want to come along?" Her youngest child of four, Matthew, was two.

"It sounds fun. Sure, I will go with you." I thought it was better being with people than being homesick alone.

I was so excited when we got to the woods. It was a new experience for me. I had a great time picking the mushrooms until I saw a worm under one. I ran out of the woods screaming so loud that it startled everyone. Mrs. McIntyre came after me holding Matthew and asked, "What happened? Are you all right?"

I was still shaking. "There was a worm!"

Everyone burst into laughter. Little two-year-old Matthew said, "Don't be scared. It won't bite!" How embarrassing!

Mrs. McIntyre was very thoughtful and helpful always. She changed sheets for me regularly. One day I noticed other roommates changed their own sheets. I asked them, "Are we supposed to change our own sheets?" I didn't even own sheets.

"Yes." They said it together.

I admired this kind, hardworking, wise American lady with great gratitude. One day I was chatting with Mrs. McIntyre. "Thank you so much for taking good care of me. I will always remember what you and your family have done for me."

"You are welcome. If my daughter were overseas, I would appreciate people being nice to her." What an empathetic caring lady!

When Don and I decided to get married, I knew nothing about the American tradition for a wedding. Don was born and grew up here, but he didn't know any more than I did. His parents were in Wisconsin. Everyone else around us assumed we knew what to do for an American wedding.

The day before the wedding, there was a house full of guests—all from out of state. After the rehearsal, it was dinner time. We didn't make any arrangements, and we didn't have any food. It was too late to do anything or to go anyplace. I didn't know what to do with our guests. Mrs. McIntyre said, "Don't worry about it. Let me see what I can do."

She went to refrigerator and took out all the food she had. She cooked the dinner for us. We even had bacon! It stills makes me laugh whenever I think about how ignorant and unprepared we were.

Mrs. McIntyre and her family also prepared everything for our wedding reception for 150 people. I will forever remember and appreciate her motherly care and kindness.

Betty Treat was another person I will never forget. She was Mrs. McIntyre's good friend and a neighbor. Betty's husband was a minister. They had two children. Both Betty and I majored in special education, and we took many classes together. She always gave me ride to and from school since all our classes were in the evening and I had no transportation. Although I lost contact with her, I never forgot her—a kind person with a beautiful heart, providing me rides to classes.

Mrs. McIntyre and Mrs. Treat were genuine caring American ladies. They helped me—a girl who had nothing to offer in return—start a new life in the U.S.

A Dear Uncle

When I was growing up in Taiwan, I was envious of people who had aunts and uncles. I always wondered how it would be—being spoiled by an aunt or uncle.

Uncle Lu was the only uncle I knew. He was the only one of Father's six siblings who went to Taiwan after the Communist took over China in 1949. He was killed in a car accident when I was very young. Mother's three brothers didn't get out of China. We had no aunts or uncles around us while growing up in Taiwan.

Shortly after I arrived in Illinois for graduate school, my family met Mr. Barry Brennon, an American businessman, in Taiwan. Father mentioned in a letter that Mr. Brennon would contact me.

One day I got a call from a man, "I am Barry Brennon. I met General, your father, in Taiwan."

I got so excited. "Yes! My father told me about you. How are they?"

"They are doing great!" He continued, "They are very worried about you. I promised General I would check on you. I will come by to see you sometime next week. I will call you before I come." His voice sounded sincere and caring.

"Great! Thank you. I look forward to meeting you."

He came to see me the following week. He was a big man—6'3" tall. He looked very kind and friendly. I called him "Uncle Barry" respectfully—my father's friend—the Chinese way.

Uncle Barry and his wife had five children, and they lived in Indiana. He owned a successful company doing business internationally. He traveled to Taiwan, Southeast Asia, and in the U.S. frequently. Whenever he had a chance, he called or came to visit me.

Uncle Barry kept his promise to my father. He checked on me and spoiled me throughout the years. I felt very close to him and could share with him whatever was on my mind—worries or happiness, like a niece sharing with an uncle. He attended our wedding; he came to see our kids; and for four decades he always made an effort to swing by wherever we lived. On June 20, 1998 he gathered his family and neighbors to cheer for me when I was awarded the American Teacher Award—Outstanding Foreign Language Teacher of the Year, broadcast on the Disney Channel.

Uncle Barry passed away peacefully in his sleep at the age of 87. He was the only uncle whom I'd really gotten to know and love.

Uncle Barry's fatherly caring brought sunshine to my life. His love made my world more wonderful. Remembering him brings warmth to my heart and smiles to my face, and missing his love brings tears to my eyes.

Noble Love

Was there anyone in your life who crossed your path briefly, and yet left a lasting effect on you? Has a selfless love moved your heart and touched your soul?

In 1972 after teaching three years in Pocatello, Idaho, we moved to Wichita, Kansas where my twin sister Irene and her husband Lawrence lived. I was offered a teaching position as a special education teacher at John Marshall Junior High School.

Jean Scott was a middle-aged English teacher. Jean embraced me and made me feel welcome instantly when we met at the first staff meeting. She took me under her wing and helped me however she could to get me situated in the new environment. She invited us to her home to meet her family, her husband Tom, and two beautiful daughters who were older than I.

Jean provided me information about the school—helpful tips and important procedures. She told me about the significant school culture. "This is a school with racial conflicts. We have police patrol the hallways." Her friendship and assistance helped me make a smooth transition at my second school in the U.S.

Mr. James Dye was our principal. He was older than my father. Mr. Dye was a pleasant, friendly, and genuinely caring gentleman. On the day when I became a U.S. citizen, he surprised me with a red-white-blue corsage. Eula May Nunemacher—the school librarian and a friend—presented it to me at the courthouse where the ceremony took place. In the evening, Mr. and Mrs. Dye invited us for dinner at their house. They also invited my friends, Jean and her husband Tom, and Eula May. They made the celebration of my special day extraordinary and memorable. How sweet and thoughtful!

In the spring of the following year, Jean found out she had terminal liver cancer. At the same time Don had a job offer from the University of Nebraska in Lincoln. We were to move and leave my dear friend Jean in the summer. I was profoundly devastated and saddened.

The following year after moving to Nebraska, we went back to Wichita a few times to check on Jean. She was in tremendous pain with a swollen liver, yet was most courageous and gracious throughout the ordeal. She greeted and welcomed us each time with sweet smiles as always.

At our last visit she told me, "Celine, I don't want Tom to be alone and sad after I am gone. I have arranged for our long-time dear friend who has been widowed for many years to marry Tom after I die." I was in awe. I was astonished and genuinely touched by my dear friend's selfless true love for her husband. What a beautiful loving soul!

Tom called shortly after our visit, "Jean has left us." A year later he married the lady Jean had picked for him.

We lived in Wichita, Kansas for only one year. But the friendship I treasured and the noble love I witnessed remains in my heart always.

Life Savers

A truly exceptional doctor to me is a doctor who not only has skills, but also has passion for the profession and compassion for his patients. A genuine caring doctor is a doctor whom you trust and feel comfortable talking to.

When I noticed my eyes were getting tired easily and words looked blurry when I read, I went to see an eye doctor. The doctor looked serious. He was very loud—almost yelling the whole time while checking on my eyes and talking to me. I wondered why he did that. I almost said to him, "I am here to check my eyes, not my ears."

Then I realized something—he assumed I couldn't understand English. Some people believe talking louder can change the language for the person who speaks a different language. Some people also tend to underestimate such a person's intelligence and abilities.

I laughed while sharing this experience with a good colleague friend, Diane Reinch. She chuckled. "Some people are funny. Go to my doctor, Dr. Mario Mota. You will like him." Dr. Mota, a doctor with Hispanic heritage, was friendly and caring. My husband and I trusted this skillful doctor. He took great care of us for many years before we moved to Wisconsin.

When I was expecting Joline, I was very sick for nine months. The principal of the school where I taught gave me a key to the nurse's office in case I got too sick to teach. But I missed only five days of school.

The gynecologist—a very cold doctor—never smiled at me throughout the care of my pregnancy. He never asked if I was going to nurse and didn't prepare me for it—physically, mentally or emotionally. I was ignorant and knew nothing about nursing. When Joline was born, I had a terrible time nursing her. Each time after half hour of nursing, my nipples were cracked and bleeding. The nurse weighed Joline after each feeding to check her intake of milk. Each time Joline had only gained two ounces.

Being an inexperienced mother, I was especially worried that Joline would starve. When I told the doctor, he responded coldly, "Maybe you shouldn't nurse." Just like that! Not a word more of comfort or encouragement. What a doctor! I felt helpless and hopeless.

When our family doctor Dr. Eugene Schwenke came to check on me and Joline shortly after the gynecologist left, he picked up my robe from the floor—gynecologist just ignored it and walked by. He smiled, "Baby looks good and well. How are you doing?"

"I have trouble nursing the baby. She will starve." I started to cry.

"Baby is doing fine. Don't worry. It will get better. I will arrange for a nurse to help you."

I stopped sobbing. "Okay. Thank you." A nurse came to help me and gave cream for my cracked nipples right away. She also showed me some tips for nursing. I felt more relaxed and relieved. What a difference between doctors.

When I was expecting our second daughter Andrea, Dr. Schwenke took care both of us. A compassionate doctor makes such a difference in people's lives. Dr. Schwenke was the doctor who was alert and took prompt action on Don's colon cancer in 1983 and saved Don's life. We are forever in debt to him. When I introduced him to my friends at Andrea's wedding in 2009, I said, "This is Dr. Schwenke. He is the doctor who saved Don's life."

He was our family doctor since we moved to Lincoln, Nebraska in 1973. When he decided to be a doctor in the emergency room of a hospital in the late 1990s, we were totally lost and devastated. We couldn't find another family doctor like Dr. Schwenke.

Before he left us, I had a female problem, Dr. Schwenke referred me to Dr. Robert Byington, a reputable gynecologist. Dr. Schwenke wrote a letter to him before my appointment. Later I found out they are good friends. Dr. Byington was just like Dr. Schwenke—kind, compassionate, and humane.

It was so easy to talk to Dr. Byington. I asked him at one of my annual check-ups when I was in my early 40s, "I heard that when a woman goes through menopause, she will have emotional changes or problems."

He looked at me for a while and smiled. "You won't have that problem!" We both laughed. Doctor knows best. I didn't have much trouble when I reached the age years later.

When I decided to take early retirement from Lincoln Public Schools in 2000, most people said, "Congratulations!"

But not Dr. Byington. He said, "Teaching is your talent, you shouldn't have retired so young." I was surprised and profoundly moved that he knew and cared about my teaching career. He must have read all the articles about me in the newspapers.

"I just need a break." I started teaching again a year later and continued for eleven more years.

When we moved to Milwaukee to join our two daughters in 2009, I went to say good-bye to him. "Thank you for taking great care of me. I will miss you. Don't retire, people need you!"

"Okay!" We laughed and hugged. I already missed him, my doctor and friend.

We are the same age. In 2012, I finally retired. In 2015, Dr. Byington is still practicing medicine and taking great care of his patients. How fortunate his patients are!

Now in Milwaukee I have a thorough, caring internist, Dr. Elizabeth Davies, as my primary doctor; Dr. R. Flickinger, a skillful and friendly doctor, to take care of my eyes; and a highly respected cardiologist to monitor my heart.

My family has been blessed with these extraordinary doctors who, not only have passion and compassion, but also have caring hearts and beautiful souls. We can always trust and lean on them.

Blessed

If the colleagues you work with closely are your friends, it not only makes your job easier but also makes your work more satisfying and your life more enjoyable. Some of them may become your life-long buddies.

New Adventure

In 1974, I started out as a special education teacher at Everett Jr. High [now Park Middle School] in Lincoln, Nebraska. The following year, Carol Nemeroff, a young lady about my age from Pennsylvania, became our assistant principal. Carol was a thorough, supportive administrator. She was intelligent with keen observations, and she was energetic and fun. Carol truly cared about the wellbeing of teachers and students.

She recognized teachers' creativity, talents, and strengths. She helped initiate many impressive programs. She identified me as a *master teacher* in an appraisal after several class observations during her first year as our assistant principal.

In 1986, an article from the Geraldine Dodge Foundation in an education publication caught her eye. The foundation offered three-year funds to help school districts that shared their vision to establish four-year Chinese language programs in secondary schools in the U.S. When Carol saw it, she grasped a great opportunity for Lincoln Public Schools [LPS].

She presented the information and a proposal to the district administration. "This will be a wonderful program for LPS students. Celine is an excellent teacher, and she had taught English as a second language in Taiwan. She is the perfect person to establish such a program."

She convinced the administration. We got the funding in 1987. At that time, there were only a handful of secondary schools offering Chinese in the U.S. I joined the pioneers to establish the Chinese program for LPS at Irving Jr. High and Everett Jr. High in 1988.

When I first started the programs, the school district world languages consultant didn't treat me professionally. She pushed me around the way I had never experienced from anyone before. She told people, "Celine is going to do whatever I want her to do!" It made me very uncomfortable and angry.

I was no longer the young girl who had just come to the U.S. and didn't know how to protect and defend herself. I decided to consult with the Lincoln Education Association [LEA], the teachers association, to see what rights I had. The LEA president said to me, "We have an issue here. I will go with you to see one of the superintendents." He then made arrangements and accompanied me to see the Superintendent of Human Resources.

I shared my concerns with the superintendent, and I made a request, "I would like to have something in writing to state that after three years of district's commitment to the Geraldine Dodge Foundation, I will have the choice either to stay with the Chinese program or go back to special education." There were many variables, and this document was my protection.

Later I heard the superintendent asked the consultant afterward, "Celine has been in the district for a long time with a good reputation. What did you do to her? "

The consultant was very angry. She called me. I responded calmly, "Don't I have the right to find out what my rights are?" It shut her up.

When Carol asked me what had happened, I trusted Carol and told her about the whole thing. Carol said to me, "Celine, she doesn't know you like I know you. She is not your superior. If she is not treating you right again, just come to me. I will deal with her." It was great to know Carol would always back me up.

In 1987, my mother had a vicious brain tumor, and I was devastated. We six siblings in the U.S. took turns to go back to Taiwan to take care of her in the hospital. Carol helped me get a one-month extended leave so that I could take care of my mother in Taiwan. What a caring administrator!

Carol and I have been good friends since we met. She moved many times, and my life had many changes. We lost contact for years. I am so glad we found each other and are reconnected again. Carol never told me about her initiative proposal to the district and all the effort she put forth for the Chinese language program until she visited me in the spring of 2015—28 years later.

I was touched and surprised. "I had no idea you were the one who made it happen." No one had told me Carol was behind everything.

She giggled and looked at me. "I was just glad that Lincoln Public Schools approved my proposal and you got to establish such a unique program."

Being a pioneer in Chinese language teaching in American secondary schools presented me not only a platform to share my heritage but also a gateway to national and international leadership. It gave me challenges, stimulation, and satisfaction. It also brought me fulfillment and honors.

Carol's belief in me provided me affirmation and opportunities. Thus, both my teaching and life have been enriched enormously. I owe all this to Carol Nemeroff—a dear friend and a superb administrator.

Visions

I am a person of many dreams and visions. When I have a dream, I make it come true. When I have a vision, I make it happen. When I have energy, I make it positive. When I have something extra or special, I always share with people.

In 1989, as my junior high students from Irving Jr. High and Everett Jr. High went to high school, I followed them to Lincoln High School [LHS].

I had envisioned a couple of new ideas I wanted to do with my students—no one had done with them previously and not likely in the future, before my first group of Chinese language students graduated from high school.

Jean Peterson, one of the assistant principals at Lincoln High School, worked closely with me. I shared my first vision with her. "I integrated many Chinese cultural activities in class. Students really enjoy learning them."

Jean smiled. "I noticed that. They are fun and interesting activities. I wish I could learn them too!"

"Wouldn't it be great if American students share the Chinese cultural activities with peers at LHS and students in other schools?"

She looked curious. "Yes, it will be wonderful if they can do that. What do you have in mind?"

I loved sowing seeds. "My students in the Chinese program can demonstrate and share with LHS students and staff the Chinese cultural activities that they learn in class. I would also like to reach out to students from other schools."

Jean looked excited. "It sounds unique! How do you do it?"

"We can set up two assemblies for LHS students and one for students from other schools."

"It would be a great experience for the whole school and students in the district. Let's do it!" Jean got more excited.

"I will name the program *Chinese Kaleidoscope*. No auditions! Every student in the Chinese program will participate."

"What a great idea! Just tell me how I can help!"

I started working on all the details. Jean helped me to set up two assemblies for LHS and one for 1,200 students from different schools in the district. In the spring of 1992, my students presented our very first *Chinese Kaleidoscope* to celebrate the Chinese New Year. It was a 40-minute Chinese cultural program including dragon dance, martial arts, Chinese history through historic fashion show, dances, and songs. Everyone in the Chinese program participated and demonstrated, including me, performing Tai Chi Sword.

Many people commented after the program. "Congratulations! It was awesome!"

My students were so proud receiving compliments throughout the year from their teachers and peers. They asked me. "Are we going to do this again?"

Jean helped us start a new tradition for LHS and Lincoln Public Schools. Every other year my students shared the Chinese cultural activities they learned in class with 3,600 people at our *Chinese Kaleidoscope* programs.

Lincoln High School Chinese Kaleidoscope Program

Fine China

Lincoln High students from Chinese foreign language classes perform the Kung Fu Fan dance as part of "Chinese Kaleidoscope," a multicultural presentation Wednesday at Lincoln High that featured music, dance and fashion from China. The program will be presented again Thursday.

Lincoln Journal Star

2000 Lincoln High School Chinese Kaleidoscope

*****

My students were also actively involved with our Chinese Club, Martial Arts Club, and the LHS Lion Dance Troupe that I sponsored. The clubs met once a month and the Lion Dance Troupe practiced weekly.

I worked closely with the Taipei Economics and Culture Office in Kansas City throughout the years when I lived in Nebraska. Whenever there was any business between Nebraska and Taiwan—the Sister States, I was the person the Office contacted.

I wanted to provide exciting meaningful experiences for my students whenever I could to broaden their horizons. Thus I set up the *Ambassador Awards* program with Taipei Economics and Culture Office in Kansas City. We sold lots of fortune cookies to raise funds for a chartered bus for the trip—three and half hours by bus. Every year students looked forward to our Kansas City trip in the spring.

Each time when we arrived at the Office, the diplomats of Taiwan welcomed us warmly with a banquet. The director, comparable to a consulate general, presented students with outstanding achievement *Ambassador Awards* in beautiful frames and unique prizes from Taiwan. All the students received different souvenirs each year. One year, the Taipei Economics and Culture Office invited our Lion Dance Troupe to perform at the Double Tenth Day [National Day] celebration in Kansas City.

Again with Jean's support, I made another vision happen—to motivate their learning and provide them an opportunity for direct contact with diplomats, and started one more tradition for my students.

Before Jean became the assistant principal at LHS, she was in charge of the gifted programs for Lincoln Public Schools. With her background in gifted education, she recognized teachers' abilities and potential. She fully supported and encouraged their innovative ideas. She truly was a gifted administrator herself.

In 1994, to my surprise, Jean Peterson nominated me for the Lincoln Public Schools Gold Star Award. It was my first professional recognition.

Jean was a sensitive genuine person. Working together closely, with mutual respect and appreciation, we became good friends. A few years later, Jean and her husband moved to Colorado. We have lost contact, and I hope to find her someday. I will always remember her—a dedicated supportive administrator and a true friend.

Buddies

Nancy Larsen joined the special education team a couple of years after I did at Everett Jr. High. Her son was an athletic kid with a learning disability in reading. She entered the field of special education so that she could work with her son. Nancy was a very dedicated and effective teacher. Her son, with her help, completed college, majoring in business while playing basketball for the school. He now is the president of his own company.

Nancy was energetic and fun. We teased and laughed so much whenever we were together. I called her *Crazy Lady,* she called me *Craziest!*

She retired early due to her heart problem. When she received treatment for her heart at Mayo Clinic, the doctor detected a brain tumor in her forehead area. It really affected her physically. I call her periodically to chat with her after we moved to Milwaukee. One day I called her, her husband Dee told me she fell and she was in a nursing home. It made me worried. I called her right away, "*Crazy Lady*, what happened? Are you okay?"

She was excited hearing my voice. She giggled. "Hi! *Craziest*! I fell backward from top of the stairs onto the basement and broke both shoulders. Can't do much. I read a lot. Don't worry, I will be fine. How are you doing? Really miss you." She was still laughing. What a positive and brave lady.

Nancy, despite her own physical problems, didn't stop helping friends and people who needed help. She often sat with friends with cancer after chemo treatments. She played piano for the patients at a hospice home weekly until her condition became unmanageable at home and moved into a special facility with 24/7 care.

I always remember what she said to me once long time ago. "Count our blessings. Compared to a lot of people, we are so blessed. We really don't have the right to complain." What a gratified positive attitude!

Since her tumor worsened, she couldn't carry on conversations anymore now. I really miss chatting with her. I miss calling her *Crazy Lady* and her calling me *Craziest*. Now I can only call her husband to check on my dear courageous and gracious friend—Nancy.

Another buddy, Lois Alward, didn't go to college until her children were all in school. She is a gentle true lady with characters I admire and respect. She was my long-term substitute when I was on maternity leave with our second daughter Andrea in 1979. She did a wonderful job. The following year, she joined our team and worked closely with Nancy and me.

Joan O'Meara, a close friend, was an energetic seventh grade reading teacher. She lived a few blocks from us. She single-handedly raised her three children. The oldest child Cindy was born a Down's syndrome child and needed special care and facilities all her life. Joan worked with the legislature closely for many years to ensure that quality facilities and services were provided for special needs adults like her daughter. She was not only a dedicated teacher but also a committed fighter for whatever she believed in.

Mary Lou, our hard-working librarian, raised two wonderful daughters on her own. I always wondered if I could be so tough to survive what she had been through. What a strong, determined lady!

Nancy, Lois, Joan, Mary Lou and I celebrated our birthdays together for many years. Lois was the one checking with everyone to set up a place and time for celebrations. One day in December, she saw me in the office and asked me, "When is your birthday?"

"I don't know." People around us heard it and looked at me with a surprised expression.

I laughed and continued, "I will let you know when I get the calendar for next year."

I then turned around and told the other people, "Chinese people use the lunar calendar. Every year my birthday is on a different date, just like Easter." A teachable moment!

Elaine, our secretary, looked relieved and laughed. "I was wondering why you didn't know your birthday."

Lois knew about this, and she checked with me every year. "Let me know when you find out."

All of them are much older than I, and they retired before I did. Lois moved to Arkansas. She is actively involved with many interest groups. May Lou travels often. Joan fought even harder for the rights of special needs adults in Nebraska. I spent eight years teaching in Beijing before moving to Milwaukee to join our two daughters. All the moments we shared still bring smiles to my face.

Diane Reinsch is another close friend and colleague. She is a little younger than I. She fully supported whatever I did for the school for over twenty some years when we taught at Park. She assisted me with Park P.O.W.E.R., sister school exchange programs, and sister city activities. She was also one of the host families for the Taiwan Youth Chinese Opera Troupe, which I arranged to tour the U.S from Taiwan.

She was one of the sister school delegates—traveling in Taiwan and visiting the Chu Lin Sister School in Taipei. Nancy and Lois were among the delegates as well. I was so happy to have my good friends visiting Taiwan with me.

I miss taking walks and chatting with Diane at the Holmes Lake Park. I miss her positive attitude and sunshine smiles. I will never forget how she and her husband John helped transport my eighteen pieces of luggage to Omaha when I first went to Beijing to teach in 2001. Diane is always willing and ready to help me whenever, wherever, and however.

Another special colleague friend is Myles Dymacek. He was a social studies teacher. Myles is a very knowledgeable, sincere, and friendly person. We often chatted about Chinese history and China's development. We became friends. He bought fortune cookies from me to help raise funds for our Kansas City trip and *Chinese Kaleidoscope* programs. He also supported the Taiping Sister City exchange program. When we were planning a trip to visit Taiping Sister City, he said to me, "I will go with you if you lead the delegation."

"I am leading the group! It will be great fun if you can go with us." He joined the Delegation of Lincoln to visit Taiping Sister City. What a great pleasure to have another friend visit Taiwan where I grew up.

Myles is a handy man. When our basement was flooded due to a sump pump problem, Myles was the one who came to our rescue. "The draining pipe is too close to the house," he explained. Myles replaced and extended the draining pipe farther away from the house and solved a major problem for us.

He used to replace roofs for people during summer break—another special trade of his. When we needed a new roof I asked him if he could replace it. "My wife does not want me to do it anymore. But I will check with Rose." Apparently when he retired from school, he also retired from the roofing trade. He and his son replaced our roof while we were in China—his last roofing job.

I went back to Lincoln during spring break in 2012, to pack and get our house ready for sale in the summer. Myles had a big van and he told me, "I can help you haul away things you want to donate or discard." Without his help, the whole process would have been more painful. I will never forget all the things Myles did for us.

Joan Marotz was the first person who welcomed me when I first started teaching at Everett Jr. High. She was a social studies teacher. She and her husband Loy were my two daughters' godparents. I called Joan to check on her two weeks before she died of breast cancer. She had battled it bravely for more than ten years. She was in good spirit, laughing and chatting with me. "Joan, I want to thank you for being my first friend at Everett. I appreciate your friendship and your love for my children," I told her. Joan will always live in my heart.

Whenever I think of Becky Martin, a physical education teacher, I see her smiles and feel her positive spirit and energy. Working with her for twenty plus years, this dear friend never seemed to have a down moment—upbeat and positive always, supporting whatever I did for our school. Our students seemed to really enjoy playing the shuttle cocks and pull bells—the Chinese games Chu Lin Sister School brought and taught our students. Becky said to me, "They are great exercise and fun games. I will integrate them as part of the curriculum."

"Great idea!" What a great way to introduce multicultural activities to her students!

Susan Hertzler was another sweet friend whom I could always lean on. She was actively involved with whatever, whenever, and however I needed her with school projects. One day a long time ago, she told me, "Do you know that you got our family eating Chinese food. We love it."

I laughed. "I am glad that you tried and liked it." Her family hosted students from Chu Lin Sister School every year for many years. She also supported the sister school exchange program and went to Taiwan with me.

I was a special education and Chinese language teacher for the Lincoln Public Schools in Nebraska for twenty-six years. My colleague buddies—both administrators and teachers—helped make my teaching and life pleasurable and meaningful throughout the years. Their genuine friendship and support made my world more amazing. What a blessing!

Spiritual Journey

Buddhist teaching was part of Chinese culture. People talked about good and bad karmas in everyday life all the time. Mother's daily morning ritual was to burn incense and pray. In high school, we studied Confucius teaching—not a religion, and we were brought up with Buddhist teaching at home.

When I was about six or seven years old, someone gave me a Christmas card with a portrait of a long-haired Westerner with a beard on it. I was curious. I asked an older neighbor, "Who is this person?"

"It's Jesus."

"He is Jesus? He is the God?" I had heard the name before from somewhere.

"Yeah, Jesus is the God for Westerners."

While growing up, I really didn't pay much attention to any religion. Although I didn't really know anything about Jesus, the funny thing was that I started to pray to Him. I never told anyone about it.

When my grandmother died, monks and nuns performed a traditional funeral ritual at a Buddhist temple. The atmosphere frightened me. The monks and nuns looked worldly and greedy, and it imprinted a very negative impression in my innocent eleven-year-old heart.

I attended a Roman Catholic college and received teachings on the Bible—mostly on the Old Testament—for four years. I went to mass regularly. I especially loved the peaceful little chapel next to the church. I felt very connected with Holy Mary.

Before graduating, our instructor, Sister Dona Marie, asked me, "Would you want to be baptized?"

There were many strict rules for Catholics. Some of them didn't make sense to me. "I don't think I can follow all the rules to be a good Catholic." She seemed unhappy. I felt bad that I disappointed her.

287

After Don and I got married, I joined his church and became a Lutheran. During the three years we lived in Idaho, we went to church every Sunday. One day the reverend asked me, "Would you teach junior high class at Sunday School?" I was teaching at a junior high school at the time.

I didn't feel comfortable teaching such a class. "Sorry. I don't think I know Bible well enough." I knew all the stories, but I couldn't relate to them.

A few years after we moved to Lincoln, Nebraska, we met Reverend Jerry Lundby. Before he served in the army during World War II, he was an engineer. Reverend Lundby was wounded and received a Purple Heart medal. While witnessing enormous suffering during the war, he had the calling to be a minister. After the war, he followed his calling and became one.

Reverend Lundby and his wife spent more than ten years doing missionary work in the remote areas in Taiwan. Their only son, Walter, was born there. He learned the language and preached in Chinese. Reverend Lundby was the most compassionate and embracing minister I have ever known. We joined his church, the American Lutheran Church. We went to church regularly again now that we had found a minister we liked. He baptized both of our daughters, Joline and Andrea. When he retired and moved to Chicago, I was devastated and felt lost. He performed the wedding ceremony for Joline and Ken in Milwaukee in 2003. He came from Chicago to Lincoln and married Andrea and Rylan at the American Lutheran Church in July 2009.

Reverend Lundby passed away at the age of 92 in June 2015. We will miss him—a special friend with a beautiful soul.

A New Gateway

In 1989, two years after Mother's surgery for a vicious brain tumor, our parents came from Taiwan to live with my three younger siblings—Eileen, Eric, and Ray—in Boston. They were all single, living together.

In that summer, I took both daughters to visit my family in Boston.

We four siblings chatted whenever we had a chance. Eileen said to me, "We met a very interesting person, Sandy Sabo, not too long ago. She shared with us something spiritual we never knew before." None of my siblings claimed any religion.

"Spiritual? It sounds interesting. What did you learn?"

"It was very different, but interesting. Through meditation you learn about yourself, the universe, and the higher power," Eric said.

I felt confused. "What do you mean?"

Eileen said to me, "You have to meet her yourself to find out about it."

"Is it possible to meet her while I am here?" I planned to stay for two weeks in Boston.

Ray was enthusiastic about it. "I will call her to make an appointment for you!"

When I first met Sandy Sabo, I didn't know what to expect. I didn't even know what to say to her. Little did I know then that our meeting would have such a great impact on my life.

Sandy seemed to be a very caring lady. We sat on the floor in her meditation room. She lit a candle, and it felt very peaceful. I asked her, "What is meditation? How does it work?"

"Meditation is a time you set aside to sit quietly by yourself or with other people to find your own inner wisdom and to communicate with higher power."

"Higher power, you mean God? How does it work? Can anyone do it?" I read about monks meditating in temples. I had not seen it or experienced it.

"Yes. Anyone who wants to learn can do it. It takes practice."

I was getting more curious and excited about it. I asked her many questions. "You mean I can do it too?"

Sandy nodded, saying to me. "If you want to learn, we can set a time and I can teach you then."

I had a strong urge to learn meditation. I set a time to meet with Sandy again the following week. She lived by the beach. "Bring your kids. They can go to the beach and play while you learn." How thoughtful.

On that day, I was excited. Eileen took Joline and Andrea to play on the beach. I spent half a day learning and practicing meditation with Sandy. It was such a fascinating experience. She opened a new gateway for me to explore something new and amazing.

After learning meditation, I started reading books on spirituality and Buddhism. I read books—from Buddhist teaching to Gary Zukav's *The Seat of the Soul*; from Wayne Dyer's *Change Your Thoughts, Change Your Life* to Louis Hays' *Totality of Possibilities*; from Dr. Brian Weise's *Many Lives, Many Masters* to Shirley McClain's *Out on A Limb*; and many more.

The more I read, the more I wanted to know. The more I read, the more I was amazed. I became more receptive not only about all religions but also about people and things happening around me.

The negative impression on Buddhist monks and nuns I had since childhood was gone. I absorbed and integrated the Buddhism teaching with my understanding of the Bible. One strange thing I noticed was that the better I understand Buddhism, the better I could relate to the Bible.

Meditation is a practice for self-cultivation, not a religion. People with any religion can practice it and benefit from it. It has helped me find my inner strength, wisdom, and guidance to live a happier, more positive life. It helped me face Mother's death and Father's passing, with different perspective. I learned to surrender and let go. It brought peace to me.

Every day is a gift. I don't take anyone or anything for granted any more, instead I appreciate them with much gratitude. My faith is stronger, and I thank God for all my blessings every day. Mindfully I live my life—making the best out of everything, everyone, and every day.

Sandy Sabo, my first spiritual teacher, has been a great friend to my siblings and me ever since we met in 1989.

Enriched

When I was younger, I felt so sad each time we had to move, leaving good friends behind to start a new life somewhere else. After multiple moves, I learned to welcome and enjoy new experiences and people who would cross my path wherever I might be.

When I first went to Beijing to teach at the International School of Beijing [ISB] in 2001, the only person I knew was Theresa Chao. She tried her best to get me situated. Don, my husband, didn't join me until two years later. I never liked to go places or do things alone, especially for fun.

New Friend

Tuanmu was a Chinese language teacher from Taiwan. She had been teaching at ISB for a few years then. I met her when I visited the school in November of the previous year.

She was so independent and knew her way around Beijing well. Biking was her transportation. One day Tuanmu asked me, "Would you want me to show you around? We can ride bikes."

I was grateful for her offer since I was such a chicken and dared not go any places by myself. "It sounds fun! Thank you." We set a time and place to meet on a Saturday.

Well, I got on my new bike and followed Tuanmu for my first expedition in Beijing. I was pretty shaky on my bike since I had not ridden a bike for at least thirty years, especially in busy streets. I was so nervous. I screamed, "Whoa! So many cars! They are so fast! Scary!"

"Come to my right side by the curb." Tuanmu tried to protect me, the chicken.

We were at the intersection of Jing Shun Road, one of the busiest and craziest streets in Beijing. Tuanmu rode across swiftly, and she stopped and waited for me. There I was, standing motionless with my bike at the same spot, frozen. "Too many cars!" I yelled.

Poor Tuanmu had to come all the way back to walk me across the street. I didn't know what she thought about all this. We had different challenges—for me it was a scary adventure; for her it was a test of patience. She was extremely patient with me. I found out later that she had no patience for timid people like me. Whenever I think of it, it still makes me laugh so hard—how dumb and scared I was on my first outing with Tuanmu.

She is a person with integrity and high expectations of herself and others. She has the most beautiful voice and can sing almost anything. She looked so charming and happy whenever she sang. I loved going to Karaoke with her. She knew how to work the machine and also what songs each person liked to sing. Sometimes she had to help me start the songs I sang. She knew all the good restaurants in Beijing. It was great fun doing things and going places with her. Tuanmu was such a caring and fun friend. I miss her.

Good Neighbor

One day after school, someone knocked on the door. A lady with a basket full of fruits was at the door. "Are you Celine? I am Rachel Chung. I live in the townhouse next to you."

"Hi! Please come in. How did you know about me?"

"Wendy Chou told me about you." How thoughtful Wendy was!

"Oh, yes. I met Wendy a few days ago at school. She mentioned she would introduce a friend to me. So you are the one!" We laughed.

Rachel is a sweet lady with many friends. She and her family lived in Beijing for years. She was an elementary school teacher in Taiwan. We hit it off and became close friends. She knew where to buy the best fruit and everything else. There was never a dull moment being with her.

When our school needed a Chinese teacher for elementary school, I encouraged her. "With your personality and experiences, you will make a great language teacher. You have had enough fun shopping and playing. Now it is time for you to do something more meaningful with your energy. Come and join us."

"You are right." She joined our department and became one of the most effective teachers at ISB.

Lost

Lirong Zhou and I started teaching at ISB in 2001. She is from China, not Beijing. She lived and taught in New Zealand for a long time. One day, we decided to explore Beijing together by subway. We tried to go to the Summer Palace. We met in the morning, and we were excited about the outing. But we got totally lost following directions given by different people.

When we got there, it didn't look right. I asked someone at the gate to make sure it was the Summer Palace. He said, "Yes, it is. This is the back gate of the Summer Palace."

We spent more than six hours on subway and bus searching, and we finally got to the Summer Palace. It was the back gate! I yelled when I saw the schedule as we were getting the tickets, "Wow! Look the schedule! It will close in one hour." What a day of expedition!

We laughed so hard whenever we shared this experience with others. After that, to save time and energy, I decided to hire a car to go anyplace I wanted to go.

Lirong became a dear friend ever since we got lost together.

Sweet Friends

Yun Li, a friendly, caring colleague, came by my classroom frequently. She is from Beijing. She knew I was so excited before our first grandchild Casey was born. "I found places for you to buy baby stuff. They are well made. I got a few pieces for you." She even bought gifts for my grandson. What a thoughtful and sweet friend.

When I took my Arrowhead students to visit China in the summer of 2011, she helped me set up an exchange program at a local school in Beijing, along with other things. I am so blessed with her genuine friendship and connections. I was so happy that she visited me twice in the U.S. since 2011.

Sophia Huang was another lovely colleague. However and whenever I needed assistance, she would go out of her way to help me throughout the years. "Do you need anything special from China now that you are going home?"

"Yes, I really would love to buy some good rugs. But I don't know much about them, and I don't know where I can get them either."

"Don't worry! I can help you to get some good rugs," without hesitation she responded.

With her family connections, I bought six most beautiful quality rugs.

How fortunate I am to have delightful Sophia as a dear friend. I miss sweet Sophia.

Invaluable Resource

You would think the non-Chinese students at ISB would have many opportunities to practice their Chinese since they lived in Beijing. It was not true at all. Our students came from 56 different countries. Most of them lived in gated villas, English speaking environments, for foreigners. The only local Chinese people they had contact with were their drivers and helpers at home. I lived in such a compound also. I knew how isolated we were from the outside world— the local Chinese community.

I taught the IB Mandarin AB classes for seven years at ISB. It is a two-year International Baccalaureate [IB] program for beginners. IB classes are compact and intensive college level classes. Students take extensive speaking, reading, and writing tests after completing the course. The passing grade is 4, and the highest score is 7. Colleges around the world will credit them the credit for the subject for the score 6 or 7. Thus it was the goal I set for my students.

We worked on listening, speaking, reading, and writing just like in any language class.

I could do all I planned for them, seventeen units, effectively and proficiently except for the speaking part. To reach the level I set for them they needed more individual or small group conversation opportunities.

I met some Chinese ladies from Taiwan, and most of them were not working outside of their homes. One day I asked Ginny Chiu, a sweet lady who lived in the same compound, "I teach IB students, they don't have enough opportunity to speak Chinese outside of the classroom. Do you think you could come to help with conversation?"

"Sure! I'd be happy to help. I have some friends who might be willing to help you too."

"That would be great. Thank you!"

Ginny lived in Beijing for a long time, and she had a lot of friends from Taiwan. Many of them became my regular volunteers during the seven years when I taught IB classes. My students appreciated their help very much, and they looked forward to conversing with these delightful ladies—my invaluable resource.

I appreciate and miss these wonderful friends and volunteers who had helped my students throughout the years—Ginny Chiu, Fang You Lin, Chelsea Wang, Yvonne Hsieh, Amy Lin, Cecilia Chang, Claudia Chiang, Erica Ho, Peggy Yen, Anita Tu, Yvonne Mu, Helen Yu, Lydia, Leming Pang, Wen Chu Lu, Shu Ming Kao, Iron Mao, Casey, Sabrina, Hui Li Hsu, and Karen Wu.

Their help inspired my students to speak Chinese and enabled them to score high with their IB tests every year. My last group's average was 6.85 out of 7.

I am forever in debt to them. My resourceful volunteers not only enriched my students' learning with their assistance, but also filled my life with the true, the good, and the beautiful colors of friendship.

China Link

China Link was the department in charge of all the China-related activities for 2000 students and staff at ISB.

The last four years when I was at ISB, I taught part-time and coordinated and supervised the China Link department part-time. The first two years I was the coordinator for high school, while Mary Lu was in charge of middle school, and Wendy Chou worked with the elementary school. We worked closely to provide programs to all the students and staff. After two years, due to the infrastructure, I became the supervisor of China Link in charge of all the China related activities for the whole school.

There were always new projects added to our on-going projects—no end to our work. Rebecca Li and Laura Liu were my two coordinators. I often encouraged them, "The more we do, the more we can do. No one can take away the skills you acquire throughout the process. You will be more capable than others no matter where you will be."

We created the Moon Cake Factory—one of the whole-school projects for the Moon Festival in the fall. Every year, more than 1,000 students made moon cakes in the cafeteria. In addition to the Moon Cake Factory, there was a Moon Festival Banquet—a dinner with performances for the community. Students also made *yuan xiao* [a dessert] for Lantern Festival, and *jiao zi* [dumplings] for Chinese New Year. Eric, our chef, was most accommodating, and Helen and Melody, the managers, were pleasant and helpful. The cafeteria staff helped make these projects successful year after year.

Right after the Moon Festival, we started the preparation for the Chinese New Year celebration—the Temple Fair for elementary school, Carnivals for middle school and high school, a traditional Chinese New Year Eve Banquet for all the staff, and a whole-school parade.

At our weekly meeting, I asked Rebecca, "Did you get a chance to find more experts for the Temple Fair?" I monitored every step of the preparation of each event.

She was always on schedule. "Yes, I found some better ones to replace a few not-so-good ones this year." She showed me all the changes.

"Great! How about the venues and dates for the carnivals and the banquet, Laura?"

"All confirmed!" Laura smiled and presented me the confirmed dates.

"Super! Thank you! All set for next step. Let's work on the timeline for each event."

I couldn't have had better helpers than Rebecca and Laura. They were my right and left hands. They were not only solid and dependable, but also delightful to work with. We did many amazing projects together.

The facilities coordinator Xiu Mei Zhang and her remarkable staff were most efficient and reliable. No matter whatever we needed to do—moving furniture, hanging lanterns and festival decorations, or setting up the stage, it was always done perfectly and timely.

Theresa Chao & Celine
Getting ready for the Chinese New Year's Eve Banquet at ISB

China Link

China Experience Trips

Summer Palace

Pingyao

Beijing

Henan

Taishan

Habitat for Humanity

Xi'an

Jingdezhen

Yangshuo

ISB China Link Program

China Link Program is one major part of the Chinese Program. China Link Program provides students and teachers with the most and the best opportunities to learn about China and its people through various curriculum integrated activities. China experience trips in the spring provide students with authentic experiences in different parts of China.

Celine leading the Chinese New Year Parade

China Connections

Mr. Ge, our purchase professional, is from Beijing. He never failed to find whatever China Link needed—molds for moon cakes, dragons for dragon dance, costumes and equipment for performances. He also is a good friend who helped me a great deal personally throughout the eight years I was in Beijing. He always told me, *"Tan Lao Shi* [Teacher Tan], just let me know whatever you need. I will get them for you."

Another special Beijing friend, Li Xin Wang, worked closely with Mr. Ge in the business office. She assisted me professionally and personally. Mr. Ge and Li Xin even helped me during the three days in Beijing when I took 22 Arrowhead students and staff to experience China in the summer of 2011. They have been my loyal friends and forever China connections.

After all the Chinese New Year celebrations, the preparation of the

Chinese Experience Trips started. In late May and early June every year, the whole school spent four days experiencing China. Elementary students stayed in Beijing while secondary students explored different places in China. In addition to elementary students' trips in Beijing, we, the China Link, made arrangements for more than twenty different trips for middle school and high school students: a camping trip in Hunan, pottery workshop in Jiangxi, Mt. Tai and Confucius hometown in Shandong, Chinese painting on top of Mt. Huang, Shanghai, marital arts workshop and Shao Lin Temple in Henan, sailing adventure in Qingdao, and more.

I carried two cell phones 24 hours during those days to ensure everything went safely and smoothly. Luckily, everything went well without any incidents or emergencies during the four years I was responsible for the China Link.

Louis Chen, the manager of the business office, always helped make our jobs easier, with all the payments involved. Sussana Fong, the asset manager, helped check all the details on every contract to be signed with travel agencies. What a thorough professional she was! I told her repeatedly, "Thank you so much. If I own a business, you will be the first person I hire."

Wendy Pan and Yan Zhen—two managers of Sunrise Travel Agency—were my most valued travel agents. I respect and appreciate them—the most honest, decent agents with great sense of honor and pride. They helped me to arrange not only many of the China Link trips but also all my personal trips. In the summer of 2011, they set up a two-week superb China Experience Trip for Arrowhead High School students and staff. I recommend them to whomever wishes to travel in China. They are my two other invaluable China connections.

Forever Gratitude

For the eight years I was teaching in Beijing, I invited my younger sister Eileen to visit us many times. "Come to visit when I am here. You don't need to worry about anything. I will make all the arrangements for you."

Eileen was single and a top notch realtor in Los Angeles. She always said, "I can't get away, maybe next year." She never came to visit us.

In the spring of 2010, Eileen finally made it to Beijing, a year after I left Beijing. She went there for alternative treatment after chemo failed to help her colon cancer in the U.S.

Theresa Chao, a dear friend, was the Chinese department principal at ISB. She squeezed time from her extremely busy schedule, and not only contacted doctors and made arrangements in different hospitals for Eileen, but also provided delicious vegetarian food for her. Theresa called me regularly to keep me posted of Eileen's condition. "There is nothing much they can do for her. Please be prepared for the worst." I am forever grateful to Theresa Chao for extending our friendship to my dying sister Eileen.

Feng Zhen Zhang—a close Beijing friend—along with her friends who didn't even know Eileen took great care of Eileen like a family member. Although we hired a 24-hour helper to take care of Eileen, they took turns to stay with Eileen for three months before I went there in June after school was out.

Sarah and Simon Mar, a lovely couple and two of my favorite friends, let us stay in their house when we—Don, my brothers Karl from Taiwan, Ken from Houston, and I—went to see Eileen. They also helped sort out and scanned all of Eileen's important documents before they went back to Taiwan for the summer.

When Eileen decided to go to Beijing for treatment, I called Chelsea Wang—another dear friend in Beijing. "Would you provide RMB [Chinese currency] for my sister Eileen to pay for her medical expenses in Beijing? I will deposit USD [US dollars] in your account in the U.S."

"Sure! Just tell me where she is and I will deliver it to her," she responded without hesitation. With total trust in me, she provided all the RMB for Eileen whenever she needed—equivalent to US$50,000—in three months.

Eileen spent her last three months of her life in Beijing. Although she didn't get to see the City of Beijing, she felt the most beautiful humanitarian love from all directions. On June 23, 2010, embraced by love and surrounded by friends, Karl and me, Eileen left this earth at the age of 60.

There are no words to describe my deepest gratitude to all of my friends in Beijing for their kindness, love, and extended friendship to my beloved sister Eileen.

After I came back from China, friends often asked me, "Do you miss Beijing?"

"Not so much the place, but I truly miss all my friends in Beijing."

It warms my heart whenever I think of all my wonderful friends in Beijing. They enriched my world and filled my life with genuine friendship, unforgettable memories, and rainbow colors.

Dairyland

I didn't think we would ever move again after living and making a home in Lincoln, Nebraska since 1973. But life is full of variables. I resigned from the International School of Beijing the moment Andrea, our younger daughter, moved to Milwaukee from Los Angeles tojoin our older daughter Joline in the fall of 2008.

When we came back from China in June 2009, we didn't go back to Nebraska. Instead we moved to Wisconsin to join our daughters. In the spring, Arrowhead High School in Hartland, Wisconsin, asked me to start a four-year Chinese language program, and I started teaching again in August.

I have friends all over the world, but I didn't have a single friend in Milwaukee.

New Challenge

I never thought that we would ever move to Wisconsin, the Dairyland, where my husband Don was born and raised. Life is full of surprises!

We moved to Milwaukee in July, and one month later I started teaching at Arrowhead High School in Hartland.

There are always adjustments wherever you move. The first thing I needed to do was to learn my way around this big city. Secondly I needed to learn to drive on the freeway since it was the only way to go anyplace from where we lived.

There is no freeway in the City of Lincoln, Nebraska. The only highway I could drive independently was to the airport. I could drive on the highway, but I was so scared of being lost. Whenever I went to Omaha, I either rode with people or someone who knew the way was with me if I drove.

I was not used to driving so fast in the city. One day, as I drove on Highway 164, Joline was with me. Joline said, "Mom, the speed limit is 55." I looked at my speed odometer, it was 45.

Arrowhead High School is a 40-minute drive each way. I was very worried about driving and finding the school. A week before school started, Joline said, "Don't worry! Let's go to Arrowhead. You drive, and I will show you the way." It was so far away.

On the first day of school, I left home early just in case I would get lost. I did pretty well with the directions until I missed the sign for Highway 16 W. I noticed it right away. I turned around and found the way. On the second day, I did the same thing again. I felt very dumb!

After a few months, I was getting braver with driving, and I could even drive on Interstate Highway 94 to most of the places I needed to go. What a giant leap for a timid chicken!

A Unique Group

In late December, I received a call from a lady speaking Chinese, "This is Amy, I got your number from your next door neighbor." I found out later our neighbor, Joan, was her son's school bus driver.

"Hi, how are you? Are you Chinese?"

"Yes, I am from Taiwan."

"Really, me too!"

"We are going to have a potluck luncheon at noon on the New Year's Day. Would you want to join us?" Amy asked.

"Sure! We would love to come." I was excited to meet someone from home.

I was so glad to meet some Chinese people at the party, and we had a grand time.

We got to know more wonderful Chinese people after the party. We enjoy sharing the past, chatting about the present, and talking about the future in our native tongue.

Gloria, a lovely lady, is from northeastern China. She is the International Customer Care Representative for Pentair Residential

Filtration LLC. Gloria is an energetic lady. She not only actively involved with the local Chinese newspaper but also the Chinese Women's Club. She has a beautiful voice. Her husband Dave is most pleasant and fun. We enjoy them very much.

Qian was a pediatrician in China, and she is getting her training in medical technology. She is a smart, courageous, hardworking lady. Her husband Steve is an engineer. They love dancing, and they dance every Saturday. They are a delightful couple.

Xiao Yun, a charming sweet lady, is from northern China. She is a Marketing Analyst at Rexnord. Her husband Darryl is also an engineer. She makes the best northern Chinese food made with flour. They are a sincere, caring couple. We are blessed with their friendship.

Alicia is a genuine, friendly lady from Taiwan. She met her husband Carl in Taiwan. They retired from GM at the same time, long ago. Carl is actively involved with the Lion's Club. They enjoy spoiling their two granddaughters. She makes the best desserts. Whenever we have a potluck dinner, I always ask her to bring dessert. I appreciate Alicia's caring friendship.

Tsui Ying, another delightful lady, met her husband Mark in Taiwan. Mark is also an engineer. They go back to Taiwan often to visit her family. She is a housewife taking care of two children, exercising, and learning different things from different sources all the time. They are a sincere and caring couple.

Tai Shiang works for the government. She is a Veterans Service Representative at the Department of Veterans Affairs. Her husband Peter is a dentist. I adore their two delightful daughters. These two mature and well-mannered young ladies are active 4H members. They compete in the horse riding at the fair. They are also very good at trap shooting, a sport I enjoyed very much. Tai Shiang is from Taiwan. She is an embracing and giving community leader among people from Taiwan.

Amy, my first Chinese friend from Taiwan in Dairyland, lives a few blocks from my daughter Joline's house. She met her husband Darryl in Taiwan. Darryl owned a successful business in Taiwan for many years. Amy is a generous and embracing lady. She takes classes constantly to learn new skills. Amy is an active member of the Muskego Women's Club and the Chinese Women's Club. I treasure her friendship.

Qiong was my student teacher at Arrowhead High School. She teaches Chinese and also works with students from China at a private school. Her husband Steve was an engineering professor at Marquette, and now owns his own consulting company. She also teaches at the weekend Chinese School. Qiong is a very sweet lady.

The new comer, Jenny, is a bright, pleasant, friendly young lady from Shanghai. Her husband Randy worked in China for many years. My husband Don met her at a barber shop while her son was getting a haircut. I invited them over to meet my family the following weekend. She then joined our group.

The wives are all Chinese and the husbands are all Americans. Whenever we get together, the ladies laugh and talk in Chinese and the guys drink and chat in English. We always have a blast.

What a unique group!

Tzu Chi

When I first moved to Milwaukee, on a Saturday, my daughter Joline and I explored in an Asian grocery store near downtown Milwaukee. As we got out, we saw two Chinese ladies at the doorway holding a sign with *Tzu Chi* on it and a bucket. They were collecting donations for an earthquake disaster in Taiwan. I put some money in the bucket.

I was very happy to see Chinese people. I said to them, "I am Celine Robertson. I am new in town."

One of the ladies laughed. "I am Celine Wang." Unbelievable! The first Chinese person I ran into is from Taiwan, with the same name. We both chuckled.

I pointed at the sign she was holding, saying, "I see you are from the Tzu Chi Foundation. I have heard so much about it, but I never had the chance to get involved."

Celine was very friendly. "There is a small group of volunteers in Milwaukee. You are welcome to join us."

"I'd be happy to help out." We exchanged contact information.

Tzu means compassion and *Chi* means relief. The Tzu Chi Foundation was founded by Dharma Master Cheng Yen in Taiwan, a Buddhist nun, in 1966.

It started with 30 housewives who put aside NT$ fifty cents from their daily grocery money in a bamboo piggy bank to help people in need in Taiwan. Now there are over 1,000,000 volunteers and donors working together to carry out Tzu Chi's mission in more than 70 countries.

Tzu Chi—with the spirit of self-discipline, diligence, prudence, and perseverance—set out to help the poor, relieve suffering, and promote peace and harmony around the world. It started with charity, and over time the Foundation extended its mission to medicine, education, and humanistic culture. It provides national and international immediate disaster relief. Tzu Chi also established the world's second largest bone marrow registration program.

The Tzu Chi Foundation in Greater Milwaukee Area provides variety of services and programs monthly—nursing home visits, character building classes, Dharma studying, promoting vegetarian diet and environmental protection, seminars on healthy living, disaster relief as well as an annual Blessing Ceremony to celebrate the Chinese New Year.

Celine Wang is in charge of all the activities. I told her, "I may not be able to assist you with all the activities. But I would be happy to support the foundation with a monthly donation."

I joined them for a Thanksgiving celebration activity at a women's shelter in Milwaukee. I was amazed how well organized and thoroughly planned they were. They provided gifts, a feast, and a fun family project for eight families, around forty people.

This small but resilient group—Celine, Shu Jen, Susan, Mike, P. J., Ginger, Pei Chi, and James—profoundly touched my heart. With Tzu Chi's spirit, commitment, and mission, the Milwaukee Tzu Chi Foundation brings warmth and humanitarian love to people in need, regularly and tirelessly.

What beautiful hearts and souls!

Yuan Fen

If you are meant to meet or encounter with someone in your life, you will meet this person no matter what, sometimes in a mysterious way. Chinese people call it *Yuan Fen* [karma].

I attended the Wisconsin World Languages Conference in Appleton for the first time in the fall of 2009. There was a Chinese Language Teachers Association membership meeting. I decided to check it out. There were not many people there. I was sitting in the second row.

As the discussion on a presentation went on, I shared some of my thoughts. The person sitting right in front of me turned around and looked at me and my name tag. There was a disbelief look on her face.

After the meeting, she came around right away and asked me, "Are you the Celine Robertson from Nebraska?"

I was surprised how she knew I was from Nebraska. "Yes, I just moved here from Nebraska."

She got more excited. "I was supposed to be your student teacher in 2001."

"Is that so?" I became curious.

During my teaching career, I had more than thirty student teachers in special education and one in Chinese language before retiring in 2000. Many of them became great teachers.

"My name is Sandra Hsiao. I was a graduate student at the University of Iowa. I wanted to be a Chinese language teacher. My professor recommended you to be my cooperating teacher. But, you were going to retire."

I didn't recognize her name since I didn't have any direct contact with her. I only remember I was surprised when I received two calls from universities out of state asking me if I would help to work with their students—one from Brigham Young University in Utah and one from the University of Iowa.

They asked me, "Would you take a student teacher next school year?" I was amazed that they would arrange student teaching for their students out of state.

I responded to them, "I'd love to work with your student, but I am retiring in June. I am sorry."

Here we were, face to face, nine years later in a different state. Incredible!

Even though I was not Sandra's cooperating teacher, she calls me *Lao Shi*. Both of us appreciated our belated *Yuan Fen* and became good friends.

Sandra is from Taiwan. She is an energetic young lady with a strong sense of responsibility and honor. Sandra sets high self-expectations and works diligently. She is a passionate, effective, well respected Chinese language teacher at a high school in Kenosha.

Her piety toward her parents touched me intensely. Sandra went back to Taiwan checking on her sick father whenever there was a break, even during one-week spring break. Now she goes back to accompany her widowed mother three or four times a year. How blessed her parents are!

I appreciate her high quality character; I enjoy her genuine friendship; and I treasure this belated *Yuan Fen* with Sandra Hsiao!

Mermaids

Joline knew that I liked to workout and always belonged to a gym. "Mom, you should go to take a look at the West Wood Health and Fitness Center. It is on the way to Arrowhead, and you can workout there on your way home."

"That sounds convenient!"

The facility is very good and people are very friendly there. I started going to West Wood on my way home every day.

I loved to workout in the water. There were some regulars in the warm therapy pool at the same time I went. Stella, a gentle lady working part-time, was there almost every day. Kay worked out in the pool regularly. Nancy and Marilyn were retired teachers. We had much to share while exercising in the water. Bernie and her husband were also regulars. Pat, a pleasant lady with a smile always, was another delightful pool-mate. We missed sweet Donna after she moved to Green Bay.

My sister-in-law Mary, a positive hardworking lady, wanted to join a gym. I told her, "Come to West Wood. You will love the warm water and the people there." She became a member and joined our group.

Eleanor, in her 90s, is alert, with good sight and hearing. She drives her red Lexus all over Milwaukee. I enjoy her and admire her spirit. Looking at her beautiful silver hair and watching her exercise in the water, I was so impressed. "You are my inspiration. I hope when I get to 90, I will be as alert and active as you."

Karen joined us the last, she is an open-minded and fun lady. We hit it off right away and became very close friends.

We referred to one another as pool-mates. One day I said to them, "Pool-mate does not sound good, we are *Mermaids*." Everyone loved it. We became *Mermaids*.

To my surprise, the wonderful *Mermaids* I met in the pool at West Wood became my first friends in Milwaukee. We celebrated Chinese New Year together. They all came to see my *Chinese Kaleidoscope* program to cheer me on at Arrowhead High School. They not only counted down the days with me but also gave me a retirement party and gifts when I finally retired. How fortunate and fun to have these lovely *Mermaids* stand by me, in water and on land.

After I retired from Arrowhead, West Wood is too far for me—a 30-minute drive each way. It broke my heart to say good-bye to the *Mermaids* at West Wood.

We kept in touch. Many saved their guest passes for me. I went back to see them once in a while. I joined them for the monthly luncheon sometimes.

Eleanor and I meet once in a while for lunch. I loved to take my granddaughter Holly to visit her. I didn't always call her beforehand. Eleanor was always excited to see us. "I love it when you drop by with your grandchildren. Please come by anytime. I am always home in the morning." Holly enjoyed telling Eleanor everything about her daycare.

Karen and I keep in close contact, she calls and emails often. Karen knew I wanted to go to Lake Geneva. "I am free Thursday next week, want to go Lake Geneva?"

"Sure!" It is always a pleasure to have an outing with her.

Fresh Water

When I first went to the brand new YMCA in Mukwonago, I wasn't sure how I would like it there. I missed the *Mermaids* at West Wood. There is no steam room or sauna. But the pools are very nice. Towels are not provided. And I didn't know anyone there.

I met Sue, a lovely intelligent lady, in the current pool. She was my first *Mermaid* friend at the Y. She even joined our Writers Club. She used to run a daycare. She didn't come to the pool for a while. When I saw her again, I asked her, "Is everything all right?"

"A good friend is sick with cancer. I stayed with her a few nights in the hospital. I was too exhausted to come." What a caring friend!

Then I met Inge, a witty loving lady. She told me, "I came to the U.S. from Germany when I was nine."

I was excited. "You are an immigrant like me! What did you do before retiring?"

"I was a high school teacher." She taught in several states as I did, even in Nebraska.

"What do you know? I was a teacher all my life too!" We both got excited and laughed.

She helps take care of her grandchildren before school like I do. She also checks on her 94-year-old father regularly. She has been actively involved with the Eastern Star—a fraternal organization for women and men offering social opportunities and a means to support a variety of state and local charities. What a loving and caring *Mermaid*!

Not long after, I met Betty, a gentle, sincere *Mermaid.* "Are you retired?" I asked her.

"Not completely. I am working a couple of hours a day."

Betty is a genuine, caring, sweet lady. She is very creative. She makes the most beautiful greeting cards and other crafts. I display all the wonderful cards she made for me.

Through Betty, we got to know Cheryl—a devoted Christian. She and her family spent a few years in Africa doing missionary work. She has written a memoir about their adventures in Africa.

When I started learning piano, she was so excited, telling me, "I am teaching myself guitar!" She also learned how to ride a motorcycle not long ago. She bought a new one, with more power and speed. I called her *Speedy Cheryl*. What an energetic and motivated *Mermaid*!

We five *Mermaids* enjoy and care about one another. After my heart attack on August 15th, 2014, I told them, "I will miss you guys. I need to have rehab three times a week for eight weeks."

Inge said, "Don't worry. We will meet you for lunch at the hospital." They met me a couple of times in the cafeteria of the hospital for lunch.

After Betty had hip surgery, she told us, "I can't workout for two months."

Sue said, "We will miss you. We will come to see you."

When Betty recovered well enough to drive, we met for lunch. We laughed and yelled, "Cheers for Betty's independence!"

These gracious *Mermaids* are my playmates, friends, and buddies.

Borrowed Eyes

I don't know exactly when writing a memoir resonated in my heart and became one of my dreams. I can't remember how long I had envisioned passing down a collection of my life stories—the roots—to my children and grandchildren. I don't recall when I had the notion to share my struggles and adventures. I do know the urge for writing such a book was getting stronger and stronger.

Intensely I felt a challenging voyage awaiting me…

*****

In June 2012, I decided to retire from Arrowhead High School in Hartland, Wisconsin—my third retirement. In September, I became a student in the Creative Writing for Publication class at Waukesha County Technical College.

A new expedition began…

When I walked into class the first day, I really didn't know what to expect. All my classmates were experienced writers. They seemed to know one another well.

I was one of the few new students in the class. Since I didn't know anyone or anything about the class, I decided to observe and see if it was the right class for me.

Gail Sweet, our teacher, pointed out to us, "Anything you write should be like a movie."

After pondering what she said, I realized the truth of her words. As I am reading, I visualize everything in front of me as if I am watching a movie—motions, colors, and sounds. This tip helped me a great deal as I started writing my stories.

It was humbling to be a student again. According to a famous saying of Confucius, you can always learn something whenever there are three people together. Here I was in class, surrounded by experienced writers. I respected all of them as my teachers.

Paul was an energetic and fun classmate. His friendly teasing helped me feel welcome. He was a talented writer with keen observations and a sensitive heart. His sharp eyes provided honest and direct feedback. His remarks sometimes seemed a bit rough, but I appreciated his straightforward critiques.

The last time I did any creative writing in English was in college practicing my English. All the writings I did in between were professional writings—reports, proposals, presentations, or speeches I had given throughout the years. Nothing was too creative, and I had never written dialogue—I had no idea how to write conversations.

Paul wrote great dialogue for his stories. He understood I was new at it. He offered, "Celine, I'd be happy to help you." Paul became my friend and mentor.

Gale Orlick—a gentle lady you would never guess was a hunter—wrote the funniest stories about hunting and her life experiences. She and I, sitting next to each other in class, became writing pals. We wanted to meet regularly outside of class. With Paul we formed "The Writers Club." Some more people joined the three of us. We had fun learning and sharing informally and sometimes formally with professionals.

During the first semester, I didn't write anything because I really didn't know how. I just observed and absorbed whatever tips and techniques I could from other people's writings and critiques.

The second semester, I applied what I had learned. I practiced those tips and techniques as I wrote the first story of my memoir, "Love and Laughter"—an experimental piece.

It took some courage to challenge myself—to face critiques from all directions. It was intimidating.

Paul showed me how to write dialogue, and others showed me how to make my writing more visual with colors, actions, and sounds. With all their suggestions and assistance, I edited and rewrote my first piece over and over throughout the whole second semester.

Finally Paul said, "Celine, you've got it. Your dialogue is very good now."

"Thanks to you! You truly are a good teacher!" It was such exciting fun to add dialogue to my stories. I appreciated all the critiques and encouragements, especially the helpful and critical ones.

I didn't start writing my memoirs until my third semester, in July 2013. Once I began, nothing could stop me—I had so many stories stored in my heart and soul.

Whenever I shared my writings in class, I always said, "Be critical! Please let me know if it is boring, dragging, or bragging." It was truly an effective way to improve—through other people's eyes.

My classmates helped me find the contradictions or vagueness I couldn't see for myself because I was too involved with the stories. They had different experiences, interests, and backgrounds—they were like readers from all over. They pre-examined my work to make sure I presented my stories effectively and clearly. What a powerful group!

After I read a few more pieces of my memoirs during the fourth semester, Paul said to me, "You wrote some powerful stories. You are honoring the people in your life."

Paul was the first person who really grasped the purpose of my stories and pointed it out to me. I felt profoundly enthused and impressed that he recognized it. "Yes, indeed my book is to honor the people whom I have loved, appreciated, and respected throughout my life."

Sometimes I didn't like the titles I had for my stories. Paul helped me with a few great titles, such as "Sweat, Blood, and Tears," "The Helping Hand," "Touchdown," and "Beyond Imagination."

Through Paul, I met Beth Hoffmann—the Grammar Guru. Beth knows the Bible so well that she even spotted errors in stories in Sunday school material. I said to Beth, "You should join us. You can write Bible stories for Sunday schools." She became my classmate, friend, and editor.

After two semesters, our instructor Gail Sweet decided to semi-retire. Our new teacher, Katie Rothschadl, was always encouraging with her positive feedback. Amazingly she caught things instantly that other people didn't see most of the time.

Ramon, a retired lawyer, had been in this class since he retired twenty some years ago. He wrote a variety of great short stories. His concise comments such as "very interesting" and "good dialogues" helped me move forward.

Sandy started the class around the same time I did. She made great progress writing her life adventures. Her sharp eyes always caught the words I used more than once. She circled every excessive "with" and "and".

Lucy raised her hand. "I found a dangler!" A dangler is a sentence missing a critical comma, or with words in an awkward order, so the meaning changes, often in a silly way.

Someone yelled, "Candy time!" Katie, our instructor, passed around a bag of candies whenever someone found a dangler.

I giggled. "Oh, no! You are so scary!" Everyone laughed. Lucy—the dangler catcher—was like a hawk, and no one could escape her piercing eyes.

Big Joe M., a great poet and writer, said to Lucy once when she offered critiques, "Be gentle, Lucy!" I was glad I wasn't the only one scared of her.

Big Joe M.'s questions on my stories helped me think and provide clearer background information whenever I wrote about my heritage and Chinese traditions.

The other Big Joe was also an innovative and strong writer. He remarked, "You have some powerful stories. I enjoy your historic background in them."

Al's characters in his stories were so creative and interesting that we all wanted to read more. I wondered if his professional background helped him write logically. He always underlined my good sentences and wrote, "Keep writing!"

Gary had just published his first book, *Grandpa Noel's Stories*—magical stories about his 23 grandchildren. He suggested, "Celine, add maps of China and Taiwan. It will help readers to see where all your stories took place." What a great idea.

Since English is my second language, Darlene once said to me, "It must be difficult for you." Writing a book—in any language—simply is not an easy task. I don't think it would be any easier if I wrote in Chinese.

"No need to repeat here," Rose pointed out. No redundancies—in any forms—escaped her notice. Rose helped me tighten my stories.

Jolene had just published her first book—*I Bring Daffodils*. She was quite an inspiration. When someone in the class suggested some changes in my writing, she said, "I wouldn't change it. It is her style."

Evan Pollock, one of my students from Arrowhead High School, always said to me, "*Lao Shi*, send me more stories." Once when I asked his opinion on something in one of the stories, he responded, "I wouldn't change it. It's your style."

Joann had been in this class a long time. Her lively personality was revealed in her writing. Everyone enjoyed her stories about Maisie. She was an inspiration to all of us. Her cheering comments meant a lot to me. "Celine, I will buy your book when it's published. Your stories are very interesting."

Joan was a retired teacher and a gentle loving soul. She wrote beautiful poems. She told me in an email, "Your book is truly a gem. I can't wait for you to finish and publish it! It will be a Must-Read!" What a sweet and supportive friend.

Connie joined the class a year ago. She is a musician and became my piano teacher. She wrote profound poems and beautiful music. She remarked, "Your personality and perseverance are reflected in your stories."

Lynn, a gifted poet, writes beautiful and amazing poems on any subject in just a short time. She made me want to write poems. She was in my first summer session when I started writing. A year later, we were in the same class again. She reminded me, "Show it with actions instead of descriptions." Once she wrote on my paper, "You are becoming a strong writer." What an encouragement.

New classmates also offered their perspectives. Meri told me what lines she liked. Maureen always cheered me on with positive notes.

Kathy Nelson, an English teacher and my pal at Arrowhead High

School, offered, "I have time in the summer. I would love to read your stories." What a caring friend.

Sandy Sabo, an old friend and a writer in Boston, was excited for me. "Celine, my background in college was editing. I would be happy to do the final check for you when it is ready for publication. I will do it for love." How blessed I am to have another pair of well-trained eyes standing by me.

I've always believed that when you are meant to do something, the right people will show up to help you. It has repeatedly been true in my life.

These people are my classmates, my friends, and my mentors. They have accompanied me every step of the way on this challenging journey.

They are my *Borrowed Eyes*. They are God-sends.

Dreams

Being a dreamer and doer, I have made many of my dreams come true throughout my life. But there were a few dreams I didn't think could ever come true.

Daydreams

Ever since I was a little girl, I pictured myself carrying a sword on my back climbing a high mountain, searching for a skillful master to teach me martial arts like I read about in books and saw in movies. I wanted to be like the heroines in the Kung Fu movies to fight the bad guys with my unbeatable piercing sword. What a dream for a little girl!

In the house where I grew up, there was a huge wooden bed—two or three feet above the floor. It took up three-fourths of the biggest room in the house. During the day, it was a play platform for us kids, and at night with padding it turned into a big bed. When I was about six or seven, one afternoon I was playing right next to my father on the big bed. He fell asleep so that I tried to be quiet. I couldn't sleep so I daydreamed, on my tummy.

I envisioned myself—a skillful martial artist flying high and jumping low, wherever I needed to be. Guess what? I flew up and landed on my father's tummy. My father screamed. He was furious. "What are you doing?"

How could I tell him I was flying like the heroines in the movies? I just looked at him, saying nothing! Till this day, I don't know how it happened.

Also when I heard music, I often danced in my imagination—wearing beautiful costumes and dancing to my own choreography. I also dreamed of playing all the songs I loved at a piano or with another instrument.

As we were growing up, those dreams were an unimaginable luxury. They could only be daydreams. We had to study and prepare all the time to pass the entrance exams for junior high, high school, and college. We lived under constant pressure to compete. In college, I studied and prepared for the Overseas Exam for another dream of mine—to attend graduate school in the U.S. and see the world.

These were a few of my impossible but beautiful childhood daydreams.

Bits & Pieces

I sometimes wonder if our childhood dreams mean anything to us when we grow older. Would they disappear and be forgotten totally? Or will we still remember and pursue them subconsciously?

When I established the Chinese language program for Lincoln Public Schools in 1988, a new adventure awaited me. I was the only channel for my students to learn the Chinese language and culture. I wanted to better prepare myself so that I could provide meaningful and memorable experiences for them. Almost every summer for seven or eight years, I went back to Taiwan to learn things that I thought my students would be interested in, such as the Lion Dance, folk dances, martial arts, and arts and crafts.

For three summers, I attended two-week Chinese opera workshops at the Fu Hsin Performing Arts Academy to learn Chinese opera. Fu Song Nan *Shi Fu* [Master] was a veteran martial arts teacher at the school. I asked him, "Would you teach me some basic martial arts? It is one of my childhood dreams."

He looked surprised. "Sure, I'd love to teach you. But we need to do it early, before class."

"No problem!" I was so excited that I could learn martial arts for a couple of weeks from him—a reputable martial artist in Taiwan.

For two weeks every morning I met him at 6:00 AM on the quiet campus to grasp whatever I could learn. He was very patient teaching me, an older person who had no background, but passion.

He taught me some basic skills the first summer. The second summer, I learned basic staff techniques. During the two weeks of the third summer, I learned a simple set of broadsword.

I brought back whatever I learned to my students. I introduced the spirit and discipline involved with martial arts to them, and I also shared with them the skills I acquired.

After *Shi Fu* retired from school several years later, he went to join his son in Venezuela in South America. In a letter, he told me he was writing a book on Chinese martial arts, and he was teaching many students.

I wrote back, "*Fu Shi Fu* [Master Fu], I am always grateful to you for helping me grasp bits and pieces of one of my childhood dreams."

Tai Chi

I played tennis with some graduate students from Taiwan regularly for many years. I enjoyed the outdoor games. The students were energetic and good sports. Being the only female and the oldest one in the group, I really needed to work harder and run faster to keep up with them.

We played doubles. My partner David Wang was a bright young man and a great tennis player. He coached me while playing. He yelled to me all the time, "Go! Go forward!" "To the left!" or "Back up!"

In the summer, we played two or three times a week. Each time, we played five sets without break. My tennis playmates became my good friends. After obtaining their master's degrees or PhD, they left me one by one. I really missed my tennis pals, and I missed playing tennis.

One day, my husband Don showed me the paper. "Hey, there is a Chinese martial artist in town teaching Tai Chi. You might be interested." Although I heard about Tai Chi all my life, my childhood impression remained—it was so slow and it was for old people.

Not long after Don showed me the paper, I met Di Ma—the young beautiful martial artist from China—we read about in the paper. Her husband was pursing his PhD degree in business. We enjoyed each other and became friends.

Di Ma was born into a martial arts family. "My father and brothers are professional martial artists. I was identified as a gifted child in the field." At the age eleven, she was recruited and became a member of the National Martial Arts Team, receiving vigorous training for competitions. She continued, "Tai Chi was my main focus. I won many titles in Tai Chi competitions."

I started learning Tai Chi from Di Ma in 1991. Di Ma had just arrived in the U.S. and was beginning to learn English. I was her translator since I was the only Chinese in class.

I learned the short form of Tai Chi Chuan and Tai Chi Sword. In 1992, I performed the Tai Chi Sword in my first *Chinese Kaleidoscope* program at Lincoln High School in Nebraska.

Twenty years later, I showed my students at Arrowhead High School in Wisconsin the application of each movement of the simplified form of Tai Chi Chuan. I told them, "When you practice as an exercise, you move slowly to train your mind and body. But when you are in a real situation, you need to apply the skills and move fast."

Students saw how powerful and fast the slow motion Tai Chi could be when applied to a combat situation. They wanted to learn Tai Chi. In 2012, I modified it with Kung Fu fans for my students to perform half a set of Tai Chi with fans at my very last *Chinese Kaleidoscope* program at Arrowhead High School in Wisconsin.

After Di Ma's husband obtained his PhD, they moved to Minnesota. I was grateful that I had a chance to learn Tai Chi for several years from Di Ma, an expert in the field. She helped me understand Tai Chi and acquire a few more bits and pieces to fulfill part of a childhood dream.

Shao Lin

I invited my family to the *Chinese Kaleidoscope* program at Arrowhead High School. After the program, my six-year-old grandson Casey asked me, "*Po Po,* would you teach me what your students did?"

Before he turned five, he asked me to teach him Chinese. And now he wanted to learn the cultural activities I taught my students. He truly is a *Descendant of the Dragon*—a Chinese.

I was delighted. "Sure! What do you want to learn?"

"I want to learn the Tai Chi Fan, flags, Lion Dance, and Dragon Dance. And also brush painting and writing. Everything your students did."

I started teaching him some basic martial arts. He was motivated and focused learning whatever I could offer. His nimble movement, flexible body, and creativity with staff [long stick], Kung Fu fan, and flags were impressive. "Good job! Anything I can do, you can do better."

I told my daughter Joline, "Casey is ready for formal martial arts training."

In the fall, Casey started his Kung Fu class, Tiny Tiger, at the ShaoLin Center. *Shi Mu* [master's wife], a dedicated martial artist, was his first instructor. Casey loved it. I watched him practice every morning. "Show me what you have learned!" He demonstrated many new skills, ones I wished I could do.

He loved to check out my collection of different weapons—swords and broadswords, once a while. "When you are older, and learn how to use them, I will give them to you."

He pointed at one gorgeous sword, his favorite. "I want this one. I can't wait to use it!"

Ever since I moved to Milwaukee in 2009, I had my eyes open to find a school for Chinese martial arts or Tai Chi. I saw some demonstrations from a couple of schools at different fairs. Although I had limited training, I could tell their schools were not for me. Their skills wouldn't challenge me.

There was a celebration for *Shi Fu* [Master] Steve Kleppe's 30th anniversary as a master in martial arts at the ShaoLin Center. I had never met him or talked to him before. I attended the program with my family.

At the program, many students demonstrated. *Shi Fu* Kleppe also did. He demonstrated Tai Chi—Wu Dang Style. It was absolutely graceful and powerful. I was so impressed, and I told Casey, my family, and many friends, "This is a true master with high level skills. Casey is in the right school."

I went to *Shi Fu* Kleppe after the program, "*Shi Fu*, superb Kung Fu! Congratulations!"

He smiled, "Thank you."

One day in May 2015, Joline told me, "*Shi Fu* would like to invite you to join Casey for the next set—Two Person Northern Staff." The class welcomes parents to learn with their children. In our case, grandma. What a creative idea.

I was surprised and excited. "Great! I love staff!"

In June, when the new set started, Casey and I became Kung Fu classmates at the ShaoLin Center. I was the only adult. According to the tradition, Casey is my *Shi Ge* [martial older brother] since he attended the school before I did. I teased him, bowing to him. "*Shi Ge*, be gentle with *Shi Mei* [martial younger sister] now that you are more skillful than I." We both giggled.

My classmates were between ages nine and eighteen. All of them had had three or four years of training. It was funny to be the oldest person and the youngest *Shi Mei* in the class. But it is better late than never to learn something you love, even at the golden age.

I was so excited that *Shi Fu* was teaching the class. In class, I had to remind Casey constantly, "Don't do it so fast. I haven't got it yet."

It was flattering that Casey fought me with the staff like fighting against a young classmate, not a golden-age *Po Po*. One time, he almost got me down to the floor if I hadn't grabbed his shoulder, just in time. As he helped me up, I said to him, "*Shi Ge*, not so rough with *Po Po!*"

I was impressed how *Shi Fu* taught us. He used task analysis to break down the movements. He showed us the application of each movement before integrating it into the set the way I taught my students. It takes a teacher to recognize an effective teacher. After my first class, I said to *Shi Fu*, "Thank you for the invitation. I really enjoyed the class. You are such a wonderful teacher. You know how to make learning fun and easy."

He laughed. "I was a high school teacher before."

"No wonder! What did you teach?"

"Science."

What a switch. "How did you become a Shao Lin Master? Where did you learn all this Shao Lin Kung Fu?"

"I started learning Chinese Ken Po and Tai Chi when I was twenty. When I received the black belt, I felt limited, no place to go. I started searching for different kinds of martial arts."

"You needed a breakthrough. You wanted to learn Chinese martial arts because there are such a wide variety of forms and styles you can learn?"

Nodding his head, he said, "You are right. That's exactly what I did." He continued, "I began a journey which led to my studying various beautiful pieces from many world renowned Chinese masters."

"Did you learn from a Shao Lin master in Wisconsin?"

"No. At first, I traveled around the country to look for a teacher. Finally, I found a Chinese martial arts teacher in Indiana. I drove to Indiana every other weekend to learn from him for three years." He continued, "After that, I wanted to learn Shao Lin Kung Fu and more Hong style martial arts, and I also wanted to continue with my Tai Chi. I started searching for a teacher again."

There were four rows of pictures on the wall at the Center. I pointed the picture above his picture on the wall and asked him, "Is he your *Shi Fu*?"

"Yes. The four people above him were his *Shi Fu*. The people of the top row were his *Shi Fu's* teachers." It is a tradition to display pictures of the masters by generation in marital arts schools.

"What is his name? Where is he?"

"My teacher's name is Kwong Wing Lam. He lives in California. He is one of the top three martial artists for Shao Lin Kung Fu, Hong Style martial arts, and Tai Chi in the U.S. I am still learning with him."

"Didn't you go to China to learn Shao Lin Kung Fu?"

"Yes. Many times from many masters." He smiled.

"How did you find all the masters in China?" It is not easy even for a Chinese person.

"I first went to Henan and Beijing with Master Lam. On another trip, my teacher referred me to a different master for Wu Dang styles. Thus I began my study of Tai Yi Tai Chi—Wu Dang Style. One referral after another, I was all over China learning a wide variety of forms." He continued, "Each time I went to China, I spent two, three or more weeks there to learn from different masters. I loved it." He beamed.

It was a joy to get to know our *Shi Fu*. It touched me deeply to see a non-Chinese person loving Chinese martial arts with enormous passion and reaching such a high level of skills. At the same time, I have great respect for *Shi Mu*, his wife, for supporting fully his passion and vision. He practices Qi Gong, meditation, and Taoism for self-cultivation. *Shi Fu* appears to be a spiritual person, living a simple, content, positive life.

The ShaoLin Center in Waukesha, Wisconsin offers many sessions of different types and levels of classes. Students can practice and get help from *Shi Fu* during Open Studio sessions. When you walk in the very traditionally decorated Center, you will feel you are in China. It was amazing to see so many students with great skills and passion doing Chinese martial arts at the Center. I appreciated it greatly when *Shi Fu* spent the last few minutes of each class teaching students about virtues, disciplines, and the history of Shao Lin as part of their training.

At the end of July, when the Two Person Northern Staff set ended, I decided to continue learning from *Shi Fu*. "Thank you again for the invitation. I had great fun. I will join ShaoLin Center, officially, this fall. Kiran and Holly, two grandchildren will also start the Tiny Tiger class."

He laughed. "I am glad you had fun. We love to have you!"

My old body may not be able to jump high, bend low or turn swiftly like Casey and other classmates. But I enjoy learning—mindfully—every technique from *Shi Fu,* a humble dedicated true master, to fulfill a childhood dream of mine.

Maybe to make another impossible dream, to play piano, come true is not so impossible after all.

The True, the Good, and the Beautiful

The true gives me faith and fortifies my trust in people. The good brings me sunshine and strengthens my hope in the universe. The beautiful touches my soul and deepens my gratitude in everything.

The true, the good, and the beautiful are what I search for in life. It is what I collect and store deep in my heart. It is what my soul treasures the most with great appreciation.

They are the joy, blessings, and gratitude stowed in me, forever...

Chapter 8
Fruitful Harvest

The Path

I was a Special Education teacher at Everett Jr. High in Lincoln, Nebraska during the eighties. One day, the manager of a successful insurance company approached me. "Would you come to work for us?"

I was surprised. "I am a teacher. Why did you come to me?"

"We need a person with your skills."

I wondered what kind of skills I had. "What are you looking for?"

"A person with organization, people, and leadership skills."

"You think I am such a person?"

"Yes, we heard great things about you. We would like to invite you to work for us."

"Thank you. But I am not interested in business." I didn't even ask what kind of job they offered me.

"Please consider it. You will double what you make as a teacher." It was very true.

Without hesitation I responded, "Money is not an attraction to me. I enjoy teaching." I turned it down.

Jing, a graduate student at the University of Nebraska from Taiwan, was a close friend during the nineties. His family had many businesses in Taiwan and in Canada. One day he asked me seriously, "We will start a new company if you'd be willing to run the business for us."

Again I was astonished. "Are you kidding? I don't know anything about running a company."

"You have all the skills needed to run a company. Besides you are so good at motivating and training people. You are also an embracing leader. With your skills and personality you can do a lot more than just teaching."

"Thank you for your trust. I am flattered," I told him. "Working with students makes me very happy." I had no interest in running a company.

When I taught at the International School of Beijing, I was approached by the administration. "Would you like to be the successor of the principal of the Chinese Department?"

"No. Thanks. I enjoy working with students." I had no desire to play politics and I didn't want to attend the countless meetings. I loved my students. I was happy teaching them and laughing with them every day.

The great joy and excitement of teaching are motivating and watching students learn and grow. It is most rewarding and priceless. Teaching keeps my heart lively and young, and it makes my soul vibrant and satisfied—the indescribable profound feelings only a person who is on the right path could feel and understand.

To teach is to touch lives forever. Teaching is my life, and it is forever for me.

Old Buddy

As I unpacked and tried to be organized with my thoughts and my stuff in the afternoon on November 6th, 2014—a day after I arrived in Taipei, Taiwan, the phone rang. It was Jie Yong Jeung. "Welcome back, *Lao Shi* [Teacher]!"

"Hi! How are you? Long time no see!" I hadn't seen him for quite a few years.

He laughed. "Yes. It has been so many years since I visited you in Beijing. When did you get in last night? How is your jet-lag?"

"I am tired, but excited. It was a long flight. It was 2:00 AM when I finally settled in the house."

"Would you want to go anyplace special? I am free for the next two days before going to Seattle." His younger son was in dental college there.

Taipei, where I grew up, has changed so much throughout the years. I had never been to this part of the city before. I didn't recognize the neighborhood. "I don't know where I am and I don't know how to get around. I heard that Taipei 101 is very unique. It is very close from where I live. Would you take me there and show me around this area?"

Taipei 101 is the first skyscraper to become the tallest building in the world. This 1,671 feet/509 meters tall building was completed in 2004. The 101-floor tower was built with steel, glass, and concrete. The skyscraper looks like an elongated pagoda, a traditional form that symbolizes protection and achievement. The tower's blue-green glass-curtain wall is the color of jade—a stone the ancient Chinese prized for its purity and vitality. It is an expression of both earthly and spiritual power. The gigantic tower is gorgeous—both daytime and nighttime. From the two observation decks, you can see not only the whole City of Taipei but also its surrounding mountains and rivers.

Jie Yong responded happily, "Sure! I haven't been up there either. I will show you around the area so that you will know where and how to take the subway and buses to different parts of the city."

"Great! Can't wait to see you!" I was excited. I gave him my address.

"Me too! I will pick you up around 9:00 tomorrow."

Here I was in Taipei, where I grew up, for my one-month vacation. I hadn't been back for many years. The first person who welcomed me—besides the good old friend Cheng De Kuo who picked me up at the airport—was Jie Yong Juang, one of the students I taught for one year when I was fresh out of college at the age of twenty-one.

The First Step

After talking to Jie Yong, the unforgettable heartwarming memories from long ago—far far away like dreams, yet vivid and clear like movies—surfaced before my eyes ...

I passed the Overseas Examination to pursue advanced studies in the U.S. after college. Since I had been away from home for college, I decided to stay home to work for one year before going abroad to study. I got my very first job. I became an English teacher at Keelung Secondary School in Badu, a little town near Keelung—the northern port in Taiwan.

As I walked onto the platform in the classroom on the first day of school, little did I realize then I was paving the first step of the way for my destiny.

Keelung Secondary School, a public school for grades 7-12 boys, was the best school for boys in the Keelung area. It took me more than an hour each way by train and bus to teach there. I was assigned to teach four seventh grade beginner English classes. There were forty or so students in each class. I was also the homeroom teacher for one of the classes I taught.

I knew how critical a teacher could be for any subject, especially for a new subject. It was my duty to make their first foreign language fun to learn. I tried different ways to provide a happy, positive, and meaningful learning atmosphere for their constant pressured, competitive lives.

It made me very happy to see the smiles and pride on those delightful little faces while learning *Twinkle, Twinkle Little Star*. Using the record to teach phonetics made it more interesting and effective for them. My English teachers taught the grammar and lessons separately. We had a hard time connecting the two. I taught them grammar while teaching the lessons. It helped them visualize the connections between the two, more clearly. It was a great pleasure to witness how some of them replaced their mental block with the confidence gained throughout the year.

I felt deeply connected with my students, especially with the liveliest class of the four. We had a ten-minute break between classes. After their classes, I never had time to return to my office. During the short break some of them played basketball and some played ping pong at the court right next to their classroom. They always wanted me to join them, "*Lao Shi*, come to play with us."

"I am not good at it." I laughed and said.

"It's okay. Come to play with us!" They were so delightful and sincere. How could I say "No"? I always joined them. Everyone passed the ball to me to shoot the basket, but I missed it most of the time. We had great fun playing and laughing together.

Being a homeroom teacher, I needed to check on each student's weekly journal. One time a student told me in his journal that several of them climbed the mountain behind school over the weekend. Together they carved my name on one of the big trees. How sweet!

One Sunday, I opened the door when the doorbell rang. I was surprised to see two students from my homeroom at the door. They looked excited. "Would you go on a picnic with us?" they asked.

Back then, not many people had telephones. They didn't know my telephone number. Without even knowing if I was home or not, they took a train ride all the way from Keelung to Taipei, a big city they were not familiar with at all. They brought food to have a picnic with me. Their innocence and sincerity touched my heart. I was genuinely moved. We spent a happy day at Bi Tan [Green Lake], and we enjoyed the delicious food they brought, as we rowed the boat.

I found goodies, sometimes cute little things on my desk in the office throughout the year. They never left their names by the food or gifts. I didn't know who gave them to me. I felt their love.

How delighted I was to see the sparkles and smiles in their eyes—a desire to learn and trust in me, every day. They loved learning English. They learned well. At the annual English competition, my four classes ranked 1-4 out of eight classes. The individual winners were also from their classes. I was very proud of them.

These were my adorable and diligent students. Their earnestness, purity, and trust touched my soul profoundly—a beauty I have treasured all my life.

Jie Yong was a student in the liveliest class. He was very quiet. He seldom talked to me. He just smiled at me whenever he saw me. Little did I know then this shy little boy would have a lifelong connection with me.

Happy time flies like a soaring arrow. My last year at home ended too soon. With tears on my face and sorrow in my heart I bid farewell to my beloved family, friends, and precious students to pursue a dream I had when I was seventeen.

Jie Yong like many students kept close contact with me. They were the ones who sent me a cookbook when they learned that I didn't even know how to boil water, let alone cooking, in the U.S. Their letters made me smile and cry at the same time. How I missed them.

I wanted my students to know the world was bigger than they could see. I planted the seeds and shared what I learned and experienced. My life in the U.S was challenging but exciting. I encouraged them to extend their visions and enlarge their worlds as I did. "The world is so big and interesting. When you have the chance, explore it."

Jie Yong turned out to be a genius student with a brilliant mind. He attended Taiwan University majoring in Electrical and Computer Engineering—a tough field at the very best university in Taiwan.

In the fall of 1979, Jie Yong brought his girlfriend, who later became his wife, to pursue advanced studies in computer science at the University of Nebraska in Lincoln, Nebraska where we lived. Jie Yong now was a confident, cheerful, and positive young man. We were so excited to be united again after so many years. I was curious how he ended up in Lincoln, Nebraska.

"To how many schools did you apply?"

"One!"

"What? Just one?"

I couldn't believe what I heard. Being such a brilliant student, he could get in any school he chose, such as Harvard, MIT, or Stanford. But he was here with me in Lincoln, Nebraska.

He smiled and said, "Yes!"

During the two years when he studied in Lincoln, he became not only one of my closest and most trusted friends but also a beloved uncle to our two daughters.

A few years later, Jie Yong received his PhD in Computer Engineering from Purdue University. After teaching four years at Northwestern University in Chicago, he decided to return to Taiwan to teach at Taiwan University, where he had studied. Later he started his own company doing business in China while teaching in Taiwan.

Although we seldom saw each other after he returned to Taiwan, we kept in touch throughout the years. Here we were together at the gorgeous tower, Taipei 101, filling our lives with precious moments of pleasure again. We shared our lives, concerns, and dreams, without any reservation, just like the good old days. The forever connection with Jie Yong is one of the amazing blessings I have cherished always.

*****

My life truly is full of surprises and unbelievable blessings.

In the fall of 1989, I received a call. "May I speak to *Tan Lao Shi* [Teacher Tan]?"

"Speaking. Who is calling, please?" I didn't recognize the voice.

"This is Yan Chun Tseng. Remember me, *Lao Shi*?"

I was so excited to hear his voice. It had been twenty-two years since I last saw him—one of the students I loved dearly.

"Hey! Of course I remember you! What a pleasant surprise! Where are you? How have you been all these years? What are you doing nowadays?"

He laughed and didn't know what to tell me first. "I am in Florida presenting my paper at an international conference."

I remembered his face and smiles clearly. "What conference? What paper?"

"It is part of my research for my dissertation on semi-conductors."

"Where are you studying now?" I was hoping he studied in the U.S.

"I am studying at Sophia University in Tokyo, Japan."

"How did you end up in Japan? Come to see me. It has been too long!"

He laughed again. "I never forgot you either. So much has happened in my life. I will tell you when I see you. I will check on the flights."

"I really want to see you!"

After a short while he called back and told me he had purchased the tickets.

He came to Lincoln to see me two days later. What an unspeakable joy to see him again. The moment we met at the airport, the missing twenty-two years disappeared. Although I had not seen him for so long, I would recognize him at any place. He still had the same grin on his happy face and the sparks in his eyes as he did when he was a seventh grader.

"How did you find me?" I wondered.

"I got your number from Long Sheng Tsai in Japan. He is studying at the same school. We talked about you a lot." Long Sheng is another student who has kept close contact with me all these years.

Yan Chun stayed for only one day. We talked about the past, the present, and the future for twenty-four hours straight, no sleep, to catch up for those missing years.

After getting his PhD in Electrical & Electronic Engineering at the Sophia University in Japan, Yan Chun went back to Taiwan to work. Later he started his own company and did business internationally.

In 1988, I started the Chinese Language Program for the Lincoln Public Schools. I was the only learning channel for my students on China and its culture. I wanted to better prepare myself to teach my students effectively and to enrich their learning with broader and meaningful experiences. In the 1990s I went back to Taiwan almost every summer—to collect materials, attend workshops, and learn cultural activities such as the martial arts, folk dances, Chinese opera, and arts and crafts.

The summer of 1993, Joline was a junior in high school, and Andrea was an eighth grader. I took them to Taiwan for a Chinese language camp. I attended a workshop at the Mandarin Center of Taiwan Normal University in Taipei.

I seemed to be allergic to something in the air. It affected my voice and throat. When the workshop ended, I got a call from Yan Chun. He heard my funny voice. "What happened to you? Are you okay?" He was concerned.

"I don't know what happened. My voice is hoarse, and my throat is irritated."

"Stay put! I will be there in two hours. I will take you to the best Chinese medicine doctor here." He lived in the Hsinchu Science Park—the Silicon Valley of Taiwan—two hours by car from Taipei where I was.

Yan Chun took me to see the doctor in Hsinchu right after picking me up in Taipei. The doctor prescribed some herb medicine for me. Yan Chun even bought an electrical herb medicine pot for me to brew the medicine.

After the doctor's appointment he showed me around in Hsinchu. When we were on top of a nearby mountain, he handed me a *hong bao* [red envelope], containing a lot of money. I was stunned, "What is this for?"

"It is some pocket money for you to use in Taiwan." He responded in a matter of fact way.

"Oh, no, no! Thank you. I have money. I appreciate your thoughtfulness."

He insisted. "It's not very much!" I refused to take his money.

We talked about a lot of things. Then he was very serious and concerned, and he asked me, "Do you have enough money to support your daughters through college?"

I was a teacher and Don was a government employee, not rich people. "We will manage." Our daughters' education was our top priority. We could always refinance the house to support them if necessary.

He said earnestly, "Be sure to let me know if you need money at any time in the future." My heart was profoundly touched by his genuine concern and care of our wellbeing. How blessed I am to have such a student and a friend in my life!

Blessed

The Youth Fu Hsing Chinese Opera Troupe was known for their outstanding training and performance for decades in Taiwan, and Mei Chiang Folk Dance Troupe was an award-winning troupe for their creative choreography and fabulous performances every year. Through workshops I attended, I got to know Tien Yu, one of the teachers and the leaders of the Chinese opera troupe and Mei Chiang Kuo, the teacher and the leader of the Mei Chiang Folk Dance Troupe. Both of them were very helpful and provided whatever resources I needed, always. I was very impressed with them and their groups.

A clear vision and a strong sense of mission resonated in my heart— to bring both troupes to the U.S.

Throughout 1990s, I arranged for both troupes to perform—in four or five states in the U.S. on each tour—many times. Each time they shared with tens of thousands of people not only their talents but also Chinese culture. The troupes didn't charge any fees for their visits and performances. Hosting schools and communities were responsible for the troupe's local transportation and room and board. With my invitation, coordination, and proposed itinerary, they could apply for a special grant for the traveling and program expenses from the government of Taiwan.

In the spring of 1998, the Youth Fu Hsing Chinese Opera Mission—a thirty-people troupe—was scheduled for another three-week tour in the U.S. One day in February I received a call from Tien Yu, my contact person at the National Fu Hsing Dramatic Arts Academy in Taipei. "*Tan Lao Shi*, I am afraid we can't make it to the U.S. this year."

"Oh, no! Why? What happened? People are looking forward to your visit." Schools and communities in five states were awaiting their arrival and performances.

"The government cut the budget. We don't have enough funds this year." This was the first time they'd had this problem.

"How much more do you need? How soon do you need it in order to make it this year?"

"We need $20,000 more, and we need it in a week." He sounded disappointed and hopeless.

"Wow! That much so soon? Let me see what I can do. I will get back to you." I wondered how and where I could get this amount of money in a week. I really didn't want to cancel their tour since people in different states had gone through a lot of coordination and preparation for their visit.

I pondered if Taiwan was like the U.S.—businesses donating for charity and sponsoring such a mission. I thought of Yan Chun Tseng since he was a successful business man in Taiwan, and he might have some connections. Hopefully he could find some sponsors for the troupe.

I called Yan Chun right away and explained the urgent situation. "Is it possible for you to check with some of your business connections to see if they would sponsor such a mission?"

He listened carefully and then asked, "How much do they need it? How soon do they need?"

"A lot! They need $20,000 in a week." It was an impossible mission, but I wanted to try if there was the slightest chance. Yan Chun was my sole resource and only hope.

He asked, "Where should I send the money?"

"To the school directly." I gave him the account number of the school.

One week later, Tien Yu called. He sounded cheerful and excited. "Your student, Mr. Yan Chun Tseng, has sent the money we need. We will be coming as scheduled. Thank you and Mr. Tseng for making our tour possible this year."

"I am happy he got the funding for you at the last minute. See you in April." What a relief! I was so glad I had thought of Yan Chun. Obtaining this partial but crucial fund of $20,000 in a week indeed was an impossible mission—truly a miracle. It enabled the troupe to share not only their talents but also Chinese culture with countless people again in the U.S. as scheduled.

When the troupe came to Lincoln, the Chinese opera artists worked with my students on martial arts. They also performed in Lincoln High School and Park Middle School where I taught. They received a standing ovation for their performance at the Asian Night that I was in charge of—a culture program for the community sponsored by the Nebraska Asian Community Center. More than four thousand people had the opportunity to appreciate the unique and colorful Chinese opera in Lincoln alone.

The troupe's next stop was Minneapolis, Minnesota. After their performance at a high school, some Chinese language students took such an interest in Chinese opera. They went to Taiwan to attend the Chinese opera workshop at the National Fu Hsing Dramatic Arts Academy in Taipei the following summer—the impact I had envisioned.

Tien Yu was a talented and creative performing artist. He was pleasant and reliable. We planned and designed workshops for the

American students and Chinese language teachers. We worked on all the details closely on all their mission tours. We became good friends.

Tien Yu stayed with me during their visit. He said to me after he got settled, "Mr. Yan Chun Tseng, the student of yours, must have great respect for you."

"Why do you say that?"

"Mr. Tseng himself donated $15,000 for our mission. Not many students will do that for a teacher." Tien Yu was a teacher himself.

"What? What did you say? Yan Chun donated $15,000? He never told me that!" I was shocked. I didn't mean for Yan Chun to donate the money himself, but to find sponsors for the troupe. I felt so bad he donated so much money because of me.

Yan Chun never mentioned a word of it. He just called and told me after accomplishing the impossible mission, "*Lao Shi*, don't worry. $20,000 has been deposited in the school account."

Tien Yu handed me a program of the mission. "Yes, he did. Here is the list of the sponsors."

My eyes welled with tears. I was speechless; I was astonished; and I was deeply moved when I looked at the list of the sponsors. Jie Yong Jeung, Long Sheng Tsai, Jing Fa Wu, and Shuo Xue Lin were among the sponsors besides Yan Chun—they all were my students.

After so many years the students I taught for one year long ago in Taiwan are still in my life and I am still in their hearts. They not only share my vision but also honor my mission. What a blessed teacher I am!

The Way We Were

Great memories with my students always warmed my heart. Back in the 70s, international travel was extremely expensive and not as common and convenient as it is today. I went back home for the first time after four long years. I was so excited.

A lot had happened during these four years. My older brother was married and became a father. My parents enjoyed spoiling their first grandchild; and both my twin sister and I got married. My younger siblings had grown up and my students were juniors in high school.

Long Sheng Tsai called shortly after I returned to Taiwan. *"Lao Shi,* welcome back! We would like to take you to the beach near Keelung for a Bar-B-Q outing. When can you go?"

"As soon as you would like to meet. I can't wait to see you." We set a date and time to meet at the Keelung train station.

As I got off the train, seven big boys ran toward me, waving, smiling, and calling, *"Lao Shi!* Here!" I was surrounded by them instantly. The first thing Long Sheng Tsai said to me, mischievously, *"Lao Shi,* you have grown up!" Everyone laughed and agreed.

They were about my size when I left them, now they were about ten inches taller than I. "You guys have really grown! You are giants now!" They burst into laughter. Each one tried to see how much taller they were—hands over my head measuring against their chests. How delightful to be with them again.

A lot to catch up on—I checked on the other students with them and got updates. They grew up by the ocean in Keelung area. They were good swimmers and divers. A few of them dove into the Pacific Ocean to get seafood, and others stayed with me on the beach to grill the food they brought.

They wanted me to get in the water—big rolling waves coming toward us. "It's fun. Come with us to the water," Long Sheng Tsai said to me.

"I am scared of water! I can't swim!" I laughed.

They all laughed and said to me at the same time, "Don't be scared. We will stay with you." They protected me like I was a little kid. With Long Sheng Tsai and Shuo Xue Lin on either side of me—holding my arms so tightly that it hurt—to keep their "chicken" teacher safe from the big waves as we approached the water. It was great fun getting all wet in the rolling waves.

A couple of them grilled the clams and other seafood from the ocean while we were in the water. When the food was ready, it was a feast. Long Sheng dipped each one in the sauce they prepared and fed me, non-stop. "Are they good? Do you like it? Try this." He fed me more. I smiled and nodded—my mouth was full.

I never knew how fun the beach near Keelung could be. With my personal divers, fishermen, and lifeguards by my side, the floating clouds in the blue sky were more gorgeous, the big waves were not as intimidating, and the beach was fun and exciting. Another unforgettable day imprinted and stored in my heart. Since then, I have gone back to the beach with my friends and daughters many times, and each time I shared the wonderful day I had with my students on this beach in the summer of 1971.

*****

Some of these students became my friends and my buddies. When I told them I decided to take early retirement from Lincoln Public Schools in 2000, Long Sheng Tsai teased me, "*Lao Shi*, you can't retire until you turn eighty!"

Yan Chun Tseng said, "Come back to Taiwan and teach, *Lao Shi*. We will open a school for you." How thoughtful and sweet.

"You are too young to retire, *Lao Shi*," Jie Yong Jung responded instantly.

They all knew me so well—being my old friends. I didn't truly retire until twelve years later in 2012, my third retirement.

Long Sheng was a lively and fun kid. He is among those who have always kept contact with me throughout the years. Long Sheng calls to check on me; he phoned whenever he moves; and he shares special events with me, always. He worked in Beijing for several years. He gave me helpful tips when I decided to teach in Beijing.

He sent me information on diabetes regularly after I told him my glucose was a little high. After my heart attack in August 2014, he comforted me and told me not to worry about my heart attack and to have a stent put in one of my arteries. "You will do fine with the stent. Many people with many stents live a normal and long life." That is my sweet caring buddy, Long Sheng Tsai.

He has lived an interesting, adventurous life. After finishing his advanced studies in Japan, Long Sheng married a wonderful Japanese lady. He worked in Tokyo for ten years in banking enterprise. He then worked for the government of Taiwan for many years. Later he spent a few years in Beijing. Then he and his family settled in Hawaii. With his three languages, currently he is an investment consultant working with clients in different countries—truly an international businessman.

In the fall of 2014, when I told him that I was going to Taiwan in November, he was in Manila, Philippines. He invited me. "*Lao Shi*, come to visit me. I will take you to the beach and show you around the Philippines."

"I will see if I have time to make a side trip. Be sure to come to Taiwan to meet me. I want to see you." I had not seen him for many years.

"For sure I will go back to see you. I have asked Chien-I Kuo to locate some classmates in Taiwan to have a reunion with you."

"Wonderful! How is Chien-I? I can't wait to see you guys." I wondered how many of them could be located in Taiwan after almost half a century. I couldn't wait to see them again.

*****

During the last week I was in Taiwan, Cheng Hui Liu [Michael] called. "Lao Shi, you are leaving soon. Do you have time to meet? I can take you wherever you wish to go."

My schedule was very tight especially during the last week. Sometimes I had three or four engagements a day. "Yeah, I want to see you. I am open tomorrow afternoon before five."

"I will pick you up at 1:00." I was looking forward to seeing him.

Michael was the president of my homeroom class. In Taiwan, each class elects a president and a few officers to assist homeroom teachers to take care of homeroom business. Michael worked closely with me throughout the school year. He has always kept contact with me.

He attended a military academy and became a computer engineer in the army. He was away from home most of the time when he was in the service. There was a family crisis—divorce, after he retired from the army. I saw him in the summer of 1996. He worked in China then and had taken his daughter with him. He was very concerned. He said,

343

"My daughter can't attend the local school in China."

"Why can't she?" I wondered.

"Schools in China don't accept her credits from Taiwan." Politics affect everything.

"Why can't she stay with her mother in Taiwan?"

He sighed. "It is complicated."

"How old is she? She can't just stay home, and not attend school." Being a teacher, I was concerned that she was not in school.

"She is an eighth grader. Is there any chance she can attend school in the U.S?"

In 1996, Melinda, Michael's youngest child, came to live with us. For one year she attended Park Middle School where I taught in Lincoln, Nebraska. I was glad I could help him at a time of need.

Eighteen years later on December 2nd, 2014, Michael and I were at a teahouse on a mountain top near Taipei. The beautiful green mountains around us made me realize how much I missed the mountains in Taiwan. We sipped tea as we remembered the past, chatted about the present, and dreamed about the future. His daughter, Melinda, got married after obtaining her master's degree in graphic designs. She had just become the mother of a baby boy. It was great to see Michael—an old friend—again, especially knowing he was content with his life, and his family was doing well.

Destiny

When I was in Taipei during the month from November 5th to December 4th, 2014, every day was a highlight. I had not been back for a long time. I didn't know when I'd be back again.

One day Chien-I Kuo called, "*Lao Shi*, remember me? I am Chien-I Kuo."

"Of course, I remember you! You were tall and skinny, and sat in the back row." I laughed.

"Good memory, *Lao Shi*! Sorry I didn't call you earlier. I just got back from a trip overseas. I was trying to locate some of the classmates to meet with you."

"Great! How many did you find?" I was excited.

"It is not easy to find everyone after so many years. I am still contacting people." It had been more than four decades since I'd seen him and most of the students.

"I know. Whoever you can locate is great. Thanks for your effort." Life really is like a dream. We were all so young then, and now some of us had retired.

"I set the date to meet in the afternoon on November 30th. Will it work for you?"

"Sure! Can't wait! Just tell me the time and place. I will be there. By the way, do you know where Yan Chun Tseng is now?"

"No. I lost contact with him a long time ago. I will check with others to see if anyone knows what happened to him."

I couldn't wait to see them even though I didn't know how many Chien-I could find. I only knew Long Sheng Tsai would come from the Philippines and Jie Yong Jung would be back from Seattle for the reunion.

Nobody seemed to know where Yan Chun Tseng was. I really wanted to see him again. He had called me from China in the fall of 2012. He sounded content and cheerful. He sold his house in Hsinchu and he was working in China.

What a pleasure to hear from him again. We had a lengthy chat to update our lives. I knew both of his children. They participated in the summer English camps I established with the English Department at the University of Nebraska for Chu Lin High School—one of the sister schools—in Taipei. His daughter became a doctor in Taiwan and his son got his PhD in the U.S. That was 2012, the last time I had heard from him.

I didn't want my time in Taiwan to pass too fast, but I was looking forward to the reunion with my students on November 30th—four days before I was scheduled to come back to the U.S.

That day two high school buddies, Mei Xin Lee and He Ying Lu, insisted on accompanying me, to ensure I could find the café where I was to meet my students. How sweet of them.

Mei Xin asked me, "Will you recognize them after so many years?"

"I really don't know. I have changed so much myself. I wonder if they will recognize me." I laughed.

"Let's just wait outside so that you are more visible. We will stay with you until they come," He Ying suggested.

After standing in the courtyard for a few minutes, I heard, "*Lao Shi!* Here! Here!" Here came Long Sheng Tsai running toward me from inside the café. We hugged and we laughed. "Long time no see! You look great, *Lao Shi!*"

"You too! I am sorry I couldn't go to the Philippines to visit you. My schedule is too tight. I am glad you made it back." We hadn't seen each other for almost twenty years.

"Of course I would come to see you. Come to visit me in Hawaii." He patted me on my back.

One by one they arrived.

Chien-I Kuo came. I had not seen him since he was a seventh grader. I could still recognize him. We hugged and then looked at each other. "You haven't changed much. You are so tall. Still skinny!"

He chuckled. "So nice seeing you after so many years. Sorry that I couldn't arrange it earlier." He is an accomplished senior consultant for a MIS company doing business internationally.

He had told me in the email who would be coming. "I wish I could have located more of the classmates for our reunion."

"Don't worry about it. Thank you for doing this. It is not an easy task to get people together after almost half a century." I couldn't wait to see whoever could make it this day.

Wen Chung [Albert] Hsu came in. He hadn't changed much since I last saw him in 1996. He looked great and handsome as before. I was thrilled to see him again. "You look the same, just more mature! How is everything with you?"

Albert embraced me and then looked at me. "You look great also. So nice to see you. Now I work in Taiwan and also in China." He is a senior consultant and a director for an IT company in Shanghai.

As we were chatting, I saw a man outside of the window—seemed lost. "Who is that? Do you know him? Is he one of ours?"

"Yeah! It's Chung Kang Tong!" We knocked on the window and

got his attention.

Chung Kang Tong ran inside toward us. He had emailed me earlier and told me he would come, and he would bring a few old pictures along. How wonderful! I had not seen him since I left Taiwan. I didn't recognize him at all.

"*Lao Shi*, do you still recognize me?" he asked me eagerly.

I giggled and patted on his shoulder. "No! I didn't recognize you. You have changed so much!"

"*Lao Shi*, do you still remember the nickname you gave to me?" His eyes were sparkling.

"Of course, *Scholar*!" He seemed surprised and happy I still remembered that. Chung Kang Tong was not as mischievous as some of the other students. He was the vice president of the class. He looked sensitive and serious like a little refined Chinese scholar for the olden days. That's how he earned his nickname. "You still look like a scholar!" I teased him. Everyone laughed and agreed.

I remembered Ming Chung Kuo clearly. He looked great, relaxed, and confident just like he did at our last reunion in 1996.

"You haven't changed! What are you up to nowadays? Are you retired? Do you have contact with Shuo Xue and Jin Fa since our reunion in 1996?"

I was hoping he knew what happened to them since I'd lost contact with them. Back in the 90s Shuo Xue Lin was doing a lot of business in Europe, and Jin Fa Wu was an engineer in Taipei. I wondered where they were and what had happened to them since our last reunion.

Ming Chung Kuo responded, "How are you, *Lao Shi*? It has been a long time. I am still in real estate business. We've all been too busy. I had lost contact with them also."

Jie Yong came back from Seattle a couple of days ago. Even though he had a bad jet-lag he joined us. "How was Seattle? How is your family?" I was happy to see him again.

"They are doing fine. All I did in Seattle was yard work." They had a house in Seattle.

A big guy I didn't recognize walked toward us, with a big smile on his face. He sat down right next to me and had his arm around my shoulders. "*Lao Shi*, remember me? I am Yu Kuo Lin."

I was delighted to see him. "Wow! Long time no see! Sure! I remember you. You were sitting in the back row also. You were very quiet. You look so different now. You are so big!" He was over six foot. I recollected how he looked when he was a seventh grader.

He grinned. "I was very shy then." In front of me was a confident and accomplished looking man, not shy at all.

"You look great! What have you been doing all these years?" I had not seen him or heard from him since I left them in 1967.

"I taught for many years. Now I work at the Central News Agency. I am the deputy managing editor for business news." We chatted to update our lives. He whispered in my ear, "*Lao Shi*, I lost my wife in June."

It made me sad. "Oh! I am so sorry. How are you doing?"

"It is very hard. I am doing better now." I wished I could comfort him.

"Take care of yourself, and be strong!" I squeezed his hand.

An average-size man I didn't recognize came toward us with a beautiful lady. Someone shouted, "Here come Shin De and his wife!" Shin De Wang was the president of the class—a well-liked and responsible president. They came all the way from Keelung.

I stood up to greet them. What a pleasure to see him and his wife. "Hey! I hardly recognized you. What have you been doing?" I couldn't wait to find out more about him. I looked at him. He still looked as sincere and friendly as I remembered.

"You look great, *Lao Shi*. This is my wife." He introduced his wife to us and continued. "I attended Taiwan Normal University and became a teacher…" His wife smiled and watched us quietly.

I was excited that he became a teacher. I interrupted him, "You did?! You are a teacher like me?! I bet your students love you."

He chuckled. "Yes. I was a teacher for many years. But now I am running my family's business in Keelung."

"You still live in Keelung?" Most of my students had moved to Taipei. "Jie Yong took me to Ye Liu. We passed Keelung. It has changed so much. Who else are still in Keelung?"

Ye Liu is one of the most popular points of interest in northern Taiwan. There are a lot of unique-shaped boulders along the coast, not far from Keelung. The most famous one is the Queen's Head. The last time I went there was in the spring of 1967.

"Chen Yao Chian is still in Keelung. He was coming today. But he got sick and couldn't make it. We can call him." They have been close friends. He dialed Chen Yao's phone number.

"*Lao Shi* is here. She wants to talk to you." He handed the phone to me.

"How are you, *Lao Shi*? I am sorry that I couldn't make it today," said Chen Yao in a nasal voice.

"Don't worry about it. Are you okay? Are you still practicing medicine at your clinic?" We chatted for a few minutes.

After I hung up the phone and I asked Chung Kang Tong, "Did you bring the pictures?"

"Yes!" He took out the pictures that he brought—eight of them. We looked at them together, chatted about the past, and laughed about silly things we did. One of the pictures was a picture of me—young, skinny (99 pounds), and happy—standing on a platform in the outdoor stadium. We had great fun as we tried to identify each person in the pictures.

Time, distance, and space disappeared—we were back in the classroom at Keelung Secondary School, and I was twenty-one and they were seventh graders, again.

I didn't ask any of them if they would have recognized me on the street, for I knew the answer! Age may change your shape and looks, and life may leave lines on your face. But our happy memories never fade, and my love for them remains the same, always.

Chung Kang Tong suggested, "We should take a trip together to Taidong for our next reunion. I am working on a rural development project there. It is gorgeous there." After his retirement, he devoted himself to Rotary Club projects and the development of the beautiful rural Taidong, in the eastern part of Taiwan.

"Yeah. Let's do that. *Lao Shi*, come back every year!" Someone responded. Everyone liked the idea.

I giggled. "Sure! You guys should meet periodically and keep in touch always."

"Let's find more classmates for our next reunion!" Chien-I suggested.

"Yes, please find more of them. Help me to find Yan Chun Tseng, Shuo Xue Lin, and Jin Fa Wu, too." I would like to see as many as they could locate for our next reunion.

It was like a dream traveling back in time to when we were all together—vibrant and joyful in the classroom. The café was filled with our laughter.

It came time to say good-bye. I said to them, "I would like all of you to know one thing. You are the reason I stayed in teaching all my life."

I hugged each one as we parted, fighting back my rolling tears. "Take care! Be sure to keep in touch! Come to visit me in the U.S."

I stored another memorable day filled with precious pleasure in my heart.

How true it is the Chinese saying about being a teacher!

Being a teacher for one day, you are a parent all your life.

When my students walked into my classroom, they walked into my life. Indeed, my love for them is like a parent's love—it goes way beyond classroom, time, distance, and space. They are always in my heart and forever in my life.

Teaching is my path. It is my destiny.

Keelung Secondary School

Assembly with homeroom class

Administration building

School main entrance

Students of Class Ping

**Second row: Wen Chung Hsu, Jie Yong Jeung, Chien-I Kuo,
Long Sheng Tsai, Yu Kuo Lin**
First row: Chung Kang Tong, Shin De Wang, Celine, Ming Chung Kuo
Reunion with students on November 30th, 2014 in Taipei

Beyond Time, Space, and Distance

The Good Life

Nebraska was a state I neither knew nor heard of before I came to the U.S. I was surprised that the capital, Lincoln, became our home for 36 years, from 1973 to 2009.

With the University of Nebraska, Wesleyan University, Union College, Southeast Community College, and a great school district, Lincoln provides quality education. With its blue sky, clean water, fresh air, low crime rate, and affordable living, for many years Lincoln was rated as one of best places to live in the U.S.

Our two daughters, Joline and Andrea, were born and raised in Lincoln. Teaching in the Lincoln Public Schools for 26 years, I was blessed with opportunities to grow professionally and initiate various programs and activities for students. In Lincoln, I was actively involved with community and professional commitments and organizations at the international, national, state, and city levels throughout the years. We became grandparents in Lincoln. We also met many of our wonderful life-long friends there.

We truly lived great lives in Lincoln—just like it says on the Nebraska license plates, *Nebraska, the Good Life*, indeed.

Open House

My first year in the U.S. as a graduate student was the hardest year of my life—I felt alone, scared, hungry, and lonely, with no friends, family, or survival skills. Tears were my daily companions for the first three months. Many people helped me to adjust and to survive the hardships in a foreign land. I decided to help people like me to have easier lives in the foreign land, wherever we might be.

After I received my master's degree in Special Education, my husband Don and I moved to Pocatello, Idaho. Don worked at the university, and I taught special needs students at Franklin Junior High.

During our three years living in Pocatello, we opened our home to the Chinese students. Idaho State University was not a big school then. There were just a few Chinese students each year. They were welcome at any time. We let them know they were never alone. We invited them to celebrate all the American and Chinese holidays—when people get homesick the most. I was more than happy to share the warmth of our home and my not-so-good Chinese food—it was during this time I learned to cook.

*****

The University of Nebraska-Lincoln (UNL) is a big university with many advanced programs in various fields. The tuition was affordable and many scholarships were available for graduate students, especially foreign students in engineering. This brought a great many graduate students from Taiwan throughout the years.

My husband was always supportive. He said to me, "Don't forget how lonely you were when you first came here."

Every year in the fall, we invited new students for a Bar-B-Q party to welcome them. The biggest group was 45 in 1980. Again we shared the warmth of our home with the new students and let them know they were welcome at any time and they were not alone.

After obtaining their master's or PhD degrees, some stayed to work in the U.S., some went to different countries, and a great number of them went back to Taiwan.

Countless couples met at our home, and some of them got married at our house. As their acting parents, we helped numerous couples with their weddings throughout the years.

Many of them became our lifetime buddies…

Reunion

I had not gone back to Taiwan for many years. I missed my brother, Karl, and all the friends there. I decided to go to Taiwan for a one-month visit in November, 2014.

Four days after I arrived, a University of Nebraska-Lincoln reunion, organized especially for me by Ming Yang Su, gathered many friends in Taipei. I was overwhelmed and delighted to see more than 40 good old friends from Lincoln, including two of my students from Lincoln High School.

Although time may leave marks on our faces or change our looks and shapes, our friendship goes beyond time, space, and distance—without any gaps. Some of these people I had not seen for more than 20 years. What a thrilling gathering!

At the reunion, with joy in my heart and a smile on my face, I relived the sweet and unforgettable memories I had with each of them…

Tennis Pals

"Wow! How long has it been since you left Lincoln?" I asked. It was such a pleasant surprise to see Patrick Chiu and his wife.

"Almost 25 years!" He laughed and hugged me.

"So happy that you could make it today!"

"I wouldn't miss it. It has been too long!" He had changed his schedule and had come back from China to meet me. I hadn't seen Patrick since he left Lincoln after obtaining his MS degree in engineering. Now he has two sons in college.

Ping Wen went back to Taiwan and took over his family's business after getting his PhD 20-some years ago. He had come to every reunion throughout the years. The last time I saw him was in Beijing when I was teaching there.

Ping Wen Liang now works in China. He and his wife also rushed back to join us.

Patrick and Ping Wen were my tennis pals. We played doubles.

Patrick and Ping Wen were partners, and my partner was David Wang. They were younger men. But they didn't treat me—a woman who was older than they—differently. We played hard. For several years the four of us played tennis two or three times a week during summer, and each time we played five sets straight without break. David was a great player. David coached and yelled at me while we played, "Go forward and kill them!" "Back up!" "To the left!" "Move to the right!"

We had great fun chatting and laughing about our games while drinking tea and eating at our place afterward. David teased me a lot. He laughed and said, "Did you guys see how fast she ran to the front to kill you guys?"

"We surely did! And she killed us!" Patrick and Ping Wen laughed and said it together. We had great fun together for several years.

Good memories never fade—stored deeply in my heart. I really miss my tennis pals and the fun we had together in the good old days.

"Let's take some pictures and send them to David," I suggested.

Patrick sent the pictures to David right away. David lives in Los Angeles. How I wish that the four of us could play tennis together again!

The Three Musketeers

Chen Te Kuo was dating Susan Chen, and Tammy Sun was their buddy when they were in graduate school. Chen Te is a man of integrity—straight forward and genuine; Susan is a bright, thoughtful, sweet lady; and Tammy is a sincere, kind, giving person.

Chen Te, Susan, and Tammy, *The Three Musketeers,* came to visit us almost every weekend. We had a lot of fun chatting, drinking tea, and cooking together.

They went back to Taiwan after obtaining their master degrees. Susan married Cheng Te. Whenever I went back to Taiwan, the time, space, and distance disappeared. We four had fun chatting and giggling just like in the good old days.

I called Chen Te and Susan before my trip to Taiwan in November 2014. "I will arrive in Taiwan very late. I am scared to take the taxi alone. Can you pick me up?" It is about a one-hour ride.

Chen Te said, "Sure! Don't worry! I will pick you up no matter how late it is." Chen Te is the kind of friend I can always count on to support me, no matter what.

When Tammy's father became very ill, she quit her job to take care of her elderly parents twenty-four hours a day, seven days a week. They lived on the third floor and there was no elevator in their apartment building. Whenever her father had a doctor's appointment, she carried her father on her back both down the stairs and up again. She is not a big person. Her love for her parents touched me immensely.

Tammy said to me, "I will make arrangements and find time to be with you. Let me know if there is anything I can help you with." She knew I always appreciated company.

One day she had asked a cousin to stay with her parents so she could spend time with me. She treated me to a great vegetarian lunch and helped me select four pairs of reading glasses in Taipei.

People change throughout the years, but not my beloved three Musketeers!

Chu Lin Schools

Ning Shi Chiu and his wife, Jin Dee, came to Lincoln for a post-doctorate position in the physics department at UNL. They were about my age. With a lot in common, we hit it off right away and became the best of friends.

Ning Shi's mother was an amazing and powerful lady who had vision. She single-handedly established a kindergarten in the suburb of Taipei, and later it became an elementary school. After the elementary school was well established, she built a reputable secondary school for students from seventh grade through twelfth grade.

Ning Shi and Dee went back to Taiwan many years ago to help his mother with the expanding schools. Ning Shi became the president of the Chu Lin Schools.

We have kept in close contact. Whenever I went back to Taiwan, we made sure to spend much time together. Since we were both in education, we talked about possible programs and activities for students.

I said to Ning Shi, "I am teaching Chinese at Lincoln High School and Park Middle School in Lincoln. My students are learning Chinese and your students are learning English. We should connect our schools for exchange programs."

"Great idea!" he responded.

I said to him, "Your students can come to visit us during spring break, and my students can host them." I continued, "And I can also work with the English department at UNL to design a summer language camp for your students. My students can be tutors and assistants for the program."

The following year, a sister school relationship was formally established between Lincoln High School and Chu Lin High School and between Park Middle School and Chu Lin Junior High. I also helped connect Pyrtle Elementary School with Chu Lin Elementary School. I worked with the director of the ESL (English as a Second Language) program and designed a summer English program especially for Chu Lin students at UNL.

Through many exchange programs between my schools and Chu Lin, I met many Chu Lin teachers. Director Yi An Hsu was one of them. She is an energetic, clear-minded, intelligent, fun lady. In her early 80s, she is still contributing at Chu Lin. She has been actively involved as a leader of the International Girl Scout organization for countless years.

Whenever I went back to Taiwan, she took great care of me. She always asked me, "What would you like to do? Where do you want to go? What are you hungry for?"

She took me places and treated me to great food that she cooked—she is a great cook. She also took me to restaurants. We had fun together. She is my inspiration and a dear friend.

Chu Lin Secondary School now provides quality education for more than 3,000 students. It was a great pleasure to visit Chu Lin again and to give a speech in English to high school students during my most recent visit there.

Peace mission

GAIL FOLDA/Lincoln Journal Star

Pei-yi Lee, left, a Taiwanese student, gives the peace sign Monday while having her picture taken with Jeremy Jewell, a Lincoln High School student. Lee is among the 20 students from Taiwan who have been visiting LHS. They are to leave today. About 70 students and teachers arrived in Lincoln last week. They have been visiting LHS, Park Middle School and Pyrtle Elementary School.

GAIL FOLDA/Lincoln Journal Star

■ **Sign in, please:** Pyrtle Elementary fifth-grader Kaitlin Schuurmans autographs a T-shirt given to Billy Lio Yo-wen, a visitor from Taiwan.

Formosa

Long ago many Portuguese settled in Taiwan. They called Taiwan *Formosa*—the beautiful island.

Ching-Ta (Ted) Chuang, a Professor Emeritus at the Taiwan National Ocean University and President of Rotary Yoneyama SY-A, has been one of my special friends.

He called me one day. "Taiwan has changed so much. Do you want to visit my hometown in the mountains and a school I tried to preserve on the coast?"

"Wonderful! I love the ocean and miss the mountains."

"I will invite Kun Nan (Jack) Lin to join us." We set a date for the adventure.

Jack also came to our reunion all the way from the southern part of Taiwan to surprise me. I had not seen him since he obtained his PhD and went back to Taiwan more than two decades ago. Jack was an engineering professor at the same university where Ted taught.

Ted had a great mission and passion in his heart—to keep the villages in the mountains alive and schools by the sea open. We visited a well-equipped elementary school in a remote but beautiful area by the ocean. There were only twelve students, with eight teachers.

Jack has a fabulous collection of sea shells from around the world. Ted and Jack brainstormed different ideas with the principal to see how to integrate Jack's collection—a special feature—to make the school a point of interest. They also talked about the incentives to attract young people with children to settle in the area to work and to raise their children, bringing energy to the villages and children to schools. I was profoundly touched and astonished by Ted's vision and Jack's full support of Ted's amazing project.

We talked about the past, we chatted about the future, and we treasured the precious moments being together again. In our car we climbed the gorgeous mountains; on the bridges we listened to the soothing music of the running rivers; and along the coast we breathed the misting fresh air of the Pacific Ocean.

Taiwan, a beautiful island the Portuguese called *Formosa*, is our home.

*****

Whenever I see the sea shells that Jack gave to me, his friendship warms my heart. The beautiful framed Chinese calligraphy hung on the wall is one of my favorite art works in our house. Ted had hand-carried it all the way from Taiwan especially for me long ago. Whenever I look at it, I think of Ted. His genuine friendship brings smiles to my face, always.

A Piece of String

When I went back to Taiwan in 1993, Ning Shi Chiu, Pu Sheng Kan, and some other friends decided to have a big welcome party for me in Taipei. Around 60 people attended the party. It felt heartwarming and overwhelming.

I love to bring people together. Seeing so many people at the party, I had a vision. "We should have an organization to connect all the

362

University of Nebraska-Lincoln alums in Taiwan. You have invaluable resources right here in this room and can network in different domains."

Many seconded my suggestion. At the party we formed a University of Nebraska-Lincoln Alumni Association. Ning Shi Chiu was elected president of the association. Since I was the only one who knew every one of them, I became the forever Honorary President of University of Nebraska-Lincoln Alumni Association in Taiwan.

A dear friend Nai Yu Chen said something very interesting to me. "You are like a piece of string stringing all of us together."

Always

Years later, when Ming-Yang Su, a younger person, went back, he took over the leadership of the alumni association. He has headed it ever since. Ming-Yang is a capable, responsible, embracing leader— with a big giving heart. He is the CFO for Mobile Energy Technology Company.

The last time we met at the reunion, he had just gotten married. Now he has two teenage children, one boy and one girl. I said to him on the phone before the reunion, "I would love to see your wife and two children." His wife brought their children to meet me briefly at the party, between events of the children's busy weekend schedules. It was great to see his whole family.

*****

Ray Hua Wan and his wife Wen-Chi, a lovely and wise lady, went back in the early 80's after he obtained his master degree in engineering, to take care of his mother when her health failed. Ray Hua has been working at National Chung-Shan Institute of Science and Technology ever since. Now he is the Chief Marketing Officer of the product commercialization office. They have never missed any reunion since the first one in 1993.

After getting his PhD in engineering and working in Lincoln for eleven years, Si Shiong Shi went back to Taiwan with his wife Mei Tsu

Kuo. Si Shiong just retired from National Taiwan Ocean University, and he is writing a textbook. Mei Tsu is a marketing director of a company. They attended every reunion whenever I went back to Taiwan. Each time they brought me beautiful gifts made in Taiwan.

*****

Richard Hsueh came to see me in Beijing the year before I came back to the U.S., but I had not seen his family since they moved away in 1980. They had moved many times since they left Lincoln.

During the two years they lived in Lincoln, we were very close. His daughter is our daughter Joline's age. They played well together when they were toddlers.

There were many changes in their family throughout the years. I knew they were Christians. But I was very surprised when his wife Yong Chen—a gentle, quiet, thoughtful lady—became a minister long ago. Their son is also a minister, and their daughter's work is related to ministry.

After he retired in the U.S. as a professor and an industrial engineer, he and his wife moved back to Taiwan. Richard is teaching at a university, and Yong Chen is a minister at a church.

I hoped to see Yon Chen, whom I had not seen since 1980. But she didn't come with Richard. I asked him, "Where is your wife?"

Richard said, "She was coming to see you, but she broke her leg a few days ago and couldn't walk."

"Oh, no! Hope to see her sometime soon!"

Long Time No See

I didn't expect to see Chuan Shion Wang and his wife Joan at the party. We had worked closely together for a couple of years when Chuan Shion was the president of the Free China Association at UNL—I was a co-founder of the association in 1975.

I was excited, asking them, "When did you get back? How long are you going to stay?" I had heard that they moved to China from San

Jose, the Silicon Valley, where they had lived since he graduated.

Chuan Shion smiled and said to me, "We are retired now. We live here now."

"What a smart move!" Taipei is such a great place to live. Taiwan is rated as Number two of the top ten safest places in the world to visit, next to Iceland.

Joan echoed, "Yeah! We love it here. It is so clean, convenient, and affordable. We are so happy to be home again—one of best decisions we ever made."

*****

I had been out of contact with Ted Kwang and Nina Chen for a long time. I couldn't believe I was seeing them at the party, "Wow! You two have become four!" Their two lovely teenage daughters were about Joline and Andrea's ages when they went back to Taiwan.

About the same time in 1990, Ted, Nina, and I became vegetarians and learned to meditate. We meditated together weekly, and we had great fun together experimenting with new dishes every weekend. After they went back to Taiwan, they moved numerous times due to Ted's work. We had lost contact for many years.

They said to me, "We will take you to the best vegetarian restaurants in Taipei." They did, many times afterward. Taiwan truly is the paradise of vegetarians.

We were so happy to be connected again after so many years. They planned to visit us in Milwaukee in the summer of 2016.

Beyond

Genuine friendship goes beyond time, space, and distance. Friends are the exquisite treasures I have been collecting throughout my life. Each of them is either a precious pearl or a gorgeous gem of some kind. I am a piece of string stringing all of them together into an irreplaceable necklace stored deeply in my heart.

Reunion with University of Nebraska - Lincoln alums in Taipei on November 8th, 2014

Friends Far and Near

Small World

One day after Mrs. Chou came back from a trip to Europe, she called me. She sounded so enthusiastic, saying to me, "Celine, guess whom we met on our trip in Europe? I couldn't wait to tell you."

I became curious and excited. "Who? Tell me!"

"We ran into a Chinese family from Brazil." She continued, "When the man heard that we were from Lincoln, Nebraska, he got so surprised and thrilled."

"Yeah?!" I wasn't sure what she was trying to tell me.

"The man asked us if we knew you."

Now I was stunned, "Who was it?" I had no friend in Brazil.

"His name is Chian Wang. He attended graduate school at UNL many years ago. They settled in Brazil."

"Wow! What a small world! I remember him. Both he and his sister were in Lincoln for a couple of years a long time ago. I always wondered where they went."

"We couldn't believe it, that the only Chinese people we ran into in Europe knew you."

*****

One day in late August 2001, shortly after I went to Beijing to teach, I received a call from an old friend, Pu Sheng Kan, whom I had not seen for years. Pu Sheng attended UNL in the 70s. I was surprised and thrilled, "Long time no see! Where are you? How did you know I am in Beijing?"

He sounded excited. "I am working in Beijing right now! Ning Shi

Chiu told me you are in Beijing. I called Don in Lincoln and got your number." Ning Shi is one of our mutual friends in Taiwan.

This old friend helped me adjust to my new life in Beijing. He took me shopping for things I needed. One time he took eight of us—all new teachers at ISB—to buy bicycles. Pu Sheng arranged a truck to transport all eight bicycles, one to each of our houses.

He took me to a big tea store in downtown Beijing. He was the manager of this store that carried tea from Taiwan. He introduced me to all his employees. "This is an old friend of mine. Please welcome her and serve the best tea whenever she comes in our store."

After that he turned around and said to me, "You can always stop and have a tea break here when you are downtown." I did many times. During my intense shopping on many weekends, I not only stored things I'd already bought, but I also enjoyed a good Taiwan tea break.

After working for a couple of years in Beijing, Pu Sheng moved to Shanghai for a new job. One day Pu Sheng called me from Shanghai. I was happy to hear from him. "Hey! How are you?"

He sounded very excited on the other end. "Do you want to know something scary?"

"What's so scary? What happened? Are you all right? "

He laughed. "I am okay. I have three friends with me right now at my house. All of them know you!"

Now I got excited. "What? Really? Who are they? Did they attend UNL?"

He giggled. "No, none of them! I will let you talk to each of them."

What a surprise! One was a good friend of my youngest brother, whom I met in Boston. One was the buddy of an old friend in Taiwan. I had helped his daughter with something a long time ago. The other one was a friend of mine in Taiwan whom I had not seen for many years.

Four people with different backgrounds—whom I met at different times and places—were together in the same house in Shanghai. A small world, indeed!

Angels

A month or so after I first went to Beijing to teach in 2001, a good old friend, Stephen Yao, called. He laughed and said, "Celine, I will always follow you! I am going to Beijing to work."

I screamed, "Really?! I can't believe it. When are you coming?" I was so excited that he was coming to Beijing.

"In two weeks!"

*****

Stephen has been a special friend for more than three decades. We met at the UNL Free China Association welcome party for new students in 1979. He was the new student I introduced to the group after a five-minute get-to-know-each-other session. He was fun, positive, and happy, my kind of people. We hit it off and became good friends.

He went back to Taiwan after getting his MBA in 1981. Since then he has been a chief executive for multinational companies for 26 years in media, financial, and legal industries in various countries in Asia.

When Andrea was a junior in college, she was in an exchange program at Sophia University in Tokyo. Stephen arranged an internship for Andrea at the Standard and Poor's in Tokyo. Andrea had three job offers after college, and Stephen was the person we consulted. He helped Andrea make the best choice for her career.

Stephen has a brilliant mind, a kind heart, and great characters. I also know his wife, Agnes, well. She was Stephen's classmate in graduate school at UNL. I was thrilled that they came back to settle in Lincoln when they immigrated to the U.S. in 1998. After settling his family in Lincoln, he continued to work in Asia. During his absence, I assisted Agnes whenever and with whatever she needed, especially with their children's education.

At that time their son Philip was a fifth grader, and Teresa was in kindergarten. They both, but especially Philip, needed help to learn and catch up in English. For three years I worked with Philip on vocabulary, spelling, reading, and writing, every Sunday morning at eight o'clock. Philip has a brilliant mind like his father. Now he is the president of his own venture capital company in Boston. Teresa is in law school with a full-ride scholarship.

*****

When I first went to Beijing to teach, my husband, Don, didn't go with me, since I wasn't sure I would like Beijing. So I was alone in China.

It was the first time that Stephen worked in Beijing also. His family, like Don, stayed in Lincoln. Stephen called me often to check on me, especially on weekends. "I found a good restaurant. You want to go and try it?" Being an old friend, he knows I am a chicken in many ways—I wouldn't go any place or eat in restaurants by myself.

I followed him like a shadow. We had great fun exploring many places and trying different restaurants in Beijing together. What a blessing to have Stephen, a trusted old friend and guardian angel, by my side for two years when I was alone in Beijing.

*****

During those two years Don was alone in Lincoln while I was in China teaching. But he was well taken care of by great friends in Lincoln. Stephen's wife, Agnes, checked on him and treated him very often. Our buddies, Theresa and Arthur Ma, work at the same place Don did. Theresa brought all kinds of good food to feed Don, at least two times a week.

Good old friends, Mei Huey and Chuan Yu, never forgot to invite Don for their parties. Te Wie Chwang, one of our oldest friends in Lincoln, picked us up and took us to the airport throughout the years. Our best neighbors and great friends Carol and Domingo Cabacungan took great care of our house for many years whenever we were not in Lincoln.

We are truly blessed with great friends—angels—in our lives.

More Than a Friend

Friends come and go in our lives. Some friends disappear throughout the years. Some of them stay connected always no matter what happens in our lives.

We met David Wong in Pocatello, Idaho, in 1970. I was a teacher at Franklin Junior High and he was a freshman at Idaho State University (ISU). David was born in Taiwan and grew up in Hong Kong.

Not many Chinese people were in Pocatello. David came to our place almost every weekend. We became very close friends. One day Don, David, and I were in the car going somewhere together. We saw a young man who looked like a Chinese, walking alone in the street. I said to Don, "Stop the car!"

We rolled down the windows, and I asked the young man, "Are you Chinese?"

He looked surprised. "Yes! I am from Taiwan."

David and I were so excited. We yelled together, "We are too!"

David asked him, "Are you a student at ISU?"

"Yes. I am a sophomore, majoring in math."

I said to him, "If you are not busy now, you are welcome to join us. We will have dinner at our place." He looked so happy and hopped in our car. Later we found out that he had been alone and very lonely, without any friend, for more than a year.

That was how we found Charlie Zee—in the street. After that, the four of us spent most weekends together at our house. Charlie was a great cook. He often made special Shanghai seafood dishes to treat us.

During their final exams week, I told them, "Come to have dinner every day and go to study afterward." I knew how stressful it could be during the finals.

In 1972, after living in Pocatello for three years, we moved to Wichita, Kansas. It was hard to say good-bye to our close friends, David and Charlie.

A year later Charlie graduated, and he went to Guam to take over his father's business there. He has been there ever since. We have kept in touch all these years, but we haven't been able to see each other.

When David graduated with a bachelor's degree in architecture in 1974, we had moved to Lincoln, Nebraska. Before he graduated, I knew he was applying for graduate school. I told him, "The architecture program at UNL is pretty good. Do you want to come here for graduate school?" He came to Lincoln in the fall. We were so happy to be reunited.

After graduate school, he found a good job in Lincoln and married a wonderful, loving lady from Taiwan, Jennifer. Our daughters became their godchildren, and we are their children's godparents. He was more than a friend. He was family. When they decided to move to Hawaii in 1988, I was devastated and sad to say good-bye to David and his family after they had been our closest friends for 18 years.

On June 26th, 2015, I received a call from his wife, Jennifer, in Seattle. This brotherly friend of mine had passed away after battling cancer and heart problems for eight years. I was so glad that Don, our younger daughter, Andrea, and I went to their son Jeremy's wedding in Toronto in April. It was the last time we spent precious moments together.

I will always remember his happy face when he hugged me and said, "It's so great to see you, my old friend!"

My old friend and a brother, David Wong, will live in my heart, always!

$$*****$$

I was deeply touched when Dah-Chuan Gong told his friends before going back to Taiwan, "Celine is the person who will always know where I am." It was January, 1983.

Dah Chuan is a brilliant, ambitious, and hardworking man, with high self-expectation and decent character. He always knows what he wants to have or to do. After he obtained his master's degree in industrial engineering at UNL in three semesters, he went back to Taiwan to work. After a couple of years, he came back to pursue his PhD at Georgia Tech in Atlanta.

He has been a reputable professor in his domain, and he is well-respected internationally. He teaches and works with many projects in Taiwan, China, and Singapore, and sometimes as a visiting professor in the U.S.

Dah Chuan has a special connection with us. Almost every summer, for more than three decades, he comes and stays with us for two or three weeks at a time. He even became a golf buddy with our good neighbor, Domingo, across street from us.

When I planned my trip to Taiwan in 2014, he said to me, "We will be in the U.S. during that time. You are welcome to stay in our house. It's at a very convenient location. My parents will take good care of you."

I had their house to myself during the month I was in Taiwan. His parents and younger brother lived one floor above. They took great care of me.

Now we are in Milwaukee, and every year he brings his wife, Lillian, and their son, Johnny, to spend the summer here. He called me not too long ago. "Happy New Year of the Monkey!"

I said, "Happy and Healthy New Year to you, too. We miss you! When are you coming back?"

"We will see you late June. I might teach a summer class at the university."

When he opened a new checking account in Milwaukee, he put my name down for a joint account. He also gave me one of his credit cards.

I laughed and asked him, "Are you sure?"

He said, "Of course! I am sure! You are my big sister!"

Dah Chuan is a brother I adopted in 1983.

*****

My friends far and near fill my life with pleasure and rainbow colors. Their friendship not only warms my heart but also enriches my life...

Joy, Agony, and Sorrow

Some friends are happy sharing joy and fun with you. Some stand by you when you are in pain or despair. Some share heartache and sorrow with you. Any friend who shares not only your happiness but also your pain and sorrow has a special spot deep in your heart and a forever bonding with you that goes beyond time, space, and distance.

Joy

1983 was an unforgettable year.

Almost every day during the week in the summer, my two daughters and I met some friends with their children at one of the swimming pools at the University of Nebraska-Lincoln (UNL). The children dived and swam happily, and the adults enjoyed chatting and playing in the water.

I knew most of the Chinese graduate students from Taiwan who were at UNL. They had a lighter load of studies during summer. Some of them worked on campus, and some of them did research for their thesis. Some of them just took a break.

Man Chan was a civil engineering graduate student from Hong Kong. He did his undergraduate work at the Taiwan University in Taipei. This summer, he worked at the maintenance department in the building where the swimming pool was. We saw him almost every day and got to know him well. Sometimes, he joined us in the pool after work. Whenever we had a gathering at our place, I invited him to join us. Man was a profound-looking young man, with a brilliant mind and a sentimental, caring heart. We enjoyed him and his company.

Eddy Cheung was from Hong Kong. He had just finished all the studies for his bachelor's degree. He started to look for a job. Eddy had been in Lincoln for several years. He had always worked on weekends when most of the students came to our place. We had met briefly before, but I didn't get to really know him until this summer.

Eddy and Man were close friends. They came by the house together or met us at the pool. I had the chance to get to know Eddy well. He was genuine, with a child's heart. He laughed a lot. Eddy was such a fun uncle to my two daughters.

Chinese children call their parents' friends respectfully, *Shu Shu* [Uncle] or *A Yi* [Aunt]. Eddy and Man became Joline and Andrea's forever Chan *Shu Shu* [Uncle Chan] and *Eddy Shu Shu* [Uncle Eddy].

In 2003 when I was in China, Andrea's car got stolen from her apartment complex in Pasadena, California. She called, and she was very upset. I told her, "Don't cry. I gave Joline my new car in 2001 when we came to China. I wanted to give you a new car also. Now is a perfect time to buy you a new car." I continued, "Call *Eddy Shu Shu* and ask him to help you buy a new car." Eddy had been living in Los Angeles since he left Lincoln.

Andrea stopped crying and said, "Okay. Thank you, Mommy!" Eddy helped her pick a nice car a few days later.

Yi Long Hsu, an engineering TA from Taiwan, did research during the summer, not taking any classes. He was a happy basketball superstar, with a big heart and gentle soul. This was his first summer in the U.S. He and many students had been to our house on weekends regularly since he had come to Lincoln the previous fall.

Yi Long played with Joline and Andrea a lot. He liked to play a bug trick with them. They loved it, and they called him *Chong Shu Shu* [Uncle Bug].

Yi Long had just learned to drive in the spring. He wanted to buy a car. "*Tan Jie* [Big Sister Tan], where can I find a reliable used car?" Since I was older than most of them, they called me *Tan Jie*, respectfully, the Chinese way. *Tan* is my maiden name.

"You are in luck. A teacher at our school is selling his old car. Let me check with him." My friend at school gave him a good deal on the car.

He said to me many times, "Thank you so much! This is such a great car! I love it!"

Randy Wu was from Taiwan, a PhD student in mechanical engineering. He was working on his research during the summer. He had been in Lincoln for a few years, and he had been to our place very often. I knew him pretty well. He was an easy-going, genuine, trustworthy friend. It was always fun to have him around.

Summer was my favorite season. I didn't have to work, and I could spend time with Joline and Andrea. We could travel and have fun outdoors.

It was always exciting to spend whole day fishing at the beautiful Branched Oak Lake, of course, not alone. On weekends, Eddy, Man, Yi Long, Randy, and I met with some other friends around five o'clock in the morning to go fishing. Sometimes there were five or six car loads of people going together. Before sunset, we brought all the fish we caught to our place. Eddy and Man were the chefs. We always had a blast while eating and drinking together, talking and laughing about the exciting moments each of us had with the fish.

One time, my fishing line moved violently, I got so excited and screamed, "Big fish! A big one!" I grabbed the fishing pole, and the jerk of the line stopped.

Eddy appeared from the rocks below from where I sat. He laughed so hard that he almost fell in the water. He was the one who moved my fishing line, not fish. Everyone burst in laughter, including me.

Yi Long loved fishing, a new sport for him. He sometimes went fishing by himself early in the morning during the week. He brought the fish over to our place whenever he caught some. We called Randy and our chefs, Man and Eddy, to come over for a seafood dinner together. We all were so happy whenever we were together. Don seldom went fishing with us, but he always had beer ready for them. He enjoyed the good food and drinking beer with them.

The students were all younger than Don and I. I was their big sister, *Tan Jie*. We were blessed with shared pleasure and one another's genuine friendship.

The summer of 1983 was the happiest and the most fun summer for us all, including Joline and Andrea.

Fishing outing at Branched Oak Lake
Second Row (Left to Right): Yi Long, Randy, & Celine
First Row (Left to Right): Man & Eddy

Agony

On Friday of the last week of my summer vacation, Don was diagnosed with colon cancer. Suddenly the sky fell, and our happy lives were shattered. I didn't know how to face such a brutal storm. Surgery was scheduled for a week later. No one would know how serious it was until the doctor checked inside. I was totally devastated and frightened. Don was in the hospital for seventeen days. I lost one pound every day.

Man, Eddy, Yi Long, and Randy were the pillars I leaned on during the most horrifying time of my life. They were with me waiting for the results of surgery in the hospital. They babysat Joline and Andrea. They did everything around the house to lighten my stress to help me survive. I was deeply touched by their friendship and support and profoundly grateful to have my four buddies—guardian angels—by my side, when I desperately needed help.

Thank God! Don's colon cancer was at the earliest stage. After the surgery, the doctors considered him cured.

Sorrow

Summer was gone, the school started again. Yi Long played basketball every Friday evening with a bunch of friends from Taiwan. This tall and strong superstar was like a flying dragon on the court. One day Yi Long had trouble raising his right arm. Later he fell and had trouble standing up.

I was concerned. "I will take you to Dr. Kwan tomorrow to see what is going on." Dr. Kwan and her husband, Kwan Gong, were like an aunt and an uncle to us. I took Yi Long to see Dr. Kwan at their house.

After Dr. Kwan checked him, she gave him a shot in his back for the pain. She suggested, "Something might be pressing on a nerve on your spine. You need to have some tests done at the hospital."

Man, Eddy, Randy, and I checked Yi Long into the university health clinic. Every day of the week he was there, we took Chinese food to him. He laughed and joked with us whenever we were there with him.

After multiple tests at the clinic, he was moved to a hospital. None of us knew how to take the shocking test result—Yi Long was diagnosed with liver cancer at the final stage, and nothing much could be done.

It saddened us all to see this strong and delightful buddy of ours face a death sentence at the age of 28. Eddy had gone to Los Angeles to look for a job. With heartache and deep sorrow, Man, Randy, and I made arrangements for Yi Long to go back home to Taiwan after Thanksgiving.

During the Thanksgiving break, the three of us decided to take Yi Long, Joline, and Andrea snow sledding in the Pioneer Park—something Yi Long had never experienced. It brought tears to my eyes when I saw how thrilled and happy Yi Long was as he flew down the snowy hills. It was the very last time we played and laughed with Yi Long—with unspeakable sorrow deep in our hearts.

My heart broke as I said good-bye to Yi Long at the airport. I whispered in his ear, with tears in my eyes, "Farewell! I will see you next summer. Be brave and hang in there." I missed him already.

After Yi Long left, we decided to do something constructive for him. Back then Taiwan had no national health insurance. Man, Randy, and I, along with some other friends, wrote a story about him and put it in many Chinese newspapers in the U.S. We collected donations to assist Yi Long with his huge medical expenses in Taiwan. With overwhelming support from the Chinese communities across the U.S, a donation of more than $10,000 went to Yi Long's family, a few months later.

Seven months later, in the summer of 1984, I took Joline and Andrea to Taiwan to see one of their favorite uncles, *Chong Shu Shu*, Yi Long. Randy also went to Taiwan with us. We had called Yi Long's family regularly to check on him. Before we left for Taiwan, his mother told me on the phone, "Yi Long hardly eats, and he doesn't talk."

"We will be there soon. Don't tell him. We will surprise him."

When Randy, Joline, Andrea, and I walked into Yi Long's room in the hospital, he looked so stunned. I saw sparkle in his eyes. He smiled, looking at Joline and Andrea. "Wow! You have grown so much. I am so happy to see you. I missed you so much."

Joline smiled and said, "We missed you too, *Chong Shu Shu*. We made something special for you." Eight-year-old Joline walked toward his bed and opened the container we brought.

"Jello! My favorite!" He looked energetic and excited again.

"We made it all by ourselves just for you!" Five-year-old Andrea was so proud.

Joline and Andrea were so thrilled that their *Chong Shu Shu* ate the whole thing. We visited him many times afterward. Each time he looked weaker. Each time he smiled and had fun with Joline and Andrea.

Shortly after we returned to Lincoln, Yi Long's mother called. "Yi Long is gone. Thank you for your loving care for him. He told us that the year when he was in Lincoln was the happiest time in his life."

1983 was a unique and unforgettable year. I had the most fun summer with my buddies. With their love, I survived the unexpected vicious storm. Together we helplessly watched our beloved Yi Long be taken, mercilessly, forever.

Although we all left Lincoln after that, we will never forget what we went through together in Lincoln. Eddy and Randy are in Los Angeles, and Man is in Hong Kong. Don and I are in Milwaukee. The five of us, including Yi Long in heaven, will always treasure the joy, friendship, and sorrow we shared in the eventful 1983—an everlasting bonding among us goes beyond time, space, and distance.

*****

My siblings are my forever best friends, and my friends are my chosen brothers and sisters. They are God-sent, and they are gifts from heaven…

The last fish Yi Long caught at the Branched Oak Lake
Man, Yi Long, Eddy, Celine, & Randy

The Pioneers

I was among the pioneers of teaching Chinese to secondary school students in the U.S. when I established the Chinese language program for Lincoln Public Schools in Nebraska in 1988.

Most of my students followed me three or four years. Many of my students became pioneers in different domains and different lands. They amazed me.

A Pleasant Surprise

After a three-week winter break, it was time to go back to Beijing to teach. As my husband and I were waiting in a long line for security check at the Lincoln airport, a very tall young man ran toward us. This handsome young man had a big smile on his face, "*Lao Shi*, remember me?"

I was very surprised and excited. "Josh Campbell! Of course I remember you!" We hugged. "You are so grown up!" I had not seen him since he graduated in 1992 from Lincoln High School, thirteen years ago.

"*Lao Shi*, I am so glad to see you. I have so much to tell you."

"What have you been doing all these years?"

He smiled, "I attended the University of Chicago after high school."

"Yeah, I heard you majored in Chinese and Asian Studies."

"Yes, I did. My major was East Asian Languages and Civilization." He continued, "After I graduated in 1996, I got a scholarship and studied Chinese at Taiwan Normal University for a year. Two years I got a job there. I have been there ever since."

"Really? You must really like it there." I was quite surprised.

"Yes." He had another big smile on his face.

I was so glad he liked it there. "Are you in Taipei? You know I grew up there."

He beamed. "Yes. I have a great job in Taipei and I love it there. I have a Chinese girlfriend. I brought her home to meet my family."

"Where is she?" I looked around.

"We couldn't get two tickets together on any airline to go back to Taipei, and she had to take a different flight." I didn't get a chance to meet her.

"I am glad you are doing so well. I am so proud of you." I always wonder about what and how my students are doing. It was great to run into Josh after so many years.

"I am so happy there. *Lao Shi*, I owe it all to you!"

The brief chat with Josh brought lots of memories and warmth to my heart.

Josh started learning Chinese when he was a ninth grader at Irving Junior High in 1988 when I first established Chinese program. He was in the program for four years.

This bright young man had the most beautiful hand-writing of Chinese. And I can still see him holding the index cards working diligently on the scripts for our very first *Chinese Kaleidoscope* program in 1992. He was one of the Masters of Ceremonies [MC] to introduce Chinese traditions and history of the performances

Ten years passed since we ran into each other at the airport. Recently we were connected again via Facebook. He married the girl he met in Taiwan, and they have two beautiful children. Currently, he is working in Shanghai. What a true pioneer!

Magic

I had great many unique students. Adam White was one of them. Ever since he was a ninth grader walking into my class, I knew this boy was a very special kid. He was much more mature and serious than his peers. He communicated well. I could tell there were profound thoughts and dreams hidden in his heart and soul.

Presenting our biennial *Chinese Kaleidoscope* programs took a lot of preparation. I was blessed with supportive students working closely with me every step of the way to ensure a quality and meaningful program to share with 3,600 in the audiences of three performances each time.

With a great sense of pride and honor, my students learned, practiced, and performed to present what they had learned in class. There was a lot of work, and the spirit of my students touched my heart. Standing by me, they shared ownership of the program. They not only strengthened my faith but also lightened my stress.

Shawn Beal told me, with a big smile, "*Lao Shi*, I got all the costumes pressed and ready for everyone. They are beautiful." She was such a loving and giving young lady.

Robert Park, our dependable handy man, single-handedly worked on the backdrop many hours after school. "*Lao Shi*, don't worry! I will get it done before you know it."

Being the president of Chinese Club and Martial Arts Club, Adam worked closely with me. He was the one who showed me how to use the computer. He learned and practiced Tai Chi Sword with me.

Adam participated in the *Chinese Kaleidoscope* program twice. Each time, he assured me throughout the process. "*Lao Shi*, you are born ready. Everything will go smoothly as always."

Besides learning Chinese language and cultural activities, Adam was passionately involved with DECA, a program providing students opportunities to learn about establishing and running a business. I could tell that there was a special seed growing steadily in his soul.

Adam had studied magic with a local magician since junior high. Whenever this handsome young man performed, he possessed the stage totally—delightful, confident, and charming. When he talked about magic, there were sparkles in his eyes. Little did anyone know then that he had already started chasing his dream!

When he was senior, his peers were busy taking SAT or ACT test and talking about college. Adam—a highly gifted, straight A student—never talked about college or the tests. One day as we chatted, I asked him, "Are you going to study business in college?"

He looked at me. "*Lao Shi*, I am not going to college."

It stunned me, but I understood. "You want to be a magician, don't you?"

Nodding his head, he said to me solemnly, "Yes, *Lao Shi*. It is my destiny."

"It is great you know what you really want to do with life. It will not be an easy journey, but follow your heart and try your best!" I was proud of him that he chased his dream wholeheartedly—without fear—at such a young age.

Persistent effort and passion frolicked magic in this brilliant young man. Adam became an amazing magician in Nebraska. He not only performs at various occasions and events, but also passes on his magic to motivate young children just like his magic teacher inspired him.

Adam posted on Facebook on Thanksgiving this year, "Made a bunch of Crab Rangoon and can't help but think of my Chinese teacher and one of my best buddies, Celine Robertson. Have a very happy Thanksgiving, *Lao Shi*!"

"Thank you! Happy Thanksgiving! Adam!"

Mission

Howie Camp, a bright, playful, motivated student, was in my class for three years. He had his mind set to be a pilot in the air force.

I can still see his happy, delightful face. He said it to me often after learning how to say it in Chinese, "*Wo ai ni!*" [I love you!]

I always said to him, "*Wo ye ai ni!*" [I love you too!] The whole class laughed with us.

Due to his eye sight, he didn't get in the Air Force Academy. He attended the University of Nebraska-Lincoln instead.

He called me one day after graduating from college. "*Lao Shi*, guess where I am going."

"Where are you going?" I was very curious.

"I am going to Taiwan to do missionary work."

I was thrilled for him. "Great! What an opportunity! You will love it there, and you will come back with fluent Chinese."

*****

One hot summer day in Taiwan a long time ago, I was upstairs looking out the window. Two Western young men in white shirts and black pants pushed their bikes under the scorching sun and knocked on the doors in the neighborhood. No one opened the door. They were missionaries.

Their spirit and faith touched me deeply. When they approached our house, I opened the door and invited them in. "It is so hot outside. Please come in to have some water."

"Thank you very much." They spoke perfect Chinese. "We are Americans, and we are from the Mormon Church."

"Yes, I heard about the Mormons." I continued, "I attended a Roman Catholic college and had four years of teaching on the Bible."

"That's great. Would you like to have a Bible from our church?" one of them asked me, handing me a Bible.

"Sure." I took the Bible and wondered if it was same as the Bible I knew. "I am going to the U.S. for graduate school next week."

They got excited, asking, "Where are you going?"

"Southern Illinois University. Where are you from?"

"We are from Salt Lake City, Utah." They had been doing missionary work in Taiwan for two years, and they were heading home soon.

We chatted a little about colleges and discussed the differences in various religions. It was quite pleasant. I was glad that I invited them in for a water break.

*****

I could see Howie and his partner on bikes in Taiwan sharing their faith and love of God.

Shortly after he came back from Taiwan, he got married. At his wedding, he looked excited, and saying to me, "*Lao Shi*, I am so glad you could come to our wedding."

"I wouldn't miss it. How was Taiwan?"

He responded in Chinese, "It was great! I loved it there. I can also speak Taiwanese dialect now." With a proud smile, he spoke a few phrases in Taiwanese.

"Super! I am impressed! I can't speak Taiwanese."

Howie Camp was another true pioneer—sharing his faith and love of God in Chinese.

Scholar

Justin Tiwald, a brilliant and motivated student, was in my Chinese program for four years. Before he graduated from high school I asked him, "What do you want to do in the future? You look like a professor to me." He seemed to be a sincere, philosophical, and knowledgeable young man.

He smiled bashfully. "I am profoundly interested in Chinese culture."

Thanks to Facebook, twenty-some years later, Justin and I reconnected.

He wrote to me, "It is good to hear from you as I have long wanted to thank you for your early influence and encouragement in my Chinese language studies at Lincoln High School. After graduation, I attended a smaller college that did not offer Chinese, and then I transferred with the support of your recommendation to Carleton College in Minnesota, where I was able to resume my Chinese studies."

He always knew what he wanted to do. He majored in philosophy and took a special interest in Confucianism. He spent a year studying literary Chinese at the University of Minnesota.

He also wrote, "I spent one great and memorable year as an exchange student in Taipei, and my wife accompanied me. Taiwan is a really extraordinary place and it will always have a special place in our hearts." It was the year of the S.A.R.S. outbreak—many people died from it in Taiwan and China, but it didn't scare Justin and his wife.

Justin commented, "After becoming a professor, I found myself increasingly interested in translation of classical and literary Chinese, so some of my current projects are related to translation of historical philosophical texts that aren't available in English. If I can have your home address I will send you a copy of an anthology of translations that a colleague and I edited."

I received his book—*Readings in Later Chinese Philosophy.*

I was amazed with the content and the quality of his work. I wrote to him, "Thank you. What an accomplishment! I am so proud of you."

He responded, "I consider myself very fortunate to have had you as my Chinese teacher. I would have been an entirely different person without your influence."

It warmed my heart especially when he commented, "I see that you continued to have much success and more adventures after your time in Lincoln. I hope you also have occasions to reflect on the wonderful contributions you have made to the lives of your students."

"I am writing my memoir. May I include you in my book?" I asked him.

"It'd be an honor, *Lao Shi.*"

Justin is a professor—a pioneer in a unique domain!

Blossoms

I saw "The Sower" on the top of the Capitol building as I drove to Lincoln High School to teach every day. It is the emblematic statue for the State of Nebraska. But it meant more than just a farmer to me. It was a symbol for my passion—sowing and nurturing the seeds I planted in my students' hearts.

It was marvelous to witness many of my students pursuing their dreams that started when they were with me in high school.

Jessie Frank spent a year in China with a full scholarship—one of a very few full scholarships—from the School Year Abroad program for high school students. In the fall of 2000, I met her and her host family when I visited Beijing. Jessie brought me a bouquet of beautiful flowers and her big smile.

"Wow! You talk like a Chinese now," I told her. We both laughed.

*****

Jessie was a positive, delightful, industrious young lady. Amanda Nelson—another outstanding student—and Jessie were best friends. They trained in fencing throughout high school. They practiced diligently and competed nationally. Amanda received a full scholarship from a college for her academic achievement and awesome performance in fencing.

When Amanda's older sister, Jeena Nelson, an excellent student, was in my program for four years, Amanda was an elementary student. She followed her big sister around all the time. I got to know Amanda then. It was such a privilege to have these two bright, motivated sisters in my program. Jessie's brilliant older brother, Josh, also took my classes for four years.

Jessie and Amanda knew I loved learning different weapons for martial arts. One day after school, they came to see me. They looked excited. I asked them, "What's up?"

Jessie said to me, "*Lao Shi*, we think you will enjoy fencing. Come to join us."

Amanda said, "Yeah, come! We will teach you."

"Do you think I can do it?"

"Yes, you will be good at it!" they said together.

"Great! I will join you." Fencing was another sport that impressed me when I was little.

Jessie was a nationally ranked fencer, and Amanda was the state champ multiple times. They became my personal coaches and provided me an opportunity to have a taste of one of my childhood dreams, with a lot of fun and giggles.

*****

Becky Banset, a mature, intelligent, outstanding student, went to Taiwan with me twice—once in high school and once in college. My two daughters, Joline and Andrea, became good friends with Becky after spending a summer together when they were in high school. Later in college, Becky and Joline participated in a summer language program together at the Mandarin Center of Taiwan Normal University.

Becky has been teaching ESL (English as A Second Language) students at a community college in Seattle. When we went there for a wedding in the summer of 2012, Becky spent a day to show us around the city.

We had not seen each other for more than 15 years. There was a lot to catch up on. She said to me, "I work with a lot of Chinese students. It is great fun to understand what they are saying."

"Do they know you understand Chinese?"

Becky laughed mischievously. "That's it. They don't know that." We both giggled.

Congress

I asked Becky, "Do you have contact with any of the other kids?" I missed my students.

"I have close contact with Amy Reger."

"Really?! Where is she? What is she doing?" I couldn't wait to find out about her.

"She is working at the U.S. Congress. She uses Chinese with her job. And she married a Chinese man from Hong Kong."

"She works at the Congress? How wonderful! Her Chinese must be very good now." Unbelievable!

Two years later, I took a two-week trip to the East Coast to visit old friends. In Washington D. C., Amy, her husband, and I spent an evening together. There was so much I wanted to know about her.

"Tell me what you have been doing for the past 21 years," I said. I couldn't wait to find out how this bright, pleasant, and hard-working student of mine ended up working at the Congress.

She smiled, and saying, "When I graduated from Lincoln High, I continued my Chinese in college. I spent a semester in Beijing in an exchange program. Then I studied in Nanking for a year after college. After that, I went to Taiwan for a year." I saw sparkles in her eyes while she shared her experiences in foreign lands.

"Wow! What an adventurer you are! What do you do at Congress?"

"I am a research associate at the Congressional Executive

Commission on China. I do research for the committee. I use my Chinese for my work." She spoke Chinese with me the whole time when we were together. Another pioneer in a very special field!

My Girls

After our meeting, Amy posted our pictures on Facebook. Since then, I have reconnected with many of the students in her class.

I still remember the cherry cheese cake, my favorite dessert; Dawn Amen made to surprise me on my birthday one year. Dawn looked as pretty and intelligent as before in the pictures she posted on Facebook. She seemed to live a content, happy life, filled with love and laughter of her children.

Jill Olson's darling daughter on Facebook has her smile. Jill is a gifted musician. She has played violin like a professional since she was a little girl. She is a freelance musician and a superb violin teacher to many students in Minneapolis.

Whenever I see the wooden bell in my display cabinet with *"My teacher, my friend"* on it, I remember how beautifully Ashley Pennington Tarter and my other girls danced the lantern dance at our first *Chinese Kaleidoscope* program. Ashley, a graceful dancer and figure skater, got married recently. They looked so happy in the Facebook pictures. This bright, diligent young lady has made her dream come true. She has her own dancing studio where she teaches and inspires young dancers with her passion.

There is a magnet on my refrigerator saying, *"To Teach is to touch a life forever."* It was a gift Lecia Taylor Mizener gave to me twenty-some years ago. I never stopped wondering how she was doing. She was not only an excellent student but also a great athlete. It is so great to know she is doing well. She and her family live in Omaha.

Lecia, Kelly, and Dawn were on the ninth grade volleyball team. They invited me to join them for a game against a different team. Dawn said, *"Lao Shi*, come and play on our team."

I said to them, "No! No! I have never played volleyball before. I will make you lose the game."

"It's okay. Do it for fun. We will help you," Lecia said.

"Yeah! We will be right next to you," Kelly reassured me.

They graciously protected and coached me throughout the whole game. They enriched my life with a new challenging experience—my first and last volleyball game. We won the game.

I checked with several people to see where Kelly was, no luck. I wonder what this positive good-natured young lady is doing nowadays. I can still see her in her cheerleader uniform cheering for her friends, with a beautiful smile.

Sarah Bench, a gifted girl, married very young. She has four children now. Before I went to China to teach, she visited me often with her children and her husband. I had great fun with her children.

When I visited my brother Ken in Houston a couple of years ago, Mandian Wei, the only Chinese girl in my program, brought her daughter and husband to meet me. She still was the same easy going lovely Mandian, with a sweet smile. Her mother, an artist, is a friend of mine.

Subha Tidball's mother was actively involved with the Save Lanka Kids organization in her home country, Sri Lanka. Subha, an intelligent, caring young lady like her mother, went to Sri Lanka after college to help children in need there. Her little boy on Facebook was so cute. Her brother, Monk, was also in my program.

Fanny Bowley had a beautiful voice. When she and Enoch Ulmer sang a beautiful Chinese love song together at the *Chinese Kaleidoscope* program, their voices touched the hearts of the audience. Many people were in tears, even though they didn't understand a word of the song. I hope both of them are still singing with their amazing voices.

Ling Nguyen, a brilliant student and creative leader, was a winner for whatever she was involved with. She was a student council member, and she was also the president of the Chinese Club. On my birthday one year, Ling gave me a big bag of peanut M & M with a cute dispenser—two smiling chubby M & M figures sitting side by side on two chairs. I still have the dispenser. She knew peanut M & M candy was one of my weaknesses. She also spent a semester in Beijing as an exchange student in college. The last time I saw her, many years ago, she had just gotten married, and she was a successful business woman in Chicago.

I still can see Candice Fryda's sweet face. She is a family nurse practitioner in Lincoln. Jennifer Smice was most pleasant and fun. She is a learning and development adviser at the Dell in Lincoln.

I miss my girls—I will always treasure the beautiful memories I had with them...

Hall of Fame

Some athletes are disciplined only with the sports they are good at, nothing else. But there are some who apply the spirit and discipline acquired through vigorous training to whatever they do. Thus they become tough, disciplined, and unbeatable winners in life. Jason Christie, one of the most unique and outstanding students I had, is one of these people. When I first started the Chinese language program for Lincoln Public Schools, Jason was a ninth grader. He was in my first Chinese language class at Everett Jr. High.

It took a couple of weeks to get to know my students. I noticed Jennifer had the same last name as Jason. I asked them, "Are you related?"

They smiled, and said at the same time, "Yes, we are twins."

I was surprised and excited. "Really? I would never have guessed that. I am a twin also." The three of us laughed.

Jennifer always had a beautiful smile on her face while Jason looked very serious. Jennifer was very actively involved with student council, gymnastics, and soccer while Jason was training and practicing diligently—three-hour training daily—in gymnastics. They both were motivated, delightful, outstanding students.

Jennifer, Jason, and their older sister Tonya were blessed with solid, supportive, and down-to-earth parents. Their mother, Kathy, devoted her life totally to them while they were in school and training in gymnastics.

When Jason started gymnastics, he was nine years old. His intensive training also started then when his potential was recognized. Since then, this little boy had a big dream in his heart—to compete in the Olympics someday.

Jason was one of the top gymnasts throughout high school while being a solid learner and exceptional student in all subjects. He was the highest achiever in Chinese among my first group of students in the program.

Jason received a full scholarship from the University of Nebraska-Lincoln for his academic achievement and remarkable exhibition in gymnastics. He competed nationally and internationally while taking a full load of courses in electrical engineering throughout college. He shared his scholarship with his twin sister, Jennifer, and attended the Chinese language program for a semester at the Beijing University.

He called me one day before graduating from college, "*Lao Shi*, I didn't make the Olympics team. There were two people ahead of me." He sounded disappointed. Although he didn't make the U.S. Olympics team, years later, he volunteered at the 2008 Olympics in Beijing to help American athletes and their families with his language skills and experiences in China.

I knew how much effort he had put forth for his dream.

"Well, you tried your best, and you won't have any regrets. What about your career?"

"I got a great offer working in Shanghai." He sounded excited again.

"Congratulations! Now you can really use your Chinese." I was so happy for him.

When we visited him in Shanghai, in fluent Chinese he introduced me to his Chinese friends, "This is my *Lao Shi* and my Chinese mother."

After working in China for several years, with his ambition, language, experiences, and background in electrical engineering, he started his own business in China. He called and told me, "*Lao Shi*, I have started my own company."

"How exciting! Good for you. How is it going?"

Jason told me, "It is going well. A lot of work! I want to get my MBA so that I know how to run a company more effectively." While managing his own company, he came back to the U.S. for a couple of years for graduate school and obtained his MBA in international business.

He always pursues whatever goals he sets for himself with a very clear vision and great effort. This industrious dream chaser has made most of his visions happen.

He called one day, sounded excited, and telling me, "Tonya is going to have triplet girls, and Jenny is going to have twin boys. They are not far apart!"

"Congratulations! You are going to be an uncle of five nieces and nephews. Are you ready?"

He laughed. "I have been ready! Can you imagine that my parents will have five grandchildren within six months?"

"What an exciting blessing!"

We have kept close contact ever since he graduated from Lincoln High in 1992. He calls me whenever there is any change or major event happening with him and in his family, no matter where he is. He was devastated when his father was diagnosed with liver cancer. A year or so later he called and told me, "My father passed away yesterday." I share his joy and feel his pain, always.

I went back to Lincoln to get our house ready to sell during Spring Break in 2012. His mother, Kathy, was also visiting from Colorado. I spent Easter with his family at Jennifer's house. He prepared a vegetarian tofu dish for me.

He told me, "When I was inducted as one of the distinguished alums for the Athletic Hall of Fame at Lincoln High School a couple of years ago, I gave a speech at the ceremony."

I was excited, and interrupted him. "What an honor! You deserved it!"

He continued, "I told the audience that learning Chinese with Mrs. Celine Robertson was the best experience I had at Lincoln High School."

"You did?"

"Yes, *Lao Shi*, I wouldn't have been on that platform without you."

This extraordinary kid of mine still works in China. Jason called recently, and told me, "I really like Taiwan. I would like to work in Taipei." He knows Asia better than I do. I know that whatever he wants to do, it will happen.

Jason Christie is one of a kind—persistent, daring, and unbeatable. He is a true winner in life and a courageous pioneer in foreign lands.

*****

My students enriched my life. They made my path colorful and my destiny spiritual…

Jason Christie & Celine in Beijing 2008

The Roaring Lion

A Seed

Not long ago, I received a call from Ray Petersen, "*Lao Shi*, this is Ray."

"Hey! How are you? What are you up to nowadays? Still working as a security guard at the Immigration Office?" I conversed with him in Chinese.

"Yes, yes! I have so much to tell you, *Lao Shi*." He spoke fluent Chinese. "First of all, I am engaged to the love of my life! You will love her."

"You have good taste. She must be wonderful! Congratulations!"

"Thank you! I started working with a group of people on the Lion Dance again."

"Great! You can drum, choreograph, and coach again. You were great at them."

"I can't stand watching people who don't know about the lions doing the Lion Dance in Lincoln. So I decided to train people the Lion Dance again to show people the right way to keep the Chinese tradition!"

"Good for you!" I was touched deeply by his passion and sense of mission.

Ray is a bright, gifted young man. He was also street-wise and well informed about whatever happened in different communities. He started learning Chinese in eighth grade. He was an eleventh grader when I retired from Lincoln Public Schools in 2000.

Ray is extremely talented with languages. He can speak Vietnamese that he learned by hanging around friends from Vietnam. He can communicate in Spanish to people who can only speak Spanish. I am not sure how he learned Cantonese—a Chinese dialect spoken in Hong Kong and Guangdong (Canton) Province. When he spent a summer in Taiwan learning martial arts, he picked up another Chinese dialect, Taiwanese. What an amazing young man.

During the eleven years I taught at Lincoln High School [LHS], I sponsored Chinese Club, Martial Arts Club, and the LHS Lion Dance Troupe. Ray was an active member of all, especially with the Lion Dance Troupe. The troupe practiced after school every Friday.

Gary, a professor at the University of Nebraska-Lincoln, was the coach. Gary was born and raised in San Francisco. He was not only a passionate martial artist but a devoted Lion Dance performer ever since he was a kid. He worked closely with my Lion Dance Troupe dancers for two years—providing training and knowledge about the Lion Dance. My students had great admiration for Gary—a devoted master. They learned diligently with passion and they respected the tradition and the lions. With great pride and honor they danced all over in Nebraska and in Kansas City for different occasions.

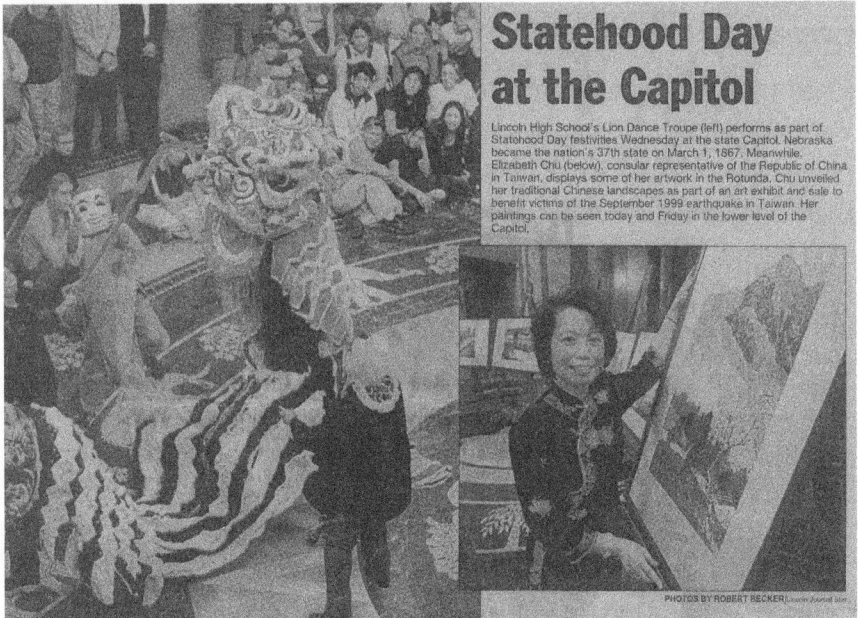

Statehood Day at the Capitol

Lincoln High School's Lion Dance Troupe (left) performs as part of Statehood Day festivities Wednesday at the state Capitol. Nebraska became the nation's 37th state on March 1, 1867. Meanwhile, Elizabeth Chu (below), consular representative of the Republic of China in Taiwan, displays some of her artwork in the Rotunda. Chu unveiled her traditional Chinese landscapes as part of an art exhibit and sale to benefit victims of the September 1999 earthquake in Taiwan. Her paintings can be seen today and Friday in the lower level of the Capitol.

PHOTOS BY ROBERT BECKER/*Lincoln Journal Star*

Courtesy of <u>Lincoln Journal Star</u>

Lion Dance

The Lion Dance has been part of the Chinese culture for thousands of years and is performed on auspicious occasions such as weddings, business grand openings, various festivals, and celebrations.

The lion—a symbol of power, wisdom, and good fortune—chases away evil spirits and brings happiness, longevity, and good luck. The Lion Dance is also performed at many business locations during the Chinese New Year's celebration to bring prosperity and good luck to their businesses for the upcoming year.

The Lion Dance is enacted by two dancers. The lions can be made in any colors—from hot pink to gold and from black to orange. One dancer handles the vibrant head, made out of strong, but light materials, paper and bamboo. The eyelids move, and the mouth opens. The other dancer plays the body and the tail under a colorfully decorated cloth that is attached to the head. A Buddha teases and accompanies the lion with a fan. The Buddha figure is significant because it represents a temple monk, who trained the lions and started the tradition.

The Lion Dance is not only looked upon as the skillful display of strength and artistry but also as the discipline of mind and body. Externally, it enhances health and can be for self-defense. It is also the cultivation of inner strength and self-discipline to receive life's challenges with grace and elegance. The lion is accompanied by musicians, playing a large drum, cymbals, and a gong.

It has traditionally been performed by martial artists. Martial arts is important for the dancers as a foundation due to the physical strain of lion dancing, as well as the fact that all the lion steps are found in the martial arts forms.

Kung Fu Kids

I was very fortunate to have some students who were motivated and strong enough to do the Lion Dance, one of the colorful Chinese traditions I introduced to my students. Todd Burnham was the leader and organizer of the troupe. He was great break dancer as well.

Todd was a strong young man, and he enjoyed the Lion Dance with great passion. Ray Petersen had creative choreography ideas and rhythm with drumming. Jeremy Jewel applied his previous martial arts training to the Lion Dance with confidence and excitement. He was an exciting dancer. Richard Jacobson was inspired and willing to learn anything using his big muscles. Jordan Devoe was a smart, hard-working, enthusiastic student. He enjoyed learning and loved the challenge. Nan Li, a bright and easy-going young man, was the only Chinese among the dancers.

They were the lions of the Lincoln High School Lion Dance Troupe. They learned Chinese together, and they trained and performed together. They became inseparable buddies throughout high school. They were my Kung Fu Kids.

Ray often said to me, "I wish I could learn Chinese martial arts. There are so many different forms and styles." He was learning Karate at the time.

"Yeah, it would be great if we learned real Chinese Kung Fu," Richard echoed.

"I agree. You can do even more tricks with the lions if you have some training in martial arts."

Learning and training for the Lion Dance is hard work, but the Kung Fu Kids never missed practice and never complained. It warmed my heart to see how creative and tough they were at the practice. When they tried new tricks, such as one person sitting or standing on another person's shoulders, I yelled, "Be careful. Don't fall!"

"Don't worry, *Lao Shi*. We got it. We are careful," they always assured me. They were my dedicated and most enduring kids!

Although I was going to retire soon, I wanted to provide them unique opportunities outside of the classroom, school and country to stretch their potentials and to broaden their horizons.

One day before I retired, my Kung Fu Kids gathered around me after school as they often did. "I have arranged something exciting for you. Are you interested?" I asked them.

"What? Tell us!" they asked it together with excitement.

I smiled. "A reputable martial arts master in Taiwan is willing to train you guys for a summer." I continued, "He will provide you room and board. There is no charge for the training. The only thing you are responsible for is your roundtrip airline ticket. Interested?"

They couldn't believe it. Ray screamed, "Wow! Really? A master trains us free in Taiwan?"

"Yeah! You will love it there!"

Jeremy had gone with me as a member of the Taiping Sister City delegation a couple of years previously. "I am going. I loved Taiwan when I went last time with *Lao Shi*."

Richard clapped his hands. "I want to go. When do you need to know?"

"Let me know as soon as possible so that I can make detailed arrangements for you."

"I am going for sure!" Jordan exclaimed.

"I need to check with my parents," Todd responded.

Nan looked disappointed. "I wish I could go. I have to go to see my grandparents in China."

It was so hard to say good-bye to my students when I decided to retire in 2000, especially to my Kung Fu Kids. On the last day of school, the Lion Dance Troupe followed me home and performed a special Lion Dance in our front yard and presented me gifts to wish me a good retirement. I already missed them.

They came to see me very often. I accepted the offer to teach at the International School of Beijing in the fall of 2001. Before they left for Taiwan, I told them, "When you get back, I will be in Beijing. I will see you in December when I come back for winter break." I continued, "Learn as much as you can and speak your Chinese there. Remember to be respectful and appreciative. Be the beautiful Americans!"

"We will be the most beautiful Americans!" They assured me.

Right after school was out in June of 2001, four of my Kung Fu Kids—Ray, Jeremy, Richard, and Jordan—boarded the plane to start a journey that changed their lives.

Master Wen Tie Tseng was a well-known martial arts master in Taiwan. He treated them like his own kids. Master Tseng took them to visit other masters, martial arts schools, and his friends. He taught them Qi Gong and martial arts.

Master Tseng provided them incredible training and experiences. They not only learned Kung Fu and Qi Gong but also absorbed the relationship and courtesy among Chinese people and the martial world traditions.

When I came home from Beijing in December, my Kung Fu Kids surprised me at the airport. They were more mature and much taller. On the way home, everyone was trying to tell me about their experiences in Taiwan. When we got home, giant Jordan said to me, "*Lao Shi*, punch me!" He pointed at his stomach.

"What?!"

"Yes, punch him!" Ray laughed and reinforced the request.

"Punch me too!" Richard said.

"Me too!" Ray and Jeremy yelled at the same time.

I looked at these four big boys in front of me. "Are you sure?" So I punched each of them in the stomach with my fist. Everyone roared in laughter. I asked, "Did it hurt?"

"No! It didn't hurt at all. Try it again! Punch harder!" Richard said. I punched him again, harder this time.

"Yeah! Harder! Punch me again too!" Jordan yelled.

We were laughing so hard. I knew what happened. "You learned Qi Gong, didn't you?"

Nodding their heads, and laughing and saying at the same time, "Yeah! We did. Master Tseng taught us. Isn't it amazing?"

"We were even in the newspaper," Ray said and showed me the paper. There was a big article about them in the newspaper when the Kung Fu Kids did demonstrations at a program in Taichung.

"*Lao Shi*, thank you for arranging this once-in-a-lifetime opportunity for us." Jordan hugged me.

Ray said, "It was wonderful! We learned so much about everything. I love the authentic food. Thank you, *Lao Shi*."

They started telling me more of their experiences in Taiwan. They looked so happy and excited.

"I am so glad you had a great time there. Be sure to thank Master Tseng and keep in touch with him." I hugged each of them when they left at midnight.

I wished that Todd and Nan could have gone with them also.

Jeremy came back with fluent Chinese and he could do a lot more Kung Fu, his passion. After college, he left Lincoln. Now he is a program manager for Nike in Portland, Oregon.

Jordan, an intelligent and clear-minded young man, always knew what he wanted. After college, he went back to Taiwan to teach English.

Richard became a professional fighter after college and won some fights internationally. Then he joined Jordan teaching English in Taipei five years ago. He surprised me.

Ray came back with fluent Chinese and some Taiwanese dialect. He continued with the Lion Dance and practiced his martial arts diligently in Lincoln.

Todd became a computer technician and moved to Omaha. There is no lion dance troupe in Omaha. He misses the Lion Dance and his buddies.

Nan went to college in another state and left Nebraska.

*****

When I went back to Taiwan in November 2014, Jordan and Richard were in Taipei. Jordan had been in Taiwan for almost ten years. He came to our gathering with his Chinese girlfriend. Jordan looked more mature, confident, and serious.

We hugged, and he introduced his girlfriend to me. I was so happy to see them. "Wow! You look so grown-up. What are you doing now? Still teaching English?"

"*Lao Shi*, so great to see you! I have been working at a computer company for five years now. How long are you going to be here?"

"One month. Do you see Richard? How is he doing?"

"Yes, we see each other often. Richard will come to meet us."

"Great! How come you never wanted to work in China?" He called to wish me happy birthday, but he never visited me during the eight years I taught in Beijing.

"I love Taiwan. Richard does too." He continued, "He is married to a Chinese girl and has a baby now."

"Are you kidding?"

Richard had been in Taiwan for five years and was teaching English in Taipei. He brought his wife and their baby girl to meet us at a coffee shop not far from where they lived.

I couldn't believe this playful young boy I remembered has become a father already. I chuckled, asking, "How old are you now?"

He smiled. "I am 32 now."

I forgot there has been almost fourteen years since I last saw Richard. "Are you really?" I teased him, "Are you a good father?"

He smiled bashfully, nodding his head. The baby woke up and opened her eyes. He gently picked the baby up from the stroller and showed me their gorgeous baby, saying, "I love her so much."

It was so touching. I chuckled, asking his wife, "Is he really a good father?"

"Yes!" There was a beautiful smile on her face.

The Roaring Lion

Ray is very bright, sensitive, and observant. One day he asked me, "*Lao Shi*, do you know you do Tai Chi in the hallways?"

"I do?" The hallways between classes at any high school are crowded and dangerous. My arm got hurt once when a student ran into me in the hallways.

He laughed. "Yeah, your arms are always up in blocking position." Only he could tell since he practiced Karate and he knew I had learned Tai Chi.

After he mentioned it, I noticed that I really did have my arms up in protective blocking mode wherever there was a crowd.

My students came to visit me often. Ray was quite a cook. He often brought fish he had caught and other food to cook for our gathering. He was our chef.

When I was their age, teachers seemed so old, serious, and boring. I never got close to any of them. I wondered why they liked to hang out with me. I asked them, "Do you guys think *Lao Shi* is old?"

They all yelled, "No! You are not old." They laughed.

Ray said, "*Lao Shi,* you are fun and energetic like a kid. That's why we love to hang out with you. You are forever eighteen!" They all agreed.

One time, seven boys took me to see a movie at the theater where Jordan worked. I felt very safe with my seven body-guards right next to me in downtown Lincoln.

*****

Ray called me in the spring this year. "*Lao Shi*, I decided to take over the Lion Dance Troupe at the Asian Community Center to keep the tradition."

"Great! You can really lead the troupe and pass on what you have learned." Super idea!

A couple of months later, Ray called again. "*Lao Shi*, I decided to establish a non-profit organization to be independent so that I can provide free lessons to people who are interested in the Lion Dance and martial arts." He continued, "We named it Jing Mo Tong Athletic Association." A great vision!

"Wonderful! Where do you get funding?"

"From donations."

"Are you going to keep your job and do this at the same time?" I worried about his livelihood.

"Oh, yes. I do it at my spare time in the evening and on weekends."

"Make sure you have everything set up legally."

"Don't worry, *Lao Shi*. Danielle, my fiancée, handled all the documents." Danielle is an intelligent and thorough young lady. It was her idea to establish such a non-profit organization.

"How can people support you?" I wanted to help him to get some funds to get started.

"We set up online with GOFUNDME. People can donate directly online."

"Send me the link. I will see what I can do."

I rounded up my family and friends, far and near, to support his vision and mission. Ching Da Chuan, a good old friend, was a professor in Taiwan. He obtained his PhD in North Carolina after receiving his master's degree at the University of Nebraska-Lincoln. When I was in Taiwan last winter, Ching Da showed me his project—preserving schools and villages including his hometown in the mountains by the ocean near Keelung. I was profoundly moved by his passion and love for the village where he was born and raised. He donated $1,000 to support Ray's mission.

*****

Ray called in the fall, "*Lao Shi*, we are invited to Master Nelson Ferreira's 20th anniversary celebration in Madison on October 18. I can come to see you in Milwaukee." He sounded excited. Master Ferreira is the founder and master of Zhong Yi Kung Fu Association in Madison.

"Great! It's an hour away," I said. "You are welcome to stay with us. Would you want to meet my *Shi Fu, M*aster Kleppe? He was impressed with the teaching CD for the Lion Dance you guys made for me and also your performances. Would you want to share and work with the lion dancers of the ShanLin Center?" ShaoLin Center is the martial arts school where Casey and I learn Shao Lin Kung Fu.

"Sure! We love to share with other people."

"I will make arrangements." I continued, "If it is possible, could you do something for my grandson Casey's school? I want them to see the beautiful authentic Lion Dance."

He laughed. "No problem! *Lao Shi*, I will do whatever you want me to do."

"Super! Just tell me how many of you are coming. I will make housing arrangements for you."

Twelve of them arrived around 6:00 PM on Friday. After dinner we went to the ShaoLin Center. They shared their dancing and drumming techniques—without hesitation and reservation—with the lion dancers at the ShaoLin Center.

Ray, the leader of the troupe, was well organized. He demonstrated different drumming techniques while his team showed how gong and cymbals accompany the drum. I was very impressed how clearly and effectively Ray shared all the information. I had told him many times before, "You will make a great teacher!" Now he is a teacher in a different classroom.

My *Shi Fu*, Master Kleppe of the ShaoLin Center, enjoyed Ray and his team and appreciated their generosity of sharing. He offered, "If you like, I can teach you whatever martial arts you wish to learn."

They were thrilled, yelling together, "Yes, we want to learn from you, *Shi Fu*!"

Early morning on Sunday, *Shi Fu* and a few skillful instructors from Wisconsin ShaoLin Center, worked with the Jing Mo Tong team from Nebraska for three hours on different martial arts forms. *Shi Fu* taught Ray *Kwan Dao*—Ray's favorite weapon since high school. *Kwan Dao* is a big broad sword like weapon attached on one end of a long stick, used by a historically famous, courageous general Kwan Gong. It touched me intensely to see these martial brothers learning respectfully and humbly from one another.

Sunday evening was the Gala for Master Ferreira in Madison. I was invited. There were masters from all over the U. S. There were also the Lion Dance and drumming masters from Singapore and Malaysia. My *Shi Fu* Master Kleppe was there also.

Nebraska Jing Mo Tong brought a brand new gorgeous hot pink lion for the Eye Dotting ceremony at the Gala, a tradition for a new lion before doing any performance. The ritual is to use a calligraphy brush and red paint to put dots on the forehead, eyes, ears, back, and four feet to bless the new lion. Thus the new dotted lion will bring good fortunes and blessings to people when it dances. It is a very important ritual—traditionally done by masters or important people.

Ray said to me, "*Lao* Shi, I want you to dot the lion too." What an honor.

"No, no! I am not a master. Besides, there are so many masters here. There may not be enough spots. I don't need to do it. Don't worry about it."

406

"It is important to me. You are my *Lao Shi*. I will talk to Master Ferreira." He insisted.

Master Ferreira, an embracing and wise master, respected and honored Ray's request. When it was my turn, he announced, "*Lao Shi*, Celine Robertson." I dotted one of the lion's feet.

There were twelve people who had the honor to participate in the ritual. Except for Master Ferreira's mother and me, the rest of them were all well-known masters in the martial world. This was the second time I saw it done, and it was the first time I had the honor to dot a lion.

After the ritual Jing Mo Tong Lion Dance Troupe did a fabulous performance with their newly dotted sexy hot pink lion. They did challenging and fancy tricks that not many lion dancers can do. Standing on the shoulders of the person who was the body and the tail of the lion, Anh Nguyen, another student of mine, demonstrated amazing skills and tricks with the heavy vibrant lion head. With impeccable communication with the drum, gong, and cymbals, the hot pink lion came alive and did a spectacular dance. They won roaring applause for their performance.

It brought tears to my eyes to watch Anh demonstrate such skillful techniques. He is the deputy director of Jing Mo Tong—actively involved with the Lion Dance and martial arts. I still remember when I first introduced martial arts to his class when he was a ninth grader. Their class demonstrated staff [long stick] at my last *Chinese Kaleidoscope* program at Lincoln High School in 2000. Now he not only shines with the Lion Dance, but also with break-dance and martial arts.

I was impressed with Ray's thorough planning for the performance and clear communication with his team to ensure an excellent exhibit of their skills with the lions. He has become a humble, embracing leader who puts his team and their mission before himself.

Masters from all over the U.S. at the Gala congratulated him, "Master Petersen, what an impressive performance!" He beamed. He became a master when people called him *Master*—an affirmation of his high level skills—at the Gala on October 18, 2015 in Madison,

Wisconsin.

Master Ferreira presented a plaque to Master Petersen for his friendship, skills, and participation at the Gala. Ray humbly received all the compliments and honor for Jing Mo Tong. He made many national and international connections with masters at this exciting event in Madison, Wisconsin.

At the whole school assembly at Casey's school, Big Bend Elementary School, Jing Mo Tang did the Eye Dotting ritual to awake and bless my two lions, gifts from my colleagues in Beijing. Several hundred students and staff had a chance to see the authentic Lion Dance ritual and performance. They also had the opportunity to see different forms of Chinese martial arts demonstrated by *Shi Fu* Kleppe and two other instructors from Wisconsin ShaoLin Center and Nebraska Jing Mo Tong warriors.

Ray introduced me to people, "This is my *Lao Shi* and my second mother since eighth grade."

I was astonished at what Ray has accomplished. When he was an eighth grader, he could never find his assignments in his backpack. One day I dumped everything out of his backpack and showed him how to organize his books and materials. Here he was, well organized, even with a system to load and unload all the Lion Dance equipment from his truck.

I commented, "I am truly impressed how organized and thorough you are with everything."

He looked at me, smiling and said, "I learned from the best, *Lao Shi*!"

This kid of mine has cultivated the seed I planted in him when he was an eighth grader. It has transformed this gifted, curious, motivated young boy, Ray Petersen, into an amazing *Roaring Lion.*

With Anh, Danielle, and his team by his side sharing his vision and mission, Nebraska Jing Mo Tong will rock the martial world with their well blessed powerful lions, for sure.

Ray Petersen (center first row), Anh Nguyen (to Ray's left), Danielle (far left of second row)

Nebraska Jing Mo Tong Lion Dance Troupe

Flying Arrows

I can still remember the first day when I met my students at Arrowhead High School. I asked them, "Who thinks Chinese is difficult?" Everyone raised their hands.

I laughed. "You guys have guts! You are here even though you think it is hard! Great! I love gutsy people!" Everybody laughed.

"Your future is now! How you prepare yourself right now will make a difference for your future." I continued, "Chinese language is the language for the century! You not only will have more opportunities with your career but also will have an enriched life. I am so excited for you."

My students listened attentively. There were sparkles in their eyes—motivation and desire to learn.

I gave a brief introduction to the language and showed them how the six different ways of Chinese characters are created and developed. In five minutes they learned how to write numbers from one to ninety-nine in Chinese. They looked amazed and proud.

Before the end of class, I asked them again, "Who thinks Chinese is easier than what you expected?"

They looked relaxed, and they smiled. Everyone raised their hands. They were ready to take their first step into an enchanted journey…

*****

Kathy Warren was my daughter Joline's colleague in Milwaukee. She had the opportunity to work in Beijing. In 2005, her son John Warren was a student in my sixth grade Chinese class at the International School of Beijing (ISB). The following summer John and his family came back to Milwaukee after living in Beijing for two years.

I always made sure to visit the Warrens whenever I came to Milwaukee to see my daughter. John's whole family missed Beijing, and they especially wished John and his sister, Mary, could continue with Chinese.

John said, "I really wish I were still in your class learning Chinese."

His sister Mary echoed, "I wish I could continue with my Chinese too." She is one year younger than John.

"Arrowhead High School is a great school, but there is no Chinese program," Kathy added.

In the summer of 2008, I casually mentioned to the Warrens that I was thinking of retiring from ISB and coming back the following year. The whole family was excited. Kathy said, "We need to get you a job here."

I was touched by their eagerness. I just smiled and didn't say anything, since I planned to come back to the U.S. to retire. But Kathy was serious about it. She arranged for me to meet the department chair of the World Languages Department at Arrowhead High School.

In the fall, Kathy, with other parents, submitted a proposal to the school board to offer Chinese as one of the world languages. The proposal was approved promptly, and the school decided to establish a four-year Chinese language program the following year.

My interview with the administrators was done via Skype from Beijing. After the interview they offered me the job and asked me to establish a four-year Chinese program for them. I started the program with three beginner classes of seventy-five students in the fall of 2009.

In 2012, the program had been successfully established—more than 150 students in the program after three years—my mission had been accomplished. I decided to retire from Arrowhead High School, earlier than my original plan. This was my third attempt to retire.

My students were sad, and they did not want me to retire.

My students asked me several times every day, "Why are you going to retire?"

"I need time to spend with my grandchildren, I want to write a book about my life, and I want to learn how to play piano."

"Bring your grandchildren to school, and we will take care of them," one student suggested.

"Yeah, and this way you can still teach us next year," another student seconded the solution.

"We will all buy your book! Let us know when it is done!" one boy yelled.

"I can teach you to play piano!" one girl called out.

It was sad to say good-bye to all my students at Arrowhead. I enjoyed them and loved them dearly.

*****

I treasured my students and teaching wherever I taught—in Taiwan, the U.S., or China. I enjoyed all my students whether they were gifted, average, or with special needs. I loved all of them whoever they were—Chinese, American, or international students from around the world.

The Chinese saying about being a teacher—*Being a teacher for one day, you are a parent all your life*—is especially true with me.

I will never forget those innocent faces of the seventh graders—my first students—in Taiwan. I will always wonder how my special needs students are doing with their lives. I will never stop missing my international students around the world. I will keep in close touch continuously with my Chinese language students from Lincoln, Nebraska, through emails and Facebook.

Cornhusker vs Badger

My Arrowhead High School students in Hartland, Wisconsin, were particularly special to me—being the very last group of students of my teaching career. They were like a bunch of new arrows—getting ready to aim at their targets.

Being part of the force for shooting these arrows, I tried to expand their vision and to provide experiences to help them explore the world and search for their targets.

I have followed my students and cheered them on by emails, Facebook, or through their parents—wherever they are and whatever targets they aim at when they are in college.

Drew Meyer, a bright, delightful, good-natured young man, was in my classes for two years. He and Charles Rusman were buddies. Sitting next to each other, they chatted constantly. I gave Drew a nickname—*Machine Gun*. Whenever I called out, "*Machine Gun*," he laughed and stopped talking. Everyone giggled.

On the last day of school before graduation, Drew said to me, "*Lao Shi,* I will be playing for the Badgers." The Badgers is the University of Wisconsin-Madison football team.

"Awesome! How exciting! Congratulations! It is not easy to get on a college team." I knew he played football, but I didn't know he had made the college team.

This tall handsome boy smiled. "I am the kicker," he continued. "We are going to play against the Nebraska Cornhuskers in October, and I wonder if you are interested in coming to watch the game." He knew we lived in Nebraska for many years.

I laughed and said to this giant in front of me, "Of course I am interested! Are you playing?"

He chuckled. "I am not sure I will start playing this year or next year. I will save two tickets for you for the Nebraska game." Later I found out he gave me two out of four tickets he had for the game—one of the most attended events.

I was touched by his thoughtfulness. I stood on tippy-toes to reach up and hug him. "Thank you! Have fun in college. Keep in touch." I already missed him—my *Machine Gun*.

One day in September, I got an email from Drew. "*Lao Shi*, are you still coming to the Nebraska game? My mother will see you at Arrowhead and give you the tickets." I knew his mother, Amy. She was a supportive and pleasant helper with all our activities.

Drew's considerate parents not only arranged and paid for the parking a block from the stadium but also brought us cushions to sit on. The Badgers won the game. I was very happy for Drew's team even though he didn't play. We even got to see him after the game—

what a privilege. I became a Badger fan because of him. After that I bought Badgers t-shirts and sweatshirts for my grandchildren to cheer for Number 90, the kicker—Drew Meyer.

Cornhusker Celine vs Badger Drew

With positive attitude and pleasant personality, this powerful arrow will fly an incredible distance.

*****

Drew's buddy Charles was a star athlete also. He made the crucial 3-pointer basket at the very last minute and won the state basketball championship for Arrowhead High School in 2011. Charles learned Chinese with great motivation and curiosity because his maternal grandmother was Chinese. He played basketball for the University of Nevada. One day last year, I got a Facebook message from him. He wrote, "*Lao Shi*, I am going to China for a semester exchange program."

I was thrilled he was still learning Chinese. "Wonderful! Speak Chinese as much as you can. Enjoy China!" This strong arrow is aiming at his target with passion and pride.

After he graduated from college, he contacted me and asked me, "*Lao Shi*, I am going to China in July to teach English in Changsha. I would like to take the Chinese Proficiency Test. Would you help me prepare before I leave?"

"Sure! I would love to help you when you come back to Milwaukee in April."

Little Buddies

Evan Pollock, a brilliant and industrious student, did an extraordinary job with the Chinese language in two years. He continued with the Chinese language at the University of Wisconsin-Madison. His high placement test scores in Chinese put him in a class equivalent to a level five class in high school—skipping two levels.

College classes are much more intensive. He was worried. "*Lao Shi*, it is so hard. I am going to have a big test next week. I am scared."

Evan is an outstanding, hard-working young man—he has known exactly what he wants and what needs to be done every step of the way ever since high school. All he needed was a little encouragement and confidence. "You will do fine. Just remember you had a very solid foundation in high school." I had more faith in him than he had in himself.

I was right—remarkably he got 90% on his big test and 98% on his composition.

After he did his internship at a local firm in the summer after his junior year, the firm offered him a job before he went back to school for his senior year. What a superb arrow!

Another excellent student, Maddie Burgdorff, and Evan have been best friends since high school. This beautiful bright young lady was born and raised in a solid, hard-working family. Her mother, Mary, was one of my treasured volunteers. We became good friends.

Maddie also continued with her Chinese in college. Although she has changed schools and majors a few times, I have faith in Maddie—this durable arrow will reach her final target.

Whenever Evan and Maddie were home from college, they always came to visit. Many others joined them for a reunion. I was happy to fix some of their favorite dishes. We had great fun catching up while playing ping pong and *ma jiang* [mah jong, a popular Chinese game on tiles].

I have known John Warren since he was a sixth grader in Beijing. It has been such a delight to watch him grow from a quiet, shy young boy to a mature, confident young man.

I finally had his younger sister, Mary, in my class for a year. She won state champion in swimming for Arrowhead and received a scholarship from Northwestern University. What a competitive arrow!

Studying at the University of Minnesota, John took advantage of the Chinese language program and joined the Chinese Students Association. He was very happy in college. "*Lao Shi*, I am the only non-Chinese member. I have made many Chinese friends. I have so much fun with them."

Now he speaks fluent Chinese. His target is to study international law and make good use of his special language skills—another energetic arrow soaring in the air.

He wrote in the fall, telling me, "*Lao Shi*, I want to spend a couple of years working in China before studying law. I really miss China."

"It is a great idea. It will be an invaluable experience for you!"

A couple of months later, John posted on Facebook the following:

> I have been formally invited and accepted the offer to join the Peace Corps as a Secondary English Teacher at a university in mainland China! Thank you to everyone who has been supporting me in my 21 years of existence on this teeny tiny planet, especially to my friends and family!
>
> The real impact started with Celine Robertson back in 2004, which inspired me to learn a language I thought was not learnable and equipped me with a lifelong skill that I am forever grateful to have. (我爱你, 老师!) [I love you, Teacher!]

This energetic, confident arrow will reach a farther distance.

The three of them—John, Maddie, and Evan—helped me produce a few Chinese teaching videos for an on-line Chinese language program. They were my Super Stars! They also are my biggest fans and supporters. They stand by my side to help me with whatever I do.

I was especially moved and surprised when Evan presented me the three book covers he designed for my book—without being asked. The Chinese characters on the book cover he picked to reflect my life were profoundly perfect. He really knew me.

How blessed I have been to have Evan, Maddie, and John in my life. They are my little buddies.

Arrows

In the fall of 2012, Evan invited me to visit him at his school. "*Lao Shi*, come to visit us in Madison. Maddie can drive you."

Maddie was excited. "Yes! I can drive. It will be fun." They know me well—a chicken. I can't handle driving to any place where I am not familiar, especially long distances.

We set a day to visit Evan and other students at the University of Wisconsin-Madison. It was such a joy to also see Jordon Fritz, Drew Meyer, and Emily Kuettner again.

As they proudly showed Maddie and me around the campus, I told them, "I love you guys and I miss you so much."

Jordan smiled and said to me, "*Lao Shi*, no teacher loves us more than you do." Everyone agreed. It warmed my heart immensely—they felt my love.

Jordan was a bright, playful, lively student. One time he had his Smart phone out in class. I smiled at him and said, "I have a 'dumb' phone. Do you want to trade with me?" He giggled and put it away instantly. Everyone burst out in laughter. I had great fun working with him for three years. With his intelligence and motivation, this strong arrow will reach whatever he aims for.

Molly Ziegler was in my class for two years. She was an active, positive, and pleasant young lady. She is Jordan's step-sister. They were very close. It touched me seeing them genuinely caring about each other like buddies. Molly is a mature, positive arrow soaring freely.

Matthew Miller was in my class for two years, and he was one year ahead of Jordan. They both were on the tennis team. I went to cheer for them at one of the tournaments when Matthew was a senior.

Jordan played against his opponent with a big smile on his face the whole time. He seemed to have so much fun. I was more excited than his parents. I yelled to cheer him on, "*Jia you!*" [Go!]

Matthew was an easy-going and sociable young man. He was a state champ. He looked so relaxed and calm. I was impressed with his endurance—which won him the championship. What an enduring and competitive arrow! He made me want to play tennis again.

Allen Prange transferred to the University of Wisconsin-Madison for its Chinese program. He is a determined arrow aiming at his target.

Super Star

Learning the Chinese language was quite a challenge for Zachery DeStael. But he was also very interested in the culture. One day, he told me he knew Chinese martial arts. I said, "Show me what you can do. If it is good, I will let you perform at the *Chinese Kaleidoscope*."

He was excited. He came early one morning and demonstrated what he could do. Surprisingly it was the genuine Chinese style of martial arts. I was impressed. "Awesome! Go to choreograph a two-minute demonstration of combined techniques and show it to me. And we will go from there."

Before long, he showed me what he had created. I worked with him to polish some of the forms to make his demonstration more impressive. I provided the opportunity for him to shine at all three of our *Chinese Kaleidoscope* programs in the spring of 2010. He did a superb job, and he was in the newspaper. He was a *Super Star*! With confidence and pride after the program, he became a different person. Zachery was a unique arrow with martial arts skills.

Blossoms

Emily Kuettner had two years of Chinese. The day before she left for her exchange program in Spain, she came to help Big Bend Elementary School celebrate the Chinese New Year in 2014. She told me, "I want to say good-bye to you before I leave for Spain."

She joined eight fellow Arrowhead students to demonstrate the Dragon Dance. She helped third graders with workshop activities and the whole school parade. She majored in Spanish and international business in college. She started working internationally right after graduating from college. This steady soaring arrow reached her target. India was her first business destination. How thrilling!

Sophie Peterson and Katherine French are two amazing, highly motivated young ladies. They are best friends. They followed me for three years and graduated from Arrowhead the same year I retired. They came to visit me on my birthday. Sophia said to me, "*Lao Shi.* You have to set up a Facebook account so that we can keep in touch always."

"I don't know how to use it." I laughed at myself being *low tech.*

"It's easy. We will set up an account for you and show you how to use it." They went to my computer and set it up in two minutes. They put down my age as 38. Since I don't really know how to update my profile or upload pictures, I am 38 always—forever young with the same old picture on Facebook.

Katherine and Sophie—active, diligent young ladies—always knew exactly what targets they were aiming at. Katherine went to Spain for an exchange program. Sophie continued with Chinese in college. She spent a semester in an exchange program in Hungary, and she wants to go to China to work after college. She did a special program about me for her class project and posted in on YouTube. They are two sharp and sturdy arrows. I know for sure they will live successful and enriched lives.

Their close friend Emily DeVal took two years of Chinese with them. She was a year ahead of them. Emily is another brilliant young lady. She graduated from college in three and a half years with a bachelor's degree in environmental science. She started working in the field shortly after—another amazing arrow reached its target.

Brittney Spakowics spent a summer in Japan. This curious arrow is exploring and searching for her final destination.

Extraordinary

I knew my retirement would have an impact on the students I left behind, especially my twelve juniors in Chinese 3. When I announced my retirement, they were stunned and looked so gloomy—nobody moved or talked. I received several emails from their parents the next day telling me how sad they and their children were.

I emphasized to my third year students, "Promise me you'll stay in the program next year for your future." Eleven out of twelve stayed in the program.

I missed them and worried about how they adjusted to their new teacher, who was so different from me. I checked on them constantly. Robin Schreck, Cody's mother, told me, "Cody talked about you and Chinese class every day when you were teaching him. Now he doesn't talk about the class anymore." It made me sad. I sometimes wondered if I should have stayed for another year.

Whenever I think of Cody, I see a bright, happy, and down-to-earth young man. I enjoyed seeing his happy face in my class every day for three years. During his sophomore year he struggled quite a bit adjusting to some changes in his family. His mother Robin and I worked closely together to monitor him. We were so pleased to see the old fun and happy Cody return to us after a semester.

Cody told me one day during his junior year, "I want to be a teacher just like you." He loved history and wanted to be a social studies teacher.

It warmed my heart. "Wonderful! With your personality, you will make a wonderful teacher! It would be a great combination if you can be a social studies and Chinese language teacher at the same time." His Chinese was quite good. His major in college is education.

Kevin LeRoy and Jake Hyland are Cody's buddies. These three

bright boys always enjoyed working together. Sometimes they had too much fun in class and forgot they needed to work on the assignments. They never held grudges against me, even though I sent them to detention at times. One Monday I laughed and asked Cody when he walked into the classroom, "Did you have fun staring at the assistant principal on Saturday? Did you take any work with you?"

He chuckled. "Yeah, I worked on the packet." His good nature made me love him more. Cody is another durable and flexible arrow.

Jake is a bright easy-going young man. He was in choir and played baseball throughout high school. "Do you speak Spanish?" I asked him one day, since it is his heritage.

He said, "Not really. I can understand."

"With three languages—Chinese, Spanish, and English, you can go anyplace in the world without a language barrier." He is an arrow with great potential, and I hoped he would pick up Spanish someday.

*****

Before this group graduated, I gave a graduation party at my house for them and their parents. It was such a joy to see them again in a group as they were in the classroom before.

At the party, Kevin LeRoy had a big smile on his face. "*Lao Shi*, I am going to the University of Wisconsin-Madison. I will continue with Chinese." Kevin is a motivated hard worker who has always taken pride being a great student.

"Terrific! You will do great in college. Be sure to combine one other field with Chinese." This 6'3" tall giant is another powerful arrow soaring confidently in the sky.

Andrew Van Gilder joined in and said, "I am going to the same school. I will also continue with Chinese." This bright young man has been very serious about learning the language since ninth grade. Andrew is a piercing arrow soaring and aiming steadily at his target.

"How wonderful you will be together in college. Who else will be going to the same school?"

"Me!" Rachael Norman raised her hand and came to join us from the other side of the table. Rachael was the only girl in this group. She is such a mature and diligent young lady. Rachael is a solid and conscientious arrow. She was among the 16 students with me in China.

*****

At the reunion in December 2015, Kevin told me, "I am going to Singapore for an exchange program. I am leaving in two weeks." He beamed.

"How exciting! Travel to the neighboring countries if you can." I was so thrilled for him.

Austin grinned, and he told everyone, "I am going to Jiao Tong University in Shanghai for a semester. I will leave mid-February."

Andrew never missed any of our reunions, at the reunion, he announced, "I am going to spend four month in Tianjin this coming summer!"

"You guys are amazing! I am so proud of you!"

China Experience Trip

In the summer of 2011, I took sixteen students and six teachers to experience China. I wanted them not only to see the beautiful country but also to experience the culture. I set up different workshops for hands-on experiences throughout the two weeks we were in China.

In Beijing, we had an exchange program with a local school where students compared Chinese and American schools and learned Kung Fu Fan—martial arts with a fan. After that, students mingled with one another—talking in both Chinese and English and laughing in the lobby. There was a piano in the lobby. When Austin Kissinger started playing the piano, all the students gathered around the piano and started to sing. They sang popular English and Chinese songs together. What a happy, touching scene. It was what I had envisioned—fun and friendship without borders.

In Shanghai, they learned to make *jiao zi* [dumpling] and *tang yuan* [a dessert made of sweet rice flour] for dinner at a restaurant. Each of us made something with clay at a pottery museum. Everyone had fun learning calligraphy and Chinese painting at the workshop held at a high school in Hangzhou.

At the martial arts workshop at a Shao Lin Kung Fu school near Shao Lin Temple, each student had one-to-one instruction on staff (a long stick) techniques for half a day from the students of the Kung Fu school. I was deeply moved watching my students seriously and humbly learning every movement from their personal instructors.

Rachel blocked with her staff on the left side and then swung her staff forcefully on the right to attack. At the break, she had a big smile on her face and came to me and said, "*Lao Shi*, it is fun. I love it. They are so good."

"They practice a lot. I wish I had a chance to learn Kung Fu when I was young. I am glad you enjoy it. You looked very good. Learn as much as you can." My students appreciated the opportunity learning from their individual instructors.

Kyle Tan is an American-born Chinese. He looked so excited and proud throughout the workshop learning the staff from his instructor. He swung his staff right and left and all over the place. He blocked and attacked his instructor like a warrior.

Unique Skill

At the *Chinese Kaleidoscope* program the following year in 2012, Rachel and Kyle were partners for the staff fighting demonstration. They applied the skills they learned at the Kung Fu workshop and choreographed an impressive staff demonstration. They fought fiercely with their staffs and won roaring applause.

Kyle is an industrious young man. He plays flute beautifully. After the China trip, he was even more motivated to learn the language and his heritage. "*Lao Shi*, I would like to go back to Beijing to learn Chinese before going to college."

"What a great idea! Go to Beijing University. The program is quite good there. I will get all the information for you." I was more excited than he.

I suggested to him, "Stay for a year if you can, you will come back with fluent Chinese."

"Okay. I will think about it."

"You are so musical, and it won't be hard to learn a new Chinese instrument when you are there. Er Hu [a small string instrument] is easy to carry around. My favorite is Gu Zen [a 21-string instrument]."

He listened carefully, nodding his head—seeming to ponder what I said. "Okay."

"Make friends there. You will meet students from all over the world. They will be your international connections." He was very shy and quiet. He was such a neat, gifted young man. I wished he could come out of his shell.

After high school, Kyle spent a year at Beijing University. He came back not only speaking fluent Chinese but also with a beautiful Gu Zen. He shared his talents playing both flute and Gu Zen when we celebrated the Chinese New Year of the Horse at Big Bend Elementary and Bright Days Daycare in 2014.

He seemed to be happier, more confident, and less bashful. "Did you make some friends there?" I asked him.

There was a big smile on his face. "Yes, I did. I have friends from different countries. We had great fun together." He responded in fluent Chinese. What a strong and flexible arrow!

Talents

I thought I knew my students very well, but I wasn't aware of some of their talents. One day in the spring of 2013, I received an email from Susan, Bill Lindenberg's mother. "Bill has a lead role in the musical, *Joseph and His Amazing Technicolor Dream-coat*. He played the part of the Pharaoh—an Elvis-like character. Would you like to see the program?"

"Definitely! I wouldn't miss it. I will bring my grandson, Casey."

"Great! Bill will be thrilled. Pick a day and I will meet you in the lobby with your tickets." How sweet and thoughtful.

Arrowhead's musicals were outstanding. Casey had loved musicals ever since he was a toddler. He didn't move the whole time as he watched the program.

I was so excited when Bill—*Pharaoh*—appeared on stage. I pointed at the Elvis-like- character Bill and said to Casey, "That is Bill, my student!" I was so proud of him. I clapped my hands until they hurt. We could have watched Bill sing all day.

During the intermission, Bill, the *Elvis-like-Pharaoh*, came out to see us. We hugged. Casey shook the superstar's hand and gave him the flowers we brought. "I wish I'd known you are such a star. I would have had you do a solo at the *Chinese Kaleidoscope* program last year."

He chuckled. "I am so glad you could come to see the program." Casey stared at Bill's hairdo and touched his shining *Pharaoh* costume.

"What a show! What a star! I wouldn't miss it." I hugged him again.

Bill is a brilliant young man—a gifted insightful student. He learned the language fast and his pronunciation was very good. In class he always asked profound questions about Chinese culture and history. He experienced and absorbed the culture thoroughly throughout our China trip. Bill—a piercing arrow—will soar straight toward his target once he finalizes his search.

Susan, Bill's mother, was one of my precious volunteers and friends. At Bill's graduation party, she took me to the display table and showed me a picture of Bill and me. "Bill loves you, and he wants to display this picture." I was profoundly moved.

Bill introduced me to his guests, "This is my overall Number 1 teacher."

*****

I meet regularly with some of my Arrowhead students' parents—who became dear friends—to enjoy their friendship and get updates on their children. At a recent gathering, Nancy Kissinger, Austin's mother, told me, "Austin had straight A again this year." He had just finished his sophomore year at the University of Wisconsin-Madison.

"Wow! You've got a winner there!"

Austin was the president of the Chinese class who assisted me with the preparation of cultural activities throughout the years. What a delight to have worked with him for three years. He always had twinkles in his eyes. He was not only a highly motivated student, but also a reliable assistant to me, even when we were in China.

In the spring of 2013, before he graduated from Arrowhead, Nancy called, "Austin is doing a solo at the spring concert. Would you like to come to see him?"

"I will be there! Just tell me the date and time."

"It will be crowded. I will go before 6:00 to get some good seats for us." The concert started at 7:00 PM.

I knew Austin played the piano—he played at the Chinese school in Beijing. But I never expected what I saw at the concert. He not only played the piano but also sang at the same time, professionally. I was in awe. This charming, talented young man brought tears to my eyes.

After the concert I hugged and congratulated Austin. "What a talent you have! I wish I knew. You would have been a Super Star for our *Chinese Kaleidoscope* last year."

"*Lao Shi*, thanks for coming." I saw twinkles in his eyes again.

"I could have watched you perform all night!"

Austin majors in business in college. He plans to study international law to combine law, business, and the Chinese language for his future. In the spring of 2016, he went to Shanghai to spend a semester as an exchange student at Jiao Tong University.

Austin is a solid gold arrow soaring happily and diligently toward his target. How exhilarating!

*****

Kristian Ashby was a quiet, well-behaved student. He played football throughout high school. He was a fighter. He never gave up or complained, no matter how challenging it was. He is a courageous arrow.

Lukas Kannenberg was another hardworking student. His had one of the most beautiful handwritings in Chinese. He always tried his best. He is a persistent arrow.

The Kelly brothers, David and Steve, were two intelligent goal-oriented young men. David did an exceptional job in my class for two years. He participated in a leadership program in China after his junior year. Steve, the younger brother, was never in my class. I got to know him on the China Experience Trip before he started learning the language. I would have loved to work with this bright and highly motivated young man. They are indeed two brilliant and vibrant arrows.

Matthew Kerschinske, an amazing and gifted young man, chose medical school as his target. His kind heart and intelligence will make him a great doctor. It will not surprise me if someday he is a doctor without borders, helping people in foreign lands. Matthew is a powerful arrow soaring with great confidence in the air—without fear or boundary.

Paul Roy, a smart and disciplined young man, was another winner. He is an assured, resilient arrow. With his abilities, motivation, and determination, he will reach whatever target he chooses.

Matthew Lindquist has a brilliant mind. With better organization skills and time management, this sharp arrow will be unstoppable.

Terry Anderson, Ryan's mother, is from Hong Kong. Ryan is a mature and responsible young man. Throughout his three years in my class, I had noticed his increased pride as he learned more about his Chinese heritage. He majors in engineering, which fits his personality perfectly. This smart and sturdy arrow will reach his target, definitely.

Jackson studies engineering at the University of Missouri. He wrote me a message on Facebook at the beginning of his sophomore year, "*Lao Shi,* I am not living in the dorm this year. I need to cook for myself. Would you give me a couple of easy Chinese recipes?"

"Sure!" I wrote back and provided him a couple of simple recipes.

Jackson has a brilliant mind. Learning Chinese was not hard for him at all, but he had trouble with time management in high school. I went after him for his assignments all the time. I jokingly gave him the nickname *Turtle*. "You are so bright. If you speed up with better organization and time management, you will be a *Shark*. Remember this. No one will go after you for your work as I do in college. They will just flunk you."

He smiled, nodding his head. "I know, *Lao Shi*."

At the reunion after their freshman year in college, he told me, "*Lao Shi*, I got a good GPA last year. I am not a *Turtle* any more. I am a *Shark* now."

"Awesome! I knew you could do it. I am so proud of you!"

"Thank you for having faith in me." He smiled and hugged me.

Inspiring

One of my Chinese 1 students, Jackson Campbell, was born with one arm. His mother Judy was another helpful volunteer and a friend.

At one of our gatherings in the spring of 2015, I asked Judy, "How is Jackson doing? What is he going to study in college?"

"He doesn't know yet. I don't know how he will do in college. I hope he will do okay." Like all parents, she worries about her children, especially now that Jackson was going to college.

I said to her, "You saw Jackson perform at our *Chinese Kaleidoscope* program. Did you see him do all the activities—Lion Dance, Dragon Dance, and flag demonstration?"

"Yes." Judy was one of my volunteers back stage.

"Weren't you impressed? They were not easy activities to do even with two arms." I continued, "Jackson is very tough. He never found excuses not to do any of the activities. Instead, he learned everything diligently and performed beautifully."

"He surely did." Judy smiled, and she looked proud.

"I have faith in him. He is a fighter, and he will do well in life," I emphasized.

After Jackson was in college for one semester, I checked with his mom, Judy, to see how he was doing. She sounded very proud when she told me, "Jackson got a GPA of 3.85!"

Jackson's strength and durability touched my heart deeply throughout the year when I taught him. He definitely is a resilient and inspiring arrow.

*****

No matter how long my students were in my class at Arrowhead, one year, two years, or three years, they all had a special place in my heart.

Teaching my students with passion, guiding them with love, cheering for them with faith, my life is forever vibrant—full of pleasure and excitement.

With blessings and love as their strings, and guidance, support, and effort as their bows, these energetic arrows—my very last group of students—will fly an incredible distance without fear or limit.

I will always follow and monitor these *Flying Arrows* as they soar in the air, aiming at their targets and beyond…

LIVING LAKE COUNTRY REPORTER

TUESDAY, FEBRUARY 16, 2010 • 75¢

VOLUME 39, NUMBER 13

Chinese New Year

COLOR IN MOTION – Students perform during the Chinese Kaleidoscope event at Arrowhead High School on Feb. 12.

PHOTOS BY SCOTT ASH/STAFF PHOTOGRAPHER

YEAR OF THE TIGER – Chinese language students perform a traditional Lion dance at Arrowhead High School during the "Chinese Kaleidoscope" event on Friday, Feb. 12. The event celebrates the beginning of the Chinese New Year, the "Year of the Tiger," which starts on Feb. 14. The Chinese language program is a brand new to Arrowhead and the "Chinese Kaleidoscope" is the first Chinese New Year celebration at Arrowhead. Juniors and seniors will present their "Chinese Kaleidoscope" program on Feb. 26 to celebrate the Lantern Festival which marks the ending of the Chinese New Year celebration.

DEMO – Senior Zak De Stael gives a demonstration of Kung Fu martial arts during the Chinese Kaleidoscope event at Arrowhead High School on Friday.

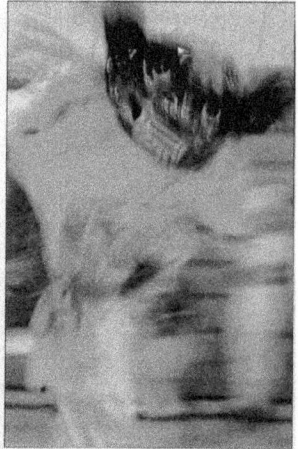

Dragon Dance at 2010 Chinese Kaleidoscope [11th & 12th graders]

Dragon Dance at 2010 Chinese Kaleidoscope [9th & 10th graders]

Third Row: Steve Kelly, Andrew Van Gilder, Evan Pollock, David Kelly, Kevin Leroy
Second Row: Bill Lindenberg, Celine, John Warren, Joe Harter
Front Row: Michael Sawall, Kyle Tan, & Madelyn Burgdorff

Reunion with Arrowhead *Arrows* (2015)

The Boulder and the Little Flower

The doorbell rang and I walked toward the door. Andrea was calling outside of the door, "Mommy! Mommy!" It sounded so urgent. Andrea, our younger daughter, was a fourth grader coming home from school.

"Coming! Coming!" I yelled and ran to the door.

I opened the door. "What is happening?"

"Do you remember my friend, Denise?" she asked me at the doorway.

I answered as I closed the door, "Yes. Something happened to her?"

"Her parents don't live in the same house. Denise doesn't see her daddy every day, only on weekends." She looked so concerned and sad for her friend.

"Oh! Her parents must have divorced."

She asked, so innocently, "What do you mean?"

"When two people, wife and husband, don't love each other anymore, they divorce."

"I thought if you love someone and get married, it is forever." She looked puzzled.

"Yes. It's supposed to be that way. But sometimes people change or things happen. They don't love each other anymore."

"Oh." The innocence about love disappeared in Andrea's pondering eyes.

True love is precious and marriage is a life-long commitment—it is supposed to be forever, just as little Andrea had understood and believed.

*****

Fruitful Harvest

Don, my husband, was born and raised on a little dairy farm near Wisconsin Dells. He is the first-born, and he has two younger sisters. His mother Grace—a German descendant was born and grew up in Milwaukee, Wisconsin. She was a school librarian. His father Percy—with a Norwegian heritage, was a farmer born and raised in a farming family of many generations.

I grew up with six siblings in Taipei, the biggest city in Taiwan. I was always fascinated with the farm life I saw in the movies. I often imagined what it was to live on a farm—cows and animals running around on a vast pasture.

When Don and I first met, I asked him many questions. "Is it fun living on a farm, like in the movies?"

He laughed. "There is a lot of work. Our farm was very small, and we couldn't afford to hire any helpers. I started helping my father when I was six."

"What? At six? What could you do?" I was totally shocked.

"Since I am the oldest and the only boy, I needed to help my father. I drove the tractor and milked the cows."

"You could drive a tractor at six? You knew how to milk the cows?" I couldn't imagine his hard childhood—doing adult chores at the age of six. Here I was, learning how to boil water at the age of 22 in the U.S.

"Yeah! We had to get up early to do all the chores. Milking cows was not too hard. But I was too small for the tractor, and I had to stand on the pedal with both feet to start it."

"Wow! Did you like living on the farm?"

"Not really."

No wonder he never enjoyed yardwork.

Growing up on a little isolated farm—no neighbors—Don had no playmates except for his two sisters. His sister Mary, one year younger, had a different personality and interests. And although Beatrice is very much like him, she is eight years younger. Books became his best and only friends—his only childhood companions. How lonesome...

I laugh when I am happy, and I cry when I feel sad or hurt, even more so when I was young. Don never laughs wholeheartedly the way

I do. I have never seen him cry, either. He said once, "Boys don't cry." I knew he felt sad and devastated when his parents died. He merely sighed, without tears.

He not only grew up as a loner, but he was also brought up suppressing his feelings. He is very knowledgeable, but not expressive. He has a tender heart, and yet it doesn't show. He seldom looks excited, angry, or unhappy—not much expression of any emotion at all.

Don is gifted linguistically. He is fluent in Chinese, and he can get by with his Japanese. He speaks some French, German, and Spanish. He taught himself Arabic and Russian while studying his coin collections. He reads like a scholar, and he enjoys his coins, alone. When we lived in Idaho, he hunted and fished all the time. Once we left Idaho—the state brimming with beautiful mountains and clean rivers—he quit hunting and fishing.

I always had friends to share or to be with me no matter what I did. When I played tennis, I had tennis pals. When I painted, I had friends painting with me. When I wrote, I had writer friends. Even in the pools at the gyms, I had *mermaid* friends by my side. A friend, Sandy, said to me many years ago, "You are like a flower, and people are the water. People make you happy." Indeed, I enjoy my friends—they fill my life with moments of different pleasures and colors.

I sometimes wonder, as most of my friends do, how different two people could be and stay married.

My schedule is usually full. I am always handling or doing more than one task at a time. For a few years, I was involved with 21 community and professional projects, committees, and responsibilities—at the international, national, state, and district levels. My mind contemplated one thing while my eyes checked on a different project and my hands worked on another task. I could work with four or five students—on different tasks—at the same time. People often asked me, "How do you do it?"

When I saw my Chinese medicine doctor, Dr. Yan, in Beijing for the first time, she remarked something amazing after checking my pulse, "Your mind is fast, your hands are speedy, and you are fast with words. 'Fast' is the word to describe you."

I chuckled. "You are absolutely right!" How fascinating she could tell my personality correctly by feeling my pulse—the myth of Chinese medicine. Maybe that is why I can handle more than one task at a time.

Don has a one-track mind and can handle only one thing at a time, slowly. If I asked Don about anything, "Is it done?" His responses were usually, "What's the hurry?" He always takes his time doing things while I'm always ahead of schedule.

One time my close friend Yi Xue came by when I was out playing tennis with a group of friends. She asked Don, "You don't mind that Celine plays tennis with other people and you stay home alone?"

Don laughed. "No! She enjoys playing tennis. She can play. I enjoy looking at my coins. I stay home to enjoy my collections." He has ancient coins from many countries around the world.

Another good friend, Richard, commented, "Don really knows how to love a person."

I could have danced all night, and Don told me, "Go dance with other people," after the first dance. I could play five sets of tennis, non-stop, on any given day, but I had to sign Don up for tennis class to get him to move physically. I worked out at the gym regularly, and Don had never gone once in four years, even though he had a membership.

*****

When Don heard me crying in the kitchen—spending more than one hour typing the very last page of a bibliography of my master's thesis and using many correction strips, Don came to check on me. "Go to take a shower and take a break." When I got out, he had finished typing it for me.

I didn't learn to boil water until the age of 22, let alone know how to cook. After we got married, I wanted to be a good wife. I remembered what Mother told me, "Don is American. He eats a lot of meat. Don't starve him!"

I tried to cook new dishes every day. I followed the recipes carefully. Sometimes the dishes I cooked didn't look like the pictures in the cookbook, and I would cry. "It didn't turn out right. It doesn't look like the picture."

Don knew how hard I tried to learn to cook. He always ate the whole thing and told me, "It doesn't matter if it doesn't look the same. It tastes very good." Poor Don!

Not long after we got married, I used a glass bowl—no common sense—to cook a soup with a lot of ingredients, and it cracked. I cried about the mess and loss of my delicious soup. Don cheered me up first, "It is okay. Don't worry about it." He cleaned up the mess. He never said a word about how dumb I was using a glass bowl on a gas stove to make soup.

*****

Don is a gentle and kind soul. He is one of the most decent and honest people I have ever known. There is not a mean bone in him. He is not expressive, but he is sincere and genuine. He is not too flexible, but he is steady and dependable. He is not talkative, but he is very knowledgeable. His expressionless face seems to be serious, but he is the most embracing person—not judgmental or discriminative at all, with the biggest heart.

Don is solid as a boulder on a cliff or a mountain top, overlooking the world quietly. He seems to have taken a vow to heaven and earth to stand by me always—to provide space for me to grow and to ensure freedom for me to enjoy life and explore the world.

I am like a little flower growing beside this boulder. This well-rooted little flower blooms freely and happily around the boulder. She is curious, and she has dreams—many of them. She follows the sunshine, enjoys the dew, explores the domain, and chases the rainbows. She extends her roots and spreads her leaves. She plays with bees and flies with butterflies. No matter what she does, where she goes, or how far she travels, the little flower always comes back to stay close to her solid and faithful boulder.

The boulder and the little flower—for better or worse, side by side—are approaching half a century and beyond...

The boulder and the little flower

Roots and Wings

A good, old friend, Chuan Yu Wang, asked me a long time ago, "How did you raise your daughters? They have no vanity at all."

A teacher told me at a parent-teacher conference at East High School, "You did a great job raising your two girls. They show their wonderful upbringing."

Nai Yu Chen and Dean Hwang have been our precious life-long friends. When their two sons were little, Nai Yu asked me more than once, "Can I send my boys to you for the summer? I want them to be like Joline and Andrea."

Carol Nemeroff, an old colleague and good friend, knew Joline and Andrea from the time they were born. She came to visit us this past summer. Joline and Andrea took us sightseeing, treated her, and brought their families to meet Aunt Carol. Carol was very impressed. "There are not many kids who would do things with their parents' friends."

Joline and Andrea are our God-sent daughters—two of the greatest blessings in our lives.

****

When Joline and Andrea started driving, I gave them credit cards so that they could put gas in the cars or for emergencies. One time, some friends and I chatted about our kids. One of them reacted with extreme surprise and concern about what I did. "You are not worried they will use it excessively?"

It never occurred to me that Joline and Andrea would do that. I said, "I trust them totally." Apparently, not all parents trust their teenage kids as I did mine.

For eighteen years, before they went to college, I taught and prepared them for whatever I could. I passed on to them what I believed and valued.

When they went to college, away from home in other states, the only thing I was worried about was their safety on campus at night, nothing else. I had faith in them that they would use good judgement with self-respect and principles.

Roots

From the time Joline and Andrea were babies, before their bedtime I read or told Joline stories in Chinese while Don read to Andrea in English. Then we switched. We did this every night until Joline was eleven years old.

Joline got a perfect score in reading on her ACT test. Andrea wrote amazing detective stories when she was in fourth grade. Reading became their life-time hobby. It is wonderful to see Joline and Andrea read to their children every night as we did with them. Joline's nine-year-old son Casey reads high level books in different fields with great pleasure and pride.

In the summer of 1982, when Joline was six and Andrea was three, I founded and established the Lincoln Chinese School for children of Chinese heritage at our church. I wanted my daughters to learn about their heritage—Chinese language and culture.

From the time Joline and Andrea were born, I taught them both Chinese and English. I talked to them in Chinese. I insisted that they respond to me in Chinese only. Whenever they spoke English to me, I said, "*Shuo zhong wen*! [Speak Chinese!] They switched it right away. I did that, like a record player, for eighteen years with each of them until they went to college. Effortlessly they acquired a special skill—to read, write, and converse fluently in Chinese.

The first time I took them back to Taiwan, Joline was eight and Andrea was five. I arranged for them to attend a local kindergarten to reinforce their language. During the 90's when they were in junior high and high school, I went back to Taiwan for workshops many summers. I always took them along. They attended a few Chinese language camps sponsored and designed by the Taiwan government especially for overseas Chinese children.

After Joline's freshman year, she participated in a summer exchange program at the Mandarin Center of Taiwan Normal University in Taipei. In a speech contest, she won second place.

Andrea became very interested in languages. In the seventh grade, she was in the highly gifted program and started learning Japanese with a mentor. In eighth grade, she wrote an incredible Kung Fu short story in Chinese.

Let It Go

When Andrea was in fifth grade, one day she came home looking upset. I asked her, "What is wrong? What happened at school?"

Tears rolled down her cheeks. "Amy is supposed to be my friend, but she told people something about me that was not true." It was very hard for her little innocent heart to understand and face such a betrayal.

"Let me ask you something. Are you a loyal and trustworthy friend?"

"Yes." She looked at me, puzzled.

"Would you do things to your friends like Amy did to you?"

"No."

"Do you like friends like Amy?"

"No."

"You know what? It is her big loss to lose a great friend like you. Do you still want to be friends with her?"

Andrea looked enlightened. "No, I don't want such a friend."

"So you should drop her and ignore whatever she does. Spend time and have fun with your decent friends instead."

"Okay!" She seemed to understand what I tried to tell her.

"A good friend brings you joy." I continued, "Always remember not to waste your energy and time on the negative people and things. They are not worth it."

"Okay!" She smiled again and nodded her head.

*****

When Joline was a freshman at the University of Illinois, one day she called, and she was crying. "Are you all right? What happened?"

She majored in electrical engineering, with minors in bio-medical engineering and international business. She was also taking pre-med classes and a Chinese class.

"A teaching assistant is teaching the Chinese class, and she is from China. She is very prejudiced toward me because of my Taiwan background. She is not professional at all, not helpful but critical." She started to cry again. Joline has always been a positive and pleasant person with a big embracing heart, and she seldom got upset like that.

It was during an era that the relationship between China and Taiwan was tense. There were huge visible gaps and differences between China and Taiwan.

I said to her, "Let me ask you something. Do you need this class for your engineering program?"

"No."

"Are you learning anything in this class?"

"No!"

"Do you enjoy the class?"

"Not at all!"

"Then, drop the class. Don't waste your precious time and energy on this class that you neither need nor enjoy and taught by an unprofessional TA! Always remember! Let no one control your emotions, and let no one make you cry!" Joline was a much happier freshman after dropping the class.

Life is very complex. It can be complicated at times when you run into difficult people or unpleasant situations. It takes wisdom and clear vision to resolve what you face. It also takes guidance and practice to learn how to protect you from negative energy.

It is crucial to be emotionally independent—one of the most essential and critical elements for total independence and happiness. I wanted my daughters to focus on the positive and let go of the negative—to be emotionally independent, always.

Compassion

Joline and her husband Ken volunteered weekly at a women's shelter for many years before they had children. After that, they didn't have time to volunteer. Instead, in addition to their annual donation, every year they supplied 30 or 40 pumpkins for the children at the shelter to celebrate Halloween. Each year Joline asked her children, "Who wants to deliver pumpkins with me?"

Both Casey and his sister Holly yelled, raising their hands in the air, "Me! Me!"

For the past few years, Casey's birthday invitations have said: *No gifts or please make a donation to Waukesha Women's Shelter.*

I am so proud of Casey for being willing to share his abundance and blessings with less fortunate people. When he was four, Casey even volunteered to ring the Salvation Army bells at a mall during the holiday season. Joline and Ken also donated to various organizations whenever their workplaces provided matching funds for their donations. When Joline nursed her three children, she donated milk for premature babies who needed human milk.

Andrea also donated to and supported different charities throughout the years. She and Rylan took their children, Kiran and Callie, to walk to support different causes every year. Sometimes we three families walked together for some charity fundraising events.

Ever since they were in high school, whenever Joline and Andrea grew their hair long enough, they cut it to donate for children who suffered with cancer and needed wigs.

It touched my heart to witness Joline and Andrea model and pass on to their children the compassion my parents showed us siblings. They share one of the principles of the way I live my life: *When you have something extra, share with people.*

Extended Love

Andrea's husband Rylan is from India. His mother Melissa comes to visit them once in a while. She usually spends a couple of months.

Melissa is a very gentle and sweet lady. She taught me how to make Indian food, and I prepared Chinese food for her sometimes. We enjoyed each other's company. We both had some kind of ache and pain throughout our *golden* bodies.

One day Andrea said to me, "Rylan's mother has a knee problem. She is in pain constantly. I wish that something could be done for her."

"Is it arthritis like mine? I have some kind of oil from China that might help her." I gave Andrea a bottle to give to Melissa.

"Thank you. I hope this will work for her."

"I am so proud of you for being genuinely caring and concerned about Melissa."

Andrea smiled and said matter-of-factly, "She is Rylan's mother. I treat her like I treat you. I care about her wellbeing."

Whenever Melissa came to visit, we made sure to spend some time together to catch up. This past October, she came to visit and stayed for a couple of months. One day as we chatted, Melissa smiled, saying to me, "Andrea has been very good to me. The oil you gave me really helped. She ordered a few more bottles for me to take back."

"You are welcome. You are a great mother-in-law, too. I know she genuinely cares about you and your wellbeing. I am glad the oil helped your knees." We both smiled.

Andrea is fortunate to have sweet Melissa as her mother-in-law. Andrea not only gets along well with Melissa but also really cares about her. I am happy for both of them.

Guardian Angels

When Joline was two, we went to the bank to get some cash every Friday. One day, she said to me, "Mommy, when I grow up, I will buy money for you!"

"Where are you going to buy money for me?" I laughed.

She tilted her little head and looked at me, saying, "In the bank!"

I had severe seasonal allergies, and the doctor told me to give shots to myself twice a week. Joline always stayed with me and watched me do it in the bathroom. I screamed whenever I poked myself with the needle. She said to me every time, "Mommy, don't scream. You will feel better." Joline was only two. She already knew how to support Mommy with her presence and love.

When Andrea was three, I started going to the doctor's office to get shots twice a week. I usually went to the clinic after picking her up from daycare. Andrea would hold one of my hands tightly with her little hand. "I will hold your hand. It won't hurt so much." It really touched my heart, and I tried not to scream.

Back in the olden days, I always had full service whenever I needed gas. When Joline was seven and Andrea was four, there was no full service any more. I needed to put the gas in my car by myself.

One day I really needed gas, and I was alone. I had never done it before. I finally got the nozzle out of the pump after twisting and joggling it for a while. I felt great that I put gas in my car by myself for the first time, successfully. But when I tried to put the nozzle back into the pump, no matter how I tried, I couldn't put it back. There was no one around to help me. I finally gave up and set the nozzle on the ground and left. I felt very dumb, and I told my family what I did. My husband Don said nothing. He just shook his head and smiled.

The next time when I needed gas, Don and kids were in the car with me. "Don't help me. Stay over there and watch me. I will try to do it myself." They stayed at a different pump and watched me from a distance.

I must have looked very awkward. Two young men came over and asked, "Do you need help?" They helped me.

After a few more times of practice, I finally felt comfortable getting gas. One time Joline and Andrea were in the car with me when I needed gas. I saw people squeezing the nozzle a couple of times after the tank was full. It looked so cool. I decided to try what they did. Guess what? I had at least three gallons of gas overflowing out of my gas tank. It frightened me, and I yelled. Joline and Andrea must have seen my horrified face and heard my scream. They got out of the car right away. They saw the mess I made. What an excitement for a cool squeeze! Never again!

After that, whenever I got gas, Joline and Andrea would say it to each other, "We'd better get out and watch Mommy do it." My two little loving guardian angels!

*****

During the past eighteen months, there were a few episodes of excitement. One morning in the spring of 2014, I got up very early. I decided to do some straightening and rearranging in the storage room downstairs. I moved boxes around, up and down, to sort things out. I suddenly felt dizzy and couldn't stand or walk straight. I managed to walk against the wall and hold on to furniture as I went to sit on the couch in the family room. The house was spinning. I was short of breath with a cold sweat—extremely miserable and frightening.

My God, I am having a stroke like my brother Ray!

Don was upstairs sound asleep, and I couldn't get to him. I called Andrea, who lives four blocks away. "I don't feel right. I am very dizzy, and I am in a cold sweat! I can't get to Daddy."

She was on her way to work, and it would take her a while to turn back. "Rylan just left the house. I will have him go over right away." Rylan, her husband, was taking their two children to daycare, not very far from where we live.

I was feeling worse. I decided to call 911. The police and Rylan arrived at the same time, and then the ambulance came.

Before I knew it, I was in the hospital emergency room. Shortly after, both Joline and Andrea arrived in the hospital. They were by my side the whole time, asking doctors questions and getting details of my condition. After many tests, it turned out I had a vertigo attack, not a stroke. What a relief!

I felt fine after a night in the hospital for observation. I resumed my daily routine. A couple of days later, I was in the garage straightening things on the shelves. After that I went to the library to return some books. As I was in the car leaving the library, I felt funny. I got dizzy again. I parked the car and called Don. It seemed hours—being miserably dizzy—before he finally arrived and drove me home. Since I couldn't walk straight, it took quite an effort for Don to get me inside the house from the car. He didn't know what to do. I told him, "Call Andrea!" Don called her, and Andrea answered.

Andrea said on the speaker, "Stay put! I will be there shortly."

On her way to our house, Andrea worked with Joline quickly and efficiently. In thirty minutes, Joline had made the necessary arrangements with the specialist. When Andrea arrived, she said to me, "Joline has made a doctor's appointment with a specialist. Let's go now."

It was vertigo again. The doctor showed me what to do about the dizziness and prescribed some medication. "Try to avoid up and down movement with your head, especially during the next two weeks."

*****

One Sunday afternoon before dinner, I had some pain in my chest. I told Joline, "I have bad heartburn." She gave me some antacid pills. The discomfort stopped. Ten minutes later, it came back. The pain was worse. I was short of breath, with a cold sweat, and it lasted longer this time.

I remembered asking my doctor a year or so before, "Dr. Davies, I sometimes feel sharp pain in the middle of my chest for just a few seconds. Do I need to worry about it? What is the difference between heartburn and a heart attack?"

Dr. Davies said, "If it goes away after you take something for heartburn, it may be just heartburn. If it doesn't go away, it is probably a heart attack. Just to be safe, I will have you take the stress test." I passed it with flying colors.

Remembering what Dr. Davies had told me, when my pain returned and was worse, I said to Joline, "The pain is getting worse. I'd better go to see a doctor." Joline was expecting Max, their third child—due any time.

"We will go to Urgent Care first. It is on the way to hospital. If there is a long wait, we will go to the hospital," Joline suggested. Urgent Care is 10 minutes away. It takes 25 minutes to get to the hospital.

When we got to Urgent Care, a couple of people were ahead of me.

I had another episode of chest pain while waiting in the lobby. Joline told the front desk, and the doctor and nurses rushed out and got me into a room right away. They did an EKG and gave me some pills. The doctor noticed something abnormal and called the ambulance to take me to the ER immediately. Here was Joline, with her big tummy, following the ambulance to the ER. Andrea came shortly after. I told Don not to come until we knew more about what was going on.

During the whole time I was in the ER, I felt fine without any more pain in my chest. After monitoring me several hours, the ER doctor said, "A heart attack won't show in the blood test until eight hours later. You can go home now, but the cardiologist ordered a blood test for you in the morning. Be sure to come early for the test."

The next day Joline worked at home, and Andrea decided to take a day off just in case she was needed. I went in for the blood test early in the morning after taking Casey to school. As soon as I came back from the hospital, Dr. Davies called. She said, "The blood test was not normal. You need to check into the hospital. A procedure is scheduled for you at three o'clock today. An excellent cardiologist, will do it for you."

I felt fine, and I was to meet with a couple of friends for lunch. "When do I need to check into the hospital?"

"Within an hour!" Wow! Urgent!

Well, Joline and Andrea took me back to the hospital right away.

After the catheterization, my cardiologist said to me, "You had a mild heart attack, but it didn't do much damage to your heart." He continued, "You are very lucky that you came in as soon as you did. There was a ninety-nine per cent blockage in the main artery—it's called the *widow-maker*. I put a stent in. You should be fine now, but you need to take medication faithfully, do not skip even one pill, to ensure the stent works well in the artery. You also need to have rehab for three months."

My cardiologist showed us the "before" and "after" pictures of my heart. It was pretty scary to see the "before" picture—the passage in the main artery was as thin as a thread.

It was a close call. I was blessed with thorough and caring doctors,

Dr. Davies and my cardiologist, who saved my life. Again, Joline and Andrea were with me throughout the whole ordeal.

Two days later, while I was waiting to be dismissed from the hospital, Joline checked in at another hospital. I was dismissed at 3:00 PM, and Joline had her third child, Max, at 7:30 PM.

Joline and Andrea are my best friends. We enjoy one another. We can talk about everything, and we will do anything for one another. They are my greatest blessings—my guardian angels.

Independence

When Joline and Andrea were old enough to understand, I said to them, "Both of you are smarter than Mommy. Something might take me an hour to learn, and it takes only ten minutes for you. You are going to spend those ten minutes." I wanted them to learn how to put forth effort. It is a skill many bright students never acquire or develop when they are young, since everything may be very easy for them.

I made my expectations very clear. "I don't expect you to get straight A's, but you can't get a C." I continued, "Always do your best, and you will not have regrets. If you haven't tried your best, you have no right to complain." One of my principles!

I encouraged them to explore activities and develop skills for fun besides studying. I told them, "Various activities will bring you different fun and diverse friends as well."

Since I was the *Chicken of the Sea,* Joline and Andrea started learning to swim when they were babies. They now are fearless fish of the ocean.

Joline played violin while Andrea learned piano. Joline was in orchestra and Andrea was in choir. One time when she was in college, Joline told me, "Playing in the orchestra is a therapy and sanctuary for me for my demanding studies." She now helps her son Casey with violin.

I was always more excited than they were about our daughters' dance recitals, where they were in beautiful costumes on stage—one of my childhood dreams. I filmed their dances and took a lot of pictures.

Whenever we skated with a bunch of friends and their children, it was hilarious to see many grown-ups fall more often than the kids. Luckily I learned how to skate when I was little.

It was very competitive get on a school tennis team in high school. Most of Joline and Andrea's friends took private lessons—$30 for a half-hour lesson. I was my daughters' coach. Both of them made the Junior Varsity team.

During the soccer season, I cheered for them. Sometimes they had games at the same time on different fields. One time, their two games were side by side. On the soccer fields, I watched Joline's game and cheered for her—loudly in Chinese—"Joline, *jia you* [Go!]!" Then I turned around to cheer for Andrea, "*Jia you* [Go!]! Andrea!" The other parents might think I was crazy! Joline has been playing on a soccer team every Sunday for the past few years.

*****

Going to college was a given when Joline and Andrea were growing up, just like it was for us siblings when we were kids.

I told them when it was time for them to choose their path for their future, "Follow the rainbows and chase your dreams. Tuition is not your problem. Your job is to select the best school for yourself."

Joline had wanted to be a medical doctor since she was three. "We will support you all the way, whatever you decide to do. We can always refinance the house to support you if you want to be a doctor." I wanted her to feel free to pursue her dreams without a burden of any kind.

I told Joline, "Don't just do pre-med. There are many variables. You might change your mind and you might not get into a medical school. If that is the case, you'll have no professional skills after college. Pick another profession besides medicine that you would love to do."

Without hesitation, Joline said, "Electrical engineering."

"Good choice for your aptitude." Joline has a logical mind, and she was very good in math and science.

Joline attended the University of Illinois, majoring in electrical

449

engineering. In four and half years, she obtained her bachelor's degree with minors in bio-medical engineering and international business. She also completed all the pre-med courses.

Since Andrea was interested in languages, she attended one of the best colleges for languages, Middlebury College in Vermont. She was double-majored in both Chinese and Japanese. In three and half years, she graduated with high honors and also received an award for her thesis.

Life is not only full of variables, but also full of impermanence. Parents will get old and leave you, and siblings can't be with you forever. Great friends get separated. There are also unpredictable factors in marriage. Nothing is permanent, and there is no guarantee anyone will always be there for you. The only person you can rely on, always, is yourself.

Being a professional and being financially and emotionally independent—the key elements for total independence and freedom— were what I instilled in Joline and Andrea as they were growing up.

Wings

One time, a student looked extremely tired in class. I asked him, "What happened to you?"

He answered, "I worked until midnight last night."

"Why do you work so late during the week?"

"I need to help my mom to pay for the rent." It was sad. I felt blessed that my children didn't need to do that.

I told my two daughters when they were in high school and college, "I don't want you to sacrifice your studying time and opportunities for school activities to work during the school year." I continued, "You may work as a tutor only if you can spare the time, and you may work full time during the summer."

Andrea tutored two Chinese students in English for a couple of years during high school. One summer, the State Farm Insurance Company provided an internship for each of the four high schools in Lincoln, and Joline was chosen from her school. She worked as an office assistant.

"How is it? Do you like it?" I asked her after a week or so.

"It's okay. People are very nice and friendly. It's not very challenging. I always finish all the work in a very short time. I get bored sometimes."

"That's it. When you don't have professional skills, you can do only routine work that is not very challenging." A teachable moment!

Ever since Joline and Andrea were old enough to understand, I encouraged them, "You will acquire various skills while doing different things. Be actively involved with school activities. Leadership will give you opportunities to develop organization and presentation abilities, a couple of critical and essential skills you will need no matter what field you are in."

Joline was the founding president of the Key Club at East High School. While studying at the University of Illinois, she was the external vice president and project leader of the Asian American Students Association. She worked with the vice chancellor to improve the menus in the cafeterias on campus for people with different dietary needs. She also served on the Illini Union Board. When Joline was a sophomore, she was nominated by the Illini Union Board for, and received, a Leadership Award for her active and effective leadership.

Andrea was also very active with various clubs in high school. In her senior year, she was the president of Junior Achievement at her school. At the annual city banquet, she was awarded in five categories, including President of the Year and Speaker of the Year.

*****

After working for a year as an engineer—Joline's first job—at the Bethlehem Steel Company in Indiana, she told me, "Mom, I decided not to pursue medical school anymore."

"Why? You enjoy engineering work? Are you sure about it?" She had taken the required test for medical school already.

"I don't think I'd like a doctor's lifestyle, especially when you have a family. I enjoy being an engineer."

"Whatever you decide to do is fine, as long as you are sure it is what you really want."

"I will start my advanced studies instead." She started a graduate program for her master's degree in Engineering Management while working full time. Later, with two children and a full time job, she never stopped pursuing a different goal she set for herself.

In December 2012, she became Dr. Joline Robertson, obtaining her PhD in Management Science—a *doctor* in a different domain.

*****

Andrea received three job offers before she graduated from college. The Capital Group Companies is one of the largest investment companies in the U.S. The company recruits six or seven college graduates each year from reputable colleges around the world for The Associate Program (TAP).

After preliminary interviews at a job fair on campus, Andrea was the only one chosen from Middlebury College to have an interview at the company in Los Angeles. A week after a series of twelve in-depth interviews with people from different departments, the human resource director called her to congratulate her and offer her a job in TAP. "You should be very proud of yourself. Only six people are selected out of numerous finalists around the world."

Andrea joined the Capital Group Companies in Los Angeles in the fall of 2000. With wide-spectrum training and experiences provided by the company, she became a compliance specialist.

After working in Los Angeles for eight years, Andrea missed the quality of life in the Midwest and decided to join Joline in Milwaukee. This brought us back from China to reunite with our daughters and their families in Wisconsin, where Don was born and raised. A greatest blessing, indeed! This fulfilled an amazingly correct prophecy.

During the eight years I taught in Beijing, Don and I traveled in China or neighboring countries whenever we had a week-long break. In the spring of 2008 on a trip in China before I thought about retiring, when I left a temple after touring inside, a monk looked at me and said to me, "You are going to have a very blessed retired life, surrounded by your family and grandchildren."

Andrea has been working at an investment company in Milwaukee for several years. She has received promotion after promotion. Now she is a senior vice president and a department manager.

When the roots grow solid and secure, the branches extend and the leaves spread. Joline and Andrea continue soaring with their well-supported wings—confidently and independently.

*****

I am proud of my two daughters, not because of their achievements, but for the women they have turned out to be. They are solid and practical without vanity. They are blessed with good nature, not petty or jealous of anyone. They live their lives with high standards and principles. They work hard always, and they keep their energy positive. With compassion, they share their abundance. Joline and Andrea are loving daughters, and they are devoted wives and mothers.

Before her second child, Holly, was born, Joline stepped down from being a supervisor of 90 people to be a project leader. Her husband Ken, an engineer also, has been a fully supportive life partner and a good father. They provide their children various opportunities to have fun and to grow intellectually and emotionally.

Andrea is very creative with art, especially pottery. She stopped doing her own hobbies after her two children were born. She and her husband Rylan provide different activities for their children to learn, to have fun, and to explore.

Mindfully, Joline and Andrea cultivate the seeds and nurture the roots in their children just as I did in them.

Someday our grandchildren will soar freely and confidently with their strong roots and wide-spread wings...

Joline, Celine, Don, and Andrea

Andrea's happy family: Callie, Rylan, Kiran, & Andrea

Joline's happy family: Casey, Holly, Ken, Max, & Joline

Chapter 9
Forever

The Prophecy
Speedy Little Monkey
Fearless Big Girl
Hollywood Holly
Diamond
Descendant of the Dragon
Forever

The Prophecy

Never Say Never

I had always told my family and friends, "I love Lincoln and I love our home. I will never move, and I will retire here."

I never thought that one day we would let go of everything we had had in Lincoln for 36 years and move to Milwaukee. *Never say never* are words of wisdom, indeed.

After our first grandchild, Casey, was born, everything changed. When Casey was three years old, we came back from China. I was willing to let go of the home we had built and the good life in Lincoln to join our two daughters in Milwaukee.

We came back in mid-June 2009. I was going full speed again as soon as I started teaching at Arrowhead High School in August. It was impossible for us to sell our house in Lincoln or to buy a house in Milwaukee.

Joline and her husband Ken foresaw this. Before we came back, Joline said to me on the phone, "Mom, don't worry about housing. There is room in our new house for you to stay as long as you wish."

They bought their new home not only for the location, acreage, and floor plan, but also for the in-law suite downstairs. It is a cozy one-bedroom apartment with a kitchen, a good-sized living room, and a little study. It also has a walk-out sliding door, big windows with good lighting, and a separate entrance—in the same house and yet privately separated. It was the perfect transition home for us.

Not until two years later, in 2011, did I finally find a brand new condo I liked at a perfect location—four blocks from Andrea and Rylan's house.

Joline and Andrea bought their houses around the same time.

Purposely they planned to live close to each other—a twelve-minute ride on local roads between their two houses.

The Prophecy

Joline and Ken now have three children. Casey is nine, Holly is four, and Max, the baby, is eighteen months. They need even more help. In order to work with the children more efficiently, I continue to live in the in-law suite in their house during the week. I go back to my own home on the weekends.

When Casey started kindergarten, I didn't want him to spend more than thirty minutes on the school bus every morning. Instead I took him to school every morning, and I used the time to work with him. I taught him Chinese and martial arts before school when he was in kindergarten through second grade.

Now that he's beyond second grade, he has more homework and sports activities. In the morning before school, he practices violin, and I help him review or study for different tests. I teach him Chinese language or games whenever there is time. Sometimes we practice martial arts or drumming for the Lion Dance. I also take Max and Holly to their music class, Singing Tree, on Fridays.

A snack is always ready for Casey when he gets home from school. He shares with me what he has learned in class, especially science. After eating, he works on his homework while I prepare and cook dinner.

Don lives in our condo near Andrea. He has been helping Andrea and Rylan with their two children—Kiran and Callie. On weekdays, Don picks them up from daycare, and they spend an hour or two with him at our house so that they don't have too long a day at the daycare. And he takes Kiran and Holly for Kung Fu class every Wednesday.

We are truly fortunate to live our retired lives just like the prophecy the monk told me at a temple in China: *You will have blessed retired lives, surrounded by family and grandchildren.* Indeed, our lives have been blessed.

Our five grandchildren fill our lives with love and laughter. They keep us young and make our lives more complete.

I have great and different fun with each of them. I call them my *toys*, my precious grandchildren.

Speedy Little Monkey

I usually get up around three or four o'clock in the morning, if not earlier. It is quiet and peaceful without any interruption—the best time to work on my writing.

Like most days, the phone rang around five o'clock as I worked on my memoir at the computer in the study. An excited voice came from the other end of the phone, yelling, "Hi! Hi! Hi!" non-stop.

I laughed and said, "Hi! I am coming!" I stopped everything and was upstairs in two minutes.

When I appeared at the door to the kitchen, in the living room on his mother's lap was a sweet little boy with a big smile—awaiting me. He clapped his little hands as soon as he saw me. He got down and crawled toward me instantly to greet me, saying the only word he could say, "Hi! Hi!" He stood up holding my legs. He smiled at me with his arms up, saying, "Hi! Hi!" again.

I picked him up and kissed his cute chubby face, saying "I love you!" This was Joline's third child, Max, before he turned one.

I talked to Max in Chinese and tickled him when I changed his diaper and dressed him for daycare. He giggled, kicked, and wiggled. I watched him make a big mess eating his breakfast.

We sat on the floor and played, waiting for his big brother and sister to come down for breakfast. When he heard their steps on the stairs, he got so excited, yelling, non-stop, "Hi! Hi!"

I start every day with laughter and lots of fun with Max early in the morning. Casey, his big brother, calls him the *Living Alarm*. Max wakes up everyone in the morning with his loud and clear, repeated, "Hi!"

Before he could walk, he crawled really fast. One time when he was crawling toward a danger zone, I tried to grab him. He was too fast, and I could only get ahold of one of his feet. He kept going and the sock came off. After turning around and giving me a big proud smile, he crawled away—full speed—again. He was nimble and active like a little monkey, without fear.

He knew how to put a little stool in front of a little table before climbing up. Before I knew it, he was standing on the table, dangerously. I said to him, "No! No! Down, down!"

He echoed, "No! No! Down, down!" I got him down from the table to the floor. I hoped he would get the message. As I turned around for one second, I heard, "Hi!" He was on the table again, with a mischievous smile on his face.

No matter what kind of high chair we put him in, he manages to get out and stands tall on the chair with a big smile, saying, "Hi!"

Max is truly a speedy, fearless little monkey!

On weekends, I go back to my own home. He always misses his *Po Po* and wants to call me. Often this little monkey takes the phone to his mother and says, "*Po Po*." He then has the longest conversation with me, repeating "Hi! *Po Po*!" and "Bye! *Po Po*!" numerous times.

Max rocks his little body whenever he hears music. His favorite song—the first song I sang to him when he was a baby—is *Twinkle, Twinkle, Little Star*. He not only sways his body but also twirls his two little hands in the air.

Whenever I say the Chinese nursery rhyme about going to *Po Po*'s house, he rocks back and forth, saying a verse of the nursery rhyme, "*Yao, yao, yao* [Sway, sway, sway]."

He wants me to play with him or to sit by him when he plays with his toys. Whenever I get up to do something, he fusses and follows me around like a shadow. I think he is spoiled, but of course, not by me!

Every day when he gets home from daycare, before his mother gets him out of his car seat, he calls, "*Po Po! Po Po!*" He knows *Po Po* is inside waiting for him.

I usually greet him at the door when I hear him and his big sister Holly come in from the garage. I ask, "Who is home?!" From his mother's arms, he reaches out to me with a grin on his face and dives into my arms for lots of love and kisses.

He leans his head against my face whenever I say, "I love you."

Our speedy little monkey, Max, knows his *Po Po* loves him unconditionally. It is forever.

Fearless Big Girl

During the week I spend much time with Joline's three children, and when I go back to my own home on weekends, I make sure to spend time with Andrea's two children. Kiran is five and Callie is two. Saturdays and Sundays early in the morning are our special times together.

Around 7:30 or 8:00 AM on Saturday, Kiran calls, asking, "*Po Po*, are you coming for coffee?"

Callie yells in the background, "*Po Po*, Mommy is making pancakes!"

"Yes, I'll be there in a little bit." I drop everything and leave for their house—four blocks away.

I usually have breakfast with Kiran and Callie at their house on Saturdays and Sundays.

Not too long ago, I started teaching Kiran and Callie some Chinese. Little Callie was very motivated and focused. She pronounced the names of family members loudly and clearly. Whenever I was there, she would say, "*Po Po*, Chinese!" Then she would go to get the little Chinese books. She sat on one side of me, with Kiran on the other side, on a Lazy Boy chair in the sunroom.

I pointed at a picture of a man, and loud and clear Callie said, "*Wo ai wo de Ba Ba* [I love my father]!"

I said, "*Wo ai...* [I love...]"

Callie said, "*Wo ai wo de Ma Ma* [I love my mother]*!*"

I said, "*Wo ai...*"

Kiran said, "*Wo ai wo de Po Po!*" After we *loved* every member of the family in Chinese, including cousins, uncles, and aunts, we did other fun things.

Big Girl

One day as I walked in the house, Callie came running and grabbed one of my hands. She looked so excited. "*Po Po*, come to see my new bed. I am a big girl now."

We raced upstairs to her newly decorated room. "Wow! You have a big girl bed now."

She pointed at the wall. "This is a big butterfly. It is from China. Mommy got it for me."

"Your room is so beautiful! I like the flowers on the sheet. Can I sleep in your bed?"

"Yes! You can." She nodded. I lay down on her bed, and Callie looked at me seriously with her big sparkling brown eyes.

"Nice! So comfortable! I like it!"

Callie beamed.

She was still in pajamas. I asked her, "Should we change your clothes? What do you want to wear?"

"I want to wear the Elsa dress and pants." She loves the movie, *Frozen.*

"Let's fix your hair also. Okay?"

"Okay!"

I dressed her and brushed her beautiful long curly hair. "All pretty now, let's go downstairs to play with *Ge Ge* [Big brother]."

We played hide-and-seek with Kiran, we read more books together, and we played with stuffed animals—sliding them down the handrail of the stairs. We danced in the living room. We giggled and raced all the way upstairs to get more toys. We counted the steps in Chinese coming down the stairs.

In the spring and summer, we played on the porch and in the backyard. We searched for baby bunnies hidden in the grass. We found birds singing in the trees, and we watched soaring airplanes in the sky. We watered the garden and we picked the tomatoes. We blew big bubbles and small bubbles, and we chased the butterflies. In the fall, we jumped on the big pile of orange leaves. We made snowmen when there was snow. We always had great fun together.

Fearless

Our little Callie has her mother's beautiful eyes and her father's curly hair. She never misses out on anything her big brother, five-year-old Kiran, does. She follows Kiran closely like his shadow. If Kiran plays with cars, Callie has a car in her hand. When Kiran runs, Callie's little legs speed up to stay right behind him. Kiran goes to the play room, and his shadow is right behind him. Whenever Kiran goes upstairs, Callie races him—with *Po Po* behind her.

One day on the playground, little Callie followed Kiran to the very top of the biggest slide, smiling and yelling, "*Po Po!* Look at me! I did it!" It looked so dangerous.

"Be careful! Don't stand too close to the big hole!" I yelled back to warn her about the big opening—right behind her—for big kids to climb up.

"Okay! I will." This fearless two-year-old Callie had a confident smile on her sweet face.

It is such great fun playing with my fearless playmate Callie. People can hear our screams and laughter a block away.

Whenever it is time for me to leave, she gives me a big hug. I kiss her and say, "Bye! I love you!"

My darling curly-haired Callie hugs me again and says, "I love you forever!"

Hollywood Holly

Big Sister

"How do you want your hair done today?" I ask Holly every morning when I fix her long hair.

"I want a big pony tail." Holly knows exactly how she wants her hair done every day.

"With a braid or not?"

"No braid today."

One day I asked her, "How do you want your hair done today?"

"I want it like Elsa's, a braid on the side." I did what she'd asked, and she looked pretty cute.

When I fix Holly's long black hair, little brother, Max, is always right next to her, with his little comb. Every morning he helps comb Holly's hair—pulling Holly's hair in all directions. I tell him, "Gentle!" He looks so happy and proud to help his big sister look pretty.

Holly never complains when Max hurts her, pulling her hair with his comb. Holly just giggles. She loves her baby brother. Ever since Max was born, whenever he cried, his big sister Holly would sing songs to him, *Silent Night; Twinkle, Twinkle, Little Star*; or other songs. The funny thing is that Max stops crying or fussing and listens attentively to Holly's sweet voice singing the songs he loves.

Love

Our petite little four-year-old Holly picks out her own clothes, socks, and shoes to wear to daycare every day. Most of the time they match and look very good, but sometimes I hope her teachers know that Holly, not I, picked her clothes.

One time, she had a fancy new dress with lace and beautiful designs on it. She looked so beautiful. "*Po Po*, did you buy this for me too?" She knows that *Po Po* buys many pretty clothes and a lot of fun stuff for her.

"Yes. Do you like it?" I asked her.

"It's so fancy. I like it very much. Thank you, *Po Po*!"

"I am glad you like it."

"*Po Po*, I know why you buy so many things for us."

I smiled and asked her, "Why?"

"Because you love us." She hugged me and said, "I love you very much, *Po Po*!"

*****

At least once a week, Holly asks me, "*Po Po*, can I go to your house?" Holly likes to play in my in-law suite—my house.

"Sure!" Then we go down together, hand-in-hand.

Every time she comes to my house, she gets her paper and bucket of crayons on the table. This four-year-old little Holly likes to draw. She is quite an artist—good color combinations and clear shapes. Then she tells me what it is about and hands me the picture. "This is for you, *Po Po*."

"It's beautiful! Thank you! I will put it on the refrigerator."

In my living room, I have toys, books, and games for her and her two brothers. Sometimes the three of them come down together. But Holly likes to come down alone. We play house. She cooks and I eat. We cuddle on the couch sharing a blanket and eating our favorite chocolate. We watch her favorite shows together.

In the middle of her favorite show, Holly turns around and hugs me, saying, "I love you very much, *Po Po*!"

Hollywood

Holly is quite a singer. When she was two, she could sing solo without missing any lyric of *Silent Night*. I sometimes wonder how this little head of hers can remember all the words and the tunes of so many songs.

Holly has a microphone that she loves to sing with. "*Po Po*, do you want to watch my show?"

"Sure! I love to watch you perform!" I sat down on the couch facing the fireplace.

She was in a fancy long dress with snowflakes like what Elsa wore in the movie *Frozen*. She stepped up on the hearth in front of the fireplace—a perfect platform. With the microphone in one hand, she started singing her favorite songs, including the song, *Let It Go,* in *Frozen*. Little Holly looked so comfortable and confident singing on the platform—with a loud, clear, sweet voice, and graceful movements—like a Hollywood star.

Last summer, Yu Li and Cindy Gong—friends in Beijing, came to visit me. I wanted them to meet my five precious grandchildren. I asked Joline and Andrea to bring their children to our place to meet my friends. Holly was in a pretty yellow dress. She was not shy at all. She carried on quite a conversation with them. I asked Holly, "Would you sing a song for *Po Po*'s friends?"

"Sure!" She went to the center of the open space between our living room and dining room. She twirled her pretty dress and changed hand gestures as she sang *Let It Go* for my friends. She was like a super star on stage.

Yun and Cindy were so impressed with my darling three-year-old Holly, they filmed the whole thing to take it back to Beijing to share with some of my friends there.

*****

Our loving Hollywood Holly is a bundle of joy and fun. If I forget to hug her or kiss her when I go down to my house, she will come chasing me down the stairs, yelling, "*Po Po*, you forgot hugs." Holly hugs me, "Goodnight, *Po Po*!"

I kiss her. "See you in the morning! I love you!"

She smiles and says, "Forever!"

Yes, forever, indeed.

Diamond

Whenever Kiran sees me, he stops whatever he is doing—even during his favorite TV show—and runs to hug me, smiling and yelling, "*Po Po! Po Po!*"

This is my charming, handsome five-year-old Kiran. He knows this *Po Po* of his loves him dearly and would do anything with him and for him.

Every Saturday and Sunday as soon as he gets up, Kiran asks his mother, "Is *Po Po* coming?"

When the answer is yes, he calls me right away. "*Po Po*, Daddy is making coffee. Are you coming soon?"

"Yes, I'll be right there." I drop whatever I am doing and go to play with my precious playmates, Kiran and Callie, who await me four blocks away.

Sometimes Kiran hears the garage door—I have their garage door opener—and he is at the door to welcome me with a big smile. On the Saturday right after his fifth birthday, he was waiting for me at the door. He looked excited, and he grabbed one of my hands. "Come to my room. I want to show you something." We raced to his room.

He looked so thrilled pointing at something by the window. "Look what Daddy and Mommy gave me for my birthday!"

"Wow! What a beautiful gift! It is green."

"My favorite color!" He beamed.

Andrea and Rylan gave their big boy a gorgeous modern desk.

"*Po Po*! Look at the chair. It turns." He got on the chair and showed me how it worked.

"How fun! It is green also! May I try it?" I sat on the chair, and Kiran turned it with both his hands. "I love it!"

Indianapolis 500

Monster trucks have been Kiran's favorite cars. Whenever I saw a cute one, I bought it for him. On weekends, car racing was an exciting climax of our time together. We lined up all the monster trucks. Each of us picked one for the big race.

Kiran knew how each one worked. He handed me a medium-sized blue one and said, "Po Po, this is for you. It runs very fast."

Little Callie picked a small hot pink one. "I want this pink one," she said.

The entryway near the front door was the starting line, and we raced our cars on the narrow runway toward the living room. We laughed when any car went too fast and rolled over. We screamed when one of our cars hit the furniture. We cheered when one passed the rug in the middle of the living room and went all the way across the room and hit the wall.

When the weather was nice, we raced in the backyard on the cement patio. After we played for a while, Kiran said, "*Po Po*! Guess what?"

"What?"

He pointed at the movable baby slide right by us. "We can start the car on the slide."

"Yeah! Great idea! Let's try it!"

He started his car on the slide.

I laughed and yelled, "Look at it go! What a smart idea!"

Callie and I tried ours, and it was so fun. Callie jumped and down. Kiran got excited and yelled, "*Po Po*, let's try the big slide."

I had more fun than they did. "Sure! I bet the cars will go even farther!" We hurried and moved the big slide to a good spot to make a longer runway for the race.

I laughed, Callie clapped her little hands, and Kiran yelled, "Wow! Look how fast and far they went! Let's try it again."

It is a great joy playing with my delightful playmates. Always!

Invitation

When I was in Taiwan during November 2014, Kiran asked her

mother, "Why is *Po Po* gone for a month? It's so long." Kiran missed his *Po Po*.

Whenever they were on vacation, I missed Kiran and little Callie. Kiran always brought something special for me. He gave me a cute elephant after they came back from India. He always remembered to bring a different sea shell for me when they went to Florida or Mexico.

After their trip to Mexico, I asked Kiran, "Did you have fun?"

After telling me what they did on each trip, Kiran always said to me, "It was fun. Would you come with us next time?"

"You want me to go with you on a vacation?" I asked.

"Yeah! I wish you were with us when we played on the beach in Mexico."

"Okay! Next time when you go to Mexico, I will go with you."

I had gone on vacations with Joline and Ken's whole family a few times, but not with Kiran and his family.

I can really see that I will have a blast with my precious playmates, Kiran and Callie, digging sand, building castles, and screaming and running from the big rolling waves on the beach!

Forever

It was Friday, two days before Valentine's Day in 2016. I was downstairs before my husband, Don, brought Kiran and Callie back from daycare. I heard Kiran yelling, "*Po Po*! I got something for you!" He came running to me holding a bag.

"What do you have there?" I asked as I hugged him.

"These are Valentine's gifts from my friends."

He started digging in the bag. "Wow! Look at all this neat stuff!" I said.

Callie came down with her bag and showed it to me. "*Po Po*! Look what I got!"

"Lucky you!" There were all kinds of little toys, candies, and stickers in her bag.

She handed me a beautiful sticker with Elsa on it. "This is for you, *Po Po*."

"Thank you! It is beautiful!"

"I got candies and many stickers. Can I eat one of the candies now?"

"Sure! Just one." Callie looked so happy and excited picking the candy she wanted to eat first.

Kiran seemed very serious searching for something in particular in his bag. Finally he found the thing that he was looking for. He got it out and smiled. "*Po Po*, this is for you."

In his hand was a huge *diamond* ring. He grabbed my right hand and put it on my middle finger. He beamed and said, "Happy Valentine's Day, *Po Po*!"

Apparently in his little head, he planned to surprise me with his special *diamond* ring when his friend gave it to him. He saved it especially for me.

I hugged him and kissed him on the forehead. "Thank you! It is so beautiful. It is the biggest diamond I have ever seen. I will put on my dresser, and I can see it every day."

He looked so proud and said, "I am glad you like it."

"I love it. Do you know a diamond is forever?"

"Yeah?!"

I hugged him and kissed him on his head. "Thank you. I love you!"

He looked at me with his beautiful shining brown eyes, and said, "Forever!"

Descendant of the Dragon

Our oldest grandchild, Casey, is nine years old now. He is focused and bright. He loves learning. When he was four, he asked me to teach him Chinese. When he started kindergarten, I started teaching him Chinese before school every day.

In the spring of 2012, before he turned six, he saw my *Chinese Kaleidoscope* program at Arrowhead High School.

That evening, Casey asked me, "*Po Po*, would you teach me all the things your students did on the stage?"

I was delighted that he wanted to learn what I taught my students.

Every day before school, I taught him basic martial arts I had acquired throughout the years. He listened attentively and practiced diligently every morning after his Chinese lesson. His young nimble body and motivation enabled him to learn fast and well. In a short time, he could do all the techniques for the fan, flags, and staff—using many of his own creative forms—better than I could do.

When Casey was ready for a professional martial arts teacher, we found the ShaoLin Center where Casey could learn Chinese martial arts. Three years later, I joined Casey to learn Shao Lin Kung Fu with him. We have had great fun learning together and fighting against each other with different weapons.

Every time we fight against each other, our teacher, Master Kleppe, laughs. "I don't know who is more dangerous, Grandma or Casey."

Supreme Skill

Casey and I spend a lot of time together every day, in the morning before school, after school, and in Kung Fu classes. Now he is old enough to understand a lot of things. We talk about everything.

We talk about what we learned in class on our way back from Kung Fu classes—twice a week.

One day I said to him, "Do you know how fortunate you are?"

"Yeah! Why?" He wasn't sure what I was getting at.

"When I was your age, I would have really liked to learn martial arts. But I never had a chance to learn because we had to study all the time. Here you are at such a young age; you not only learn Chinese Kung Fu but also learn from a true Shao Lin master."

Our teacher, Master Kleppe of ShaoLin Center, is a humble, dedicated, and skillful master. He knows how to make difficult techniques easy for us to learn.

"Yes. I am very lucky. I really like it, especially when we learn different weapons."

"Do you know what Kung Fu means?"

He looked puzzled. "Isn't it martial arts?"

"Kung Fu means a supreme skill achieved with great effort. It is not just limited to martial arts. But it commonly refers to martial arts nowadays, especially in the Western world."

"You mean if I am very good with soccer, I have soccer Kung Fu?" He understood.

"Yes. Whatever you want to achieve at a high level, you need to put great effort into it. Now you see our master being such a skillful master, but you didn't see the effort he put into it before becoming a master. He continues to learn new skills."

"I can't imagine how hard he must have practiced. It takes so much for us to learn simple techniques with our weapons."

I laughed. "Look how sore our arms and shoulders are after one hour of class using the Kwan Dao [a broadsword on a long stick]!"

"I know!" Casey touched his upper arm and moved his shoulders.

"Try to learn as much as you can when you are young. Do you see those martial big brothers and sisters in the other class? They work so hard at it, and they are so good. They are not even Chinese. Some of them have been learning since they were little kids."

"I hope I can do all what they can do someday."

"Be humble! There is always something new to learn, and there is always room for improvement. Never quit, and you will be as good as they, someday!"

"I will not quit!"

I emphasized, "Remember that without effort, no matter how intelligent a person might be, nothing will happen. You are very blessed. You are not only smart but also hardworking. You will always be a winner!"

Casey grinned.

Risk

In addition to teaching Casey the Chinese language, I taught him the two most popular Chinese games—*ma jiang* [mah jong—a gambling game on tiles] and Chinese chess, a board game similar to Western chess.

You can find people playing Chinese chess in any park in China. It takes strategy, observance, and intelligence to win the game. When I was little, I played with my older brother Karl and younger brother Ken. Both of them are smarter than I. They had strategies. They always won.

When I first started teaching Casey, I noticed that he was very careful with every move. "Why didn't you take my horse?"

"You will get my cannon if I take your horse." He was very observant, but very conservative with his moves. He was in defense mode most of the time.

"Sometimes you need to trade one for another. Move some of them across the river to be more offensive."

"Okay." He foresaw many of my possible moves, but he still was too hesitant.

Casey is a very careful young lad. I wanted him to loosen up and learn to take some risk with the game.

When we started a new game, I said to him, "Let's be more aggressive and change our strategies. Both of us are too cautious!"

Once Casey got the hang of it, being aggressive and taking some risk, he had more fun playing Chinese chess. He beats me half of the time now.

I always laugh when I lose a game. "Wow! You won again!" I want

Casey to learn that winning or losing is all good and fun—always be a good sport and enjoy the process. Learn from your mistakes, and try again.

"See what you can do now. In real life, we need to take some risk in order to move forward with our visions, dreams, or inventions, just like all inventors and scientists do with their ideas and experiments."

Casey nodded his head. "Yes, I can see that."

Dragon

Every morning I take Casey to school, and we chat on the way. One day I asked him, "Do you know what the dragon stands for?"

"Does it represent the Chinese emperor?"

"Yes, it does. It is also the emblem of China. Whenever you see a dragon, you know it has something to do either with China or with Chinese people."

"No wonder I see dragons in Chinese restaurants."

"Do you remember one of the songs you played when you practiced Kung Fu when you were six?"

"Kind of."

"One of the songs is called *The Descendants of the Dragon*. It is about Chinese people."

"Right! I remember that in the song Chinese people call themselves the *Descendants of the Dragon*."

Casey looked at me and asked, "So you are a *Descendant of the Dragon?*"

"Yes. You are a *Descendant of the Dragon* also. It is your heritage. I am so glad you want to learn Chinese and Kung Fu, and you enjoy playing Chinese chess."

Casey grinned, "Of course! I am a *Descendant of the Dragon!*"

"Yes, all five of you are *Descendants of the Dragon*—it's in your blood."

As I dropped him off at the front door of the school, I said, "Have fun! I love you!"

Casey said, "Forever!"

Forever

When my parents passed down their treasured traditions, wisdom, values, and principles, their teaching took root in my heart and the hearts of my six siblings. My deep roots and their love have helped me face challenges without fear and stand tall with pride and honor. Always!

I passed my roots with love to my two daughters, and they have blossomed beautifully. They now plant the seeds and cultivate the roots in their growing seedlings—our grandchildren. Someday the nurtured seeds will take root. The reinforced roots will accompany our precious grandchildren—the little miracles in action and motion—on incredible journeys...

With their strengthened roots, our grandchildren will chase their dreams with passion, follow their rainbows with hope, and climb their high mountains without fear. Their strong roots will give them the courage to face any obstacles they might have along the way. So they soar.

Love will support the wings of my fabulous *Descendants of the Dragon* and straighten the feathers as they fly against the winds. Our love will accompany them always as they soar freely and independently to search for their destinies. My love for my precious grandchildren is unconditional. It is eternal.

My Precious Ones,
You are miracles in action.

Fear not!
Dream big!
Spread your wings!
Soar high and far!

If you have a dream, make it come true.
If you have a vision, make it happen.
If you have energy, make it positive.
If you have something extra, share with people.

Your roots will support you.
Your wings will take you.
Our love will escort you.

My love for you is forever...

Callie, Holly, Kiran, & Casey (2013)

The Descendants of the Dragon
Kiran, Callie, Holly, Max, and Casey (2015)

Appendix
Awards and Honors

Professional Honors and Awards

1999 U.S.-Newly Independent States (former USSR) Excellence in Teaching Award; spent two weeks in Kazakhstan

1999 Fulbright Memorial Fund Scholar; spent three weeks in Japan

1998 Walt Disney American Teacher Award—Outstanding Foreign Language Teacher of the Year

1998 Lincoln Public Schools Scottish Rite Distinguished Educator of the Year (Hall of Fame)

1997 Nebraska Teacher of the Year—Honored by President Clinton at the White House

1997, 1992 Lincoln Public Schools Gold Star Award

1998, 1994, 1992 Who's Who Among American Teachers

Additional Honors and Awards

2005 Distinguished Alumnus of Providence University in Taiwan

2000, 1999, 1995, 1982 Taiwan Service Award

1995 Significant Ethnic Woman of Nebraska

1994 Nebraska Asian Woman of the Year

1993 Honorary President of University of Nebraska-Lincoln Alumni Association in Taiwan

Leadership Service

Professional Involvement

1998-2000 Governor's Teacher Advisory Cabinet on Quality Education in Nebraska

1996-1997 President of Chinese Language Association of Secondary-Elementary Schools (CLASS)

1989-1999 Chinese Language Association of Secondary-Elementary Schools (CLASS) Executive Board Member

1995-1999 Established sister school relationship with schools in Taiwan for four public schools in Lincoln, Nebraska

1992-2012 Director and producer of the "Chinese Kaleidoscope," a 40-minute cultural program, performed by Chinese language students at Lincoln High School, Lincoln, Nebraska (1992, 1994, 1996, 1998, & 2000) and at Arrowhead High School, Hartland, Wisconsin (2010 & 2012)

Community Involvement

1998-2001 Lincoln Human Rights Commissioner

1997-1998 President of Nebraska Asian Community and Culture Center

1997 Established sister city relationship for Lincoln, Nebraska and Taiping, Taiwan

1997-2001 Liaison of sister cities—Lincoln, Nebraska and Taiping, Taiwan

1997, 1999 Leader of Lincoln delegation to Taiping, Sister City in Taiwan

1995 Leadership Lincoln XI Trustee

1993, 1996 Leader of the Asian Community and Cultural Center 100-people Lion Dance Troupe, the first Asian troupe at the Nebraska Star City Parade, and won the Best Specialty Unit Award

1993 Co-founder of University of Nebraska-Lincoln Alumni Association in Taiwan

1992 Co-founder of Nebraska Asian Community and Cultural Center

1982 Founder of Lincoln Chinese School

1975 Co-founder of University of Nebraska-Lincoln Free China Association

Teacher at Park School named best in the state

BY ED RUSSO
Lincoln Journal Star

Celine Robertson, who introduces Chinese language and culture to Lincoln students, has been named Nebraska Teacher of the Year by the state Department of Education.

Robertson, who teaches Chinese at Park Middle School and Lincoln High School, was selected for her professional development, community involvement and teaching philosophy.

"I feel very honored to be recognized for what I've done with my students and my community," Robertson said.

A native of China, Robertson said she is proud of her students, including those who travel to China, Taiwan and Hong Kong so they can learn more about those countries and cultures.

ROBERTSON loves kids

"They can motivate, educate and share what they have experienced with many people," Robertson said in her application to the education department. "I truly believe that if everyone had a broadened vision and world concept it would make the world a better place for everyone."

The state Department of Education gave "awards of excellence" to four other teachers: Clayton Erwin, a counselor at Valparaiso Elementary School; Bev McKillip, Oakland-Craig High School; Nancy Jane Koch, Morton Elementary, Hastings; and Tom Shield, Kearney High School. The teachers will be honored at a luncheon Friday at the Nebraska Club, at the top of the First Bank building, 13th and M streets.

The department said the honored

More on TEACHER, Page 6A

LINCOLN Journal Star

LINCOLN, NEB. · SATURDAY

NOVEMBER 2, 1996

Teacher/Began LPS Chinese program

Continued from Page 1A

teachers are selected on the basis of their professional development activities, community involvement, philosophy of teaching, engagement in critical education issues and professional leadership. First Bank Nebraska gives the teacher of the year a $1,000 prize and the other four honored teachers $250 each.

Robertson began the Lincoln Chinese School in 1982 to meet the needs of Chinese children and other people who wanted to study Chinese. The school meets Sunday afternoons at American Lutheran Church. She began the Lincoln Public Schools Chinese language program in 1988 after LPS received a $40,000 grant from the Geraldine Dodge Foundation.

Among other activities, Robertson has been instrumental in organizing a multicultural conference for 800 students and staff at Park Middle School, and she produced and directed "Chinese Kaleidoscope," a Chinese cultural program that has been performed by Chinese language students every other year since 1992.

"It's really rewarding," she said. "I just love my kids."

Robertson, 51, was born Yu Hua Tan in China. She fled the country with her family after the Communist revolution. She was raised in Taiwan and became an English teacher there before receiving a scholarship

to Southern Illinois University in 1967.

Robertson and her husband, Donald, moved to Lincoln in 1973. She began teaching special education students at Everett Junior High School (now Park Middle School) the next year.

Robertson is involved in 21 different groups or activities, including the Chinese Language Association of Secondary-Elementary Schools and the Chinese Language Teachers Association. She helped start sister-school relationships between Lincoln High School and Park Middle School and Chu Lin High School in Taiwan, and she currently chairs a committee seeking to establish sister city ties between Taiping, Taiwan, and Lincoln.

She is a member of the Lincoln Commission on Human Rights and the LPS multicultural enrichment committee.

Among other honors, Robertson has received a service award from the consulate general of Taiwan; a Gold Star award from LPS; a Taiwan Chinese cultural workshop achievement award; Who's Who Among American Teachers award in 1992 and 1994; Nebraska Outstanding Asian American Woman of the Year in 1994; and Taiwan Chinese Opera and Martial Arts Workshop Achievement award. She received a LPS Barbara Buckingham Patronsky scholarship for 1996.

1997 Nebraska Teacher of the Year

NEBRASKA

NEWS FROM ACROSS THE STATE

Lincoln teacher in line to be No. 1 in nation

Celine Robertson, Chinese language teacher at Lincoln High School and Park Middle School, shares a laugh with a Disney Channel camera crew filming her in class Friday. Robertson is one of 36 finalists in 12 categories for the Eighth Annual American Teacher Awards. A committee will choose winners in each category after viewing videotapes of the teachers in their classrooms and presentations from the teachers in Los Angeles. The 12 winners and the Outstanding Teacher of 1998 will be honored during a taped broadcast to air June 20 on the Disney Channel.

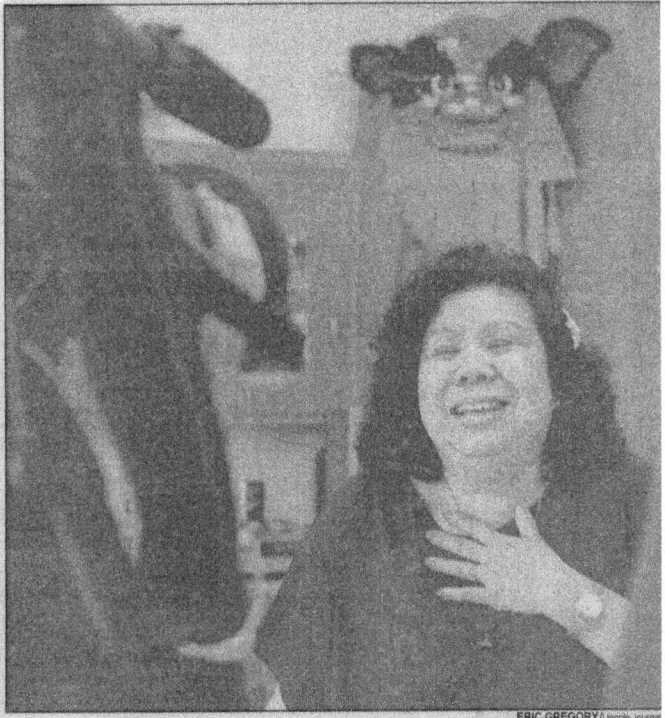

ERIC GREGORY/*Lincoln Journal*

A finalist for 1998 American Teacher Awards

Lincoln teacher receives national award

BY JOURNAL STAR WRITERS

Lincoln High School teacher Celine Robertson Wednesday received the national foreign language teacher of the year award during a taped Disney Channel celebration.

Robertson was named one of three finalists in the foreign language category in February. Last week, Disney flew her to California for the star-studded "Eighth Annual American Teacher Awards."

The awards show will be televised June 20 on the Disney Channel at 6 p.m.

The selection committee named an outstanding teacher in each subject after viewing videotapes of the teachers in their classrooms and a presentation by them in Los Angeles.

ROBERTSON

Robertson could not be reached Thursday.

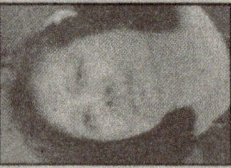

Born in China and raised in Taiwan, she helped establish the Lincoln Public Schools' Chinese language program in 1988. She has been recognized many times during her career. Last year, she was honored at the White House as the Nebraska Teacher of the Year.

"I feel very honored to be recognized for what I've done with my students and my community," she said in 1996 when she won the state Department of Education's award.

But she is even more proud of her students, including those who travel to China, Taiwan and Hong Kong to learn more about those countries and cultures.

"They can motivate, educate and share what they have experienced with many people," Robertson said in 1996. "I truly believe that if everyone had a broadened vision and world concept it would make the world a better place for everyone."

1998 Walt Disney American Teacher Award
Outstanding Foreign Language Teacher of the Year

Robertson joins LPS hall of fame

Lincoln High and Park Middle School teacher Celine Robertson officially became part of Lincoln Public Schools history on Monday, Nov. 16, when her portrait was hung among the other 33 winners for the annual Scottish Rite Teacher of the Year.

Robertson was selected last spring as the 34th recipient of this prestigious award.

"We are here to celebrate teaching and learning, and excellence in both," said Marilyn Moore, associate superintendent for instruction at LPS, presiding over the ceremony.

"There are many awards for outstanding teaching, but the Scottish Rite Award is the most distinguished."

Robertson teaches Chinese Language at both Park Middle and Lincoln High schools, and was recognized as Nebraska Teacher of the Year in 1997. She also has taken groups of students and teachers to China and has started a Lion Dance Troupe at Lincoln High.

The purpose of the Scottish Rite Teacher of the Year award is to honor an outstanding classroom teacher in Lincoln's public schools. It carries with it a $1,500 award from the Scottish Rite.

Celine Robertson slides her portrait onto the wall in the LPSDO lobby with a little help from the Scottish Rite folks.

A Few Extraordinary Achievements

1998 Scottish Rite Distinguished Educator of the Year

Celine Tan Robertson
譚渝華
(Tan Yu Hua)

Celine Robertson, teacher at Park Middle School and Lincoln High, was chosen as Scottish Rite Teacher of the Year and received the Walt Disney Teacher Award in the foreign language category.

A Yi （阿姨）– Aunt

Ba Ba （爸爸）– Father

Bao （抱）– Hold or embrace someone

Bao bei （寶貝）– Precious treasure

Bu hao wan （不好玩）– Not fun

Chun juan （春捲）– Spring/egg rolls

Dou fu （豆腐）– Tofu

Ge Ge （哥哥）– Older brother

Gong Gong （公公）– Maternal grandfather

Hao wan （好玩）– Fun

Hong bao （红包）– Red envelope

Jia you （加油）– Cheer for someone

Jiao zi （餃子）– Dumplings

Jie Jie （姐姐）– Older sister

Jiu xiang lao shu ai da mi （就像老鼠愛大米）– Just like mice love rice

Lao da （老大）– First born

Lao Shi （老師）– Teacher

Long （龍）– Dragon

Ma Ma （妈妈）– Mother

Ma jiang （麻將）– A gambling game on tiles

Mei Mei （妹妹）– Younger sister

Nai （奶）– Milk

Nai Nai （奶奶）– Paternal grandmother

Peking （北京）– Beijing

Po Po （婆婆）– Maternal grandmother

Qing Long (青龍) – Green Dragon

Shi Fu (師父) – Master

Shi Ge (師哥) – Martial older brother

Shi Mei (師妹) – Martial younger sister

Shi Mu (師母) – Master's wife

Shou zu (手足) – Siblings

Shu Shu (叔叔) – Uncle

Shui (水) – Water

Shuo zhong wen (说中文) – Speak Chinese

Tan Jie (譚姐) – Big Sister Tan

Tang yuan (汤圆) – A dessert made of sweet rice flour

Tao Lao Shi (譚老師) – Teacher Tan

Tie mu (鉄幕) – The Iron Curtain

Wo ai ni (我爱你) – I love you

Wo men xiang ni (我們想你) – We miss you

Xi (囍) – Double happiness

Xie xie ni (謝謝你) – Thank you

Xiao Mei (小妹) – Youngest sister

Yao (摇) – Sway or shake

Ye Ye (爺爺) – Paternal grandfather

Yi Yuan (藝園) – Garden of Art

Yuan fen (缘份) – Karma

Yuan xiao (元宵) – A dessert for Lantern Festival made of sweet rice flour

Zhu (竹) – bamboo

Zuo gong (做工) – Laboring as a blue-collare work

www.ingramcontent.com/pod-product-compliance
Lightning Source LLC
Chambersburg PA
CBHW030532100426
42813CB00001B/231